T0256205

Intelligent Systems and Machine Learning for Industry

The book explores the concepts and challenges in developing novel approaches using the Internet of Things, intelligent systems, machine intelligence systems, and data analytics in various industrial sectors such as manufacturing, smart agriculture, smart cities, food processing, the environment, defense, the stock market, and healthcare. Further, it discusses the latest improvements in the industrial sectors using machine intelligence learning and intelligent systems techniques, especially robotics.

Features:
- Highlights case studies and solutions to industrial problems using machine learning and intelligent systems.
- Covers applications in smart agriculture, smart healthcare, intelligent machines for disaster management, and smart manufacturing.
- Provides the latest methodologies using machine intelligence systems in the early forecasting of weather.
- Examines the research challenges and identifies the gaps in data collection and data analysis, especially imagery, signal, and speech.
- Provides applications of digitization and smart processing using the Internet of Things and effective intelligent agent systems in manufacturing.
- Discusses a systematic and exhaustive analysis of intelligent software effort estimation models.

It will serve as an ideal reference text for graduate students, post-graduate students, IT professionals, and academic researchers in the fields of electrical engineering, electronics and communication engineering, computer engineering, and information technology.

Computational Methods for Industrial Applications
Series Editor- Bharat Bhushan

In today's world IoT platforms and processes in conjunction with the disruptive block-chain technology and path breaking AI algorithms lay out a sparking and stimulating foundation for sustaining smarter systems. Further computational intelligence (CI) has gained enormous interests from various quarters in order to solve numerous real-world problems and enable intelligent behavior in changing and complex environment. This book series focuses on varied computational methods incorporated within the system with the help of artificial intelligence, learning methods, analytical reasoning and sense making in big data. Aimed at graduate students, academic researchers and profession-als, the proposed series will cover the most efficient and innovative technological solu-tions for industrial applications and sustainable smart societies in order to alter green power management, effect of carbon emissions, air quality metrics, industrial pollution levels, biodiversity and ecology.

Blockchain for Industry 4.0: Emergence, Challenges, and Opportunities
Anoop V.S, Asharaf S, Justin Goldston and Samson Williams

Intelligent Systems and Machine Learning for Industry: Advancements, Challenges, and Practices
P.R Anisha, C. Kishor Kumar Reddy, Nguyen Gia Nhu, Megha Bhushan, Ashok Kumar, Marlia Mohd Hanafiah

Intelligent Systems and Machine Learning for Industry

Advancements, Challenges, and Practices

Edited by

P.R Anisha
C. Kishor Kumar Reddy
Nhu Gia Nguyen
Megha Bhushan
Ashok Kumar
Marlia Mohd Hanafiah

CRC Press
Taylor & Francis Group
Boca Raton London New York

CRC Press is an imprint of the
Taylor & Francis Group, an **informa** business

Front cover image: Jirsak/Shutterstock

First edition published 2023
by CRC Press
6000 Broken Sound Parkway NW, Suite 300, Boca Raton, FL 33487-2742

and by CRC Press
4 Park Square, Milton Park, Abingdon, Oxon, OX14 4RN

CRC Press is an imprint of Taylor & Francis Group, LLC

ISBN: 978-1-032-26144-7 (hbk)
ISBN: 978-1-032-26145-4 (pbk)
ISBN: 978-1-003-28674-5 (ebk)

DOI: 10.1201/9781003286745

Typeset in Sabon
by Deanta Global Publishing Services, Chennai, India

Contents

Preface

With the improvements of intelligent systems and machine intelligence systems, a huge volume of information is composed successfully, and making use of such information is of complete benefit to researchers, academicians, practitioners, scientists, governments, and end customers. The innovative concepts and practices such as intelligent systems, machine intelligence systems, deep learning, edge computing, cognitive analytics, and so on cast light on creating decent conventions of huge amounts of information through great difficulty. The individuality of this book lies in the appropriate collection and presentation of an emergent multi-disciplinary research trend of intelligent systems and machine intelligence that spans a wide area and has established a substantial influence on our industry and science community.

This book consists of 16 chapters, mainly covering concepts, applications, and challenges of the Internet of Things, virtual reality, machine learning, deep learning, and image processing techniques in various applications. Further, the book covers advanced concepts like ensemble methods, fuzzy systems, intelligent systems applications in software engineering, and sentiment analysis. The book covers major applications like classification of pandemic diseases, medical diagnosis, latest technologies in healthcare education, smart farming, monitoring marine environment conditions, managing agriculture pollution, prediction of crop selection, food processing industry applications, smarter defense service, speech recognition for Indian-accent English, stock market prediction, and intelligent software effort estimation models.

The main focus of this book is to provide insights and complete knowledge of machine learning, deep learning, and the Internet of Things and their integration into various industrial applications. We trust that the proposed book will let readers find innovative ideas that are helpful to their research in various aspects.

About the editors

P.R. Anisha is a TEDx Speaker and is currently working as an Associate Professor in the Department of Computer Science and Engineering at Stanley College of Engineering and Technology for Women, Hyderabad, India. She holds teaching experience of over nine years. She received her doctoral degree from KL University, Guntur, India. Her areas of interest include artificial intelligence, machine learning, and image processing. She has over 35 research articles published in international conferences and journals. She has co-authored two books named *Introduction to C Programming* and *Introduction to C++ Programming*. She has acted as the special session chair for international conferences for Springer – INDIA 2019 and 2022, SCI 2021, and FICTA 2020 and 2022 – as well as the IEEE conference ICCSEA 2020. She is a member of the ACM and IAENG professional bodies.

C. Kishor Kumar Reddy is currently working as an Associate Professor in the Department of Computer Science and Engineering at Stanley College of Engineering and Technology for Women, Hyderabad, India. He obtained his PhD in Computer Science Engineering from KL University, Guntur, India. He has research and teaching experience of more than nine years. He has published more than 50 research papers in national and international conferences, book chapters, and journals indexed by Scopus and others. He is the author of two textbooks and two co-edited books. He acted as the special session chair for Springer FICTA 2020 and 2022, SCI 2021, INDIA 2022, and IEEE ICCSEA 2020 conferences. He is a member of ISTE, CSI, IAENG, UACEE, and IACSIT.

Nhu Gia Nguyen received a PhD degree in Mathematics for Computer Science from Ha Noi University of Science, Viet Nam National University, Vietnam. Currently, he is Dean of Computer Science at Duy Tan University, Vietnam. He has a total academic teaching experience of 20 years with more than 60 publications in reputed international conferences, journals, and online book chapter contributions (indexed by SCI, SCIE, SSCI, Scopus, and DBLP). His area of research includes healthcare informatics, network performance analysis, and simulation and computational intelligence. Recently, he has been on the technical program committee and review committee and been the track chair for international conferences: FICTA 2014, ICICT 2015, INDIA 2015, IC3T 2015, INDIA 2016, FICTA 2016, IC3T 2016, IUKM 2016, INDIA 2017, FICTA 2017, FICTA 2018, INISCOM 2018, and INISCOM 2019 under the Springer-ASIC/LNAI Series. He has nine computer science books published by Springer, IGI Global, CRC Press, and Wiley Publications. Presently he is the Associate Editor of the IGI-Global *International Journal of Synthetic Emotions (IJSE)*.

Megha Bhushan is currently an Assistant Professor (Senior Grade) in the School of Computing at DIT University, Dehradun, India. She received her PhD degree from Thapar University, Punjab, India. She has four years of research experience as a Junior Research Fellow and Senior Research Fellow under the University Grants Commission (UGC), New Delhi, Government of India. She was awarded a fellowship by UGC, Government of India, in 2014. In 2017, she was a recipient of the Grace Hopper Celebration India (GHCI) fellowship. She has filed four patents and published many research articles in international journals and conferences of repute. Her research interests include software quality, software reuse, ontologies, artificial intelligence, and expert systems. She is also the reviewer and editorial board member of many international journals.

Ashok Kumar is currently an Assistant Professor in the Research and Innovation Network (CURIN) Department at Chitkara University, Punjab, India. He has a PhD in Computer Science and Engineering from Thapar University, Punjab, India. He also worked as a project fellow in a UGC-funded project during his stay at Thapar University. He has over 15 years of teaching and research experience. He has filed three patents and published many articles in international journals and conferences of repute. His current areas of research interest include cloud computing, the Internet of Things, and mist computing. His teaching interests include Python, Haskell, Java, C/C++, advanced data structures, and data mining.

Marlia Mohd Hanafiah is an Associate Professor and Head of the Centre for Tropical Climate Change Systems at the Institute of Climate Change of the National University of Malaysia, Malaysia. Her areas of research expertise are life-cycle impact assessment (LCA) and environmental footprinting of green materials and energy, environmental engineering, wastewater treatment and water management, and green technology and sustainability. She has a total academic teaching experience of over 15 years with more than 100 publications in reputed international conferences, journals, and online book chapter contributions (indexed by SCI, SCIE, SSCI, Scopus, and DBLP). She received a research grant and consultation (as project leader and team member) of RM 7,284,719.00.

Contributors

Mukil Alagirisamy
Faculty of Engineering
Lincoln University College
Petaling Jaya, Malaysia

P.R. Anisha
Department of Computer Science
and Engineering
Stanley College of Engineering and
Technology for Women
Hyderabad, India

Manickavasagan Annamalai
Department of Biological
Engineering
University of Guelph
Canada

Ninja Begum
Department of Food Engineering &
Technology
Tezpur University
Assam, India

Shubham J. Bhanderi
Department of Applied Computer
Science
Concordia University
Montreal, QC

Udayini Chandana
Faculty of Engineering
Lincoln University College
Petaling Jaya, Malaysia

Masoud Daneshtalab
Division of Intelligent Future
Technologies
Mälardalens University
Sweden

Wilfrido Gómez-Flores
Center for Research and
Advanced Studies
Tamaulipas Campus
Ciudad Victoria, Mexico

Anjali Gupta
Department of Computer Science
and Engineering
PES University
Bengaluru, India

Marlia Mohd Hanafiah
Department of Earth Sciences &
Environment
Faculty of Science and Technology
The National University of
Malaysia
Bangi, Selangor, Malaysia

and

Centre for Climate Change System
Institute of Climate Change
The National University of Malaysia
Bangi, Selangor, Malaysia

Siti Norliyana Harun
Centre for Climate Change System
Institute of Climate Change
The National University of Malaysia
Bangi, Selangor, Malaysia

Manuj Kumar Hazarika
Department of Food Engineering &
    Technology
Tezpur University
Assam, India

V. Jeyalakshmi
Department of Electronics and
    Communication Engineering
College of Engineering, Guindy
Anna University
Chennai, India

Mohammad Nasfikur R. Khan
Department of Systems Engineering
University of South Alabama
Mobile, AL

V. Ravi Kishore
Department of Computer Science
    and Engineering
Aditya Engineering College
Surampalem, India

S. Kripa
Department of Electronics
    and Communication
    Engineering
College of Engineering, Guindy
Anna University
Chennai, India

Abhay Krishan
Electrical & Instrumentation
    Engineering Department
Thapar Institute of Engineering and
    Technology
Patiala, India

Kari J. Lippert
Department of Systems
    Engineering
University of South Alabama
Mobile, AL

Monica Madan
Department of Computer Science
    and Engineering
Amity School of Engineering and
    Technology
Noida, India

Khairul Nizam Abdul Maulud
Department of Civil Engineering
Faculty of Engineering and Built
    Environment
Universiti Kebangsaan Malaysia
Bangi, Malaysia

Ibomoiye Domor Mienye
Department of Electrical and
    Electronic Engineering Science
University of Johannesburg
Johannesburg, South Africa

Kezia Joseph Mosiganti
Department of Electronics and
    Communication Engineering
Stanley College of Engineering and
    Technology for Women
Hyderabad, India

Nhu Gia Nguyen
School of Computer Science
Duy Tan University
Danang, Vietnam

Noorashikin Md. Noor
Earth Observation Centre
Institute of Climate Change
The National University of
    Malaysia
Bangi, Selangor, Malaysia

Ashish Patel
Department of Artificial Intelligence
  and Machine Learning
Cygnet InfoTech
Gujarat, India

Darshil P. Patel
Department of Information
  Technology
Gujarat Technological University
Gujarat, India

Kinjal A. Patel
Faculty of Computer Application
  and IT
Gujarat Law Society University
Gujarat, India

Mathang Peddi
Department of Computer Science
  and Engineering
PES University
Bengaluru, India

Telagarapu Prabhakar
Electronics and Communication
  Engineering
GMR Institute of Technology
Rajam, India

Ashima Rani
Department of Computer Science
  and Engineering
Amity University
Haryana, India

C. Kishor Kumar Reddy
Department of Computer Science
  and Engineering
Stanley College of Engineering and
  Technology for Women
Hyderabad, India

Shagufta Rizwana
Department of Food Engineering &
  Technology
Assam, India

Sakshi
Department of Computer Science
  and Engineering
PES University
Bengaluru, India

S. Rama Sree
Department of Computer Science
  and Engineering
Aditya Engineering College
Surampalem, India

Yanxia Sun
Department of Electrical
  and Electronic Engineering
  Science
University of Johannesburg
Johannesburg, South Africa

K. Swaroopa
Department of Computer Science
  and Engineering
Aditya Engineering College
Surampalem, India

P. Teja
Department of Computer Science
  and Engineering
PES University
Bengaluru, India

Sachin Umrao
University of California San
  Francisco
San Francisco, CA

A. Vanathi
Department of Computer Science
  and Engineering
Aditya Engineering College
Surampalem, India

Chapter 1

A framework for a virtual reality-based medical support system

Mohammad Nasfikur R. Khan and
Kari J. Lippert

CONTENTS

1.1 INTRODUCTION

The healthcare system seems to have remained relatively unchanged for hundreds of years despite changes in devices and processes [1]. Even though conventional models foster highly skilled support systems, there is a push to reform clinical paradigms in response to the rapid technological advances

DOI: 10.1201/9781003286745-1

transforming healthcare globally. The healthcare mechanism is changing: an entire century of tradition is being challenged by ethical and legal concerns regarding healthcare quality, excessive work restrictions, surgical procedure costs, and their repercussions [2]. Although skills are taught to real human beings during routine training, patients are still at continuous risk [3, 4]. In addition to the increasing demand for healthcare workers, there is a need to find viable substitutes for traditional instructional skills that reduce the reliance on experienced supervisors' guidance. In order to improve the performance and reliability of the medical system [5], virtual reality healthcare and medical assistant systems are going to play an important role. This chapter proposes a VR-based healthcare system that assists healthcare professionals in providing medical care to patients. Moreover, this chapter addresses a few important issues regarding the VR technology-based medical system.

- What is virtual reality (VR)?
- How can VR be implemented in medical education?
- What are the uses of VR in healthcare systems?

The technology may be utilized with various devices, including VR glasses, sensors, and wristwatches. Users can access the system according to their needs. This system allows users to contact medical professionals based on their requirements, exchange data with them, receive feedback, pre-medical care, surgical assistance, psychological support, and finally, emergency aid. This chapter begins with a background description of the system, next moves on to stakeholder analysis, then to developing the operational concept in order to extract user desirements and system requirements through use cases, and finally to key performance indicators.

1.2 BACKGROUND

1.2.1 What is VR?

Zhang et al. define virtual reality as a simulation of a three-dimensional world generated using a computer. Electrical equipment such as goggles and a headpiece with sensors may enable users to interact in a seemingly tangible manner [6]. As defined by Sacks et al., VR is a technology that employs computer-based operating systems and other technologies to present users with a virtual experience [7]. According to the definitions, VR systems offer an immersive, interactive presence inside a virtual world. Individuals may engage with this simulated alternate world with various devices increasing their perception of realism [8]. According to Gadelha, VR technology has changed how teachers train and students understand [7]. By leveraging it, teacher-centered instruction can become student-centered. The Multimedia

Cone of Abstraction (MCoA), which is based on Dale's Cone of Experience (CoE), illustrates how learners become active learners through engaging with a purposeful virtual world in which they learn through a variety of activities [9]. VR was effectively used to replace the CoE's foundation level, "Direct Purposeful Experiences," the most abstract level, suggesting it can deliver highly realistic representations of things learners might interact with and learn best from. Individual students can understand work or concepts when they are given proper conditions, such as timely feedback and the opportunity to improve at their own pace [10]. Its use also encourages people to keep working hard to improve their skills [11]. Students may also receive timely feedback on their present ability level in a virtual learning environment. Students can see what they need to focus on to master a skill or activity, and visual programming is utilized to construct a virtual learning environment suited to their needs [12].

1.2.2 **VR in healthcare education**

Various research has shown that simulation training improves knowledge acquisition and competencies in healthcare education [13]. VR technology is regarded as a valuable interactive and practical, experiential learning tool for medical students to develop the skills and confidence required in a real-life situation and as a cost-effective learning approach for repeatedly practicing a variety of simulated clinical scenarios in healthcare [14]. As a result, VR enables medical students to practice without fear of making real-life fatal mistakes, preparing for diagnosing sickness indicators, and even performing complicated procedures.

The VR system allows trainee surgeons to experience various operations and procedures, including endoscopic surgery, laparoscopic surgery, neurosurgery, and epidural injections [15]. According to Vaughan et al., orthopedic VR training simulations provide surgeons with a wonderful opportunity to grow and improve their operative and decision-making abilities in a safe, risk-free realistic operating theater [16]. Consequently, implementing VR simulations to teach essential orthopedic and other types of surgery may be an effective tool for doctors with less surgical experience. Traditional instructional approaches, such as offering a vocal presentation of information or conveying written data to patients and their primary caregivers, may be less ineffective [16]. Language proficiency, ethnic and socioeconomic origins, levels of education and comprehension, and language or cognitive disability should all be considered when interacting with a patient. Studies have shown that these patient characteristics influence risk factors and patient outcomes [16]. Education must be designed to represent the specific needs of various patients experiencing an acute or chronic condition to deliver relevant and intelligible patient knowledge [17]. Thompson-Butel et al. developed guided and tailored virtual reality education sessions for stroke survivors and their primary caregivers to reduce recurrent stroke and maximize rehabilitation. They investigated the effectiveness of these VR sessions in delivering post-stroke education [18]. According to the study, the use of the VR sessions resulted in "various significant improvements in technical expertise in areas such as neurodevelopment and physiology, cognitive impairment and healing, and stroke-specific instructions like as personalized stroke risk factors and acute therapy advantages" for the survivor and the caregivers [19].

The present condition of virtual reality simulations in dentistry training was investigated by Roy et al. [20]. They suggest that the use of VR equipment in dentistry education provides significant opportunities for flexibility and self-learning. As a result, learners can participate in their education in several ways VR devices to perform simulations whenever and wherever they choose and store and revisit their work after it is over. Furthermore, incorporating virtual reality technology into the classroom reduces anxiety and boredom, making learning more exciting and compelling. Finally, since VR's rapid technological advancements, students in all dental disciplines may enjoy more efficient and realistic pre-clinical experiences [20].

1.2.3 Utilization of VR in the medical sector

Medical VR researchers regularly assess a patient's experience of physical presence (the feeling of "being there") in virtual worlds to test the effectiveness of various immersive settings. To go beyond this, Felnhofer et al. evaluated if social presence in VR affects therapeutic efficacy in a study of persons with social anxiety disorder. Three social tasks were assigned to participants in an interactive virtual world [21]. The findings demonstrate that the VR scenario might be used as a diagnostic and therapeutic tool for those who suffer from social paranoia. Virtual Reality Cue Exposure Therapy (VR-CET) has been showcased in multiple trials to be an effective treatment for weight-related disorders due to its experiential aspect. In a six-month follow-up study on previous research, Ferrer-Garcia et al. looked at a randomized clinical trial with bulimia nervosa who still experienced frequent binge-eating symptoms after completing a structured cognitive-behavioral therapy program. Subjects were randomly assigned to two further treatments: further CBT or VR-CET. Virtual reality-CET outperformed A-CBT in terms of dimensional (attitudinal and behavioral variables, stress, appetite) and classified outcomes after therapy (abstinence rates) [22].

In another study by Riches et al., their two-phase inquiry focused on the potential of VR to enable real-time monitoring of paranoid thoughts and accompanying social performance. This study suggested that virtual reality (VR) could help promote relaxation among the general population, significantly when stress levels are increasing internationally, such as during the COVID-19 outbreak. These findings, however, need to be approached with care due to methodological constraints, such as the lack of randomized clinical studies and longer-term evidence [23]. Recent studies have attempted to demonstrate the effectiveness of virtual reality (VR) for elderly individuals across the care continuum, from evaluation to prevention to rehabilitation. For example, Gamito et al. studied an aged group of volunteers to investigate if VR technology might be used to prevent or slow the neurodegenerative diseases that come with age. According to the study's findings, the intervention group's concentration and memorization abilities improved much more than those of the control group [24]. For cognitive testing function, Negro Causa et al. compare immersive and non-immersive 360° circumstances. Memorizing items from one's surroundings is part of the cognitive study. The findings suggest that memory retention was only improved in a non-immersive environment. These findings and prospective future research areas in the cognitive assessment are discussed in their research. The results suggest that immersive 360° technology is not as effective as previously anticipated in improving episodic memory preservation; further research is needed to grasp the ramifications of this technology [25] correctly. Finally, Riva et al. focus on augmented reality (AR) and virtual reality (VR) and examine their applications in behavioral health and the findings of the 28 systematic reviews and meta-analyses currently available. Afterward, the study explores how VR and AR bring an additional level of value to modifying external experiences, focusing on the degree of self-reflection and personal efficacy generated by their feeling of presence and emotional involvement. It describes how virtuality can be used to reshape our inner experience in the future by organizing, changing, and replacing our bodily self-consciousness [26].

Ultimately, a new breed of transformative experiences may emerge that uncover previously experientially hidden knowledge while simultaneously transforming an individual's view [27, 28]. This is a small sampling of various applications of VR in medical, surgical, clinical, and training situations. There is considerable potential for using virtual reality in medical evaluation with training methodology [29]. Applying systems engineering principles to this domain, the remainder of this chapter will work through the steps necessary to design a system for stakeholders based on their preferences and desires. While not complete, the requirements and technical performance measures for a simple integrated structure will be discussed through a few use cases [30]. A spoof of non-directional psychotherapy, Weizenbaum's ELIZA, appeared in an initial psychotherapy interview. The doctor's instructions and data dictate the speech patterns of ELIZA despite her reputation as a psychotherapist. On the other hand, the phrase "virtual patient" refers to interactive computer simulations used in healthcare education [31]. A particular emphasis is placed on the simulation of clinical processes using virtual patients. Virtual patients bring together scientific excellence, cutting-edge technology, and the novel concept of game-based learning. Virtual patients allow the learner to assume the role of a healthcare professional and practice clinical skills such as diagnosis and treatment decisions. Computer-based simulations of virtual patients have also been considered to supplement clinical training [32–34]. The use of virtual patient programs in healthcare is growing, partly in response to increased demands on healthcare professionals and student education, but also because they allow students to practice in a safe environment [35]. Kononowicz et al. conducted a literature review to identify all articles that used the term "virtual patient" in the title or abstract. This study looked at 536 articles published between 1991 and December 2013. Three hundred and thirty of them were thought to be educational. As VPS, Interactive Patient Scenarios were used in three-quarters of the articles [31]. Over time, an assessment of the literature reveals a general trend toward using web-based patient setups as the most common type of VP in clinical training. Researchers and VP creators in healthcare education can use this modified classification to describe better the kind of VP they are focusing on and avoid misunderstandings [36–39].

1.3 STAKEHOLDERS OF THE SYSTEM

The first step in designing a system is to define its requirements. An individual, an entity, or another subsystem is considered a stakeholder if they have a significant impact on, are influenced by, connected to, or contribute in some way to the system's outcomes. Our proposed design examines two types of stakeholders, active and passive. Users, commercial enterprises, and other participating platforms in the proposed system are engaged stakeholders. Passive stakeholders are individuals, organizations, rules and processes, and standards that impact the system's efficacy.

Active stakeholder groups included the user (patient, student), management (financial and management authority), doctors or other providers, supporting staff, and hardware and software maintenance individuals. The system's developers, researchers, local and global markets, VR devices, and government entities are all passive stakeholders. Table 1.1 shows active stakeholders and their responsibilities, whereas Table 1.2 shows passive stakeholders and their responsibilities. Figures 1.1 and 1.2 represent active and passive stakeholders, respectively.

Table 1.1 Roles and responsibilities of active stakeholders

Stakeholders	Responsibilities
User	A user will run the system and use it according to his or her needs.
Administrators	The system's funding and management will be overseen by administrators.
Service providers	The system will be serviced by medical providers (like doctors, nurses, and pharmacists).
Supporting personnel	Pre-medication professionals and lab technicians are examples of supporting personnel.
Maintenance	Maintainers oversee the repair and upgrade services for the VR devices and software.

Table 1.2 Roles and responsibilities of passive stakeholders

Stakeholders	Functions
Designers	In possession of the system's development, distribution, and maintenance.
R&D officers	Investigation period statistics and support with modifications for the designers.
Local clients	Capturing local clients will help capture the local market.
Global market	Globally, the system will be introduced on the international market.
VR devices	Immersive, virtual experiences will be created through the use of VR devices.
Other devices	The VR device can be connected to other devices to collate, store, and exchange data.
Authorities	Medical regulations and guidelines are regulated by a variety of government authorities.

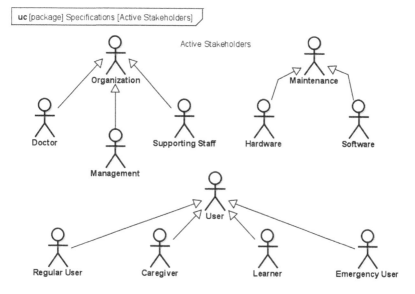

Figure 1.1 Illustration of active stakeholders.

1.3.1 Desirements of the stakeholders

A desire or need expressed by a stakeholder that a current system cannot meet is the starting point for developing a new system. When stakeholder expectations are only desired rather than required, those are referred to as stakeholder desirements. Research shows that the stakeholders for a VR medical system are looking for specific features fundamental to their pre-conceived notions. This section focuses on capturing stakeholder desires, expectations, and requirements representing the foundation of system validation – what system they want.

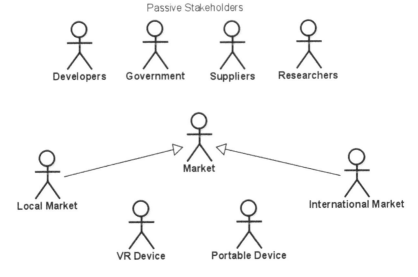

Figure 1.2 Demonstration of passive stakeholders.

Table 1.3 represents a sample of stakeholder desirements. Some desires are based on a virtual reality implementation and utilize multiple sensors and devices. Uses include therapeutic solutions, healthcare for children, surgical aid, training for medical support staff and users, pre-medication, robotic surgery, psychiatric counseling, and autism therapy. The cultural

Table 1.3 Summary of stakeholder desires

Stakeholder desires
A VR healthcare system with several sensors can be employed.
A treatment system based on a portable gadget.
Children's healthcare system based on virtual reality.
A surgical trial using a VR medical app system.
Virtual reality-based robotic surgery.
Medical support employees can receive training in a virtual reality-based healthcare system.
Training for patients and users in a virtual reality-based healthcare system.
Psychological intervention via virtual reality treatment.
Pre-medication technology based on virtual reality.
Virtual reality technology is being used to treat autism.
On the VR-based healthcare system, client data is kept private.
Patients should be treated according to their ethnicity.
Virtual patients are being created for training purposes.

requirement expresses the concern for patient differences. Additional system requirements (not shown here) include data security, privacy concerns, etc.

1.4 SYSTEM PURPOSE AND CONCEPT OF OPERATIONS

1.4.1 Concept of operations

There are various ways to describe a system, including virtual reality [30]. This section will highlight the intention and operational concept of the system through the mind map in Figure 1.3 and the following discussion. The mind map is showcased with several parts to design the system, like actions of the users and the system, goals, features of the system, preservation, and guidelines for the user. The entire system will receive data from the human body, share data with medical support personnel, and provide medical solutions using virtual reality and numerous sensor-based devices. This system of interest (SoI) comprises a few instruments, a software-based application, and a data-sharing system. The method does not need a physical location to find medical workers because VR technology is incorporated. Users may utilize VR devices with goggles and portable, multiple sensor-based devices like a watch and a smartphone app. High-level system operation can be determined based on stakeholder desires. The system allows users to choose recommended medical staff, medical staff can provide feedback, emergency assistance can be provided through the system, a medical team can evaluate regular health reports, and one-on-one sessions with medical professionals can be arranged. Additionally, medical associates will be able to receive surgical aid demonstrations.

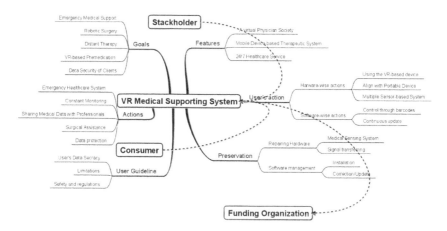

Figure 1.3 A mind map of the proposed system.

1.4.1.1 Current and planned system

A range of therapeutically supportive systems is accessible in today's world, some of which rely on intelligent frameworks. A good example is ScenicSoft, an IT-based firm that has spent the previous ten years working in clinical therapy and has produced a fantastic VR-based item for cancer trials. They have created a methodology for creating a training program for healthcare workers, including virtual reality. However, the paradigm is of little use to patients, focusing on clinical professional training rather than the patient's perspective [40]. On the other hand, Ghost Productions offers training frameworks to reduce catastrophic human mistakes in almost all mission-critical services. Learn how virtual reality improves medical and surgical training while decreasing medical errors, the third most significant cause of mortality in the United States. In response, they created a very successful virtual reality (VR) medical and surgical teaching system based on simulations, Wraith [41]. Despite this, our stakeholders and research team believe that no system delivers realistic medical and surgical virtual-assisted aid advantageous to clinical personnel and patients.

1.4.1.2 Functions of the system

The system will be segmented into several components, including a chronic patient, psychiatric patient, and emergency (acute) assistance. All users must register and choose appropriate options to begin using the system. Figure 1.4 summarizes, at a high level, the system's functionality for providing medical

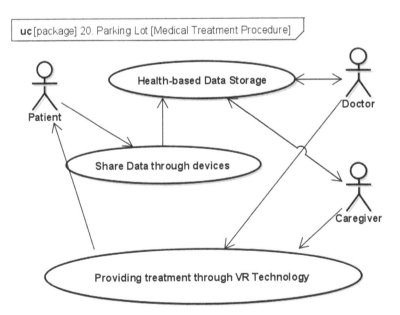

Figure 1.4 An illustration of the medical treatment procedure of the proposed system.

treatment. Depending on the user's role, various functions will be available in the system.

- In order to update essential family and health information, a patient-user must first register and open an account.
- Following that, sensors will be incorporated into mobile and wrist-worn devices. The health data of patients will be regularly updated through these devices.
- Medical support staff can review data when the system detects a problem.
- The system will inform and suggest taking the initiative during any situation that has been defined for such actions
- The user can select to share their data with a specific specialist.
- The user can directly contact the doctor and get the medication utilizing the systems.

1.4.1.3 Critical system requirements

Critical system requirements make the system usable and acceptable to the users. There are many types of users for this system, and each will have its requirements. Share among all users will be the need for data security and privacy. This is an essential exemplar requirement: no one will desire to use the system without it. Another critical requirement would be that the system must be highly responsive to the user and be obvious regarding system malfunctions. The user interface will be required to present information in a timely and informative fashion for each category of users, tailored to their specified preferences. For all users, the system and user profile data and preferences will be a critical part of proper system functioning and will require review frequently. The system will have multiple help options – for system operation, acute patient care, and guidance about a particular medical condition or concern. In the last two of these, the system can guide the patient-user about what services are available and assist the user in obtaining timely medical assistance. Emergency services can be notified if the patient is in such poor condition that they cannot use the help option properly, or the user can request emergency help as needed. Finally, users' clinical data should be updated periodically to reflect any activity within the system (and external to the system) to enable appropriate treatment as required. Outdated information in the system – both system knowledge and patient data – will render the system useless.

1.4.2 Context diagram

A context diagram in Figure 1.5 shows the scope, bounds, and links between the system of interest and its environment. There are four terminators in the

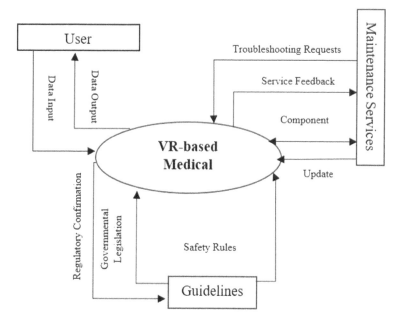

Figure 1.5 Context diagram for the VR-based medical support system.

system, each of which is an external part of functions that take place outside of the proposed methodology.

1.4.2.1 First terminator

The user is the first terminator in the system. By sharing information with the medical support staff, they can obtain knowledge and guidance or receive treatment.

1.4.2.2 Second terminator

Maintaining the system correctly throughout its lifetime is the company's second terminator. Using troubleshooting requests, one can determine whether or not there are any system malfunctions, as well as determine what those malfunctions are; components are used to correct damaged parts within the system, and updates keep the operating system updated and enhance it.

1.4.2.3 Third terminator

Information about the malfunction and even the parts that need replacing is provided by service feedback. The output amounts flowing to maintenance services are components, which are the parts that need to be replaced. There will be a wide variety of maintenance and support required by the system and its various components, all of which may not be provided by the same entity.

1.4.2.4 Fourth terminator

The final termination point is a set of guidelines. From this terminator, input variables include system-based safety standards, health regulations, and environmental regulations. It is necessary to produce regulatory confirmation in order to comply with all guidelines, rules, and laws. Complying with these guidelines will be a critical task for the system.

1.5 SYSTEMS REQUIREMENTS AND USE CASES

The system requirements specify the configuration that a system will need – hardware, software programs, or processes – to perform accurately and successfully. The inability to satisfy stakeholder requirements will prevent the system's adoption by those stakeholders. A team of systems engineers develops system requirements in concert with other specialty engineers to meet the stakeholders. As the system requirements are derived, care is given to ensure that systems thinking is applied to innovate as required, but the system behaves as desired. A sample of system requirements is shown in Table 1.4.

The system was built by identifying specific system requirements to satisfy stakeholder expectations. Since the system shall have multiple sensor-based VR solutions and portable devices such as smartphones, wrist watches, and VR goggles aligned with the system, the client will be able to share data with the system. Still, the system must provide a safe environment, adequate medical staff, adequate pre-medical support, adequate pre-medication, exceptional psychological support to children, the training of users, and robotic surgical training, and the system must be updated regularly to achieve the desired outcome.

1.5.1 Use cases

The use case map details the possible interaction between a user and a system. Use case diagrams typically represent several types of users and multiple use cases of a system in their simplest form, an extension of which may be another diagram. Figure 1.6 illustrates how users can send or receive data between specific medical support staff members. According to the transfer data use case, users choose a medical provider and provide treatment requirements. The system then shares its clinical data with the provider. However, a simple use case illustrates the condition that the user

Table 1.4 The system's requirements are listed

ID	Requirements	Brief description
01	Multiple sensors	The system shall utilize various sensors.
02	Support staff	The system shall make support available 24/7.
03	Sharing data	The system shall allow the user to share data with specified other users.
03.1	Data secrecy	The system shall ensure that privacy is maintained for all users.
04	Pre-medical support	The system shall provide pre-medical support.
04.1	Pre-medication	The system shall provide pre-medication information and support to the user.
05	Child support	The system shall have a separate child healthcare section.
06	Portable medical support	The system shall be compatible with portable devices.
07	Psychological support	The system shall have psychological therapy.
07.1	Autism treatment	The system shall prove VR autism treatment.
08	Regular data update	The system shall require user review and update of information at a minimum of once every 30 days.
09	Training for healthcare provider	The system shall provide training for support staff.
09.1	Surgical experiment	The virtual environment shall support surgical experimentation.
09.2	Robotic surgery	The system shall include support for VR-based robotic surgery.
10	Training for patients	The system shall provide training for patients.
12	System response time	The system response time shall be no longer than two seconds under normal operating conditions.
12.1	Support staff	The system shall provide support staff responsible for patient users within ten minutes.
12.2	Max time to response	The system shall respond within 25 seconds.
12.3	Emergency support	The system shall provide emergency support within two minutes.
13	System update	The system shall update the knowledge base every 60 days.
13.1	Regular system update	The system shall update every ten months and update as a new version.
13.2	Correction	The system shall respond to user correction within two hours.
14	Data storage	The data storage shall be expandable as needed.
14.1	Minimum space	The minimum storage capacity shall be 1 GB for the individual user.
14.2	Maximum space	The maximum storage capacity shall be 5 GB for the individual user.
15	Treatment based on ethnicity	The system shall have configurable profile options to allow the user to select their ethnicity.
16	Virtual patient	The system shall have virtual patients from different ethnicities for training and educational purposes for healthcare givers.

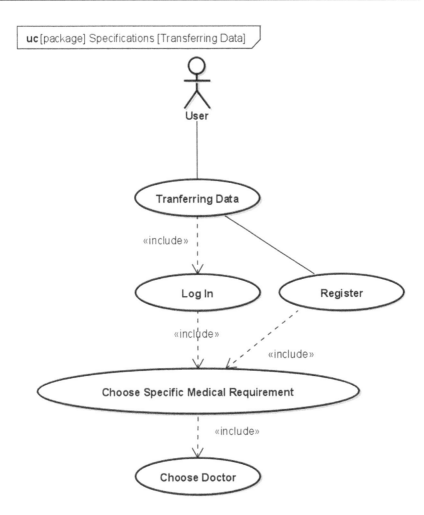

uc [package] Specifications [Transferring Data]

User

Tranferring Data

«include»

Log In

Register

«include»

«include»

Choose Specific Medical Requirement

«include»

Choose Doctor

Figure 1.6 Use case of transferring data.

must select a doctor to whom data is to be transferred. The use case shown in Figure 1.7 is a high-level use case capturing the variety of treatments and services available through the use of the system. This use case is not all-inclusive but highlights the more important design aspects from the user perspective.

1.5.2 Block definition diagrams

In block definition diagrams (BDD), system components (properties, behaviors, and constraints), interfaces, and relationships are displayed in a static format. In BDD, there are five parts to a system: blocks, agents, ports, dependencies,

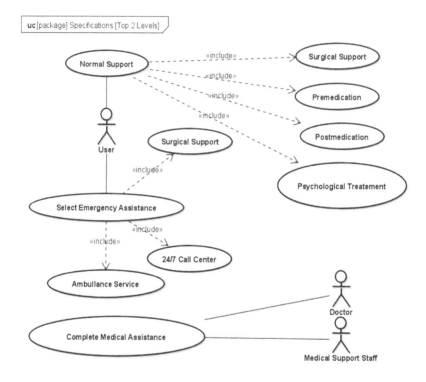

Figure 1.7 Top-level functionality of the proposed system.

and flows. Figure 1.8 demonstrates how to configure system dynamic frameworks for control, data, and interface objects using the BDD shown. This BDD is drawn in Astah by using Systems Modeling Language (SysML).

1.6 TECHNICAL PERFORMANCE MEASURE (TPM)

Technical performance measures (TPMs) are derived from system requirements. A TPM approach is a method of predicting the future significance of a major conceptual evaluation metric of a higher-level end design process based on current evaluations of lower-level goods in a system structure [42]. TPMs are important because they ensure that the system reflects the customers' demands, providing metrics that the system engineers can use as guidelines during the design and construction of the system. TPMs demonstrate how the approach satisfies the system requirements, and as such, are measurable. They will form the foundation of verification and validation testing performed on the system to satisfy the users' desires. It meets the required measures of technical performance. The systems engineering maintenance team

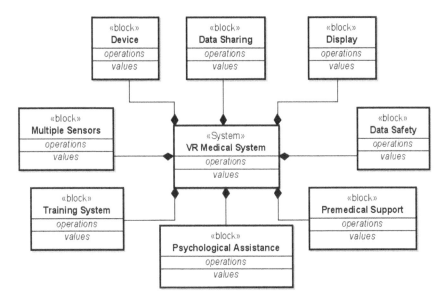

Figure 1.8 BDD for the proposed system.

will collect, analyze, check, and react to TPM indicators [43–45]. Several technical performance measures will be developed during the prototype of the system, which is demonstrated in Table 1.5. In addition to existing simulations and VR-based interactive approaches, the proposed system can gain insights from existing simulations and VR-based interactive techniques.

Table 1.5 An illustration of the five crucial TPMs

	TPM		Description
1	System response time	Max time to response	The system shall respond within 25 seconds.
		Support staff	The support staff shall take a maximum of ten minutes to respond.
		Emergency support	The system shall take a maximum of two minutes for emergency support.
2	Data storage	Minimum space	The system shall have a minimum of 1 GB storage capacity for the individual user.
		Maximum space	The system shall have a maximum of 10 GB storage capacity for the individual user.
3	Support staff	Medical assistants	The system shall have a minimum of 15 medical assistants.
		Available doctors	The system shall have a minimum of four specialist doctors in each category.
4	System update	Correction	The system shall correct every 30 days.
		System update	The system shall update every ten months.
5	Regular data update		The system shall update every 30 days.

1.7 CONCLUSION

VR is a platform that lets individuals engage with one another in an immersive fashion in a computer-generated world. VR has enormous potential in the world of medical sciences. Currently, however, virtual reality in the medical field is relatively limited. There are just a handful of VR-based systems available for teaching doctors and other medical support professionals. VR can be used to treat and manage several conditions and provide training. According to this study, existing systems were generally built-in isolation. The optimal use of VR and associated technologies and devices can only be determined through a systems engineering approach. The use of VR systems in healthcare can assist caregivers, train clinicians, and help patients. There is a common goal shared by all these perspectives: helping people live better lives. Besides, the virtual hospital would simulate a wide range of healthcare scenarios in real-time, with advanced technology as well as proven safety standards, in order to simulate a wide range of healthcare systems. An evaluation of a virtual reality-based system for medical assistance is presented in this chapter. The technology is integrated into many devices, including VR goggles, sensors, and smartwatches. The system can be accessed by users based on their preferences. The service enables users to exchange data with medical personnel, receive feedback, and obtain pre-medical treatments, surgical assistance, psychological advice, as well as emergency support.

This chapter also covers a background discussion of why VR-based medical support systems are important, the proposed system's objective, a stakeholder analysis, the development of an operational concept, the extraction of user needs, and finally a discussion of essential technical performance measurements. Based on the results of the research so far, VR systems within the medical field are highly promising. To sum up, VR systems in the healthcare industry are suitable for on-the-job training, designing a suitable environment, reducing patient risk, and treating patients through virtual environments. Moreover, it can be argued that future endeavors might include developing stakeholder-based approaches for developing new protocols and experimental therapies that would otherwise be difficult to assess due to safety issues. The current technological advancements are being harnessed to support the continual transformation of medical treatment through VR, which makes a modest but significant impact on healthcare.

REFERENCES

1. Gallagher, Anthony G., & Christopher U. Cates. "Virtual reality training for the operating room and cardiac catheterization laboratory." *Lancet* vol. 364,9444 (2004): 1538–40. https://doi.org/10.1016/S0140-6736(04)17278-4.
2. Roberts, Brent W. et al. "Patterns of mean-level change in personality traits across the life course: a meta-analysis of longitudinal studies." *Psychological Bulletin* vol. 132,1 (2006): 1–25. https://doi.org/10.1037/0033-2909.132.1.1.

3. Johnson, Julie K., & Paul Barach. "Patient care handovers: what will it take to ensure quality and safety during times of transition." *The Medical Journal of Australia* vol. 190,S11 (2009): S110–2. https://doi.org/10.5694/j.1326-5377 .2009.tb02614.x.

4. Haller, Guy et al. "Quality and safety indicators in anesthesia: a systematic review." *Anesthesiology* vol. 110,5 (2009): 1158–75. https://doi.org/10.1097/ ALN.0b013e3181a1093b.

5. Pathan, Sayeedakhanum, Megha Bhushan, & Anita Bai. "A study on health care using data mining techniques." *Journal of Critical Reviews* vol. 7,19 (2020): 7877–7890. https://doi.org/10.31838/jcr.07.19.896.

6. Zhang, Juhua, et al. "LeNup: learning nucleosome positioning from DNA sequences with improved convolutional neural networks." *Bioinformatics* vol. 34,10 (2018): 1705–12. https://doi.org/10.1093/bioinformatics/ bty003.

7. Rafael Sacks, Amotz Perlman, & Ronen Barak. "Construction safety training using immersive virtual reality." *Construction Management, and Economics* vol. 31,9 (2013): 1005–17. https://doi.org/10.1080/01446193.2013.828844.

8. Wiederhold, Brenda K., & Giuseppe Riva. "Positive technology supports the shift to preventive, integrative health." *Cyberpsychology, Behavior and Social Networking* vol. 15,2 (2012): 67–8. https://doi.org/10.1089/ cyber.2011.1533.

9. Gadelha, Rene. "Revolutionizing education: The promise of virtual reality." *Childhood Education* 94:1,40–3. https://doi.org/10.1080/00094056.2018 .1420362.

10. Baukal, C. E., Ausburn, F. B., & Ausburn, L. J. "A proposed multimedia cone of abstraction: updating a classic instructional design theory." *Journal of Educational Technology*, 9,4 (2013): 15–24. Retrieved February 5, 2022, from https://www.learntechlib.org/p/194433/.

11. Bloom, B. S. "Time and learning." *American Psychologist*, 29,9 (1974): 682–688. https://doi.org/10.1037/h0037632.

12. Sánchez-Cabrero, Roberto et al. "Improvement of body satisfaction in older people: an experimental study." *Frontiers in Psychology* vol. 10 (2018): 2823. 12 Dec. 2019. https://doi.org/10.3389/fpsyg.2019.02823.

13. Norris, Michael W., Kristen, Spicer, & Byrd, Traci. "Virtual reality: The new pathway for effective safety training." *Professional Safety* vol. 64 (2019): 36–9.

14. Bracq, Marie-Stéphanie et al. "Virtual reality simulation in nontechnical skills training for healthcare professionals: a systematic review." *Simulation in Healthcare: Journal of the Society for Simulation in Healthcare* vol. 14,3 (2019): 188–94. https://doi.org/10.1097/SIH.0000000000000347.

15. King, Christopher L et al. "A trial of a triple-drug treatment for lymphatic filariasis." *The New England Journal of Medicine* vol. 379,19 (2018): 1801–10. https://doi.org/10.1056/NEJMoa1706854.

16. Vaughan, Neil et al. "A review of virtual reality-based training simulators for orthopedic surgery." *Medical Engineering & Physics* vol. 38,2 (2016): 59–71. https://doi.org/10.1016/j.medengphy.2015.11.021.

17. Khan, M. N. R., Shakir, A. K., Nadi, S. S., & Abedin M. Z. (2022) "An android application for university-based academic solution for crisis situation." In: Shakya, S., Balas, V. E., Kamolphiwong, S., & Du, K. L. (eds)

Sentimental Analysis and Deep Learning. Advances in Intelligent Systems and Computing, vol 1408. Springer, Singapore. https://doi.org/10.1007/978-981-16-5157-1_51.

18. Thompson-Butel, Angelica G et al. "The role of personalized virtual reality in education for patients post stroke-a qualitative case series." *Journal of Stroke and Cerebrovascular Diseases: The Official Journal of National Stroke Association* vol. 28,2 (2019): 450–7. https://doi.org/10.1016/j.jstroke cerebrovasdis.2018.10.018.

19. Hoffmann, Tammy, & Kryss McKenna. "Analysis of stroke patients' and carers' reading ability and the content and design of written materials: recommendations for improving written stroke information." *Patient Education and Counseling* vol. 60,3 (2006): 286–93. https://doi.org/10.1016/j.pec.2005.06.020.

20. Roy, Arnab et al. "Correction: The evolution of cost-efficiency in neural networks during recovery from traumatic brain injury." *PloS One* vol. 13,10 (12 Oct. 2018): e0206005. https://doi.org/10.1371/journal.pone.0206005.

21. Felnhofer, Anna, et al. "Is virtual reality emotionally arousing? Investigating five emotion-inducing virtual park scenarios." *International Journal of Human-Computer Studies* vol. 82 (2015): 48–56.

22. Ferrer-García, Marta et al. "A randomised controlled comparison of second-level treatment approaches for treatment-resistant adults with bulimia nervosa and binge eating disorder: assessing the benefits of virtual reality cue exposure therapy." *European Eating Disorders Review: The Journal of the Eating Disorders Association* vol. 25,6 (2017): 479–90. https://doi.org/10.1002/erv.2538.

23. Riches, Simon et al. "Virtual reality relaxation for the general population: a systematic review." *Social Psychiatry and Psychiatric Epidemiology* vol. 56,10 (2021): 1707–27. https://doi.org/10.1007/s00127-021-02110-z.

24. Gamito, Pedro et al. "Cognitive training on stroke patients via virtual reality-based serious games." *Disability and Rehabilitation* vol. 39,4 (2017): 385–8. https://doi.org/10.3109/09638288.2014.934925.

25. Negro Causa, Erica et al. "New frontiers for cognitive assessment: an exploratory study of the potentiality of 360° technologies for memory evaluation." *Cyberpsychology, Behavior and Social Networking* vol. 22,1 (2019): 76–81. https://doi.org/10.1089/cyber.2017.0720.

26. Riva, Giuseppe et al. "Transforming experience: the potential of augmented reality and virtual reality for enhancing personal and clinical change." *Frontiers in Psychiatry* vol. 7 (30 Sep. 2016): 164. https://doi.org/10.3389/fpsyt.2016.00164.

27. Kirmse, Sebastian et al. "A comprehensive commercialization framework for nanocomposites utilizing a model-based systems engineering approach." *Systems* vol. 9, 4 (2021): 84.

28. Lagassé, Lisa P et al. "How accessible was information about H1N1 flu? Literacy assessments of CDC guidance documents for different audiences." *PloS one* vol. 6,10 (2011): e23583. https://doi.org/10.1371/journal.pone.0023583.

29. Badarudeen, Sameer, and Sanjeev Sabharwal. "Assessing readability of patient education materials: current role in orthopedics." *Clinical Orthopedics and Related Research* vol. 468,10 (2010): 2572–80. https://doi.org/10.1007/s11999-010-1380-y.

30. Mostashari, A., McComb, S. A., Kennedy, D. M., Cloutier, R., & Korfiatis, P. Developing a stakeholder-assisted agile CONOPS development process. *Systems Engineering* vol. 15 (2012): 1–13. https://doi.org/10.1002/sys.20190.

31. "Adrianne Wortzel; *ELIZA REDUX*: A Mutable Iteration." *Leonardo* vol. 40,1 (2007): 31–6. https://doi.org/10.1162/leon.2007.40.1.31.

32. Dafli, Eleni et al. "Virtual patients on the semantic Web: a proof-of-application study." *Journal of Medical Internet Research* vol. 17, (22 Jan. 2015): 1 e16. https://doi.org/10.2196/jmir.3933.

33. Isaza-Restrepo, Andrés et al. "The virtual patient as a learning tool: a mixed quantitative, qualitative study." *BMC Medical Education* vol. 18,1 (6 Dec. 2018): 297. https://doi.org/10.1186/s12909-018-1395-8.

34. Huang, Grace et al. "Virtual patient simulation at US and Canadian medical schools." *Academic Medicine: Journal of the Association of American Medical Colleges* vol. 82,5 (2007): 446–51. https://doi.org/10.1097/ACM .0b013e31803e8a0a.

35. Kononowicz, Andrzej A. et al. "Virtual patients--what are we talking about? A framework to classify the meanings of the term in healthcare education." *BMC Medical Education* vol. 15 (1 Feb. 2015): 11. https://doi.org/10.1186/ s12909-015-0296-3.

36. Devi, T. (2021). *Securing IoT in Industry 4.0 Applications with Blockchain* (P. Kaliraj, Ed.) (1st ed.). Auerbach Publications. https://doi.org/10.1201 /9781003175872

37. Mondal, J., & Das, A. (2021). *Medical Internet of Things: Techniques, Practices, and Applications* (A. Mitra, Ed.) (1st ed.). Chapman and Hall/ CRC. https://doi.org/10.1201/9780429318078

38. Linger, Richard C., & Hevner, Alan R. "Flow semantics for intelligent control in IoT systems." *Journal of Decision Systems* vol. 27,2 (2018): 63–77. https://doi.org/10.1080/12460125.2018.1529973.

39. Dimitrov, Dimiter V. "Medical internet of things and big data in healthcare." *Healthcare Informatics Research* vol. 22,3 (2016): 156–63. https://doi.org/10 .4258/hir.2016.22.3.156.

40. Di Meglio, Alberto, & Estrella, Florida. (2012). *ScienceSoft: Open Software for Open Science.* 032. https://doi.org/10.22323/1.153.0032.

41. *Highly Effective VR Medical & Surgical Training*, Ghost Productions, 14 May 2020. https://ghostproductions.com/medical-vr-virtual-reality/surgical -training/.

42. Erasmus, L. D., & Doeben-Henisch, G., "A theory for the systems engineering process." *IEEE Africon '11*, 2011, pp. 1–5. https://doi.org/10.1109/AFRCON .2011.6071989.

43. Kim, H., & Ben-Othman, J., "Toward integrated virtual emotion system with AI applicability for secure CPS-enabled smart cities: AI-based research challenges and security issues." In *IEEE Network*, vol. 34,3 (May/June 2020): 30–6. https://doi.org/10.1109/MNET.011.1900299.

44. Demir, I. E., Ceyhan, G. O., & Friess, H. "Surgery and the kings of medical science." *Langenbecks Arch Surg* vol. 406 (2021): 1669–71. https://doi.org/10 .1007/s00423-021-02242-5.

45. Kyaw, B. M., Posadzki, P., Paddock, S., Car, J., Campbell, J., & Tudor Car, L. "Effectiveness of digital education on communication skills among medical students: Systematic review and meta-analysis by the digital health education collaboration." *Journal of Medical Internet Research*, vol. 21,8, (2019): e12967. https://doi.org/10.2196/12967.

Chapter 2

ConvMax

Classification of COVID-19, pneumonia, and normal lungs from X-ray images using CNN with modified max-pooling layer

Kinjal A. Patel, Ashish Patel, Darshil P. Patel, and Shubham J. Bhanderi

CONTENTS

2.1 INTRODUCTION

The coronaviruses are frequently transmissible to birds, but in past years they have become proficient at transmitting to humans as well. The novel coronavirus is identified from its genome composition as it has a similar genome structure to severe acute respiratory syndrome (SARS) infection [1]. Therefore, it is also recognized as SARS-CoV-2, that is, a novel variant of the SARS virus. The infectious virus called corona was initially discovered in inhabitants of China and quickly extended over the earth. The novel coronavirus is hastily spread from one living being to many more within a small period.

The symptoms of coronavirus have varied for each human being based on their immunity. The major symptom of this infectious virus is high fever. In addition, a person may have a loss of sensation and weariness, as well as a few symptoms such as dry cough with a sore throat, problems breathing, aching in the chest, headache, and diarrhea [2]. Due to symptoms of dry cough and chest aching, in some cases, it is considered a pneumonia infection instead of a COVID-19 infection. The symptoms of coronavirus

DOI: 10.1201/9781003286745-2

are similar to pneumonia and malaria disease. Thus, it is required to distinguish between them. In some cases, a person may carry the COVID-19 virus, but that person does not feel any symptoms of COVID-19 due to strong immunity. Thus, the infectious one may not be aware that he/she has a coronavirus infection due to strong immunity, but the coronavirus is spread by this person to others who may get in contact with that person. Due to the transmissible behavior of COVID-19, several countries applied strict lockdowns to prevent the transfer of COVID-19.

COVID-19-positive patients number 610,393,563 globally. At least 6,508,521 fatalities had been confirmed in the year 2022 [3]. Because of the large number of coronavirus-infected illnesses, the World Health Organization declared an international public health emergency [4]. By February 2020, the World Health Organization (WHO) had named this disease COVID-19 [5]. A total of 1,83,54,342 positive COVID-19 cases and 6,96,147 deaths were confirmed globally by 5 August 2020 around the world [6]. A total of 19,08,254 positive COVID-19 cases and 39,795 deaths were confirmed by 5 August 2020 in India only [6]. India is in third position with a huge number of COVID-19-positive cases across the globe [7]. The doctors, nurses, healthcare workers, cleaning staff, police officers, and municipal health officers are also getting infected while treating and working around COVID-19-positive patients.

The research community from various fields is working to find proper treatment and antibiotics for the COVID-19 cure. As coronavirus has symptoms of pneumonia and malaria also, it is tough to identify the COVID-19 infection. Due to the unavailability of proper drugs and medicine, the initial discovery of the coronavirus-infected person is required to avoid the spreading of coronavirus. The majority of nations have imposed strict lockdowns to avoid the increase in the infection of COVID-19 among their people. Many government agencies have declared open competitions for innovative ideas from brilliant minds from every domain to handle the situation of the COVID-19 global pandemic [8–11]. Gujarat, Maharashtra, Andhra Pradesh, Delhi, and Tamil Nadu are the most affected states in India [12]. Thus, there is a requirement for the management of patient care, hospitality resources, and sterilization on a large scale. The other challenges are the detection of fake news, online education for youth, and maintaining social distance while applying lockdown. Also, business stabilization, tracking the movement of groups, and online conferences for study, discussions, and making a decision about extending lockdowns are challenges [8–11].

Before unlocking the country, the Government of India divided the areas into three zones, the red zone, orange zone, and green zone, for the highly COVID-19-affected area, moderately COVID-19-affected area, and low COVID-19-affected area respectively. After that, the Government of India declared a containment zone where a COVID-19-positive person is identified, and nowadays the Government of India has closed only limited areas called micro-containment zones where only a COVID-19-positive person and the related limited area are blocked. Also, the concept of herd immunity is applied in India.

The vast explosion in COVID-19-positive cases leads to medical equipment and tools storage. The test utilized to check whether a person is COVID-19-positive or not is a real-time reverse transcription-polymerase chain reaction (RT-PCR) test. But this test is not considered to be precise. The RT-PCR test provides low sensitivity along with high false-negative rates [13]. Due to less accuracy of the RT-PCR test, it might possible that a COVID-19-infected person was declared negative but that person may carry coronavirus. So, that person can spread the virus to other people.

As opposed to RT-PCR, radiographic imaging of the ribs and lungs computed tomography (CT) and X-ray is more sensitive and accurate in detecting and studying COVID-19, which can manifest as chest pain and dry cough [13]. The chest or ribs X-ray and CT are some of the best solutions to detect COVID-19-positive people at the initial phase. But as positive cases increased, there was a lack of RT-PCR tools, radiologists, and medical professionals to examine chest X-ray reports. Therefore, a coronavirus-affected world requires an involuntary instrument capable of determining whether a chest X-ray image has a COVID-19 infection, pneumonia, or is normal (uninfected). This automated technique for diagnosing COVID-19 infection or pneumonia or normal should be considered in situations when there is a dearth of medical personnel.

The main goal of this research is to categorize COVID-19 infection, pneumonia, and normal (uninfected) cases from X-ray chest pictures. Deep learning, a sophisticated branch of artificial intelligence, is employed to distinguish between people infected with COVID-19, pneumonia, and non-infected people. The CNN deep learning architecture is used for binary class classification between COVID-19 and normal, as well as multi-class classification between COVID-19, pneumonia, and normal. The CNN is trained using dataset-1 and consists of three 2D convolutional layers. The dataset-1 consists of the X-rays of chest images – COVID-19 and normal. Another CNN is applied with three 2D convolutional layers and trained by considering dataset-2. The dataset-2 consists of the X-rays of chest images – COVID-19, pneumonia, and normal. Different estimate methods, including confusion matrices, are used to assess the CNN model's performance. In terms of broader features map extraction, a novelty is that a size 3×3 filter is used instead of a 2×2 filter in the max-pooling layer. The modified max-pooling layer of the convolutional neural network is coined as ConvMax. The novelty of ConvMax – modification in the size of max-pooling layer of convolutional neural network is added while training of CNN model.

The structure of the chapter is as follows: works regarding this field will be discussed in the "Literature review" section; afterward, the "Proposed work" section will discussed the implemented CNN model for dataset-1 with the classification of binary classes and dataset-2 with the classification of multi-class. The enactment of the CNN model and its performance comparison with different fractions of datasets is discussed in the section on "Results and discussion"; the chapter is finished in the "Conclusion" section.

2.2 LITERATURE REVIEW

Specific patterns have been identified by researchers from the COVID-19-positive person's chest and lungs X-ray images [14]. They have released the uniqueness of features on the data of chest CTs and radiographic images of COVID-19 infection [14]. The RTPCR kits were limited as compared to the increased ones in positive cases. The comparative study was held by Xie et al. [15] with 167 patients with COVID-19. Of those 167 COVID-19 patients, 3% of them tested negative by RT-PCR. However, chest CT and X-rays revealed that just 3% of patients were COVID-19-positive.

Another survey was conducted by Bernheim et al. [16] by investigating chest CTs of a total of 121 COVID-19-infected patients. The infection was found to be increased compared to the initial stage. Two patients were inspected by Fang et al. [17] for their symptoms along with their history of traveling. The chest CT gives advanced sensitivity as compared to the RT-PCR test to recognize the infection.

Khan et al. [18] established a model such as COVIDRENet and custom visual geometric group (VGG) for the categorization of positive or negative diseases from X-ray images. The feature extracted from CNN is given as input to SVM for improvement of model performance. While evaluating the results, the five-fold cross-validation is applied to the dataset. The concept of contacting the features of both the models gives 98.3% accuracy, 0.99 AUC, 0.97 F-score, 98% recall, and 96.67% precision.

Wang et al. [19] designed COVID-Net as a CNN with extremely minimal convolution and computation as compared to VGG-19 and ResNet-50. Firstly, an ImageNet dataset is used to pre-trained the developed COVID-Net. After that, the model is trained using the COVIDX dataset. COVID-19, pneumonia, and normal are the three categories in the model. The accuracy of categorization was 93.3% achieved by COVIDNet. On another side comparatively, classification accuracy was 83.0% achieved by the VGG-19 model, and classification accuracy was 9.06% achieved by ResNet-50.

The ResNet50, InceptionV2, and Inception-ResNetV3 were used by Narin et al. [20] along with the concept of transfer learning. These models classify between COVID-19 and normal X-ray images. To reduce the inadequate data and overcome the time required during training, the transfer learning technique is applied to the data of ImageNet. ResNet-50 achieved a classification accuracy of 98%, whilst InceptionV3 and Inception- ResNetV2 achieved a classification accuracy of 97% and 87%, respectively.

The deep learning–based Q-deformed entropy algorithm is developed by Ali et al. [21] which extracts the features from images of lungs. After that, extracted features were applied to the LSTM neural network. The model was trained by extracted features that classify between pneumonia, fit lungs, and COVID-19 with an accuracy of 99.68%.

Abbas et al. [22] used DeTrac, short for Decompose, Transfer, and Compose, with custom-developed CNN. To classify between SARS cases and normal cases from images of X-rays the DeTrac method is applied with CNN. The dataset of irregular images is handled by the DeTrac. For classification, the model scores 93.36% with precision, 95.12% with accuracy, 97.9% with sensitivity, and 91.87% with specificity.

Dipayan et al. [23] developed a truncated Inception Net which classifies among positive of COVID-19, pneumonia, tuberculosis, and healthy cases. The developed truncated Inception Net model gives 99.96% accuracy for classifying the positive cases of COVID-19 and the other classes.

To identify COVID-19 pneumonia, Hoonko et al. [24] built an FCONet – a fast-track COVID-19 classification network, which is a 2D deep learning structure. The FCONet is proposed to classify X-rays of chest images among COVID-19 pneumonia, other, and no diseases. Among all four pre-trained models of FCONET, ResNet-50 provides 99.58% sensitivity, specificity of 100%, and 99.87% accuracy. The additional pre-trained model such as ResNet-50 gives 96.97% accuracy which was tailed by the 90.71% accuracy of the Xception model, 89.38% accuracy of the Inception-V3 model, and 87.12% accuracy of the VGG16 model.

Yoo et al. [25] developed a decision-tree classifier centered on deep learning for identifying an infection of coronavirus by X-ray images of the chest. The classifier contains a total of three decision trees trained with the CNN model. Each decision tree is binary. The first decision tree classifies between CXR normal or abnormal with 98% accuracy. The abnormal images that may contain an indication of tuberculosis were detected by a second decision tree with 80% accuracy and another abnormal image that may hold an indication of COVID-19 was identified by the third decision tree with 95% accuracy.

The CNN was used to categorize COVID-19-infected or else non-infected patients using chest CT images by Singh et al. [26]. Using an accuracy of 1.9789%, an F-measure of 2.0928%, sensitivity of 1.8262%, specificity of 1.6727%, and Kappa statistics of 1.9276%, the CNN trained with multi-objective differential evolution gives a significant performance.

The DarkCovidNet model was developed by Ozturk et al. [14]. The DarkCovidNet model has a total of 17 layers of convolutional and different filtering at each layer. The DarkCovidNet model developed by Ozturk et al. [14] was used for binary class categorization such as COVID and no findings along with multi-class categorization such as COVID, pneumonia, and no findings. A 98.08% accuracy of classification on COVID and no findings and an 87.02% accuracy of classification on COVID, pneumonia, and no findings are given by the DarkCovidNet model.

By this comparison of existing studies, it has been investigated that CT and X-ray scans of the chest can be useful in determining if COVID-19 is infectious at an early stage [27]. The consequence of this is that in this study, a CNN deep learning architecture is created from the ground up to recognize binary and multi-class patients from chest X-ray images, including COVID-19, pneumonia, and normal conditions.

2.3 PROPOSED WORK

2.3.1 Proposed methodology

The proposed approach consists of various phases that must be completed in order to achieve precise classification. The phases are as follows: data collection, total input samples, training and testing dataset fractions, classification of the model, training of the model with a variety of training dataset sizes, testing and assessment of the model, and final evaluation. In this study, the classification model is trained and tested independently for binary classification and multi-class classification, using different amounts of train:test datasets. Figure 2.1 demonstrates the proposed approach for binary classification and multi-class classification.

2.3.2 Dataset collection

Data is the prime parameter to develop any computer-aided diagnostic device. The open datasets used for these experiments were collected from various open sources. For the trials, two different datasets were used. Dataset-1 comprises 1,298 pictures of chest X-rays with COVID-19 infection and 1,583 images of chest X-rays in normal posture [28–31]. Dataset-2 comprises 1,298 pictures of COVID-19 infection, 4,273 pneumonia infection images, and 1,583 images of the normal position on chest X-rays [28–32]. Sample images from datasets-1 and 2 are shown in Figures 2.2 and 2.3, respectively. Dataset-1 was used for binary classification, and dataset-2 was used for multi-class classification, with dataset-1 being used for both.

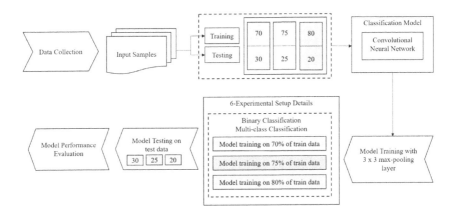

Figure 2.1 Framework of the proposed method.

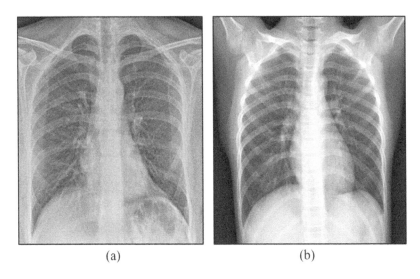

(a)   (b)

Figure 2.2 Dataset-1: (a) COVID-19 X-ray image; (b) normal X-ray image. Sources: (a) [28–31]; (b) [32].

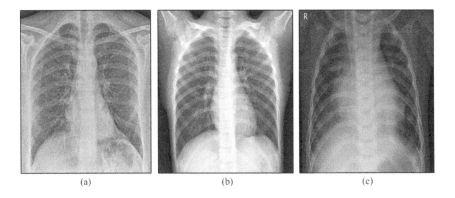

(a)   (b)   (c)

Figure 2.3 Dataset-2: (a) COVID-19 X-ray image; (b) normal X-ray image; (c) pneumonia X-ray image. Sources: (a) [28–31]; (b) [32]; (c) [32].

2.3.3 Novel contributions of this study

Herein, we propose a peculiar architecture of CNN that enables improved results from the existing paradigms. Herein, a finer filter is applied, i.e, 3 × 3 in contrast with 2 × 2, the major utility of which can be seen in the max-pooling layer. Max-pooling is defined as the sampling process in CNNs. The major ambition of max-pooling is to down-sample the image representation (of input) in CNN to detect the features from the feature maps. Selecting a pooling operation is like applying a filter to the feature map. In this experiment, we leveraged the attributes of a 3 × 3 feature map. The

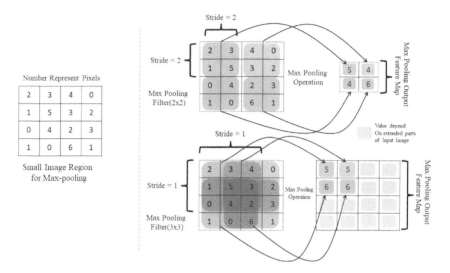

Figure 2.4 Comparative max-pooling.

improvement of the bigger feature map over the smaller one can be seen in Figure 2.4.

2.3.4 System flow and related concepts

Figure 2.5 depicts the system flow of the CNN architecture. Here the image as well as the kernel are given as input to the feature extractor.

The results of the former are then given to the neural network for the final prediction. The CNN convolution operation is given in equation 2.1.

$$s[t] = (x * w)[t] = \sum_{a=-\infty}^{a=\infty} x[a]w[a+t] \tag{2.1}$$

where $s[t]$ is a feature map, x is an input image, and w is a kernel. The feature map results are calculated according to equation 2.2. Here I denotes

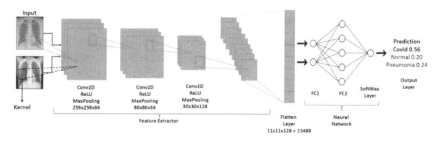

Figure 2.5 System flow diagram.

the input image and K is the kernel. The p_1 and p_2 represent the indexes of the resulted matrix. Herein, equation 2.3 depicts the cross-correlation function of equation 2.2.

$$S(p1, p2) = (I * K)(p1, p2) = \sum_m \sum_n I(m, n) K(p1 - m, p2 - n) \qquad (2.2)$$

$$S(p1, p2) = (I * K)(p1, p2) = \sum_m \sum_n K(m, n) I(p1 - m, p2 - n) \qquad (2.3)$$

CNN uses pooling a lot of times in order to reduce the size of the tensor so that the calculations speed up. Pooling layers divide the image into distinct regions so that calculative operation can perform divide and conquer. Max-pooling is one such pooling method that allows selecting the maximum values from each region so as to capture the most prominent features of the image. And the dimension of the feature map as a function of the input image size (W), feature detector size (F), stride (S), and zero padding on image (P) is given by equation 2.4.

$$(W - F + 2P) / S \qquad (2.4)$$

2.3.5 Proposed CNN architecture

CNN is an accurate dominant tool that is broadly employed for image classification. The main functionalities of CNN such as structure with a hierarchical manner and effective extraction of features from an image make it a prime model for the classification of the image.

The examined factors include total convolution layers, filters, pooling dimensions, kernel dimensions, total fully connected layers, and total neurons present in fully connected layers as well as other CNN parameters [33–35]. In addition, the three fundamental parameters of depth, height, and width are noticed in association with the layers of CNN. These parameters are nominated after carrying out an analysis of works by analyzing obtainable pre-trained structures used by researchers as yet [18–20, 23]. As per the examination of the observation, this study organized CNN structural design with all the parameters of CNN from scratch.

Using dataset-1 (COVID-19 and normal X-ray images), the proposed CNN model is presented in Figure 2.6, and using dataset-2 (COVID-19, normal, and pneumonia X-ray images), the proposed CNN model is demonstrated in Figure 2.7. Using datasets-1 and 2, the identical settings of a model as in Table 2.1 were applied to datasets-1 and 2.

The developed model contains three 2D convolutional layers. Each layer is tailed by the ReLu activation function and pooling layer. Thus, these

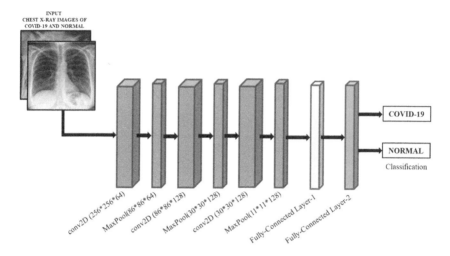

Figure 2.6 Architecture for proposed CNN model for dataset-1.

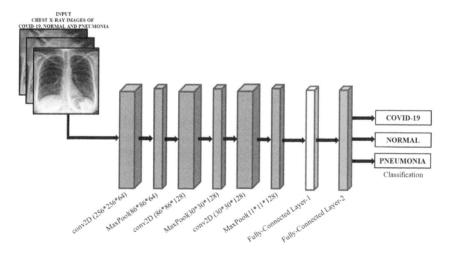

Figure 2.7 Architecture for proposed CNN model for dataset-2.

three convolutional layers are followed by three pooling layers. It also contains two fully connected layers. Each fully connected layer is tailed by a ReLu activation function. The fully connected layers were also tailed by the drop-out method with 0.3 rates. The drop-out method arbitrarily drops the connections from the previous layer which is used to elude overfitting. The last output layer is tailed by the sigmoid activation function (dataset-1) and Softmax activation function (dataset-2).

The size of 2 × 2 zero paddings is used to avoid dimension shrinkage. Also, the size of the 3 × 3 kernel is used throughout the experiments. The

Table 2.1 Proposed CNN model

Layer	Sequence of units	Input size	Output size	Kernel dimension	Batch dimension	Padding zero
1	Convolutional 2D layer 1	256×256	$256 \times 256 \times 64$	3×3	64	2×2
2	Max-pool	$256 \times 256 \times 64$	$86 \times 86 \times 64$	3×3	64	–
3	Convolutional 2D layer 2	$86 \times 86 \times 64$	$86 \times 86 \times 128$	3×3	128	2×2
4	Max-pool	$86 \times 86 \times 128$	$30 \times 30 \times 128$	3×3	128	–
5	Convolutional 2D layer 3	$30 \times 30 \times 128$	$30 \times 30 \times 128$	3×3	128	2×2
6	Max-pool	$30 \times 30 \times 128$	$11 \times 11 \times 128$	3×3	128	–
7	Fully connected: layer 1 with 1,024 neurons Activation function: ReLu Dropout rate: 0.3					
8	Fully connected: layer 2 with 1,024 neurons Activation function: ReLu Dropout rate: 0.3					
9	Final output layer for dataset-1 with activation function: Sigmoid Final output layer for dataset-2 with activation function: Softmax					

larger batch size leads to enhanced gradient and avoids jumping nearby, but the too large size of the batch may lead to memory problems. In this CNN model, 64 batch sizes were used. One of the hyper-parameters of CNN model architecture is steps per epoch. The total number of training samples divided by the batch size can be used to compute the set of trips per epoch. The input pictures were 256 by 256 pixels in size. Several picture dimensions were reduced to 256 by 256 pixels. Table 2.1 lists the specifics of CNN architecture.

The proposed model was evaluated on dataset-1 [28–31] and dataset-2 [28–32]. Both datasets were divided into three sets of train and test: 70:30%, 75:25%, and 80:20%. The learning rate of 0.001 with an Adam optimizer was used for the experiments. The value of Adam's learning rate was nominated after the experienced training loss. The 60 epochs were considered for model training. Every experiment was executed using Google Collaboratory with Tesla K80 GPU. This configuration of GPU was used for TensorFlow and Keras Library.

2.4 RESULTS AND DISCUSSION

This study has conducted a research experiment with the novelty of a CNN max-pooling layer on the COVID-19 dataset with three different volumes such as 70:30%, 80:20%, and 90:10% train:test splits. The CNN structure is shown in Figure 2.3 for dataset-1 and dataset-2. The CNN model trained up to the number of epochs to avoid overfitting. This experiment investigated different max-pooling sizes which is a novel approach, such as 2 × 2 and 3 × 3 filters, producing different feature map sizes. Through the implementation, the observed results with both sizes of the max-pooling kernel were that the 3 × 3 max-pooling layer size generated a bigger feature map, which leads to more accuracy than the 2 × 2 max-pooling layer size yield. All tables' results have been trained with a 3 × 3 max-pooling layer size and demonstrate the experiment outcome for COVID-19 images. This theoretical understanding of this result is discussed in the novelty section about the reason the 3 × 3 max-pooling produced a larger feature map than the 2 × 2 max-pooling layer.

Tables 2.2 and 2.3 show the statistics of the train and test images from datasets-1 and 2, as well as different percentages. Tables 2.2 and 2.3 show that the evaluation metrics which were used in this experiment to estimate the credibility of the model increased significantly with an increase in sample size in both datasets. The various test:train splits also performed exceptionally well in determining the target attribute in this experiment, as shown by the results in Tables 2.2 and 2.3.

The results depicted in the respective tables are quite promising. Corresponding confusion matrices for datasets-1 and 2 can be perceived in Figures 2.8 and 2.9 respectively. The magnitude of the true positives and true negatives are forming the majority in both matrices. The evaluated

Table 2.2 Results achieved from dataset-1 (three different splits applied on proposed CNN models)

Experiment number	Train:test split	Total training images	Total testing images	Confusion matrix with performance outcome in % on the test set			
				Precision	Recall	F1 score	Accuracy
1	70:30%	2,016	865	99	99	99	99
2	75:25%	2,160	721	99	99	99	99
3	80:20%	2,304	577	96	96	96	96

Table 2.3 Results achieved from dataset-2 (three different splits applied on proposed CNN models)

Experiment number	Train:test split	Total training images	Total testing images	Confusion matrix with performance outcome in % on the test set			
				Precision	Recall	F1 score	Accuracy
1	70:30%	5,007	2,147	97	97	97	97
2	75:25%	5,368	1,786	97	97	97	97
3	80:20%	5,622	1,532	96	95	95	95

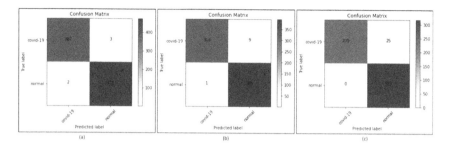

Figure 2.8 Evaluated confusion matrix from dataset-1 (binary-class): (a) confusion matrix for 70:30% split; (b) confusion matrix for 75:25% split; c) confusion matrix for 80:20% split.

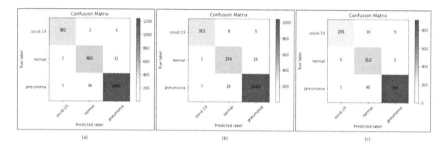

Figure 2.9 Evaluated confusion matrix from dataset-2 (multi-class): (a) confusion matrix for 70:30% split; (b) confusion matrix for 75:25% split; c) confusion matrix for 80:20% split.

metrics hence show performance above 95% which shows that the trained model performed very well during the testing.

The results obtained by the proposed CNN architecture from dataset-1 and dataset-2 along with all the splits are demonstrated in confusion matrices in Figures 2.8 and 2.9 respectively, which have also demonstrated healthy results.

2.5 CONCLUSION

Herein, a classification model, the CNN, is implemented to categorize COVID-19, pneumonia, and normal in chest X-ray images. Dataset-1 and dataset-2 of X-ray images are split 70:30%, 75:25%, and 80:20% for train and test respectively. Each fragmented data distinctly applied to a CNN. Each split data is executed for the training of CNN with 50 epochs. As a concluding opinion, the evaluations are stained from each split of training and testing from dataset-1 and dataset-2. All-encompassing trial consequences show that the proposed model overtakes with regard to accuracy, recall, precision, and F1-score by 96% in the 80:20% split and 99% in the other two data splits 70:30% and 75:25% of dataset-1 (COVID-19 and normal). Also, the projected model overtakes in terms of precision, accuracy, F1-score, and recall by 95% for the 80:20% split and 97% for the other two data splits 70:30% and 75:25% of dataset-2 (COVID-19, normal, and pneumonia). Following that, the suggested framework is advantageous for the rapid diagnosis of COVID-19 infectious disease from X-ray pictures of the chest. This study also includes a comparison examination of the three-max-pooling method vs. the two-max-pooling method. Experiment results show that increasing the dimension of the max-pooling layer has an additional benefit in terms of enhancing the results. The novelty discussed in the previous sections can be used to automate the flow of the healthcare industry amid the pandemic. The healthcare domain has suffered enough in the past two years and hence this proposed solution deployment in the real world can lead to at least detecting the medical condition immediately. AI is making its way in all possible industries and aims to perform this experiment in real-time in the near future. This study aims to deploy this model in a dynamic environment and see its capabilities. The medical laboratory industry can definitely exploit the benefits of leveraging deep learning technology to advance its current working dynamics. The classification of normal lungs vs. pneumonia vs. COVID-19 using neural networks (CNN precisely) would indeed make medical science grow intelligent artificially.

REFERENCES

1. T. G. Kinjal, and A. Patel, "Automatic detection and classification of corona infection (covid-19) from x-ray images using convolution neural network." https://www.technoarete.org/commonabstract/pdf/IJSEM/v8/i5/   Ext14268 .pdf. Accessed: 2020.
2. "(2020, may) world health organization - who." https://www.who.int/health -topics/coronavirus. Accessed: 2020.
3. "(2020, january) world health organization - who." https://www.who.int/ health-topics/coronavirus. Accessed: 2020.
4. "(2020, january) world health organization-who." https://www.who.int/ news-room/detail/30-01-2020-statement-on-the-secondmeeting-of-the-inter-national-health-regulations-(2005)-emergencycommittee-about-the-novel-coronavirus-(2019-ncov. Accessed: 2020.
5. "(2019) world health organization-covid-19technicalguide." https://www .who.int/emergency/diseases/novel-coronavirus-2019/   technical-guidance/ naming-the-coronavirus-disease-(covid-2019)-andthe-virus-that-causes-it. Accessed: 2020.
6. "(2020, may) worldometer." https://www.worldometers.info/coronavirus/ country/india/. Accessed: 2020.
7. "(2020, may) world health organization - who status - daily reports." https:// www.who.int/docs/default-source/coronaviruse/situationreports/20200525 -covid-19-sitrep-126.pdf?sfvrsn=887dbd662. Accessed: 2020.

8. "(2020, may) the challenge of designing a video conference solution." https://startups.meitystartuphub.in/public/application/inc/ 5e92ec-1269e3401cd7bc6db7. Accessed: 2020.

9. "(2020, may) introducing india.." https://www.startupindia.gov. in/content /sih/en/ams-application/challenge.html?applicationId= 5e79126ee4b055bfae-a9ef66. Accessed: 2020.

10. "(2020, may) mygov covid-19 solution challenge.." https://www.mygov.in/ task/covid-19-solution-challenge/. Accessed: 2020.

11. "(2020, may) student open innovation challenge." http://www.ssipgujarat.in /soic/index.php. Accessed: 2020.

12. "(2020, may) world health organization - who status - daily reports." https:// www.mygov.in/corona-data/covid19-statewise-status/. Accessed: 2020.

13. T. Ai, Z. Yang, H. Hou, C. Zhan, C. Chen, W. Lv, Q. Tao, Z. Sun, and L. Xia, "Correlation of chest ct and rt-pcr testing for coronavirus disease 2019 (covid-19) in china: a report of 1014 cases," *Radiology*, vol. 296, no. 2, pp. E32–E40, 2020.

14. T. Ozturk, M. Talo, E. A. Yildirim, U. B. Baloglu, O. Yildirim, and U. R. Acharya, "Automated detection of covid-19 cases using deep neural networks with x-ray images," *Computers in Biology and Medicine*, vol. 121, p. 103792, 2020.

15. X. Xie, Z. Zhong, W. Zhao, C. Zheng, F. Wang, and J. Liu, "Chest ct for typical coronavirus disease 2019 (covid-19) pneumonia: relationship to negative rt-pcr testing," *Radiology*, vol. 296, no. 2, pp. E41–E45, 2020.

16. A. Bernheim, M. Chung,X. Mei, N. Zhang, M. Huang, X. Zeng, J. Cui, W. Xu, Y. Yang, Z. A. Fayad, et al., "Ct imaging features of 2019 novel coronavirus (2019-ncov)," *Radiology*, vol. 295, no. 1, pp. 202–207, 2020.

17. Y. Fang, H. Zhang, J. Xie, M. Lin, L. Ying, P. Pang, and W. Ji, "Sensitivity of chest ct for covid-19: comparison to rt-pcr," *Radiology*, vol. 296, no. 2, pp. E115–E117, 2020.

18. S. H. Khan, A. Sohail, M. M. Zafar, and A. Khan, "Coronavirus disease analysis using chest x-ray images and a novel deep convolutional neural network," *Photodiagnosis and Photodynamic Therapy*, p. 102473, 2021.

19. L. Wang, Z. Q. Lin, and A. Wong, "Covid-net: A tailored deep convolutional neural network design for detection of covid-19 cases from chest x-ray images," *Scientific Reports*, vol. 10, no. 1, pp. 1–12, 2020.

20. A. Narin, C. Kaya, and Z. Pamuk, "Automatic detection of coronavirus disease (covid-19) using x-ray images and deep convolutional neural networks," *Pattern Analysis and Applications*, vol. 24, pp. 1–14, 2021.

21. A. M. Hasan, M. M. Al-Jawad, H. A. Jalab, H. Shaiba, R. W. Ibrahim, and A. R. AL-Shamasneh, "Classification of covid-19 coronavirus, pneumonia and healthy lungs in ct scans using q-deformed entropy and deep learning features," *Entropy*, vol. 22, no. 5, p. 517, 2020.

22. A. Abbas, M. Abdelsamea, and M. Gaber, "Classification of covid-19 in chest x-ray images using detrac deep convolutional neural network. medrxiv," *Preprint Posted Online May*, vol. 18, 2020.

23. D. Das, K. Santosh, and U. Pal, "Truncated inception net: Covid19 outbreak screening using chest x-rays," *Physical and Engineering Sciences in Medicine*, vol. 43, no. 3, pp. 915–925, 2020.

24. H. Ko, H. Chung, W. S. Kang, K. W. Kim, Y. Shin, S. J. Kang, J. H. Lee, Y. J. Kim, N. Y. Kim, H. Jung, et al., "Covid-19 pneumonia diagnosis using a simple 2d deep learning framework with a single chest ct image: model

development and validation," *Journal of Medical Internet Research*, vol. 22, no. 6, p. e19569, 2020.

25. S. H. Yoo, H. Geng, T. L. Chiu, S. K. Yu, D. C. Cho, J. Heo, M. S. Choi, I. H. Choi, C. Cung Van, N. V. Nhung, et al., "Deep learningbased decision-tree classifier for covid-19 diagnosis from chest x-ray imaging," *Frontiers in Medicine*, vol. 7, p. 427, 2020.

26. D. Singh, V. Kumar, M. Kaur, et al., "Classification of covid-19 patients from chest ct images using multi-objective differential evolution–based convolutional neural networks," *European Journal of Clinical Microbiology & Infectious Diseases*, vol. 39, no. 7, pp. 1379–1389, 2020.

27. Y. Chang, C. Yang, Y. Chien, and Y. Hsu, "Author reply to letters to the editor 'ct chest findings in coronavirus disease (covid-19)'." https://coronavirus.1science. com/item/92b2e06e21c079fcce2ed0bb4658c948ba15 2909, 2020.

28. "Shoroqqazanalimohammadalqudah. (2020, march) progress." https://data .mendeley.com/datasets/2fxz4px6d8/4#folder-2eec69c79b6c-4864-b9d5 -bd059e2dd24b. Accessed: 2020.

29. "Bganglia and ieee8023 / covid-chestxray-dataset." https://github.com/ ieee8023/covid-chestxray-dataset. Accessed: 2020.

30. "Bachir - covid-19 chest x-ray." https://www.kaggle.com/bachrr/covidchest -xray. Accessed: 2020.

31. "Saimansa-c." https://www.kaggle.com/saimanasachadalavada/covid19chest -xray-analysis/. Accessed: 2020.

32. "Paulmooney." https://www.kaggle.com/paultimothymooney/. Accessed: 2020.

33. K.A. Patel, K.K. Gandhi, and A.S. Vyas An Effective Approach to Classify White Blood Cell Using CNN. In: Thakkar F., Saha G., Shahnaz C., Hu Y.C. (eds) *Proceedings of the International e-Conference on Intelligent Systems and Signal Processing. Advances in Intelligent Systems and Computing*, vol 1370. Springer, Singapore, (2022). https://doi.org/10.1007/978-981-16-2123 -9_49

34. S. Pal, N. Mishra, M. Bhushan, P.S. Kholiya, M. Rana, and A. Negi, Deep Learning Techniques for Prediction and Diagnosis of Diabetes Mellitus. In: *Proceedings of the 2022 International Mobile and Embedded Technology Conference (MECON)*, IEEE, pp. 588–593, doi: 10.1109/ MECON53876.2022.9752176, 2022.

35. M. Rana and M. Bhushan, "Advancements in Healthcare Services using Deep Learning Techniques," In: *Proceedings of the 2022 International Mobile and Embedded Technology Conference (MECON)*, 2022, pp. 157–161, doi: 10.1109/MECON53876.2022.9752020.

Chapter 3

Biorthogonal filter-based algorithm for denoising and segmentation of fundus images

Udayini Chandana, Kezia Joseph Mosiganti, and Mukil Alagirisamy

CONTENTS

3.1 INTRODUCTION

In the field of medicine, due to the variation in the opinions of the field experts and the uncertainties introduced in medical images, it becomes extremely difficult and challenging to diagnose and then apply a prognosis for a medical condition. This also increases the probability of misdiagnosis of diseases. To help the medical experts, the images acquired should be as detailed and clear as possible. Hence, various image processing methods must be explored to make precise and automatic interpretations of the acquired medical images, with uncertainties, ambiguities, and vagueness

DOI: 10.1201/9781003286745-3

shown in detail. The initial process includes image acquisition and then image segmentation of the near noise-free images.

To obtain a suitable segmentation output, the image should undergo partial or total noise removal during the preprocessing stage. The noise in the image acquired through a digital camera [1] can be typically categorized into three types: a fixed-pattern noise, due to differences in the gain and offset of each pixel of the sensor; a random noise, which can be averaged out with multiple exposures; and a banding noise, due to small differences in the gains of a sensor's column amplifiers. In different medical image modalities, different types and levels of noise are present due to the variation in the functional characteristics of the acquisition devices, the technology, and the environment in which the device is utilized. Primarily, Gaussian noise, which is a white or normal noise, is introduced during this process. Also, the impulse noise is introduced during the use of an analog-to-digital converter, the result of which includes bit errors during the data transmission. A magnetic resonance image (MRI) is dominated by the Rician noise with a Gaussian distribution while mammogram and radiography images contain quantum noise. Some of the properties of noise that are mostly seen in medical images include those correlated to additive, multiplicative, and quantum noise [2]. The additive noise, like Gaussian, impulse, and salt-and-pepper noise, is independent of the contents of the image, in which the noise will be added to each pixel, thus varying its intensity, and is independent of its neighboring pixels. Unlike additive noise, in multiplicative noise like speckle noise, the pixel intensity is varied according to the intensity level of the noise. Due to its independent nature, the additive noise is a little easier to remove than the multiplicative noise. The increase in noise may also be caused by factors related to the environment, and it is very crucial for the noise to be diminished by utilizing suitable filtering algorithms. High-frequency filters can be used in image processing to obtain enhanced and sharpened edges or to reduce the noise content through image smoothing. In the spatial domain, the same operations are performed using point and mask processing. All the image de-noising techniques aim at removing the noise and restoring the original image with maximum effort to preserve all significant features of the original image.

Fundus imaging [3] is the two-dimensional representation of the retina captured with a fundus camera. It captures the optic nerve, the regions of the macula and the fovea, along with the main retinal blood vasculature. The light that gets reflected from the retinal tissue is stored in the form of variations in the intensities of this reflected light, which may produce random noise. The result depends on the sensitivity of the camera sensors. As there is no source of illumination internally in the retina, only an external source of light is to be considered. The reflected light must follow a path that should not overlap with the incident ray path and it must be captured separately through the pupil, which is 2 to 8 mm in diameter, in order to obtain an insight into the status of the inner portion of the eye. There is a possibility of poor contrast capture during acquisition.

Different methods are employed to denoise and segment fundus images and to analyze the result for a more accurate diagnosis in the field of ophthalmology. In the past five to six years, several varied approaches have been proposed for segmentation, such as iterative enhancements [4], pixel-based feature vector [5], adaptive thresholding [6], region growing [7], imperialism competitive algorithm [8], bowler-hat transform [9], Zernike moments [10, 11], neural network-based segmentation methods [12], and bendlets [13]. Also, methods based on transforms and texture are found to be in use substantially. Many of the aforementioned techniques either deliver the simplified solution or are computationally intensive both in time and resources, still falling short of delivering the desired performance. A biorthogonal wavelet [14] is a generalized version of the orthonormal wavelet with an associated invertible and non-orthogonal wavelet transform. It consists of two bases that are orthogonal to each other but do not form an orthogonal set. Key properties for any efficient wavelet include displaying translation and shift invariance. If there are non-zero coefficients due to the shift, the energy would be seen over several coefficients and hence becomes smaller in value, thereby resulting in a degradation in denoising. To overcome this, a system consisting of the wavelet and its shifted orthogonal version is used to obtain a translation invariant wavelet. The biorthogonal wavelets provide the flexibility for the construction of symmetric wavelet functions or the introduction of scaling functions, wherever required.

3.1.1 Motivation

The processing of medical images requires experience and expertise from multiple fields like applied mathematics, physics, feature engineering, computer science, medicine, and biology. Several types of modalities are utilized for effective and timely disease diagnosis. The major challenge observed during the diagnosis includes the noisy images acquired. Currently, study of the analysis of images through wavelet decomposition is being conducted to understand the intricacies of the acquired image content. Wavelets provide the channel for analysis in both the time and frequency domains simultaneously. The periodic characteristic of the signals is retained while its energy is concentrated in time. Hence, wavelet decomposition is a very useful mathematical tool for a comprehensive analysis of the non-stationary signal with several regions of discontinuities where the statistical analysis cannot be done. Over the past three decades, wavelet transforms, especially the stationary wavelet transform, have been widely used in varied fields like medical imaging, weather forecasting, remote sensing, and computer vision. Several sub-bands are formed upon decomposition of the digital signal through wavelet transform. The lower frequency sub-bands are utilized for frequency resolution analysis and the higher frequency sub-bands are used for time resolution analysis. The non-dependency observed between the various components of the image is increased when filtering is done in the wavelet domain, and hence several features of the medical images may be highlighted better in the sub-bands. This helps to obtain better segmentation results and hence, improved accuracy in the classification of images.

A versatile image processing tool is the discrete wavelet transform (DWT) due to its flexibility in providing a multi-resolution representation of signals through wavelet decomposition. Mathematical morphology [15, 16] has been a popular post-processing step to improve the segmentation results where a few discontinuities may occur at the edges of the image due to different factors. In general, orthogonal wavelets are used to perform denoising by removing small amplitude coefficients, resembling noise in nature. The orthogonal wavelet transform is not the most efficient approach for image denoising as it is a translation variant and requires the wavelet and scaling filter to be of the same length. The length of the filters also should be even. So, reconstruction artifacts are observed in the denoised image. A translation invariant wavelet transform reduces the artifact effect by increasing the redundancy of the transform. And this would increase the execution time for denoising. The foreground and the background information in an image can be identified across the edges which carry important anisotropic information [17]. This information includes the geometric characteristics of the shape, which are not secured through isotropic wavelets, and hence, can be improved by taking basis functions as nearly parallel to the edges as possible. The approach through wavelets allows the retention of most of the details of the digital image during denoising or segmentation.

For a retinal image, the focus areas are the optic disc, the fovea, and the retinal blood vessels. The fundus image which is acquired through a digital camera is an image of the retinal vasculature and may be corrupted by salt-and-pepper noise. The variation seen in the retinal vasculature [18] indicates an underlying cardiac condition or any eye disease which may not be prominent to the naked eye. The process of segmentation is important for identifying the structural characteristics and changes. There exists communication between the retina and the brain through the optic nerve to which the blood vessels in the retina are connected [19, 20]. The color of the fundus obtained through imaging varies widely from one patient to the other and is based on the person's iris color which depends on that individual's race and ethnicity. Also, in a colored fundus image, there are several regions that do not display clear contrast between the foreground and background of blood vessels. So, an appropriate color space must be defined for the best representation of the fundus image for segmentation. Hence, preprocessing the images is highly recommended. The pixels are clustered into clearly defined regions with as little overlapping of intensity values as possible for effective utilization of the resulting image through segmentation.

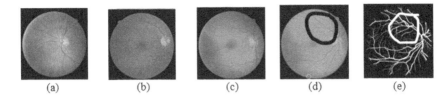

(a)   (b)   (c)   (d)   (e)

Figure 3.1 Fundus images with different levels of tortuosity: (a) normal; (b) slightly tortuous; (c) highly tortuous; (d) region of overlapping; (e) differentiation required
between vessel crossing, bifurcation, or branching.

A variation in the width or diameter of the retinal blood vessels (from
0.1 mm to 300 mm width) is observed as the body is trying to adapt to the
different levels of pressure required for the functionality of different parts
of the body. As a result, there will be a difference in the pressure of the
flow of blood through the vessels. This variation in the pressure may lead
to cloudiness in the vision, and in extreme cases, partial blindness, or even
total blindness. Challenges in fundus images are shown in Figure 3.1: the
overlapping of vessels and the difficulty in estimating the width of the vessels as shown in Figure 3.1(a) to (c), where the images with different levels
of tortuosity are shown in comparison with a fundus image with normal
vasculature. In Figure 3.1(d) and (e), a comparison is made between a fundus image from the DRIVE database and its ground truth to highlight the
problem of identifying the cross-over properly.

Another challenge faced during the segmentation of the blood vessels
is due to their extremely narrow and non-uniform structure. In the process, many thin vessels go missing and some of the regions are difficult
to analyze due to the conditions of tortuosity of the blood vessels. Hence,
the proposed system focuses on obtaining an image of higher contrast and
accuracy through wavelet transforms.

3.1.2 Major contribution

The wavelet used for the experimentation is the biorthogonal wavelet transform. The scaling equation related to the biorthogonal transform is shown
below in Equation (3.1) to indicate the relation between the scaling and the
wavelet functions:

$$\frac{1}{\sqrt{2}} \psi\left(\frac{t}{2}\right) = \sum_{n=-\infty}^{+\infty} g[n]\emptyset(t-n) \qquad (3.1)$$

where $\psi(t)$ represents the wavelet function and $\emptyset(t)$, the scaling function.
The notation used for these wavelets is x.y with x representing the number of reconstruction filters and y related to that of the decomposition
filters. These wavelets are distinguishable from the orthogonal wavelets

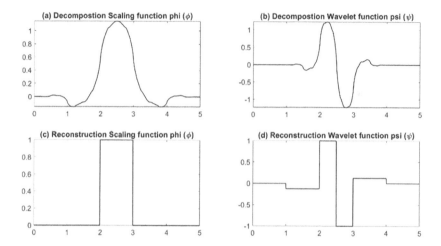

Figure 3.2 Functions for biorthogonal wavelet 1.3: (a), (b) decomposition scaling and wavelet functions; (c), (d) reconstruction scaling and wavelet functions.

by the difference in the weights of the functions (scaling, wavelet). Hence, bior1.3 would represent a wavelet with one reconstruction filter and three decomposition filters. The level of linearity in the phase of the signal will determine the final performance. A biorthogonal wavelet system with a nonorthogonal basis and dual basis is used. The threshold values can be obtained from the histogram values and the set of optimal values between the peaks. The decomposition (a–b) and reconstruction (c–d) scaling and wavelet functions for the biorthogonal wavelet 1.3 are shown in Figure 3.2.

Before the implementation of the aforementioned wavelet transform, preprocessing steps through the extraction of the green channel and then the contrast enhancement process are conducted to provide an effective image for denoising followed by segmentation. The orthogonality property of the wavelet helps to have a separate identity for the sub-bands which can be processed independently to improve the segmentation outputs. A near-perfect reconstruction of the image after the processing is attributed to the biorthogonal wavelet transform.

3.1.3 Outcomes

A simple and fast method is proposed for the noise removal and segmentation of retinal fundus images through the biorthogonal wavelet transform. The transform produces sub-bands of frequencies through decomposition. Denoising and segmentation operations are performed on the decomposed components and then reconstruction is accomplished to produce the retinal vasculature after post-processing through morphological operations. The comparison is made with the ground truth images after determining the performance metrics of sensitivity, specificity, and accuracy. An improvement in the accuracy of the output is observed when compared to other existing methods. This approach can be used for segmentation in several applications like chest images, leaf vein extraction, image compression, registration, and classification.

3.1.4 Chapter organization

The remaining contents of the chapter are organized as follows. In section 3.2, some of the existing approaches for image denoising and segmentation, especially for retinal images, are briefly described. The various performance metrics that can be used for comparison of the approaches are listed in section 3.3. Then, the approach under discussion is explained in section 3.4. The experimental results and evaluation are illustrated in section 3.5. Section 3.6 includes the discussion and conclusions in which the summary of the outputs of the approach in focus is provided.

3.2 LITERATURE REVIEW

3.2.1 Denoising of medical images

Various types of noises affecting the medical images are discussed, namely, Gaussian noise, quantum noise, and Rician noise [21, 22], and the design of filters used for denoising images is elaborated. The effect of the noise in images can be observed as the random noise and the artifact. The random noise is an internal noise, whose source could be the instrument, detector, defect in the design, device-generated noise, pixel values (missing or spurious), etc. On the other hand, the artifact is an external interference, due to various reasons like due to motion, etc. Essentially, any type of noise in an image results in distortions in the image.

3.2.2 Segmentation techniques for medical images

The last two decades have witnessed several methods for the segmentation process of the blood vasculature. The conventional process of segmenting blood vessels results in noise being introduced into the branch because the algorithms are susceptible to the convex shape of the vessels. An iterative technique based on global thresholding is used for effective estimation of the vasculature structure in [4] and is only applicable to images of moderate resolution as an initial estimate of the major blood vessel is required before the two thresholds can be determined. This is not applicable for images with very high standards of resolution. A cross-curvature analysis [23] is done by creating a connected linear structure to identify the points of bifurcation, followed by its evaluation, with the drawback of a number of false detections. A study related to the uniformity in the retinal vessel structure [24, 25] shows that the arteries and veins vary widely in diameter in every region of the fundus but still follow a certain model or form and are independent of gender or age. An example of how the characteristics of the retinal blood vessel width and its tortuosity change with the condition of retinopathy of prematurity is discussed [26]. The fiducial points for vessel bifurcation or crossing are highlighted in this method. The vessel tortuosity [27, 28] is identified and each of the blood vessels is partitioned into different segments differentiated based on the sign of the curvature. The output is then combined with their number to obtain a number that indicates whether it is part of the vessel or a separate one. The dependency of the output is on the scaling factor and forms a drawback of the method when the tortuosity is to be measured for the entire image. The curvelet transform makes a good representation of the edges [29]. The fuzziness and vague information present in medical images make their segmentation and classification based on the process of feature extraction very challenging and time-consuming [30]. The set, in terms of fuzzy sets, is a popular method in image processing to include the spatial context of the pixels for segmentation. This is important for understanding the noise and artifacts in medical images. The wavelet transform is used to decompose a single channel into multiple frequency modes and then simple independent component analysis is applied to each of these modes. This is multiscale ICA [31] and it helps to reduce the noise by decorrelating the data in the image for processing.

Techniques based on wavelets that are anisotropic in nature [32] are used to obtain the scores related to the orientation of the vectors. The output is a pair of real and imaginary parts representing local symmetric and antisymmetric features respectively. Techniques involving the removal or reduction of noise through adaptive contrast enhancement followed by morphology-based segmentation [33] show improvement in the specificity of the algorithm. Applying a simpler Daubechies wavelet reduced the MSE with improved specificity and accuracy but with minimal improvement in the peak signal-to-noise ratio as compared to the basic Haar transform at the second level but very thin vessels are not easily extracted. The modern-day tools can be utilized to enhance the rural healthcare service sector [34, 35, 36]. Some of the more recent image segmentation methods along with the author(s) are listed in Table 3.1.

3.3 PERFORMANCE EVALUATION

Some of the image quality indicators normally used for the quantitative evaluation of the performance of the algorithm are discussed in the following, for both the process of denoising and segmentation.

Table 3.1 Summary of various approaches in major recent publications related to retinal image segmentation

S. no.	Author [reference] and year	Approach	Important findings
1	Farokhian et al. [8], 2017	Gabor filter, imperialist competitive algorithm (ICA)	• Required number of directions reduced to 20 • Selection of directional parameters requires thresholds to be determined • Incorrect determination of threshold levels will lead to a failure of the technique
2	Câmara Neto et al. [15], 2017	Smoothing through Gaussian filter, curvature, mathematical morphology	• Performance evaluated for conditions of abnormalities and disorders related to blood vessels • Results in high specificity but also leads to several false positives as the diameter of the blood vessel is not taken into consideration
3	Dash and Bhoi [6], 2018	Gamma correction, contrast-limited adaptive histogram equalization, adaptive thresholding, double enhancement	• Threshold calculated dynamically • Results in numerous discontinuities in the blood vasculature images of certain pathological conditions
4	Sazak, Nelson, and Obara [9], 2019	Bowler-hat transform	• Utilizes structuring elements of different sizes and shapes for image enhancement • Blob is not identified easily • Sensitive to salt and pepper and speckle noise
5	Adapa et al. [10], 2020	Zernike moment-based features	• Extraction of features based on the shape with very low rates of redundancy of features • Fails to extract very thin vessels of one or two pixels width as higher-order moments with greater complexity are required
6	Zhou, Zhang, and Chen [37], 2020	Weighted line detector and hidden Markov model	• Used to identify the centerline and trace the blood vessel along its width • Dependent on image resolution and hence requires customized values of parameters for high-resolution images

(*Continued*)

Table 3.1 (Continued) Summary of various approaches in major recent publications related to retinal image segmentation

S. no.	Author [reference] and year	Approach	Important findings
7	Maji and Sekh [38], 2020	Feature vector generation through transfer learning	• Based on the statistical properties the image has improved accuracy as a number of the characteristics of the pixels and their relative intensities are captured as a vector • Validated on a small set of data • Complex process requiring heavy resources
8	Gao et al. [39], 2020	Wavelet segmentation method (WSM)	• Three-level decomposition through wavelet transform with a threshold determined by valley point
9	Toptaş and Hanbay [5], 2021	Features extracted based on pixel properties	• Different statistical and pixel properties from five groups for the segmentation process are considered • Accuracy levels are not the best
10	Kaushal, Patil, and Birajdar [40], 2021	Fractional DWT	• A combination of DWT and fractional Fourier transform • A fractional angle α range from 0.1 to 1 to decompose the image into spectral components • Eight features based on image textural properties are extracted to identify the pixel/non-pixel output to reduce the rate of misclassification
11	Reddy, Anisha, and Apoorva [41], 2021	Convolutional neural networks	• Deep learning techniques to classify the images
12	Saha Tchinda et al. [12], 2021	Features based on classical edge detection filters, neural networks	• Blood vessels of different widths and images of different luminosity levels are handled • Noise levels are amplified

3.3.1 Denoising performance metrics

Removal of noise from the images results in an image with greater clarity but also results in the loss of some of the data. The performance metrics [42] will help the user to judge the algorithm to be used for the particular applications, depending upon the kind of information loss.

a) Mean square error (MSE) represents a metric for the measurement of the average of the error of the squares of the difference between the original and the estimated images. This parameter is indicative of the loss in the image information [43]. In Equation (3.2), $m \times n$ are the dimensions of the image in the form of the number of pixels, $I(i,j)$ is the original image, and $I'(i,j)$ is the image obtained through the estimation process. The terms i and j represent the coordinates of the image pixel location.

$$MSE = \frac{1}{m \times n} \sum_{i=0}^{m-1} \sum_{j=0}^{n-1} \left[I(i,j) - I'(i,j) \right]^2 \tag{3.2}$$

b) Peak signal to noise ratio (PSNR) is defined by Equation (3.3), where $Max(i)$ represents the maximum image pixel intensity. It is also the log of the ratio between the corrupted noise power of the blurry image versus the signal's practical maximum power [44].

$$PSNR = 10 * \log_{10} \frac{Max(i)^2}{MSE} \tag{3.3}$$

c) The structural similarity index measure (SSIM) is employed to compare two images in terms of similarity. The image contrast and the luminance are key to determining the changes in the information of the image structure. Both these factors are considered to determine the degradation of the image [45]. In Equation (3.4), μ_F and $\mu_{F'}$ are average of F and F', σ_F and $\sigma_{F'}$ are the variance of F and F', $c1$ and $c2$ are variables to stabilize the division using weak denomination, while F and F' are input images.

$$SSIM = \frac{\left(2\mu_F\mu_{F'} + c1\right)\left(2\sigma_{FF'} + c2\right)}{\left(\mu_F^2 + \mu_{F'}^2 + c1\right)\left(\sigma_F^2 + \sigma_{F'}^2 + c2\right)} \tag{3.4}$$

3.3.2 Segmentation performance metrics

The effectiveness of an algorithm is based on certain primary parameters used for comparison of a proposed method to the existing ones.

a) Accuracy: in the case of images, it indicates the amount by which the output matches the standard output point to point [46]. In Equation (3.5), Acc denotes accuracy, *Sen* the sensitivity, and *Spe* the specificity. These are statistical performance metrics.

$$Acc = \frac{Sen + Spe}{2} \tag{3.5}$$

with *Sen* = TP/(TP + FN) and *Spe* = TN / (TN + FP).
Accuracy can also be defined as Acc = (TP + TN)/(TP + TN + FP + FN).

b) Dice metric (D_m): this metric is a quantitative measurement of the commonality between the segmented area and the ground truth [47]. In Equation (3.6), A indicates a segmented image area and B indicates an area of ground truth to be compared.

$$D_m = \frac{2x\,\text{Area}(A \cap B)}{\text{Area}(A) + \text{Area}(B)} \qquad (3.6)$$

The more false positives exist, the smaller this value will be. Similarly, the greater the number of positives that are missed also affects this parameter adversely.

c) Area overlap (A_o): it is a metric that indicates an intersection over the union of the areas between the segmented portion of the image and the corresponding area of the ground truth image [48]. In Equation (3.7), the segmented area of the image is given by A_{seg} while the corresponding area of the ground truth is represented by A_{gt}.

$$A_0 = \frac{A_{seg} \cap A_{gt}}{A_{seg} \cup A_{gt}} \qquad (3.7)$$

d) The Matthews correlation coefficient (MCC) [49] is a statistical metric in terms of the correlation coefficient defined between the manually segmented result and the ground truth, ranging from -1 (completely incorrect classification) to 1 (perfect classification). The relationship between the two is given by Equation (3.8):

$$MCC = \frac{\dfrac{TP}{N-S} XP}{\sqrt{[PXSX(1-S)X(1-P)]}} \text{ with } S = (TP+FN)/N, P = (TP+FP)/N \qquad (3.8)$$

e) F1-score (F1) within the field of view (FOV) gives the harmonic mean of precision and recall shown in Equation (3.9), ranging from 0 (completely incorrect classification) to 1 (perfect classification).

$$F1 = \frac{2\left(\dfrac{TP}{TP+FP}\right) \cdot \left(\dfrac{TP}{TP+FN}\right)}{\dfrac{TP}{TP+FP} + \dfrac{TP}{TP+FN}} \qquad (3.9)$$

(d) and (e) are metrics used for evaluating an unbalanced dataset where the retinal vessel segmentation with vessel pixels comprises only 9–14% of the image.

f) The receiving operator characteristics (ROC) curve utilizes the probability map of any vessel and is calculated as the true positive fraction

(Se) versus the false positive fraction (1 – Sp), with respect to the varying threshold T. This quantifies the performance of the operation. The area under this curve (denoted by AUC) can be calculated to evaluate the parameter.

3.4 BIORTHOGONAL WAVELET TRANSFORMS AND FILTERS

Wavelets provide the channel for analysis in both the time and frequency domains simultaneously. The periodic characteristic of the signals is retained while its energy is concentrated in time. Hence, wavelet decomposition is a very useful mathematical tool for a comprehensive analysis of the non-stationary signal with several regions of discontinuities where the statistical analysis cannot be done. The mathematical representation of the additive and the multiplicative noise models is generally given by Equations (3.10) and (3.11):

$$I'(i,j) = \text{Sum}(I(i,j), \eta(i,j)), \text{ for all } i,j \tag{3.10}$$

$$I'(i,j) = \text{Product}(I(i,j), \eta(i,j)), \text{ for all } i,j \tag{3.11}$$

where I'(i,j) is the noisy image, I(i,j) is the noise-free or original image, and $\eta(i,j)$ is the noise added to the original noise-free image.

The four filters for biorthogonal transforms (for analysis and synthesis filters for the scaling and wavelet coefficients) are related by Equation (3.12) given here:

$$\tilde{g}(n) = (-1)^n h(1-n); \quad g(n) = (-1)^n \tilde{h}(1-n) \tag{3.12}$$

where $\tilde{h}(n)$ and $h(n)$ are analysis and synthesis filter coefficients. Now when $\tilde{h}(n) = h(n)$, then $g(n) = (-1)^n h(1-n)$. This will result in a condition defined by Equation (3.13) as shown here:

$$\sum_n \tilde{h}(n) \cdot h(n+2k) = \delta(k) \tag{3.13}$$

Now $h(n)$ is orthogonal to even translation of itself. Here $\tilde{h}(n)$ is orthogonal to h and so it is named biorthogonal [50].

If $\tilde{h}(n)$ is non-zero for $\tilde{N}_1 \leq n \leq N_2$ and $h(n)$ is non-zero for $N_1 \leq n \leq \tilde{N}_2$, then the relation of the number of analysis and synthesis filter coefficients is related by Equation (3.14) as:

$$N_2 - \tilde{N}_1 = 2k+1 \text{ and } \tilde{N}_2 - N_1 = 2\tilde{k}+1, k, \tilde{k} \in \mathbf{Z} \tag{3.14}$$

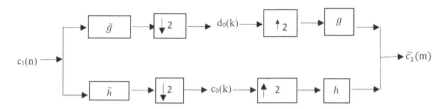

Figure 3.3 Representation of the two channels in filter bank (biorthogonal).

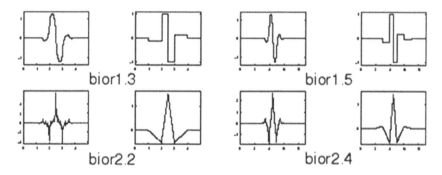

Figure 3.4 Sample of different biorthogonal wavelets and their wavelet coefficients.

The difference in the lengths of $\tilde{h}(n)$ and $h(n)$ must be even, i.e., these lengths must be both even or both odd to get an even length. Symmetric and odd-length filters will result in even-length and symmetric scaling and wavelet functions. Symmetric and even-length filters have symmetric scaling and anti-symmetric wavelet functions. Figure 3.3 is a representation of the biorthogonal filter bank.

The decomposition and reconstruction wavelet coefficients of biorthogonal wavelets with different lengths are shown in Figure 3.4.

These biorthogonal wavelets must satisfy the following conditions in Equation (3.13) and Equation (3.15):

$$\sum_n h(n) = \sum_n \tilde{h}(n) = \sqrt{2} \qquad (3.15)$$

Filters can further be categorized as linear and non-linear. The filters used prominently in medical image processing are listed in Table 3.2.

3.5 INVESTIGATIONAL RESULTS

The publicly available Digital Retinal Images for Vessel Extraction (DRIVE) database [17, 52] with available gold-standard images is used

Table 3.2 Filters used commonly in image processing

S. no.	Name of the filter (spatial or frequency domain)	Linear/ non-linear	Results in	Type of noise removed/reduced
1	Mean/average/ convolution (spatial)	Linear	Smoothing	Grain noise
2	Median (spatial)	Non-linear	Sharpening	Edge blurring/salt and pepper/ impulse noise
3	Wiener filter/ optimal filter (frequency domain and spatial)	Linear (mean square error ideal)	Gaussian white noise	Additive noise/ blurring
4	Bilateral filter [51]	Non-linear	Edge preserving; noise reduction; smoothing filter	Gaussian noise

to test the algorithm. It is a dataset comprising a total of 40 color fundus images that were captured under standard illumination conditions using a Canon CR5 non-mydriatic 3-CCD camera with a field of view of 45°. Each image was captured by 8 bits per plane at 768 × 584 pixels and stored as a jpeg file. The set of 40 images is divided into test and training sets, each consisting of 20 images, with seven cases of abnormalities. The patients lie in the range of 25 to 90. The ground truth images that were manually segmented by the individual observers are also included in the dataset, which can be used for research work. The experimental setup used consisted of an Intel Core i7 (8th Gen) PC with a RAM of size 4 GB and at 2.20 GHz with Windows 10 64-bit operating system, using MATLAB 2018a software for visualization.

The transform is applied to various standard images to understand the result on different coefficients. Upon decompositions, different features are observed in different sub-bands. Based on these features, the requirements of the wavelet transform can be varied across the sub-bands. Relating to the eye, the focus areas are the fovea, the macula, the optic disc, and the blood vessels. The area in the fundus image with the maximum variation in the pixel intensity in comparison to the neighboring pixels is the optic disc.

3.5.1 Noise suppression in images using the wavelet transform

A two-step preprocessing is performed. The first preprocessing step includes an enhancement of the contrast between the foreground and the background through local contrast enhancement [53]. The mathematical representation of this relation is expressed in Equations (3.16) and (3.17).

$$\text{New pixel } p_n = 255^* \left(\frac{[\phi_w(p) - \phi_w(\min)]}{[\phi_w(\max) - \phi_w(\min)]} \right) \tag{3.16}$$

$$\text{with } \phi_w(p) = \left(1 + \exp\left(\frac{\mu_w - p}{\sigma_w} \right) \right)^{-1} \tag{3.17}$$

The terms min, max, μ_w, and σ_w denote the minimum and maximum values of intensities of the image pixels, the mean, and the standard deviation of the local window respectively.

It is observed that for low contrast (σ_w is low), the exponential produces significant enhancement and for high contrast (σ_w high), it provides little enhancement.

As part of the second preprocessing step, it is seen that the blood vessels are also clearly visible when the green channel with reduced noise at this wavelength is used. The size of 512×512 pixels is used for the green channel and with a median filter of size 30 to remove the non-uniform illumination. Also, the tone of the RGB is not uniform in the image and the Euclidean distances in this color space do not represent the difference in color as perceived by the human eye. The grayscale image is obtained through contrast enhancement. To produce a normalized color range through histogram specification, a (3×3) median filter is normally used to suppress the noise and for background exclusion. Here, instead, the wavelet transformation with level-dependent thresholding is used for denoising the image.

3.5.2 Contrast enhancement of the images for improved segmentation

Through the process of contrast enhancement, the narrow-ranged image intensity values are changed to have a distribution covering a wide range of intensities. The contrast of an image can be studied through its histogram. Intensity equalization or normalization includes methods to produce uniformity in the intensity distribution in the images. This important step helps to identify the foreground and background. The process of outlier equalization involves the removal of mismatched pixels in the neighborhood. The other methods that help to improve the segmentation process are bias compensation, time/space filtering, and iterative processing method.

3.5.3 Findings

Some of the distinct features that are considered to differentiate between the blood vessel and non-vessel regions are the diameter of the blood vessel,

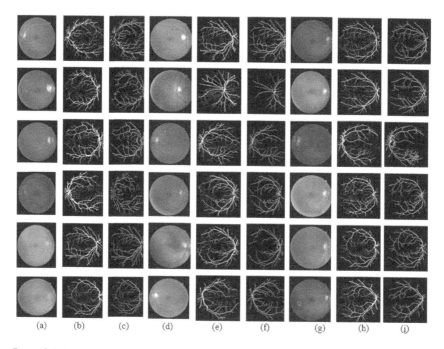

Figure 3.5 Results of the approach on normal and affected retinal images: (a), (d), (g) original image; (b), (e), (h) annotated image; (c), (f), (i) segmented output. Source: (a), (b), (d), (e), (g), (h) images taken from DRIVE database.

its compactness, the length of the structure, its diameter, strength of the edge, and so on [5]. Each of these features is extracted for the image at various pre-defined points.

The image visual outputs obtained from the images of the DRIVE database using the aforementioned approach are shown in Figure 3.5.

The implementation of this algorithm produces the output with good accuracy for the images, as seen by visual inspection of the outputs. The parameters used for quantitative comparison are sensitivity, given by *Sen* = TP/(TP + FN), specificity defined by *Spe* = TN/(TN + FP), and accuracy as Acc = *Sen+Spe*/2, which can also be defined as Acc = (TP +TN)/(TP + TN + FP + FN). The terms TP, TN, FP, and FN represent true positive, true negative, false positive, and false negative, where true positive indicates that the algorithm recognizes the positive object correctly and true negative when the algorithm recognizes the object correctly as not belonging.

On the other hand, false positive is when the algorithm indicates the object incorrectly as belonging and false negative is when the algorithm indicates the object incorrectly as not belonging. The dice metric or dice coefficient is a measure of the number of positives that exists in samples and is given as $D_m = 2*TP/(2*TP + FP + FN)$.

Table 3.3 Comparison of sensitivity (Sen%), specificity (Spe%), accuracy (Acc%), dice metric (D_m), and Matthews correlation coefficient (MCC) of biorthogonal wavelet-1.3 for a sample of the DRIVE dataset

DRIVE image	Sen%	Spe%	Acc%	D_m	MCC
01_test.tif	63.97	92.19	96.60	0.7858	0.7679
02_test.tif	73.62	96.30	97.60	0.7682	0.7612
03_test.tif	64.84	95.02	97.52	0.7421	0.6464
04_test.tif	68.72	94.25	97.73	0.7224	0.6456
05_test.tif	67.63	93.04	96.87	0.7288	0.6676
06_test.tif	72.46	96.62	97.80	0.7072	0.5274
07_test.tif	67.72	92.06	97.18	0.7164	0.6356
08_test.tif	76.16	96.19	97.78	0.6471	0.6124
09_test.tif	73.62	96.30	97.60	0.6882	0.6353
10_test.tif	70.47	93.70	97.81	0.6784	0.6506
11_test.tif	65.14	93.07	96.08	0.6832	0.6597
12_test.tif	67.64	94.57	97.41	0.6686	0.6564
13_test.tif	69.08	94.04	97.36	0.7275	0.6273
14_test.tif	66.60	92.83	97.72	0.6934	0.7636
15_test.tif	62.46	91.61	97.31	0.7377	0.6319
16_test.tif	67.46	93.12	97.73	0.6434	0.6893
17_test.tif	72.91	96.26	97.95	0.7612	0.7045
18_test.tif	69.96	94.01	97.44	0.7550	0.6305
19_test.tif	67.82	94.05	97.78	0.7178	0.7099
20_test.tif	74.81	95.42	97.85	0.7175	0.6532
Average	63.97	92.19	97.46	0.7140	0.6645

A comparison of the aforementioned metrics for a sample of 20 images from the DRIVE database is tabulated in Table 3.3.

From the table, the average values of the sensitivity, specificity, accuracy, dice metric, and the Matthews correlation coefficient are observed to be at around 64%, 92%, 97%, 0.7140, and 0.6645 respectively, with the approach discussed earlier.

Table 3.4 shows a comparison of the accuracy obtained when the biorthogonal wavelet transform with variation in the number of decomposition and reconstruction filters is applied to a subset of the DRIVE dataset. It is noted that the accuracy of the segmentation process improves as the length of the filters of the biorthogonal transform is increased (as seen in bior1.3 and bior1.1). However, contrary to the expectation, when bior1.5 with a more complex structure is used, there is very minimal improvement in the accuracy.

The quantitative analysis in comparison with the previous methods is tabulated in Table 3.5, which shows an improvement in the accuracy of the outputs obtained through the aforementioned wavelet transform approach.

Table 3.4 Comparison of accuracy (%) of biorthogonal wavelets of different filter lengths for a sample of the DRIVE dataset

DRIVE image	Biorthogonal-1.1	Biorthogonal-1.3	Biorthogonal-1.5
01_test.tif	76.87	96.60	96.61
02_test.tif	77.14	97.60	97.06
03_test.tif	78.73	97.52	97.52
04_test.tif	83.37	97.73	97.71
05_test.tif	77.91	96.87	96.81
06_test.tif	76.73	97.80	97.80
07_test.tif	77.26	97.18	97.17
08_test.tif	76.24	97.78	97.78
09_test.tif	77.14	97.60	97.63
10_test.tif	77.56	97.81	97.81
11_test.tif	76.92	96.08	95.93
12_test.tif	77.06	97.41	97.38
13_test.tif	76.88	97.36	97.38
14_test.tif	76.92	97.72	97.72
15_test.tif	76.37	97.31	97.29
16_test.tif	76.93	97.73	97.69
17_test.tif	76.98	97.95	97.95
18_test.tif	76.65	97.44	97.35
19_test.tif	83.46	97.78	97.77
20_test.tif	77.32	97.85	97.87
Average	77.72	97.46	97.41

From Table 3.2, the sensitivity results of the method under study yielded an average value compared to a few of the methods in the literature. The specificity, however, is much above the average value of the different approaches, while there is much-needed improvement in the accuracy of the method.

3.6 DISCUSSION AND CONCLUSIONS

A vessel segmentation method based on the biorthogonal wavelet transform algorithm is discussed to understand its efficiency and its limitations. This is part of the ongoing work to identify a universally applicable segmentation process for the retinal blood vessels in fundus images of different eye conditions or varying resolution or quality. The abnormal signs in the retinal images complicate the process of performing the blood vasculature segmentation. The wavelet transform algorithm is highly successful in obtaining distinguishable sub-bands of an image. This is the simplest and

Table 3.5 Analysis of different approaches

S. no.	Author name [references]	Year	Sensitivity (Sen)%	Specificity (Spe)%	Accuracy (Acc)%
1	Proposed method (biorthogonal wavelet -1.3)	–	70.62	94.54	96.68
2	Miri and Mahloojifar [29]	2011	73.53	97.96	94.59
3	Fraz et al. [54]	2012	71.53	97.69	94.31
4	Imani, Javidi, and Pourreza [17]	2015	75.25	97.54	95.23
5	Roychowdhury, Koozekanani, and Parhi [4]	2015	73.91	97.81	94.90
6	Farokhian et al. [8]	2017	69.34	97.78	93.92
7	Câmara Neto et al. [15]	2017	78.07	96.29	87.19
8	Zhang et al. [32]	2017	81.15	98.47	96.26
9	Jiang et al. [55]	2017	83.76	96.94	95.98
10	Dash and Bhoi [6]	2018	74.11	98.62	95.73
11	Sazak, Nelson, and Obara [9]	2019	71.82	98.11	95.92
12	Kushol et al. [13]	2020	75.88	97.48	94.56
13	Adapa et al [10]	2020	69.95	98.12	94.50
14	Toptaş and Hanbay [5]	2021	84.36	97.17	96.16
15	Saha Tchinda et al. [12]	2021	73.53	97.76	94.81
16	Manual evaluator [52]	–	77.65	97.43	94.71

fastest biorthogonal wavelet transforms, which is a family of unsupervised techniques. A comparative graph is represented in Figure 3.6 to show the improvement in the accuracy when bior1.3 is utilized.

The experimental outputs indicate the potential improvement in segmenting blood vessels in the retinal images of patients with different eye diseases, including diabetic retinopathy. Moreover, the method is robust to noise as the wavelet transform algorithm can separate noise from the image also. After removing the noise from retinal images, the vessels are extracted by the biorthogonal wavelet transform. In the last stage, the final binary vessel vasculature is obtained through mathematical morphology. The average accuracy of the vessel segmentation output using the biorthogonal wavelet on the DRIVE dataset is 96.68%.

It is concluded that for biorthogonal wavelet transforms of higher lengths, even though more complex in structure, there is minimal improvement in the accuracy of images in the DRIVE database beyond the biorthogonal transform 1.3. However, in cases where the conditions of severe diabetic retinopathy or the presence of very high levels of blood vessel tortuosity occur, the aforementioned approach does not yield good results. The metrics related to the different segmentation techniques are shown graphically in Figure 3.7 for (a) sensitivity, (b) specificity, and (c) accuracy.

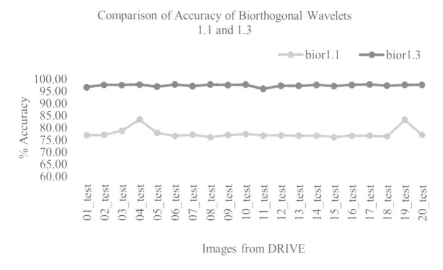

Figure 3.6 Comparison of the biorthogonal wavelets of different filter lengths.

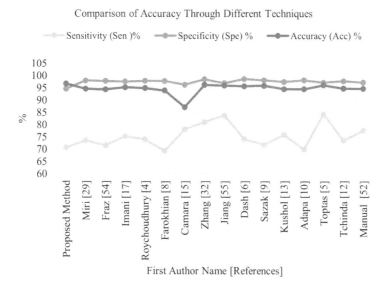

Figure 3.7 Comparison of the average sensitivity, specificity, and accuracy for different approaches (including the one under study) applied on the DRIVE database.

The aforementioned approach generates better quantitative and qualitative results. The advantage of the biorthogonal wavelets is that there is stability in the system even with an exchange of the primary and the dual filters with no change in the system output. But its disadvantage is that the norm of the coefficients is not the same as the norm of the functions that were traversed. One other area requiring focus is the Gaussian white noise being converted to a colored or correlated noise when using a biorthogonal (non-orthogonal) filter, which would require additional care to address the colored noise. In the future, to overcome the limitation of the approach, the redundancy of the wavelet transform can be increased to improve the quality of the denoised image before the segmentation process. This will help to produce a better translation invariant transform, thus reducing the artifacts produced during reconstruction. This approach can be used to detect other diseases involving blood vessel–like structures, such as the case of cardio disease. Wherever the finer and narrower vessel structures are to be detected, more refined and effective preprocessing and post-processing methods can be applied.

REFERENCES

1. W. Huang and Z. Xu, "Characteristics and performance of image sensor communication," *IEEE Photonics J.*, vol. 9, no. 2, pp. 1–19, Apr. 2017, doi: 10.1109/JPHOT.2017.2681660.
2. C. Gokilavani, N. Rajeswaran, K. Senthilvel, and R. Sathishkumar, "Noise Adaptive Fuzzy Switching Median Filters for Removing Gaussian Noise and Salt & Pepper Noise in Retinal Images," Jan. 2016, doi: 10.5829/idosi.mejsr .2016.24.02.22884.
3. G. Lim, V. Bellemo, Y. Xie, X. Q. Lee, M. Y. T. Yip, and D. S. W. Ting, "Different fundus imaging modalities and technical factors in AI screening for diabetic retinopathy: a review," *Eye Vis.*, vol. 7, no. 1, p. 21, Dec. 2020, doi: 10.1186/s40662-020-00182-7.
4. S. Roychowdhury, D. D. Koozekanani, and K. K. Parhi, "Iterative vessel segmentation of fundus images," *IEEE Trans. Biomed. Eng.*, vol. 62, no. 7, pp. 1738–1749, Jul. 2015, doi: 10.1109/TBME.2015.2403295.
5. B. Toptaş and D. Hanbay, "Retinal blood vessel segmentation using pixel-based feature vector," *Biomed. Signal Process. Control*, vol. 70, p. 103053, Sep. 2021, doi: 10.1016/j.bspc.2021.103053.
6. J. Dash and N. Bhoi, "An unsupervised approach for extraction of blood vessels from fundus images," *J. Digit. Imaging*, vol. 31, no. 6, pp. 857–868, Dec. 2018, doi: 10.1007/s10278-018-0059-x.
7. M. Vijaya Maheswari and G. Murugeswari, "Empirical evaluation of retinal vessel segmentation techniques," *J. Comput. Theor. Nanosci.*, vol. 17, no. 9–10, pp. 4671–4677, Jul. 2020, doi: 10.1166/jctn.2020.9297.
8. F. Farokhian, C. Yang, H. Demirel, S. Wu, and I. Beheshti, "Automatic parameters selection of Gabor filters with the imperialism competitive algorithm with application to retinal vessel segmentation," *Biocybern. Biomed. Eng.*, vol. 37, no. 1, pp. 246–254, 2017, doi: 10.1016/j.bbe.2016.12.007.
9. Ç. Sazak, C. J. Nelson, and B. Obara, "The multiscale bowler-hat transform for blood vessel enhancement in retinal images," *Pattern Recognit.*, vol. 88, pp. 739–750, Apr. 2019, doi: 10.1016/j.patcog.2018.10.011.

10. D. Adapa, A. N. Joseph Raj, S. N. Alisetti, Z. Zhuang, G. K., and G. Naik, "A supervised blood vessel segmentation technique for digital Fundus images using Zernike Moment based features," *PLOS ONE*, vol. 15, no. 3, p. e0229831, Mar. 2020, doi: 10.1371/journal.pone.0229831.

11. A. Praharsha, D. S. P. Lanka, and U. Chandana, "Expression tuna: World of expressive music," *Turk. Online J. Qual. Inq.*, vol. 12, no. 7, Art. no. 7, Aug. 2021.

12. B. Saha Tchinda, D. Tchiotsop, M. Noubom, V. Louis-Dorr, and D. Wolf, "Retinal blood vessels segmentation using classical edge detection filters and the neural network," *Inform. Med. Unlocked*, vol. 23, p. 100521, 2021, doi: 10.1016/j.imu.2021.100521.

13. R. Kushol, M. H. Kabir, M. Abdullah-Al-Wadud, and M. S. Islam, "Retinal blood vessel segmentation from fundus image using an efficient multiscale directional representation technique Bendlets," *Math. Biosci. Eng. MBE*, vol. 17, no. 6, pp. 7751–7771, Nov. 2020, doi: 10.3934/mbe.2020394.

14. M. Misiti, Ed., *Wavelets and their applications*. London; Newport Beach, CA: ISTE, 2007.

15. L. Câmara Neto, G. L. B. Ramalho, J. F. S. Rocha Neto, R. M. S. Veras, and F. N. S. Medeiros, "An unsupervised coarse-to-fine algorithm for blood vessel segmentation in fundus images," *Expert Syst. Appl.*, vol. 78, pp. 182–192, Jul. 2017, doi: 10.1016/j.eswa.2017.02.015.

16. K. Sun, Z. Chen, S. Jiang, and Y. Wang, "Morphological multiscale enhancement, fuzzy filter and watershed for vascular tree extraction in angiogram," *J. Med. Syst.*, vol. 35, no. 5, pp. 811–824, Oct. 2011, doi: 10.1007/s10916-010-9466-3.

17. E. Imani, M. Javidi, and H.-R. Pourreza, "Improvement of retinal blood vessel detection using morphological component analysis," *Comput. Methods Programs Biomed.*, vol. 118, no. 3, pp. 263–279, Mar. 2015, doi: 10.1016/j.cmpb.2015.01.004.

18. G. Liew and J. J. Wang, "Retinal vascular signs: A window to the heart?," *Rev. Esp. Cardiol. Engl. Ed.*, vol. 64, no. 6, pp. 515–521, Jun. 2011, doi: 10.1016/j.rec.2011.02.017.

19. A. Osareh, B. Shadgar, and R. Markham, "A computational-intelligence-based approach for detection of exudates in diabetic retinopathy images," *IEEE Trans. Inf. Technol. Biomed.*, vol. 13, no. 4, pp. 535–545, Jul. 2009, doi: 10.1109/TITB.2008.2007493.

20. R. GeethaRamani and L. Balasubramanian, "Retinal blood vessel segmentation employing image processing and data mining techniques for computerized retinal image analysis," *Biocybern. Biomed. Eng.*, vol. 36, no. 1, pp. 102–118, 2016, doi: 10.1016/j.bbe.2015.06.004.

21. B. Shinde, D. Mhaske, and A. R. Dani, "Study of noise detection and noise removal techniques in medical images," *Int. J. Image Graph. Signal Process.*, vol. 4, no. 2, pp. 51–60, Mar. 2012, doi: 10.5815/ijigsp.2012.02.08.

22. Dr. L. D. C, "Noise removal in magnetic resonance images using hybrid KSL filtering technique," *Int. J. Comput. Appl.*, vol. 27, Aug. 2011, doi: 10.5120/3324-4571.

23. F. Zana and J.-C. Klein, "Segmentation of vessel-like patterns using mathematical morphology and curvature evaluation," *IEEE Trans. Image Process.*, vol. 10, no. 7, pp. 1010–1019, Jul. 2001, doi: 10.1109/83.931095.

24. M. E. Martinez-Perez et al., "Retinal vascular tree morphology: a semi-automatic quantification," *IEEE Trans. Biomed. Eng.*, vol. 49, no. 8, pp. 912–917, Aug. 2002, doi: 10.1109/TBME.2002.800789.

25. S. Wang, L. Xu, Y. Wang, Y. Wang, and J. B. Jonas, "Retinal vessel diameter in normal and glaucomatous eyes: the Beijing eye study: Retinal vessel diameter in adult Chinese," *Clin. Experiment. Ophthalmol.*, vol. 35, no. 9, pp. 800–807, Dec. 2007, doi: 10.1111/j.1442-9071.2007.01627.x.

26. C. Heneghan, "Characterization of changes in blood vessel width and tortuosity in retinopathy of prematurity using image analysis," *Med. Image Anal.*, vol. 6, no. 4, pp. 407–429, Dec. 2002, doi: 10.1016/S1361-8415(02)00058-0.

27. W. Lotmar, A. Freiburghaus, and D. Bracher, "Measurement of vessel tortuosity on fundus photographs," *Albrecht Von Graefes Arch. Klin. Exp. Ophthalmol.*, vol. 211, no. 1, pp. 49–57, 1979, doi: 10.1007/BF00414653.

28. E. Grisan, M. Foracchia, and A. Ruggeri, "A novel method for the automatic grading of retinal vessel tortuosity," *IEEE Trans. Med. Imaging*, vol. 27, no. 3, pp. 310–319, Mar. 2008, doi: 10.1109/TMI.2007.904657.

29. M. S. Miri and A. Mahloojifar, "Retinal image analysis using curvelet transform and multistructure elements morphology by reconstruction," *IEEE Trans. Biomed. Eng.*, vol. 58, no. 5, pp. 1183–1192, May 2011, doi: 10.1109/TBME.2010.2097599.

30. K. Mondal, P. Dutta, and S. Bhattacharyya, "Fuzzy logic based gray image extraction and segmentation," *International Journal of Scientific & Engineering Research*, vol. 3, no. 4, p. 14, 2012.

31. M. K. Nath and S. Dandapat, "Multiscale ICA for fundus image analysis," *Int. J. Imaging Syst. Technol.*, vol. 23, no. 4, pp. 327–337, Dec. 2013, doi: 10.1002/ima.22067.

32. J. Zhang, Y. Chen, E. Bekkers, M. Wang, B. Dashtbozorg, and B. M. ter H. Romeny, "Retinal vessel delineation using a brain-inspired wavelet transform and random forest," *Pattern Recognit.*, vol. 69, pp. 107–123, Sep. 2017, doi: 10.1016/j.patcog.2017.04.008.

33. U. Dikkala, M. K. Joseph, and M. Alagirisamy, "A comprehensive analysis of morphological process dependent retinal blood vessel segmentation," in 2021 International Conference on Computing, Communication, and Intelligent Systems (ICCCIS), Feb. 2021, pp. 510–516. doi: 10.1109/ICCCIS51004.2021.9397095.

34. S. Pathan, M. Bhushan, and A. Bai "A study on health care using data mining techniques," *Journal of Critical Reviews*, vol. 7, no. 19, p. 7877–7890, 2020, doi: 10.31838/jcr.07.19.896.

35. V. J. Singh, M. Bhushan, V. Kumar, and K. L. Bansal, "Optimization of segment size assuring application perceived QoS in healthcare," in Proceedings of the World Congress on Engineering,Vol. 1, p. 5, 2015.

36. Mangla, A., Kumar, V., Mehta, M., Bhushan and S. N. Mohanty. *Real-Life Applications of the Internet of Things: Challenges, Applications, and Advances*, Apple Aademic Press, 1st edn, pp. 536, 2022. DOI: https://doi.org/10.1201/9781003277460

37. C. Zhou, X. Zhang, and H. Chen, "A new robust method for blood vessel segmentation in retinal fundus images based on weighted line detector and hidden Markov model," *Comput. Methods Programs Biomed.*, vol. 187, p. 105231, Apr. 2020, doi: 10.1016/j.cmpb.2019.105231.

38. D. Maji and A. A. Sekh, "Automatic grading of retinal blood vessel in deep retinal image diagnosis," *J. Med. Syst.*, vol. 44, no. 10, p. 180, 2020, doi: 10.1007/s10916-020-01635-1.

39. J. Gao, B. Wang, Z. Wang, Y. Wang, and F. Kong, "A wavelet transform-based image segmentation method," *Optik*, vol. 208, p. 164123, Apr. 2020, doi: 10.1016/j.ijleo.2019.164123.

40. B. Kaushal, M. D. Patil, and G. K. Birajdar, "Fractional wavelet transform based diagnostic system for brain tumor detection in MR imaging," *Int. J. Imaging Syst. Technol.*, vol. 31, no. 2, pp. 575–591, Jun. 2021, doi: 10.1002/ima.22497.

41. C. Kishor Kumar Reddy, P. R. Anisha, and K. Apoorva, "Early prediction of pneumonia using convolutional neural network and X-ray images," in Smart Computing Techniques and Applications, Singapore, 2021, pp. 673–681. doi: 10.1007/978-981-16-1502-3_67.

42. J. Gupta, S. K. Saini, and M. Juneja, "Survey of denoising and segmentation techniques for MRI images of prostate for improving diagnostic tools in medical applications," *Mater. Today Proc.*, vol. 28, pp. 1667–1672, 2020, doi: 10.1016/j.matpr.2020.05.023.

43. E. L. Lehmann and G. Casella, *Theory of point estimation*, 2nd ed. New York: Springer, 1998.

44. Q. Huynh-Thu and M. Ghanbari, "Scope of validity of PSNR in image/ video quality assessment," *Electron. Lett.*, vol. 44, no. 13, p. 800, 2008, doi: 10.1049/el:20080522.

45. Z. Wang, A. C. Bovik, H. R. Sheikh, and E. P. Simoncelli, "Image quality assessment: From error visibility to structural similarity," *IEEE Trans. Image Process.*, vol. 13, no. 4, pp. 600–612, Apr. 2004, doi: 10.1109/TIP.2003.819861.

46. N.-M. Tan, Y. Xu, W. B. Goh, and J. Liu, "Robust multi-scale superpixel classification for optic cup localization," *Comput. Med. Imaging Graph.*, vol. 40, pp. 182–193, Mar. 2015, doi: 10.1016/j.compmedimag.2014.10.002.

47. F. Yin et al., "Automated segmentation of optic disc and optic cup in fundus images for glaucoma diagnosis," in 2012 25th IEEE International Symposium on Computer-Based Medical Systems (CBMS), Rome, Italy, Jun. 2012, pp. 1–6. doi: 10.1109/CBMS.2012.6266344.

48. N. M. Tan, J. Liu, D. W. K. Wong, F. Yin, J. H. Lim, and T. Y. Wong, "Mixture model-based approach for optic cup segmentation," in 2010 Annual International Conference of the IEEE Engineering in Medicine and Biology, Buenos Aires, Aug. 2010, pp. 4817–4820. doi: 10.1109/IEMBS.2010.5627901.

49. D. Chicco and G. Jurman, "The advantages of the Matthews correlation coefficient (MCC) over F1 score and accuracy in binary classification evaluation," *BMC Genomics*, vol. 21, no. 1, p. 6, Dec. 2020, doi: 10.1186/s12864-019-6413-7.

50. A. Aldroubi, P. Abry, and M. Unser, "Construction of biorthogonal wavelets starting from any two multiresolutions," *IEEE Trans. Signal Process.*, vol. 46, no. 4, pp. 1130–1133, Apr. 1998, doi: 10.1109/78.668563.

51. M. Zhang and B. K. Gunturk, "Multiresolution bilateral filtering for image denoising," *IEEE Trans. Image Process.*, vol. 17, no. 12, pp. 2324–2333, Dec. 2008, doi: 10.1109/TIP.2008.2006658.

52. J. Staal, M. D. Abramoff, M. Niemeijer, M. A. Viergever, and B. van Ginneken, "Ridge-based vessel segmentation in color images of the retina,"

IEEE Trans. Med. Imaging, vol. 23, no. 4, pp. 501–509, Apr. 2004, doi: 10.1109/TMI.2004.825627.

53. C. Sinthanayothin, J. F. Boyce, H. L. Cook, and T. H. Williamson, "Automated localisation of the optic disc, fovea, and retinal blood vessels from digital colour fundus images," *Br. J. Ophthalmol.*, vol. 83, no. 8, pp. 902–910, Aug. 1999, doi: 10.1136/bjo.83.8.902.

54. M. M. Fraz et al., "An approach to localize the retinal blood vessels using bit planes and centerline detection," *Comput. Methods Programs Biomed.*, vol. 108, no. 2, pp. 600–616, Nov. 2012, doi: 10.1016/j.cmpb.2011.08.009.

55. Z. Jiang, J. Yepez, S. An, and S. Ko, "Fast, accurate and robust retinal vessel segmentation system," *Biocybern. Biomed. Eng.*, vol. 37, no. 3, pp. 412–421, 2017, doi: 10.1016/j.bbe.2017.04.001.

Chapter 4

Deep learning-based automatic detection of breast lesions on ultrasound images

Telagarapu Prabhakar, Wilfrido Gómez-Flores, and C. Kishor Kumar Reddy

CONTENTS

4.1 INTRODUCTION

Breast cancer is the most common cancer in women, affecting one in every eight of them. It starts with abnormal cell development in the breast, and these cells travel out of the ducts or lobules and into adjacent tissues, where they proliferate swiftly and spread throughout the breast and even into other

DOI: 10.1201/9781003286745-4

regions of the body [1]. Female death rates are increasing day by day in the world due to diseases like breast cancer. For reducing the death rates early detection is important [2]. Most people can use the mammography technique for screening as well as for detection. It is considered a standard technique for early detection, but this process involves ionization radiation, namely, X-rays. However, it is uncomfortable and painful for women [3]. To overcome this type of drawback, we are using an ultrasound imaging technique. Any patient can get good treatment if he/she can have awareness regarding the disease at its early stage [4]. In the medical image field, many techniques are available, but ultrasound has many advantages compared to other techniques: it is available at a lower price, it is very comfortable for the patients compared to mammography, it is safer because of no radiation process being involved, and it has more sensitivity than others [5]. But the information that is present on the BUS images will purely depend upon the radiologist's experience. CAD systems are available to the radiologist for getting information regarding the diagnosis of a symptomatic lump that varies from the rest of the breast, which is a sign of breast cancer [6]. The patient may develop later stages of breast cancer because of their ignorance about the condition, which may be highly dangerous [7]. As a result, early identification of breast cancer may save a person's life by preventing the illness from spreading to other regions of the body. Kumar et al. built a single segmentation mask using numerous U-nets [8].

After removing speckle noise from the images, the contrast is increased to highlight the tumor spots. Probabilistic categorization of region growth employing the autonomously formed seed point [9]. The regions are then grown from these seed points to adjacent points depending on a region membership criterion. The adaptive reference point production technique may automatically generate RPs depending on breast anatomy during the region of interest (ROI) development stage, and the multipath search strategy grows the seeds consistently and quickly [10].

A rule-based technique and a single-valued thresholding segmentation phase are then used to find the lesion ROI and the seed point. The inverted, original ultrasound image is now subjected to an isotropic Gaussian function [11], a computerized breast lesions segmentation method based on ultrasound images. The images are first pre-processed [12]. Before applying a segmentation approach to the ultrasound images, they must first be pre-processed using the anisotropic diffusion method [13]. A breast segmentation approach based on ultrasound scans was proposed for the detection of breast cancer. Cropping and a median high-boost filter to sharpen the malignant area are part of the preprocessing for segmenting the breast region [14]. The filter's output is processed for picture segmentation using the watershed transform method. In the segmentation phase, the watershed transform approach is utilized to determine the position of the malignancy and may identify things based on their background [15, 16]. For eliminating breast fat tissue, the watershed method is recommended. Singh et al. look at how ultrasound images may be used to diagnose and categorize breast cancer [17, 18]. The morphologic and texture qualities will be used to extract features from the ROI [19]; this is a segmentation method that is completely automated and does not require human intervention [20]. An ROI is automatically created using empirical data and breast anatomical characteristics [21]. By using the u-net deep learning architecture to develop a breast ultrasound segmentation system [22], they developed a tumor segmentation method that was totally automated from start to finish [23]. To begin, image quality may be improved by using preprocessing techniques like contrast augmentation and speckle removal [24], a method for segmenting breast lesions using limited ultrasound imaging data sets, which can help in breast cancer diagnosis [25, 26].

The tumor areas were initially segregated and the segmented BUS pictures were sent into a VGG-19 network that was trained on the ImageNet dataset to determine if the breast tumor was benign or malignant [27]. This is an expanded RDAU-Net model in which the WGAN-RDA-U-Net tumor segmentation technique is built on a generative adversarial network (GAN) [28]. To identify automatic lesions, an adaptive median filter is used during the pre-processing stage, and an adaptive thresholding method is used during the segmentation stage [29]. This is an algorithm for automatically segmenting lesions in ultrasound pictures. An anisotropic diffusion approach is used to reduce speckle noise in the pictures at first. The lesion locations are accentuated by raising the edge. A normalized cut is a graph theoretic approach for image segmentation that allows different attributes to be combined [30].

A sophisticated and automated approach for segmenting breast ultrasound images includes preprocessing breast ultrasound pictures (SRAD), defining the iterative threshold, filtering potential regions, and rating remaining areas to confirm the ROI was an effective method for preliminary contour selection (ROI) [31]. T. Prabhakar and S. Poonguzhali reported using feature extraction based on filtering to detect benign and malignant tumors in breast ultrasound pictures [32]. In this work, breast lesions were detected on ultrasound images using feature-based artificial segmentation. The ability to autonomously separate breast tumors is a key feature of CNN-based techniques.

The following is a breakdown of how this chapter is structured. Section 4.1 depicts a literature review on deep learning–based automatic breast lesion detection on ultrasound images. The approach for automatic detection of breast lesions on ultrasound images using a deep learning algorithm is described in section 4.2. The findings from the separate steps of the speckle reduction and segmentation are combined in section 4.3. Finally, section 4.4 summarizes our findings.

4.2 METHODOLOGY

This chapter explains the suggested approach for CNN-based segmentation of breast lesions on ultrasound images. The suggested study work's block diagram is also presented in detail. Image capture, preprocessing, and segmentation are the three steps of the proposed study. In each of these three steps, a fresh method is used. Various performance measures are used to assess the correctness and efficiency of the planned task.

The methods used in each of these steps are explored in depth. In addition, this chapter delves into the dataset and implementation environment utilized in our research. The block diagram is used to explain the architecture for the automated identification of breast lesions. This chapter highlights the procedures involved in each of the three stages. The previous sections go through the details of each step as well as the assessment measures. The technique of segmentation divides a picture into areas. This is an early step in identifying the image's ROI.

One of the most challenging problems in digital image processing is automatic segmentation. The success or failure of automated analytic processes is determined by segmentation accuracy [27]. Medical image segmentation is useful in applications including visualization, image-guided surgery, and computer-aided diagnosis, and it's used to diagnose breast cancer, lung cancer, colon cancer, prostate cancer, and coronary artery disease. It's also utilized to diagnose other abnormal masses in the organs described.

To differentiate the aberrant breast masses from their background in computer-aided diagnosis of breast masses, segmentation is necessary. The ultrasound (US) picture is marred by speckle noise that leads to poor segmentation results. Hence the noise needs to be eliminated from the picture. This chapter discusses the approaches used in this study to eliminate speckle noise and segment aberrant masses in filtered US pictures.

4.2.1 Block diagram of proposed method

The suggested segmentation method's block diagram is shown in Figure 4.1. The segmentation method may be used to determine the ROI. Various performance measures are used to assess the correctness and efficiency of the planned task.

4.2.2 Breast ultrasound dataset

Breast cancer is one of the world's top causes of mortality among women. The decrease in early mortality is aided by early detection. The information examines medical pictures of breast cancer obtained by an ultrasound scan. The Breast Ultrasound Dataset contains pictures that are categorized into three categories: normal, benign, and malignant. Breast ultrasound images, when combined with machine learning, may provide outstanding results in the classification, diagnosis, and segmentation of breast cancer. Only female patients were included in the dataset. 500×500 pixels is the typical picture size. PNG is the image file format. Ground truth pictures for the real input images are included in the dataset. Normal, benign, and malignant lesions can be divided into three categories.

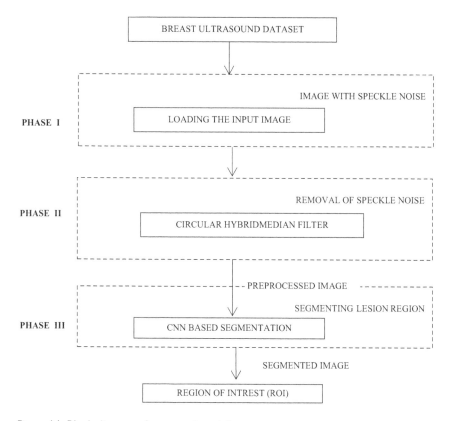

Figure 4.1 Block diagram of proposed model.

4.2.3 Preprocessing

4.2.3.1 Overview

A transmitted US pulse interacts with an anatomical area of interest throughout the picture generation process, delivering information about tissue structures in the form of an echo signal. The coherent summation of signals from US scatterers positioned in the tissue structures of the area of interest produces this echo. These scatterers are caused by inhomogeneities and features in the tissue microstructure that are smaller than the wavelengths of US. Speckle is an interference pattern created by the coherent accumulation of such echo signals. The grainy appearance of essentially homogeneous tissues is due to speckle, which may hide information in the picture. However, because of the poor contrast between tissues in US pictures, calculations that lead to segmentation are problematic. Speckle is a strange granular pattern of white and black specks that attempts to reduce tissue resolution and contrast. Because speckle does not allow for the accurate extraction of textural information, it is difficult to identify or classify aberrant masses in US pictures of various organs.

Ultrasound is a widely used non-invasive, real-time, convenient, and low-cost medical imaging technique. The widely used method for diagnosing breast cancer is breast ultrasound (BUS) imaging, but the interpretation will vary based on the experience of the radiologist. Nowadays, CAD systems are available to provide information regarding BUS image segmentation. But the understandability of information that is present on the BUS images will purely depend upon the radiologist's experience. CAD systems are available to the radiologist for getting the information regarding diagnosis. CAD systems analyze mainly two components regarding BUS images. As a result, speckle reduction is a crucial step in the preprocessing of ultrasound pictures. Furthermore, speckle may be seen as a locally correlated noise that affects picture quality by masking tiny features and lowering SNR. Due to the low contrast between the backdrop and the structures to be segmented, speckle will make it more difficult to locate the edges of distinct components during segmentation operations. As a result, one of the biggest drawbacks of breast ultrasound imaging is speckle interference. Speckle must be reduced without obliterating critical aspects of breast ultrasound imaging.

4.2.3.2 Block diagram of the proposed speckle reduction method

As illustrated in Figure 4.2, the goal of this research is to create a circular hybrid median filtering algorithm for speckle noise reduction.

4.2.3.3 Speckle reduction by circular hybrid median filter technique

Due to the existence of multiplicative noise known as speckle noise, the ultrasound pictures exhibit poor contrast. As a result, speckle noise should

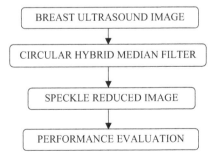

Figure 4.2 Overview of the proposed speckle reduction method.

be minimized while maintaining characteristics. The filtering methods used here are based on the circular hybrid median filter. Linear or nonlinear spatial filters are the most common speckle filters used for breast ultrasound pictures. Linear filters are the most basic filters, replacing values with a local average value or other local measurements to reduce unexpected peaks in pixel intensity.

The basic and easy-to-implement linear filters were the max filter, min filter, mean filter, and Lee filter. Linear filters, on the other hand, tend to smooth and blur the picture, and tiny and low-contrast lesions may vanish along with the noise. Image processing applications are increasingly using nonlinear filtering methods. Nonlinear filters have the virtue of being able to smooth noise while preserving fine structural details. In the nonlinear category, the median filter is a popular filter. The median filter works by replacing each pixel value with the median of surrounding pixel values as it passes across the picture pixels.

A predetermined window, based on neighboring patterns, moves pixel by pixel over the whole picture. The median filter has the advantage of reducing blur and keeping edge sharpness. Figure 4.3 shows the median filter selection of new pixel intensity.

The hybrid median filter maintains edges better than the square median filter, as seen in Figure 4.4. The circular hybrid median filter was employed to better preserve the fundamental geometry of key structures, as seen in Figure 4.5.

In the median filters of size 15 × 15, "R" represents vertical and horizontal pixels, "D" indicates diagonal pixels, and "C" is the center pixel, as illustrated in Figure 4.4. Figure 4.5 shows median filters of size 15 × 15 corresponding to a circular hybrid window.

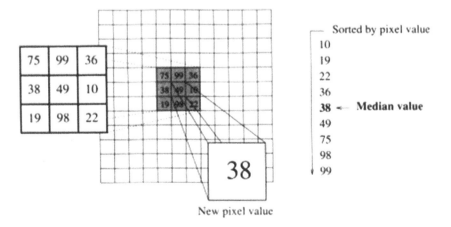

Figure 4.3 Median filter selection of new pixel intensity.

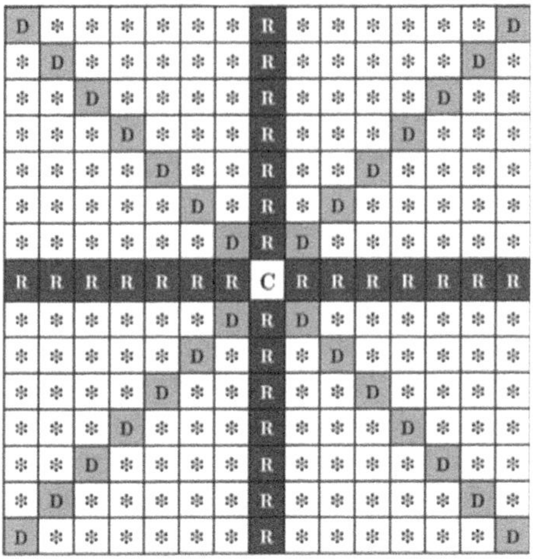

Figure 4.4 Median filters of size 15 × 15 corresponding to hybrid window.

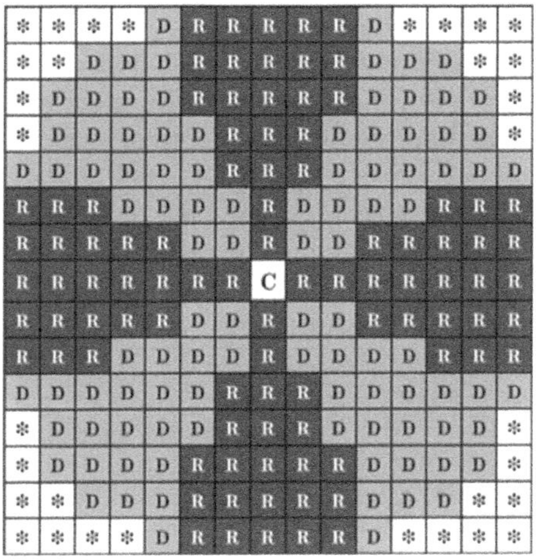

Figure 4.5 Median filters of size 15 × 15 corresponding to circular hybrid window.

4.2.3.4 Algorithm

Use the breast ultrasound image as input.
Step 1: Open the dataset and load the original image.
Step 2: Set the window size of the circular hybrid median filter to w = 7.
Step 3: If the window size is even, go to the next step. "Window size w × w must be odd" error ("Window size w × w must be odd")stop.
Step 4: If not, create three circular filtering windows: WD, WR, and C.

Step 5: Calculate the WD window's median by overlaying it over the input picture.
Step 6: Calculate the WR window's median by overlaying it over the input picture.
Step 7: Arrange the three windows in a three-dimensional array.
Step 8: Add the medians of the three windows WD, WR, and C to get the result.
Step 9: Replace the image's median value with the generated center pixel.

4.2.3.5 Performance indices

Various amounts of speckle were intentionally injected into the picture to test the performance of the suggested approach quantitatively. As a quantitative performance metric for this approach, the signal-to-noise ratio (SNR), peak signal-to-noise ratio (PSNR), and structure similarity index measure (SSIM) were determined.

$$\overset{x}{\underset{i=1}{\sum}}\overset{y}{\underset{j=1}{\sum}}\frac{\left(\mid I_{ij}-J_{ij}\right)^2}{x*y} \qquad (4.1)$$

J is the preprocessed picture, while I is the original image. The image's width is x, and its height is y.

$$\text{PSNR} = 10\log_{10}\left(\frac{Max^2}{MSE}\right) \qquad (4.2)$$

$$\text{SSIM} = \frac{\left(2\mu_x\mu_y + c_1\right)\left(2\sigma_{xy} + c_2\right)}{\left(\mu_x^2 + \mu_y^2 + c_1\right)\left(\sigma_x^2 + \sigma_y^2 + c_2\right)} \qquad (4.3)$$

4.2.4 Segmentation

4.2.4.1 Need for image segmentation

Cancer has traditionally been seen as a fatal disease. Even in today's technologically advanced world, cancer may be lethal if it is not detected early. Rapid detection of malignant cells has the potential to save millions of lives. The morphology of the malignant cells is crucial in evaluating the cancer's aggressiveness. Object detection will not be particularly helpful here, even if you have put the parts together. It will simply provide bounding boxes and will not assist us in determining the geometry of the cells. Image segmentation methods have a significant influence in this case. They enable

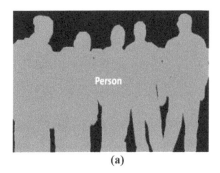 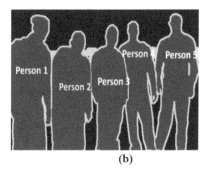

Figure 4.6 (a) Semantic segmentation; (b) instance segmentation.

us to take a more detailed approach to the issue and provide more useful outcomes. It's a win-win situation for everyone involved in the healthcare business. Image segmentation is also affecting businesses in a variety of different ways:

- Traffic management systems.
- Autonomous vehicles.
- Object detection in satellite images.

Image segmentation methods may be divided into two categories:

- Every pixel, as illustrated in Figure 4.6(a), corresponds to a certain class (either background or person). Furthermore, all pixels belonging to the same class are represented by the same color (background as black and person as pink). This is a case of semantic segmentation in action.
- Each pixel in the picture has been allocated a specific class, as seen in Figure 4.6(b). Distinct items of the same class, on the other hand, have different hues (Person 1 as red, Person 2 as green, background as black, etc.). This is an example of a segmentation instance.

Both images are using image segmentation to identify and locate the people present in the figure.

4.2.4.2 CNN-based image segmentation

All other machine learning algorithms function by taking labeled training data and processing incoming input and making judgments based on the training. Deep learning, on the other hand, works with neural networks and may come to its own conclusions without the requirement for labeled training data [33, 34]. This strategy may be used by a self-driving automobile to

Table 4.1 Comparison of image segmentation techniques

Advantages			
Region-based	**Edge-based**	**Cluster-based**	**CNN-based**
Simple calculations and fast operation speed	Ideal for images with more contrast between objects	Performs well on tiny datasets and produces nice clusters	Provides the most accurate results
Disadvantages			
Region-based	**Edge-based**	**Cluster-based**	**CNN-based**
It's tough to produce precise portions when there's no considerable grayscale	When there are too many edges in the picture, it's not a good idea to use it	The computation time is very long and costly	It takes a similar amount of time to train the model

distinguish between a signboard and a pedestrian. Neural networks use algorithms that coexist in the network, with the output of one algorithm influencing the result of another. This results in a system that can make choices as if it were a person. As a result, we have a model that is a wonderful example of a machine learning system. In the area of image segmentation, CNN-based segmentation is now the state-of-the-art approach. It works with photos that have three dimensions: height, breadth, and channel count. The picture resolution is represented by the first two dimensions, while the number of channels (RGB) or intensity values for red, green, and blue hues are represented by the third dimension. The size of the pictures supplied into the neural network is usually lowered to minimize processing time and prevent the issue of underfitting. Table 4.1 states the comparison of image segmentation techniques.

4.2.4.3 Residual network

Computer vision has seen a flurry of innovation in the recent few years, including state-of-the-art outcomes on tasks like picture classification and image recognition, especially with the advent of deep convolutional neural networks. As a result, academics have been working to build more complicated neural networks (with more layers) to tackle more difficult problems. However, it has been shown that as the number of layers in a neural network increases, training gets more complex and accuracy decreases. This is where ResNet comes to the rescue.

Adding more layers to deep neural networks improves accuracy and speed when dealing with difficult problems. As layers are added, they are expected to learn more and more complicated characteristics. A good illustration of this would be in picture recognition, where the first layer might learn to recognize edges, the second layer could learn to identify textures,

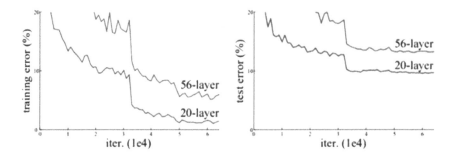

Figure 4.7 Training and testing errors without skip connections.

and so on. Traditional convolutional neural network models, on the other hand, have a maximum depth threshold. For a 20-layer network and a 56-layer network, Figure 4.7 shows the percentage of errors in training and testing data.

In both training and testing data, we can observe that the error percentage for a 56-layer network is higher than that of a 20-layer network. This shows that the performance of a network declines as additional layers are added on top of it. The optimization function, the network's initialization, and the vanishing gradient issue might all be to fault. Overfitting is a possibility; however, the 56-layer network's error percentage is the worst on both training and testing data, which does not happen when the model is overfitted, as you would expect. Figure 4.7 infers the training and testing errors without skip connections.

4.2.4.3.1 Disappeared gradient

When building neural networks, stochastic gradient descent is a common training method. First, the model's prediction error is calculated, and then the error is used to estimate a gradient that is then used to update each weight in the network in order to reduce prediction error in the future. From the output layer to the input layer, this error gradient travels backwards across the network. A big training dataset and the ability to express more sophisticated mapping functions between inputs and outputs are two reasons why it is beneficial to train neural networks with multiple layers of representation. The gradient drops substantially as it is carried backward through the network, which is an issue when training networks with many layers (e.g., deep neural networks). Depending on the size of the mistake, the model may not notice it until it reaches layers near the model's input. As a result, the "vanishing gradients problem" is the name given to this issue. In addition to the disappearing gradients, there is another reason why we employ them so often. Several tasks (such as semantic segmentation, optical flow estimation, etc.) need information that was collected in the first layers, and we would want to enable the latter layers to learn from them. Researchers have shown that the learned traits correlate to lower levels of semantic information in the input at a deeper level of processing. Unless we employed the skip connection, the information would have been too abstract.

4.2.4.3.2 Blockage remaining

With the development of ResNet or residual networks, the difficulty of training extremely deep networks has been addressed using residual blocks. In Figure 4.8, the first thing we notice is that there is a direct link that bypasses various levels (this may change in different models). It's called a "skip connection," and it's what makes up the heart of the remaining blocks.

ResNet's skip connections address the issue of gradients disappearing in deep neural networks by providing an additional shortcut channel for gradients to go through during training. Comparing ResNet-enhanced neural networks to neural networks with plain layers, the plot of error percentage shows how much better ResNet-enhanced networks perform.

In networks with 34 layers, ResNet-34 has a substantially lower error rate than plain-34, which is clear. Plain-18 and ResNet-18 have almost identical error rates. Figure 4.9 shows the training errorr of plain and ResNet networks.

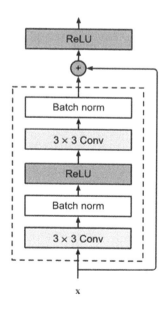

Figure 4.8 Residual building block.

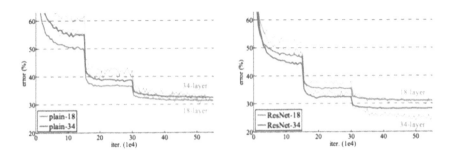

Figure 4.9 Training error of plain and ResNet network.

Its 18 weight layers, 17 convolutional layers, and one fully linked layer give it the name ResNet-18 (Figure 4.10).

4.2.4.4 Implementation

Deep learning will be used to create a semantic segmentation network once all photos in the dataset have been pre-processed. To create a segmented picture, we use a semantic segmentation network to classify each pixel.

The transfer learning technique and the deep network designer supplied by the deep learning toolbox in MATLAB R2020a are used to create a semantic segmentation network in deep learning. Segmentation is carried out by using the pre-trained network ResNet-18. In the ResNet-18 neural network, there are 18 layers. We have access to a network that has already been pre-trained on over one million photos in the ImageNet database. The pre-trained network can categorize photos into 1,000 item categories, such

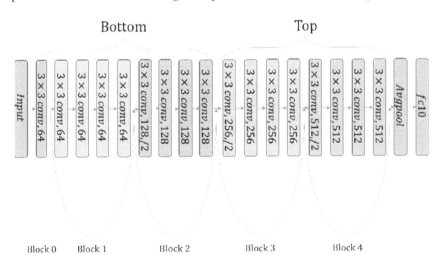

Figure 4.10 ResNet-18 architecture.

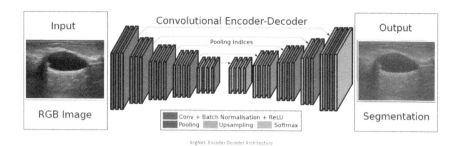

Figure 4.11 Overview of semantic segmentation network.

as a keyboard, mouse, pencil, and a wide variety of animal species. Thus, the network's feature representations for a broad variety of pictures have become more complex. The network accepts images with a resolution of 224 by 224 pixels. Figure 4.11 is an overview of the semantic segmentation network.

4.2.4.4.1 Semantic segmentation in deep learning: a step-by-step guide

- From the deep network designer, choose the pre-trained network (ResNet).
- To use the dataset, you must first load the input photos and then the labeled/ground-truth images.
- Modify the downsampling layers and build the encoder network to retrain the pre-trained network for segmentation.
- Use the decoder network after the upsampling layers have been added.
- Use semantic segmentation to alter the final layers of the image.
- Modify the training settings if required by selecting the training options from the training tab.
- Train the network and export it.
- Test the trained network by selecting new images for segmentation.

Use segmented photos to verify the ground truth. Because they were pre-trained on color pictures from the ImageNet database, CNN models need a three-channel image for their input layer. Consequently, we suggest that the original BUS grayscale picture be rescaled to 128 by 128 pixels. After that, the scaled picture is duplicated twice more to create the three layers of a color image that are fed into the neural network of CNN. Because of this, the input layers of all semantic segmentation models have been rescaled to 128 by 128 by 3. Using a SoftMax layer, the probabilities of each pixel belonging to a class are calculated. If the probability value is higher than 0.5, the input pixel is categorized as a tumor pixel; otherwise, the pixel is classed as normal tissue. As a result of this imbalance, tumor pixels tend to be in smaller areas of the BUS than normal tissue pixels. A local minimum of the loss function may occur if CNNs are trained from classes that are not equally balanced, resulting in network predictions that are heavily skewed in the direction of the dominant class. As a result, the tumor site is either completely overlooked or only partly identified. As a result, the Dice loss function is maximized and stated to minimize the impact of class imbalance.

$$D_L = \frac{2\sum_{i=1}^{n} p_i g_i}{\sum_{i=1}^{n} p_i^2 + \sum_{i=1}^{n} g_i^2} \tag{4.4}$$

Summarizing the predicted probabilistic map (p_i = P) and the ground truth binary mask (g_i = G), we get the following result: data normalization is essential since the BUS pictures were taken with various ultrasound equipment that had varied dynamic ranges. A normal distribution with zero mean and unit variance is approximated here by applying standardization to the z-score distribution in input pictures. This aids the activation and gradient descent process. Stochastic gradient descent with a learning rate of 0.001 is used to train the CNN models over a period of ten epochs in this way. Overfitting might occur because of a lack of data, hence data augmentation is utilized to alleviate this issue. According to the notion that more information may be gained by data augmentations, this operation is carried out. During CNN training, geometric alterations are randomly applied to the mini-batches to enhance the data. To put it another way, it's possible to think of this on-the-fly procedure as a kind of implicit regularization that decreases overfitting. Several different geometric transformations are considered, including scaling and rotation in the [22.5 deg] and [22.5 deg] ranges, as well as vertical and horizontal translations and reflections in the [32, 32] range.

4.2.4.5 Analyzing the network

Number of layers: 100
Number of connections: 113
Optimizer: stochastic gradient descent momentum (sgdm)
Learning rate: 0.001
Layers used: input layer, batch normalization layer, convolution layer, ReLU layer, addition layer, pooling layer, transposed convolution layer, softmax layer, and Dice pixel classification layer

4.2.4.6 Performance indices

The segmentation accuracy is assessed by comparing the similarity between the radiologist-performed ground-truth segmentation and the CNN result.

Table 4.2 Confusion matrix for binary segmentation

		Predicted class	
		Tumor	Normal tissue
Actual class	Tumor	True positive (TP)	False negative (FN)
	Normal tissue	False positive (FP)	True negative (TN)

Using the two-class confusion matrix, the following fundamental segmentation performance indices may be computed:

1. Table 4.2 infers the confusion matrix for binary segmentation in that accuracy informs us how many pixels are successfully classified by dividing the total number of subjects or pixels by the number of subjects or pixels that are correctly categorized:

$$\text{Accuracy} = \frac{(TP + TN)}{(TP + TN + FP + FN)} \times 100 \tag{4.5}$$

- To measure our program's precision, we look at the percentage of positive pixels accurately identified as tumor pixels compared to the total number of positive labels.

$$\text{Precision} = \frac{TP}{(TP + FP)} \times 100 \tag{4.6}$$

It quantifies the percentage of positives that are properly recognized (i.e., the proportion of those who have a condition [affected] that is appropriately identified as having the condition).

$$\text{Recall}\,(\text{Sensitivity}) = \frac{TP}{(TP + FN)} \times 100 \tag{4.7}$$

- Precision (true negative rate) is an indicator of how many false negatives (i.e., those who do not have the ailment [unaffected]) are accurately diagnosed as being false.

$$\text{Specificity} = \frac{TN}{(TN + FP)} \tag{4.8}$$

- The F_1-score (also known as the Dice similarity coefficient) is the weighted average of the precision, $\dfrac{TP}{(TP + FP)}$, and recall $\dfrac{TP}{(TP + FN)}$, that considers class imbalance:

$$F_1 - \text{score} = \frac{2 * \text{Recall} * \text{Precision}}{(\text{Recall} + \text{Precision})} \qquad (4.9)$$

$$F_1 - \text{score} = \frac{2\text{TP}}{(2\text{TP} + \text{FP} + \text{FN})} \qquad (4.10)$$

IOU (also known as the Jaccard index) is a measure of the overlap ratio between the ground-truth mask and the segmented image:

$$\text{IoU}(\text{Jaccard Index}) = \frac{\text{TP}}{\text{TP} + \text{FP} + \text{FN}} \qquad (4.11)$$

A segmentation performance that is close to 100% in accuracy, specificity, and recall is considered sufficient. Results in the range of [0, 1] for F1 and IoU indices suggest that segmentation is performing adequately.

4.3 RESULTS AND DISCUSSIONS

4.3.1 Preprocessing results

Breast ultrasound pictures may be pre-processed using a low-pass filtering method known as speckle noise reduction. MATLAB is used to simulate the preprocessing procedure, which is tested using 256-level 2D grayscale ultrasound breast pictures. There were 12 benign masses and 13 malignant masses in the 25 breast ultrasound pictures that were used to evaluate the algorithm. The photos for diagnostic purposes that include speckle noises have been selected. Figure 4.12 shows the preprocessed picture findings after the ultrasound images have been selected and processed with the circular hybrid median filter.

MSE, PSNR, and SSIM equations 2.1, 2.2, and 2.3 were used to assess performance after filtering. In Table 4.3, the MSE, PSNR, and SSIM values for the images were determined.

From Table 4.2, it is observed that MSE, PSNR, and SSIM values for the images were determined for 25 breast ultrasound images. For Image1 the MSE value is 43.76, PSNR value is 34.31, and SSIM value is 0.9. For Image2 the MSE value is 21.57, PSNR value is 37.80, and SSIM value is 0.93. For Image3 the MSE value is 24.31, PSNR value is 37.28, and SSIM value is 0.91. For Image4 the MSE value is 34.15, PSNR value is 35.81, and SSIM value is 0.87. For Image5 the MSE value is 28.25, PSNR value is 36.63, and SSIM value is 0.89. For Image6 the MSE value is 29.88, PSNR value is 36.39, and SSIM value is 0.88. For Image7 the MSE value is 23.63, PSNR value is 37.41, and SSIM value is 0.93. For Image8 the MSE value is 34.69, PSNR value is 35.74, and SSIM value is 0.88. For Image9 the MSE value is 34.35, PSNR value is 35.07, and SSIM value is 0.90. For Image10

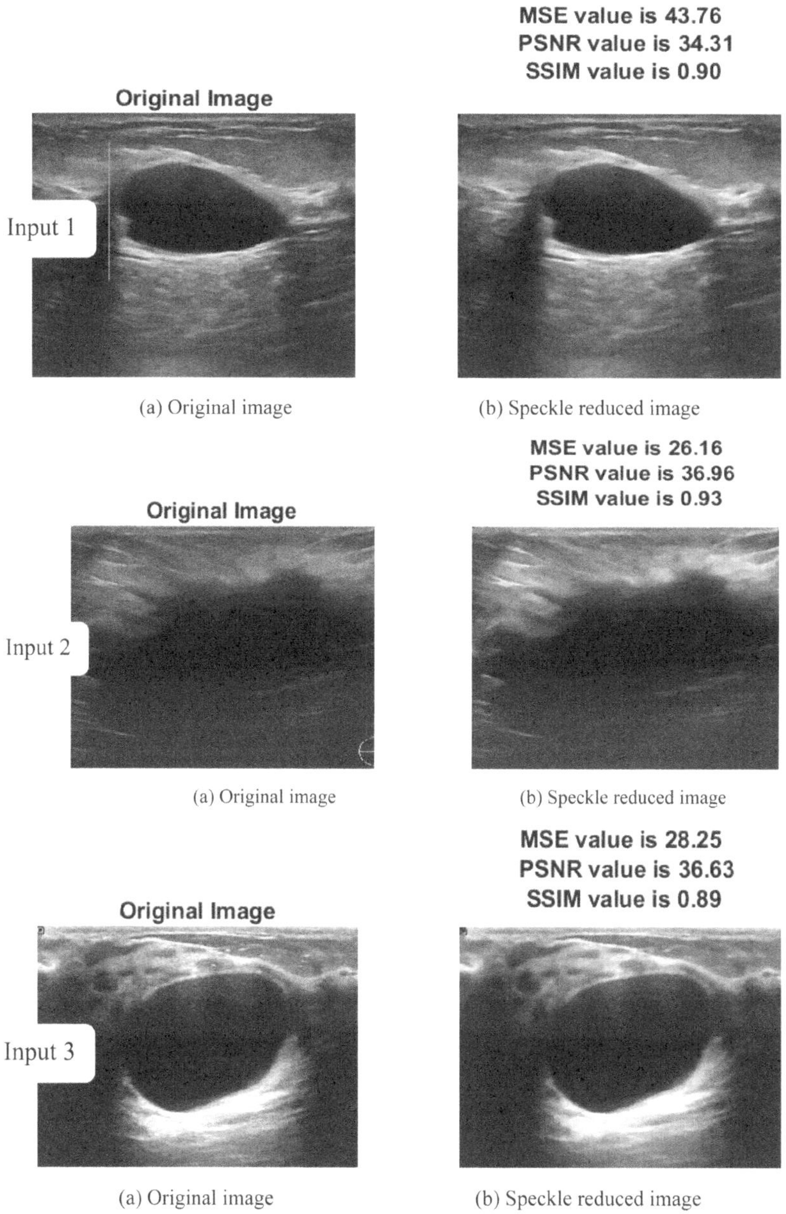

MSE value is 43.76
PSNR value is 34.31
SSIM value is 0.90

Original Image

Input 1

(a) Original image

(b) Speckle reduced image

MSE value is 26.16
PSNR value is 36.96
SSIM value is 0.93

Original Image

Input 2

(a) Original image

(b) Speckle reduced image

MSE value is 28.25
PSNR value is 36.63
SSIM value is 0.89

Original Image

Input 3

(a) Original image

(b) Speckle reduced image

Figure 4.12 Original image and resultant despeckled image.

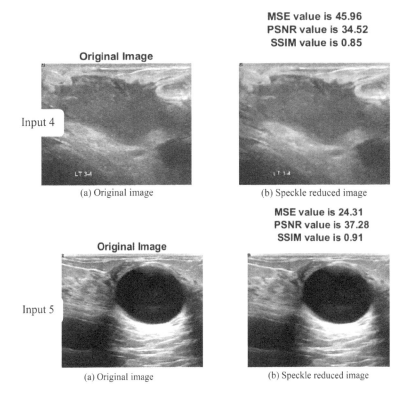

MSE value is 45.96
PSNR value is 34.52
SSIM value is 0.85

Original Image

Input 4

(a) Original image   (b) Speckle reduced image

MSE value is 24.31
PSNR value is 37.28
SSIM value is 0.91

Original Image

Input 5

(a) Original image   (b) Speckle reduced image

Figure 4.12 (Continued).

the MSE value is 45.96, PSNR value is 35.52, and SSIM value is 0.85. For Image11 the MSE value is 27.23, PSNR value is 36.79, and SSIM value is 0.89. For Image12 the MSE value is 26.87, PSNR value is 36.85, and SSIM value is 0.88. For Image13 the MSE value is 146.88, PSNR value is 29.26, and SSIM value is 0.80. For Image14 the MSE value is 47.60, PSNR value is 34.36, and SSIM value is 0.88. For Image15 the MSE value is 47.60, PSNR value is 34.36, and SSIM value is 0.88. For Image16 the MSE value is 155.57, PSNR value is 28.95, and SSIM value is 0.82. For Image17 the MSE value is 22.57, PSNR value is 37.36, and SSIM value is 0.90. For Image18 the MSE value is 26.50, PSNR value is 36.88, and SSIM value is 0.91. For Image19 the MSE value is 108.51, PSNR value is 30.79, and SSIM value is 0.87. For Image20 the MSE value is 26.25, PSNR value is 36.95, and SSIM value is 0.87. For Image21 the MSE value is 18.04, PSNR value is 38.16, and SSIM value is 0.90. For Image22 the MSE value is 17.51, PSNR value is 38.71, and SSIM value is 0.93. For Image23 the MSE value is 26.16, PSNR value is 36.96, and SSIM value is 0.93. For Image24 the MSE value is 48.36, PSNR value is 34.30, and SSIM value is 0.86. For Image25 the MSE value is 39.87, PSNR value is 35.14, and SSIM value is 0.87.

Table 4.3 Summarizes the various MSE, SSIM, and PSNR values computed for 25 breast ultrasound images

S. no.	Mean square error (MSE)	Peak signal-to-noise ratio (PSNR) in dB	Structural similarity index measure (SSIM)
1	43.76101	34.31155	0.895214
2	21.57339	37.80192	0.925035
3	24.31374	37.28259	0.912248
4	34.14930	35.80729	0.871919
5	28.24643	36.63147	0.893959
6	29.87666	36.38778	0.878072
7	23.62987	37.40649	0.925189
8	34.69325	35.73865	0.880947
9	34.35061	35.07231	0.895915
10	45.96238	34.51708	0.847537
11	27.22993	36.79064	0.887265
12	26.87422	36.84774	0.882241
13	146.8777	29.26473	0.802555
14	47.60202	34.36485	0.882037
15	47.60202	34.36485	0.882037
16	155.5658	28.94510	0.815897
17	22.56669	37.36465	0.902814
18	26.49572	36.87522	0.914452
19	108.5137	30.78626	0.865318
20	26.25447	36.94907	0.869038
21	18.03809	38.16052	0.900301
22	17.50832	38.70866	0.928040
23	26.16454	36.96397	0.926919
24	48.36332	34.29594	0.861799
25	39.86625	35.13505	0.870721

4.3.2 Segmentation results

The ResNet CNN architecture's segmentation results are shown in this section. In order to make it easier for you to understand the findings, we've organized our discussions here. ResNet architecture's segmentation performance is shown in Table 4.4. The ResNet segmentation model with F1s > 0.90 and IoU > 0.81 is noteworthy. Due to the fact that more subtle information is recovered as the network depth increases, this finding implies that network depth is an important consideration when trying to obtain improved segmentation quality. Training hyperparameters may be tweaked to increase segmentation quality. Figure 4.13 infers tumors segmented by the ResNet CNN model, and the ground-truth segmentation is given by the radiologist outlining taken from the dataset

Table 4.4 Segmentation performance results in terms of the F1-score, Jaccard index, accuracy, specificity, recall, and precision

S. no.	F1 -score	Jaccard	Accuracy (%)	Specificity (%)	Precision (%)	Recall (%)
1	0.97	0.95	97.46	96.36	96.31	98.60
2	0.96	0.92	95.87	94.10	93.97	97.76
3	0.97	0.95	97.45	96.28	96.23	98.67
4	0.94	0.88	93.89	96.66	96.34	91.03
5	0.96	0.92	95.95	92.61	92.58	99.57
6	0.92	0.86	92.40	88.95	88.57	96.28
7	0.96	0.92	96.00	93.19	93.13	99.02
8	0.93	0.88	93.64	93.73	93.32	93.54
9	0.96	0.93	96.14	93.85	93.77	98.57
10	0.89	0.81	90.23	97.34	96.80	89.93
11	0.98	0.96	97.81	97.40	97.35	98.24
12	0.96	0.92	95.83	98.21	98.08	93.40
13	0.86	0.75	87.52	98.17	97.63	76.66
14	0.92	0.85	91.87	89.23	88.71	94.82
15	0.93	0.86	93.97	90.24	89.70	95.83
16	0.90	0.82	90.76	95.95	95.28	85.34
17	0.94	0.88	94.08	95.56	95.21	92.54
18	0.90	0.83	90.63	88.83	88.35	96.22
19	0.93	0.86	92.58	89.18	89.18	97.22
20	0.91	0.84	91.51	87.63	87.17	95.93
21	0.93	0.86	92.94	94.38	93.89	91.41
22	0.95	0.91	95.30	94.51	94.31	96.13
23	0.94	0.88	94.04	93.47	93.12	94.66
24	0.91	0.83	91.24	96.60	96.05	89.69
25	0.94	0.88	94.21	98.78	98.64	89.59

Table 4.4 infers segmentation performance results in terms of the F1-score, Jaccard index, accuracy, specificity, recall, and precision. F1-score varies in range from 0.86 to 0.98. Jaccard value varies in range from 0.75 to 0.96. Accuracy varies in range from 87.52 to 97.81. Specificity value varies in range from 87.63 to 98.78. Precision value varies in range from 87.17 to 98.64. Recall value varies in range from 76.66 to 99.57.

Table 4.5 shows the performance comparison of deep learning models to detect breast lesions on ultrasound images. It is observed that segmentation performance obtained from the ResNet-18 model is increased compared with AlexNet and VGG16. Suggested that ResNet-18 gives good accuracy to detect breast lesions on ultrasound images.

ResNet

| Input Images | Ground Truth Images | Binary Images (ROI) | Segmented Images (ROI) |

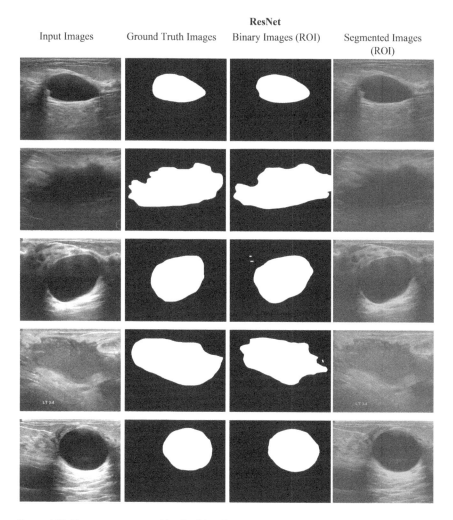

Figure 4.13 Tumors segmented by ResNet CNN model and the ground-truth segmentation given by the radiologist outline taken from the dataset.

4.4 CONCLUSION

The circular hybrid median filter is used as a de-speckling method for the removal of speckle noise present in ultrasound images. The circular hybrid median filter gives good performance with its average PSNR of 36.47 dB, MSE of 44.24, and SSIM of 0.884 for the images. It reduces the speckle noise while the edges are preserved, and a large number of pixels is covered when compared to median and hybrid median filters. The aforementioned results are further used in the segmentation process. Resnet-18 CNN architecture is used for the automatic segmentation of lesion regions

Table 4.5 Comparison of deep learning models to detect breast lesions on ultrasound images

S. no.	Transfer learning model	Accuracy (%)
I	AlexNet	84.46
2	VGG16	86.39
3	ResNet-18	93

present in the breast ultrasound images. Hence, the segmentation performance obtained from the ResNet-18 model gives an accuracy, specificity, precision, and recall of 93%, 90.2%, 89.7%, and 95% respectively, along with F1 -score and IoU equal to 0.92 and 0.85 respectively. As expected, the segmentation performance is improved with the increase in depth of the network of the deep learning model. An alternative to downscaling the picture to suit the CNN input layer is to use block-dividing algorithms to increase the image's quality. It is also possible to construct an automated post-processing step to improve the CNN result further. Using smart data augmentation to highlight certain dataset properties such as tumor size and textural pattern is another research avenue to pursue.

REFERENCES

1. Kumar, V., J. M. Webb, A. Gregory, M. Denis, D. D. Meixner, M. Bayat, D. H. Whaley, M. Fatemi, and A. Alizad, "Automated and real-time segmentation of suspicious breast masses using convolutional neural network." *PLOS ONE* 13, no. 5 (2018): 1–18.
2. Yap, Moi Hoon, Eran A. Edirisinghe, and Helmut E. Bez. "A novel algorithm for initial lesion detection in ultrasound breast images." *Journal of Applied Clinical Medical Physics* 9, no. 4 (2008): 181–199.
3. Madabhushi, Anant, and Dimitris N. Metaxas. "Combining low-, high-level and empirical domain knowledge for automated segmentation of ultrasonic breast lesions." *IEEE Transactions on Medical Imaging* 22, no. 2 (2003): 155–169.
4. Xian, Min, Yingtao Zhang, and Heng-Da Cheng. "Fully automatic segmentation of breast ultrasound images based on breast characteristics in space and frequency domains." *Pattern Recognition* 48, no. 2 (2015): 485–497.
5. Moon, Woo Kyung, Yi-Wei Shen, Min Sun Bae, Chiun-Sheng Huang, Jeon-Hor Chen, and Ruey-Feng Chang. "Computer-aided tumor detection based on multi-scale blob detection algorithm in automated breast ultrasound images." *IEEE Transactions on Medical Imaging* 32, no. 7 (2012): 1191–1200.
6. Drukker, Karen, Maryellen L. Giger, Karla Horsch, Matthew A. Kupinski, Carl J. Vyborny, and Ellen B. Mendelson. "Computerized lesion detection on breast ultrasound." *Medical Physics* 29, no. 7 (2002): 1438–1446.

7. Yap, Moi Hoon, Eran A. Edirisinghe, and Helmut E. Bez. "Fully automatic lesion boundary detection in ultrasound breast images." In *Medical Imaging 2007: Image Processing*, vol. 6512, p. 65123I. International Society for Optics and Photonics, 2007.

8. Gomez, W., L. Leija, A. V. Alvarenga, A. F. C. Infantosi, and W. C. A. Pereira. "Computerized lesion segmentation of breast ultrasound based on marker-controlled watershed transformation." *Medical Physics* 37, no. 1 (2010): 82–95.

9. Verma, Kanupriya, Sahil Bhardwaj, Resham Arya, Mir Salim Ul Islam, Megha Bhushan, Ashok Kumar, and Piyush Samant. "Latest tools for data mining and machine learning." *International Journal of Innovative Technology and Exploring Engineering* 8, no. 9S (2019): 18–23. https://doi.org/10.35940/ijitee.I1003.0789S19.

10. Kholiya, Pankaj Singh, Akshat Kapoor, Meghavi Rana, and Megha Bhushan. "Intelligent process automation: The future of digital transformation." In *2021 10th International Conference on System Modeling & Advancement in Research Trends (SMART)*, pp. 185–190. IEEE, 2021. https://doi.org/10.1109/SMART52563.2021.9676222.

11. Singh, Vikram Jeet, Megha Bhushan, Vikram Kumar, and Kishori Lal Bansal. "Optimization of segment size assuring application perceived QoS in healthcare." In *Proceedings of the World Congress on Engineering*, vol. 1, pp. 1–3, 2015.

12. Shan, Juan, Yuxuan Wang, and Heng-Da Cheng. "Completely automatic segmentation for breast ultrasound using multiple-domain features." In *2010 IEEE International Conference on Image Processing*, pp. 1713–1716. IEEE, 2010.

13. Almajalid, Rania, Juan Shan, Yaodong Du, and Ming Zhang. "Development of a deep-learning-based method for breast ultrasound image segmentation." In *2018 17th IEEE International Conference on Machine Learning and Applications (ICMLA)*, pp. 1103–1108. IEEE, 2018.

14. Behboodi, Bahareh, Mina Amiri, Rupert Brooks, and Hassan Rivaz. "Breast lesion segmentation in ultrasound images with limited annotated data." In *2020 IEEE 17th International Symposium on Biomedical Imaging (ISBI)*, pp. 1834–1837. IEEE, 2020.

15. Zhao, Yijun, Dashun Que, Jiaqi Tan, Yang Xiao, and Yanyan Yu. "Automated breast lesion segmentation from ultrasound images based on PPU-net." In *2019 International Conference on Medical Imaging Physics and Engineering (ICMIPE)*, pp. 1–4. IEEE, 2019.

16. Liao, Wen-Xuan, Ping He, Jin Hao, Xuan-Yu Wang, Ruo-Lin Yang, Dong An, and Li-Gang Cui. "Automatic identification of breast ultrasound image based on supervised block-based region segmentation algorithm and features combination migration deep learning model." *IEEE Journal of Biomedical and Health Informatics* 24, no. 4 (2019): 984–993.

17. Zhuang, Zhemin, Nan Li, Alex Noel Joseph Raj, Vijayalakshmi GV Mahesh, and ShunminQiu. "An RDAU-NET model for lesion segmentation in breast ultrasound images." *PloS One* 14, no. 8 (2019): e0221535.

18. Negi, Anuja, Alex Noel Joseph Raj, Ruban Nersisson, Zhemin Zhuang, and M. Murugappan. "RDA-UNET-WGAN: an accurate breast ultrasound lesion segmentation using wasserstein generative adversarial networks." *Arabian Journal for Science and Engineering* 45, no. 8 (2020): 6399–6410.

19. Amiri, Mina, Rupert Brooks, Bahareh Behboodi, and Hassan Rivaz. "Two-stage ultrasound image segmentation using U-Net and test time augmentation." *International Journal of Computer Assisted Radiology and Surgery* 15, no. 6 (2020): 981–988.

20. Sahar, Muzni, Hanung Adi Nugroho, IgiArdiyanto, and Lina Choridah. "Automated detection of breast cancer lesions using adaptive thresholding and morphological operation." In 2016 International Conference on Information Technology Systems and Innovation (ICITSI), pp. 1–4. IEEE, 2016.

21. Liu, Xu, Zhimin Huo, and Jiwu Zhang. "Automated segmentation of breast lesions in ultrasound images." In 2005 IEEE Engineering in Medicine and Biology 27th Annual Conference, pp. 7433–7435. IEEE, 2006.

22. Li, Xilin, Chunlan Yang, and Shuicai Wu. "Automatic segmentation algorithm of breast ultrasound image based on improved level set algorithm." In 2016 IEEE International Conference on Signal and Image Processing (ICSIP), pp. 319–322. IEEE, 2016.

23. Hu, Yuzhou, Yi Guo, Yuanyuan Wang, Jinhua Yu, Jiawei Li, Shichong Zhou, and Cai Chang. "Automatic tumor segmentation in breast ultrasound images using a dilated fully convolutional network combined with an active contour model." *Medical Physics* 46, no. 1 (2019): 215–228.

24. Xian, Min, Yingtao Zhang, Heng-Da Cheng, Fei Xu, Boyu Zhang, and Jianrui Ding. "Automatic breast ultrasound image segmentation: A survey." *Pattern Recognition* 79 (2018): 340–355.

25. Moldovanu, S., and L. Moraru, "Mass detection and classification in breast ultrasound image using K-means clustering algorithm." In Proceedings of the IEEE 3rd International Symposium on Electrical and Electronics Engineering, pp. 197–200. IEEE, 2010.

26. Zhang, Y., H. D. Cheng, J. Tian, and J. Huang, "Novel speckle reduction and contrast enhancement method based on fuzzy anisotropic diffusion." In Proceedings of the IEEE 17th International Conference on Image Processing, pp. 4161–4164. IEEE, 2010.

27. Gonzalez, R. C., and R. E. Woods, *Digital Image Processing*, Pearson Prentice Hall, New Jersey, 2008.

28. Cardoso, F. M., M. M. S. Matsumoto, and S. S. Furuie. "Edge-preserving speckle texture removal by interference-based speckle filtering followed by anisotropic diffusion." *Ultrasound Medicine and Biology* 38, no. 8 (2012): 1414–1428.

29. Deng, J., Dong, W., Socher, R., Li, L. J., Li, K., and Fei-Fei, L. "Imagenet: A large-scale hierarchical image database." In 2009 IEEE Conference on Computer Vision and Pattern Recognition, pp. 248–255. IEEE, 2009, June.

30. Zhuang, Z., N. Li, A. N. Joseph Raj, V. G. V. Mahesh, and S. Qiu. "An RDAU-NET model for lesion segmentation in breast ultrasound images." *PLOS ONE* 14, no. 8 (2019): 1–23.

31. Nalavade, A., Anita Bai, and Megha Bhushan "Deep learning techniques and models for improving machine reading comprehension system", *International Journal of Advanced Science and Technology*, vol. 29, no. 04, pp. 9692–9710, Oct. 2020. http://sersc.org/journals/index.php/IJAST/article/view/32996

32. Prabhakar, T., and S. Bpoonguzhali. "Filtering based feature extraction to classify the benign and malignant lesions from breast ultrasound images."

Journal of Medical Imaging and Health Informatics, 6, no. 6 (2016): 1469–1474.

33. Pal, Someswar, Navneet Mishra, Megha Bhushan, Pankaj Singh Kholiya, Meghavi Rana, and Arun Negi. "Deep learning techniques for prediction and diagnosis of diabetes mellitus." In 2022 International Mobile and Embedded Technology Conference (MECON), pp. 588–593. IEEE, 2022. https://doi.org/10.1109/MECON53876.2022.9752176

34. Rana, Meghavi, and Megha Bhushan. "Advancements in healthcare services using deep learning techniques." In 2022 International Mobile and Embedded Technology Conference (MECON), pp. 157–161. IEEE, 2022. https://doi.org/10.1109/MECON53876.2022.9752020

Chapter 5

Heart disease prediction using enhanced machine learning techniques

Ibomoiye Domor Mienye and Yanxia Sun

CONTENTS

5.1 INTRODUCTION

Heart diseases are among the leading causes of death worldwide [1–3]. An estimated 17 million deaths yearly are attributed to heart-related conditions, accounting for 31% of the reported global deaths, and it is projected to increase to 22 million by 2030 if not curtailed [4–6]. Cardiovascular disease (CVD) is the term given to the condition which affects the heart and blood vessels, such as heart diseases [7]. Heart diseases have a high impact on the world economy, with an estimated economic burden of 3.7 trillion dollars from 2010 to 2015 [8]. In South Africa, heart diseases cause the most deaths after HIV/AIDS [9]. The main cause of CVDs remains unknown; however, there are known risk factors behind it, including physical inactivity, poor diet, diabetes, and too much tobacco intake [10]. However, these risk factors can be reduced through lifestyle changes such as regular physical activity, rich diet, and reduced salt, tobacco, and alcohol intake [11].

DOI: 10.1201/9781003286745-5

Machine learning (ML) techniques are constantly being applied in diverse industries due to the advances in computing power and the availability of data [12–14], and they have recorded success in medical diagnosis, including the prediction of heart disease [15–18], chronic kidney disease [19, 20], and different cancers [21–24]. Meanwhile, ML is a branch of artificial intelligence (AI) centered around using data and algorithms to emulate the learning process of humans. In recent times, ML systems have outperformed humans in image processing [25–27] and many other applications [28–32]. Also, there are numerous research works and applications of machine learning in predicting cardiovascular diseases (CVDs) [33–35].

The early detection of heart diseases is vital in successfully managing and treating these conditions, thereby reducing the mortality rate [36–39]. The use of ML in predicting people at risk of heart disease has been highly recommended to assist clinicians in their diagnosis and treatment. Furthermore, the introduction of ML-based predictive models in the detection and diagnosis of diseases could potentially aid clinicians in efficiently evaluating a patient's heart disease risk and recommending necessary treatments to minimize the risk [40]. Machine learning has shown great potential in predicting heart diseases compared to the usual heart disease risk factors detection tools such as Framingham, Reynolds, and QRISK2, which gives poor results if the sample population differs from the sample used in building the tool [8].

This study presents recent advances in machine learning–based heart disease prediction. Notably, the study evaluates well-performing ML techniques in current literature. Furthermore, this study implements some well-known ML algorithms to predict heart disease. Meanwhile, the class imbalance that occurs in most medical datasets hinders the classification performance of ML models. Therefore, this study implements a hybrid resampling technique to balance the datasets and enhance the classifiers' prediction performance.

The rest of this chapter is structured as follows: section 5.2 presents a background and brief overview of machine learning. Section 5.3 discusses the heart disease datasets and section 5.4 presents some recently proposed methods for predicting heart disease. Section 5.5 discusses the proposed heart disease prediction method and examines the selected algorithms. In section 5.6, the simulation results are presented, and the chapter is concluded in section 5.7.

5.2 OVERVIEW OF MACHINE LEARNING TECHNIQUES

Machine learning involves using computers to make sense of data, such as classifying if a person has heart disease [41]. ML algorithms tend to

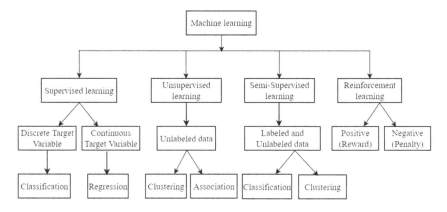

Figure 5.1 Different types of machine learning techniques [42].

optimize the performance of a specific task using past data [13]. Most machine learning tasks fall into one of the following groups: supervised, semi-supervised, unsupervised, and reinforcement learning. The different ML categories and methods are shown in Figure 5.1. In supervised learning, ML algorithms learn a function that maps the independent variable to the corresponding dependent variable. Usually, a labeled dataset is used in this type of learning. Supervised learning is performed when a specific goal is defined to be achieved using some labeled data, such as in most heart disease prediction tasks. Furthermore, supervised learning tasks are generally divided into classification and regression. Classification techniques categorize a set of input data into classes, while regression techniques are used to predict continuous values.

Meanwhile, unsupervised learning tasks are those where the ML algorithm is required to extract and detect similarities in the input data in order for similar inputs to be categorized together. In unsupervised learning, the labels or output variables are not known. Clustering, dimensionality reduction, and feature learning are some popular unsupervised learning tasks. Furthermore, semi-supervised learning employs labeled and unlabeled data for building ML models, and it is a popular learning approach usually employed for text classification, fraud detection, and data labeling [42]. Lastly, reinforcement learning is an approach where the ML algorithm rewards desired actions and punish undesired ones.

Furthermore, several learning methods can be used to develop efficient ML models depending on the available data. Most heart disease prediction tasks fall into the supervised learning category [43], which is the focus of this study. Figure 5.2 demonstrates the workflow of a supervised learning technique, which depicts the data collection, data preprocessing (i.e., cleaning and labeling), and data splitting steps.

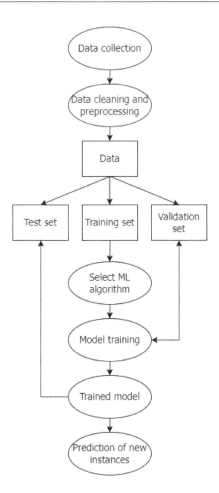

Figure 5.2 The workflow of supervised learning techniques [12].

5.3 HEART DISEASE DATASETS

Recently, several research works have developed numerous methods for predicting heart disease using different datasets. Cleveland [19] and Framingham [20] are the most widely used heart disease datasets [44–46]. Tables 5.1 and 5.2 describe the Framingham and Cleveland datasets, respectively. These datasets contain several attributes that are risk factors and are utilized for heart disease identification. Also, the attributes include modifiable and non-modified risk factors. The modifiable risk factors include blood pressure, cigarette intake, and cholesterol which can be controlled through lifestyle changes and medications. The non-modifiable risk factors are family history, age, and race which cannot be changed [47].

Table 5.1 Framingham dataset

S/N	Features	Description
1	Age	Age
2	Sex	Gender
3	Education	Educational level
4	BMI	Body mass index
5	Diabetes	The person's diabetes status
6	currentSmoker	The person's smoking status
7	totChol	Total cholesterol level
8	Heartrate	Heart rate
9	diaBP	Diastolic blood pressure
10	BPMeds	Whether the individual is taking BP medications
11	sysBP	Systolic blood pressure
12	Glucose	Glucose level
13	PrevalentHyp	Whether the individual is hypertensive
14	cigsPerDay	The average number of cigarettes the patient smokes each day
15	PrevalentStroke	If the patient had a stroke in the past
16	TenYearCHD (TargetVariable)	Whether or not the person has a risk of heart disease

Table 5.2 Cleveland dataset

S/N	Feature	Description
1	Sex	The sex of the individual
2	Age	The patient's age, in years
3	Number of vessels	The number of major vessels
4	Category of Chest pain	The category of chest pain
5	Resting ECG	ECG diagnosis category
6	Thalassemia	The category of thalassemia disorder
7	MaxHeart rate	The person's maximum heart rate
8	Resting BP	The resting BP measurement of the individual
9	Slope	The slope of the peak exercise ST segment
10	Fasting Blood Sugar	Fasting blood sugar > 120 mg/dL (1 = yes; 0 = no)
11	ST depression	ST depression caused by physical activity
12	Serum Cholesterol	Serum cholesterol measurement
13	Angina	If there is angina caused by exercising (1 = yes; 0 = no)
14	Target variable	The status of heart disease diagnosis (0 = absent; 1, 2, 3, 4 = present)

There are 303 rows and 14 features in the Cleveland dataset. Among the 303 samples, there are 138 healthy and 165 unhealthy patients. The Framingham dataset contains 4,238 instances and 16 attributes. Also, there are 3,594 healthy patients and 644 unhealthy patients in the Framingham dataset. Both datasets comprise patients' medical records and demographic details, including cholesterol level, diabetes diagnosis, blood pressure, age, and gender [48].

5.4 NOTABLE HEART DISEASE PREDICTION STUDIES

This section discusses some well-performing techniques proposed for predicting heart disease in recent literature. The datasets used in the studies will also be noted and the results tabulated for ease of reference. Mohan et al. [49] introduced a novel approach for predicting heart disease. The authors called the proposed technique a hybrid random forest via linear model (HRFLM). The HRFLM uses an artificial neural network (ANN) and backpropagation technique. Also, it employs the three data mining association rules, including predictive, apriori, and Tertius, in order to obtain the most relevant risk factors. The authors utilized the Cleveland dataset, and the insights derived from the proposed method indicate that women are less likely to have heart conditions than men. Furthermore, the authors used other classifiers in their study as a baseline for performance comparison, and the proposed HRFLM outperformed the classifiers, having achieved an accuracy of 88.7%.

Fitriyani et al. [50] used the Cleveland dataset to implement an ML model to identify heart disease. The model comprises an enhanced heart disease prediction method (HDPM). The proposed HDPM identifies and eliminates outliers and performs data resampling and prediction using a hybrid synthetic minority oversampling technique – edited nearest neighbor (SMOTE-ENN) and XGBoost, respectively. The proposed method's performance was benchmarked with other classifiers, including a multilayer perceptron (MLP), SVM, and random forest. The results demonstrate that the HDPM achieved a classification accuracy of 98.4%, which is superior to other classifiers. Furthermore, the authors implemented a prototype CDSS tool for heart disease prediction to assist clinicians in detecting patients' heart disease status.

Mienye et al. [48] utilized the Cleveland and Framingham datasets to develop a robust heart disease prediction model. Their novel approach involves integrating particle swarm optimization (PSO) technique and stacked sparse autoencoder network (SSAE). The PSO was used to optimize the SSAE to achieve excellent prediction results, resulting in a classification accuracy of 96.1% and 97.3% for the Cleveland and Framingham datasets, respectively.

Ghosh et al. [51] presented robust models for heart disease prediction. They combined the Cleveland dataset and other publicly available datasets. The authors used relief and LASSO techniques to identify the most relevant attributes. Meanwhile, the classifiers used in the study include KNN, gradient boosting, adaptive boosting, and random forest bagging method (RFBM). The authors conducted a performance comparison of the various classifiers, and the RFBM with the relief technique got the highest accuracy of 99.05%.

Mienye et al. [52] developed an enhanced ensemble technique to classify heart disease. The algorithm uses a mean-based method to split the training data into small partitions that are used to train decision tree classifiers. After fitting the decision tree classifiers, an accuracy-based weighted aging classifier was employed as the weighting mechanism to create a homogeneous ensemble. The experimental results using the Framingham dataset resulted in a classification accuracy of 91%.

Rahim et al. [47] proposed a framework to detect heart disease effectively. The framework handles missing data and class imbalance using mean imputation and synthetic minority oversampling technique (SMOTE), respectively. After that, feature selection was conducted using the feature importance technique, an inbuilt class in Sklearn. Lastly, an ensemble classifier was developed to achieve optimal performance. The authors used KNN and logistic regression algorithms to develop the ensemble classifier, and their method achieved a classification accuracy of 99.1%.

Javeed et al. [53] utilized the Cleveland dataset to implement a technique to detect heart disease. The study aimed to solve the overfitting problem common in most machine learning applications. The technique involves selecting the most significant risk factors using the random search algorithm (RSA). After selecting the features, the classification task was performed using a random forest classifier, which obtained a classification accuracy of 93%.

Budholiya et al. [54] introduced an approach for predicting heart disease. The model was trained using an XGBoost classifier and optimized by a Bayesian optimization algorithm, and it achieved an accuracy of 91.8%. In a similar study, Patro et al. [55] used the Cleveland dataset to build some heart disease prediction models. The models were developed using a Bayesian optimized SVM (BO-SVM), naïve Bayes, and KNN algorithms. The classification results indicate that the BO-SVM got the best accuracy of 93.3%.

Deepika and Balaji [27] proposed a heart disease detection method based on feature selection and a novel MLP approach. The information gain method was employed for the feature selection, while the prediction model was trained using the improved MLP. Meanwhile, the enhanced MLP was achieved using the dragonfly algorithm, and it obtained an accuracy of 94.28%. In Ali et al. [4], a comparative study of ML algorithms with application to heart disease prediction was conducted. The study aimed to identify ML algorithms with the best classification accuracy. The classifiers used

Table 5.3 Comparison of different heart disease studies in recent literature

Reference	Year	Dataset	Method	Accuracy (%)
[49]	2019	Cleveland	HRFLM	88.7
[50]	2020	Cleveland	HDPM	98.4
[48]	2021	Cleveland	SSAE with PSO	96.1
[48]	2021	Framingham	SSAE with PSO	97.3
[51]	2021	Cleveland	RFBM with relief technique	99.05
[52]	2020	Framingham	Ensemble learning	91
[47]	2021	Cleveland	MaLCaDD	95.5
[47]	2021	Framingham	MaLCaDD	99.1
[53]	2019	Cleveland	RSA and random forest	93.33
[56]	2020	Cleveland	FCMIM with SVM	92.37
[54]	2020	Cleveland	Optimized XGBoost	91.8
[57]	2020	Cleveland	Optimized deep belief network	94.61
[58]	2019	Cleveland	Optimized deep neural network	93.33
[55]	2021	Cleveland	BO-SVM	93.3
[4]	2021	Framingham	MLP, KNN, and RF	100
[59]	2021	Cleveland	Optimized RF	97.52
[60]	2022	Cleveland	Enhanced MLP	94.28

in the study include decision tree, MLP, KNN, and random forest. The study employed the feature importance score to rank the attributes, and the KNN, random forest, and decision tree obtained classification accuracies of 100%.

Valarmathi and Sheela [29] used the Cleveland dataset to build heart disease prediction models. The method involved a feature selection step using the sequential forward selection technique. Secondly, genetic programming, grid search, and randomized search were employed to tune the parameters of XGBoost and random forest classifiers. The results indicate that the random forest model that is optimized using genetic programming obtained the best classification accuracy of 97.52%. The methods discussed in this section and the results obtained are tabulated in Table 5.3.

5.5 PROPOSED HEART DISEASE PREDICTION APPROACH

This research employs the supervised learning framework shown in Figure 5.2 to develop heart disease prediction models using the Cleveland and Framingham datasets. Meanwhile, both datasets contain missing values.

Therefore, the mean imputation method is employed as a preprocessing step to fix the missing values. The mean imputation technique computes the mean of the non-missing values of an attribute and imputes this mean into the missing values of that attribute. Imputation is crucial because deleting missing rows from a dataset could result in reduced sample size and bias in the data, leading to poor models [61].

Furthermore, both datasets contain an uneven class distribution, which could impact the performance of the classifiers. The imbalanced class problem is a huge challenge in machine learning research and application. It occurs when samples belonging to one class exceed those belonging to the other class. For example, in the medical domain, most datasets contain more samples belonging to the negative class than those of the positive class.

In order to obtain balanced datasets for effective heart disease prediction, this study uses the SMOTE-ENN method to resample the Framingham and Cleveland datasets. The SMOTE part of the technique oversamples the minority class instances, while the ENN discards overlapping samples [62]. Furthermore, the algorithm uses the neighborhood cleaning method in the ENN to delete samples different from two among the three nearest neighbors [63]. The resampled datasets are then used to train some popular ML classifiers, including decision tree (DT) [64], logistic regression (LR) [65], SVM [66], random forest (RF) [67], XGBoost [68], and AdaBoost [69]. The ten-fold cross-validation method [70] is chosen to train and evaluate the performance of the classifiers. The ML algorithms used in this study are presented in the following subsections.

5.5.1 Decision tree

Decision tree algorithms use a tree structure similar to a flowchart to show the classifications that occur from a succession of attribute-based splits. The algorithm begins at a root node and terminates in a leave node, where the classification is made [71, 72]. This study uses the classification and regression tree (CART) [73], which employs the Gini index to calculate the probability that a randomly selected example will be incorrectly predicted. Assuming p_i is the probability that a sample is predicted to belong to a given class. Therefore, for an example with J classes, and if $i \in \{1, 2, ..., J\}$, then the Gini index is represented mathematically as:

$$\text{Gini} = 1 - \sum_{i=1}^{J} p_i^2 \tag{5.1}$$

5.5.2 Logistic regression

This algorithm uses statistical techniques, and it is a popular algorithm for binary classification problems such as heart disease prediction. It uses the logistic function to fit a machine learning model. The algorithm computes the probability of an event using a given feature set. Meanwhile, the probability is a ratio; hence, the algorithm models the logarithm of the probability instead:

$$\log\left(\frac{\pi}{1-\pi}\right) = \beta_0 + \beta_1 x_1 + \beta_2 x_2 + \ldots \beta_m x_m \tag{5.2}$$

where π denotes the probability of a certain end result such as sick or healthy, β_i is the regression coefficients, and x_i denotes the predictor variables [74].

5.5.3 Support vector machine (SVM)

The SVM is a robust ML algorithm derived from the field of statistics. Initially, SVM was mostly employed for linear classification tasks but can be used for nonlinear classification through a method known as kernel trick [75]. Different SVM kernels include Gaussian, sigmoid, radial basis function (RBF), linear, and nonlinear kernels.

5.5.4 Random forest

The random forest algorithm [67] builds several decision tree models and combines them to form an ensemble classifier to obtain high performance. It employs bootstrap aggregating to generate random subsets of the input feature that ensures the individual trees are not highly correlated. After building the decision tree models, an unseen sample is classified through voting by all the individual trees that make up the forest [76, 77]. Then the algorithm selects the class that has the highest votes.

5.5.5 XGBoost

The XGBoost algorithm is a variant of gradient boosting developed by Chen and Guestrin [68]. Similar to most ensemble algorithms, the XGBoost uses decision trees as base learners in creating a powerful ensemble model. The XGBoost technique uses parallelized implementation to build decision trees sequentially. Assuming the number of decision trees is denoted as T and the predicted class variable for a sample i_{th} is $\hat{y}_i^{(T)}$, then the main mathematical formulation of the XGBoost is:

$$\hat{y}_i^{(T)} = \hat{y}_i^{(0)} + \sum_{t=1}^{T} f_t(x_i) \tag{5.3}$$

where $f_0(x_i) = \hat{y}_i^{(0)} = 0$ and $f_t(x_i) = \omega_{q(x_i)}$, and ω denotes a weight vector related to the leaf node [78].

5.5.6 Adaptive boosting

The AdaBoost technique [69] is a type of ensemble learning approach employed for developing robust classifiers via voting the weighted classifications of the base learners. It is used with different ML algorithms as base learners [79]. The selected base algorithm is used to fit a classifier using the initial training set when building an ML model using the AdaBoost technique. Then the weights of the various instances are adjusted, and the misclassified instances are given higher weights. These samples with modified weights are used to train subsequent classifiers that try to correct the misclassified samples from the previous model, and this process goes on iteratively [80].

5.6 EXPERIMENTAL RESULTS AND DISCUSSION

The evaluation metrics employed for assessing the model's performance include accuracy, precision, recall, and F-measure. These metrics are widely used in binary classification, and they effectively demonstrate the performance of classification models [81–84] and are represented mathematically as:

$$\text{Accuracy} = \frac{TP + TN}{TP + TN + FP + FN} \tag{5.4}$$

$$\text{Precision} = \frac{TP}{TP + FP} \tag{5.5}$$

$$\text{Recall} = \frac{TP}{TP + FN} \tag{5.6}$$

$$F\text{measure} = \frac{2 \times \text{Precision} \times \text{Recall}}{\text{Precision} + \text{Recall}} \tag{5.7}$$

where true positive (TP) represents the sick patients that were correctly identified, and false-negative (FN) denotes the sick patients that were wrongly classified. True negative (TN) indicates the healthy patients that were correctly classified, and false-positive (FP) represents the healthy patients that were wrongly classified. After training the classifiers with the original Cleveland and Framingham datasets, the performance of the models is tabulated in Tables 5.4 and 5.5.

From Tables 5.4 and 5.5, the XGBoost classifier showed higher performance than the other classifiers, with a classification accuracy of 0.86 when trained with the Cleveland dataset and 0.90 when using the Framingham dataset. However,

Table 5.4 Classification results using the Cleveland data

Classifier	Accuracy	Precision	Recall	F-measure
DT	0.70	0.69	0.74	0.71
LR	0.76	0.80	0.73	0.76
SVM	0.80	0.83	0.78	0.81
RF	0.84	0.81	0.86	0.83
XGBoost	0.86	0.90	0.88	0.89
AdaBoost	0.84	0.87	0.83	0.85

Table 5.5 Classification results using the Framingham data

Classifier	Accuracy	Recall	Precision	F-measure
DT	0.75	0.77	0.74	0.75
LR	0.83	0.83	0.84	0.83
SVM	0.82	0.82	0.78	0.80
RR	0.85	0.84	0.87	086
XGBoost	0.90	0.86	0.92	0.89
AdaBoost	0.84	0.82	0.89	0.86

Table 5.6 Classification results using the resampled Cleveland data

Classifier	Accuracy	Recall	Precision	F-measure
DT	0.75	0.88	0.77	0.83
LT	0.81	0.89	0.86	0.88
SVM	0.86	0.90	0.90	0.90
RF	0.91	0.91	0.92	0.91
XGBoost	0.93	0.96	0.94	0.95
AdaBoost	0.91	0.94	0.90	0.92

in both instances, the models performed poorly with respect to the sensitivity metric. The sensitivity indicates the number of sick patients detected accurately. Furthermore, the poor sensitivity observed in the models results from the imbalance class problem inherent in both datasets. Therefore, this study attempts to resample the datasets to enhance the classification performance. The SMOTE-ENN technique is employed to resample the datasets. Tables 5.6 and 5.7 display the models' performance after resampling the datasets.

From Tables 5.6 and 5.7, the XGBoost achieved better performance than the other classifiers. Lastly, to validate the superior performance of the XGBoost, it could be beneficial to use different performance evaluation metrics. Therefore, the receiver operating characteristic (ROC) curve shown in Figures 5.3 and 5.4 is utilized to visualize the predictive ability

Table 5.7 Classification results using the resampled Framingham data

Classifier	Accuracy	Recall	Precision	F-measure
DT	0.81	0.90	0.84	0.87
LR	0.86	0.89	0.88	0.89
SVM	0.85	0.91	0.83	0.87
RF	0.91	0.94	0.94	0.94
XGBoost	0.94	0.96	0.95	0.96
AdaBoost	0.89	0.93	0.91	0.92

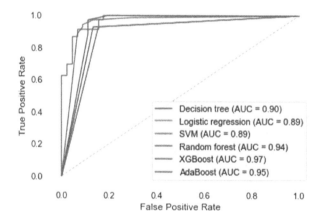

Figure 5.3 Classifiers performance using the resampled Cleveland data.

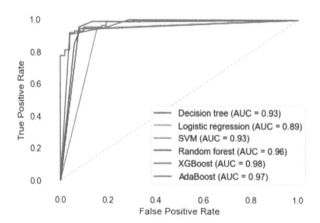

Figure 5.4 Classifiers performance using the resampled Framingham dataset.

of the models. The ROC curve plots true positive rate versus false-positive rate at different threshold values, and it demonstrates a classifier's ability to distinguish one class from another in a two-class problem such as heart disease prediction. However, the area under the curve (AUC) provides a summary of the ROC curve, and its value ranges from 0 to 1. It evaluates the diagnostic ability of ML models [85–87]. An AUC of 1 indicates a perfect model, while 0 indicates an unskilled model.

The ROC curves further indicate that the XGBoost model achieved superior performance. Furthermore, the XGBoost obtained the highest AUC value of 0.97 and 0.98 for the Cleveland and Framingham datasets, respectively, indicating that it has a good performance in identifying if a person has heart disease.

5.7 CONCLUSION

Machine learning has demonstrated its effectiveness in assisting clinicians in detecting diseases using the numerous data available in the health sector. This research discusses some recent advances in the application of ML for heart disease prediction. The study focused on the use of the well-known Cleveland and Framingham datasets. In the process, some ML models were implemented. Furthermore, the study employed a hybrid resampling technique to balance the datasets, which enhanced the performance of the ML models. The XGBoost classifier obtained accuracies of 93% and 94% for the Cleveland and Framingham datasets, respectively, which outperformed the other classifiers used in the study.

REFERENCES

1. R. Bharti, A. Khamparia, M. Shabaz, G. Dhiman, S. Pande, and P. Singh, "Prediction of Heart Disease Using a Combination of Machine Learning and Deep Learning," *Comput. Intell. Neurosci.*, vol. 2021, p. e8387680, Jul. 2021, https://doi.org/10.1155/2021/8387680.
2. D. Bertsimas, L. Mingardi, and B. Stellato, "Machine Learning for Real-Time Heart Disease Prediction," *IEEE J. Biomed. Health Inform.*, vol. 25, no. 9, pp. 3627–3637, Sep. 2021, https://doi.org/10.1109/JBHI.2021.3066347.
3. C. Martin-Isla et al., "Image-Based Cardiac Diagnosis With Machine Learning: A Review," *Front. Cardiovasc. Med.*, vol. 7, 2020, Accessed: Feb. 20, 2022. [Online]. Available: https://www.frontiersin.org/article/10.3389/fcvm.2020.00001
4. M. M. Ali, B. K. Paul, K. Ahmed, F. M. Bui, J. M. W. Quinn, and M. A. Moni, "Heart Disease Prediction Using Supervised Machine Learning Algorithms: Performance Analysis and Comparison," *Comput. Biol. Med.*, vol. 136, p. 104672, Sep. 2021, https://doi.org/10.1016/j.compbiomed.2021.104672.

5. K. V. V. Reddy, I. Elamvazuthi, A. A. Aziz, S. Paramasivam, H. N. Chua, and S. Pranavanand, "Heart Disease Risk Prediction Using Machine Learning Classifiers with Attribute Evaluators," *Appl. Sci.*, vol. 11, no. 18, Art. no. 18, Jan. 2021, https://doi.org/10.3390/app11188352.

6. Y. Muhammad, M. Tahir, M. Hayat, and K. T. Chong, "Early and Accurate Detection and Diagnosis of Heart Disease Using Intelligent Computational Model," *Sci. Rep.*, vol. 10, no. 1, Art. no. 1, Nov. 2020, https://doi.org/10.1038/s41598-020-76635-9.

7. D. Chicco and G. Jurman, "Machine Learning Can Predict Survival of Patients with Heart Failure from Serum Creatinine and Ejection Fraction Alone," *BMC Med. Inform. Decis. Mak.*, vol. 20, no. 1, p. 16, Feb. 2020, https://doi.org/10.1186/s12911-020-1023-5.

8. J. Maiga, G. G. Hungilo, and Pranowo, "Comparison of Machine Learning Models in Prediction of Cardiovascular Disease Using Health Record Data," in 2019 International Conference on Informatics, Multimedia, Cyber and Information System (ICIMCIS), Oct. 2019, pp. 45–48, https://doi.org/10.1109/ICIMCIS48181.2019.8985205.

9. A. E. Schutte, "Urgency for South Africa to Prioritise Cardiovascular Disease Management," *Lancet Glob. Health*, vol. 7, no. 2, pp. e177–e178, Feb. 2019, https://doi.org/10.1016/S2214-109X(18)30476-5.

10. K. N. Likitha, R. Nethravathi, K. Nithyashree, R. Kumari, N. Sridhar, and K. Venkateswaran, "Heart Disease Detection using Machine Learning Technique," in 2021 Second International Conference on Electronics and Sustainable Communication Systems (ICESC), Aug. 2021, pp. 1738–1743, https://doi.org/10.1109/ICESC51422.2021.9532705.

11. C. Krittanawong et al., "Machine Learning Prediction in Cardiovascular Diseases: A Meta-analysis," *Sci. Rep.*, vol. 10, no. 1, Art. no. 1, Sep. 2020, https://doi.org/10.1038/s41598-020-72685-1.

12. K. Verma, S. Bhardwaj, R. Arya, M. S. U. Islam, M. Bhushan, A. Kumar, and P. Samant, "Latest tools for data mining and machine learning," *Int. J. Inno. Tech. Exp. Engi.*, vol. 8, no. 9S, pp. 18–23, July 2019, https://doi.org/10.35940/ijitee.I1003.0789S19.

13. P. S. Kholiya, A. Kapoor, M. Rana, and M. Bhushan, "Intelligent Process Automation: The Future of Digital Transformation," in 2021 10th International Conference on System Modeling Advancement in Research Trends (SMART), Dec. 2021, pp. 185–190, https://doi.org/10.1109/SMART52563.2021.9676222.

14. K. Verma, A. Kumar, M. S. Ul Islam, T. Kanwar, and M. Bhushan, "Rank Based Mobility-aware Scheduling in Fog Computing," *Inform. Med. Unlocked*, vol. 24, p. 100619, Jan. 2021, https://doi.org/10.1016/j.imu.2021.100619.

15. I. D. Mienye and Y. Sun, "Effective Feature Selection for Improved Prediction of Heart Disease," in Pan-African Artificial Intelligence and Smart Systems, Cham, 2022, pp. 94–107, https://doi.org/10.1007/978-3-030-93314-2_6.

16. M. Marimuthu, S. Deivarani, and R. Gayathri, "Analysis of Heart Disease Prediction Using Various Machine Learning Techniques," in *Advances in Computerized Analysis in Clinical and Medical Imaging*, Chapman and Hall/CRC, 2019.

17. L. L. R. Rodrigues et al., "Machine Learning in Coronary Heart Disease Prediction: Structural Equation Modelling Approach," *Cogent Eng.*, vol. 7, no. 1, p. 1723198, Jan. 2020, https://doi.org/10.1080/23311916.2020 .1723198.

18. N. Louridi, S. Douzi, and B. El Ouahidi, "Machine Learning-based Identification of Patients with a Cardiovascular Defect," *J. Big Data*, vol. 8, no. 1, p. 133, Oct. 2021, https://doi.org/10.1186/s40537-021-00524-9.

19. R. Aggarwal and P. Thakral, "Diagnosis and Prediction of Type-2 Chronic Kidney Disease Using Machine Learning Approaches," in *Cancer Prediction for Industrial IoT 4.0: A Machine Learning Perspective*, Chapman and Hall/ CRC, 2021.

20. I. D. Mienye, G. Obaido, K. Aruleba, and O. A. Dada, "Enhanced Prediction of Chronic Kidney Disease Using Feature Selection and Boosted Classifiers," in Intelligent Systems Design and Applications, Cham, 2022, pp. 527–537, https://doi.org/10.1007/978-3-030-96308-8_49.

21. G. Sharma and C. Prabha, "Applications of Machine Learning in Cancer Prediction and Prognosis," in *Cancer Prediction for Industrial IoT 4.0: A Machine Learning Perspective*, Chapman and Hall/CRC, 2021.

22. K. Pradhan and P. Chawla, "Medical Internet of Things Using Machine Learning Algorithms for Lung Cancer Detection," *J. Manag. Anal.*, vol. 7, no. 4, pp. 591–623, Oct. 2020, https://doi.org/10.1080/23270012.2020.1811789.

23. M. Avanzo et al., "Electron Density and Biologically Effective Dose (BED) Radiomics-Based Machine Learning Models to Predict Late Radiation-Induced Subcutaneous Fibrosis," *Front. Oncol.*, vol. 10, 2020, Accessed: Feb. 06, 2022. [Online]. Available: https://www.frontiersin.org/article/10.3389/ fonc.2020.00490

24. I. D. Mienye, Y. Sun, and Z. Wang, "Improved Predictive Sparse Decomposition Method with Densenet for Prediction of Lung Cancer," *Int J Comput*, vol. 19, no. 4, pp. 533–541, 2020.

25. T. A. Tuan, T. B. Pham, J. Y. Kim, and J. M. R. S. Tavares, "Alzheimer's Diagnosis Using Deep Learning in Segmenting and Classifying 3D Brain MR Images," *Int. J. Neurosci.*, vol. 132, no. 7, pp. 689–698, Oct. 2020, https:// doi.org/10.1080/00207454.2020.1835900.

26. K. Aruleba et al., "Applications of Computational Methods in Biomedical Breast Cancer Imaging Diagnostics: A Review," *J. Imaging*, vol. 6, no. 10, Art. no. 10, Oct. 2020, https://doi.org/10.3390/jimaging6100105.

27. X. Wu, Y. Zheng, C.-H. Chu, and Z. He, "Extracting Deep Features from Short ECG Signals for Early Atrial Fibrillation Detection," *Artif. Intell. Med.*, vol. 109, p. 101896, Sep. 2020, https://doi.org/10.1016/j.artmed.2020.101896.

28. V. J. Singh, M. Bhushan, V. Kumar, and K. L. Bansal, "Optimization of Segment Size Assuring Application Perceived QoS in Healthcare," in *Lecture Notes in Engineering and Computer Science*, Jan. 2015, vol. 2217, pp. 274–278. Accessed: Feb. 15, 2022. [Online]. Available: https://espace.library.uq .edu.au/view/UQ:709139

29. B. Niepceron, A. Nait-Sidi-Moh, and F. Grassia, "Moving Medical Image Analysis to GPU Embedded Systems: Application to Brain Tumor Segmentation," *Appl. Artif. Intell.*, vol. 34, no. 12, pp. 866–879, Oct. 2020, https://doi.org/10.1080/08839514.2020.1787678.

30. S. Kedia and M. Bhushan, "Prediction of Mortality from Heart Failure using Machine Learning," in Proceedings of the 2nd International Conference on Emerging Frontiers in Electrical and Electronic Technologies (ICEFEET), 2022, pp. 1–6, https://doi.org/10.1109/ICEFEET51821.2022.9848348.

31. R. Arya, A. Kumar, and M. Bhushan, "Affect Recognition using Brain Signals: A Survey," in Computational Methods and Data Engineering, Singapore, 2021, pp. 529–552, https://doi.org/10.1007/978-981-15-7907-3_40.

32. S. Pathan, M. Bhushan, and A. Bai, "A Study on Health Care using Data Mining Techniques," *Journal of Critical Reviews*, vol. 7, no. 19, pp. 7877–7890, 2020, https://doi.org/10.31838/jcr.07.19.896.

33. M. Laad, K. Kotecha, K. Patil, and R. Pise, "Cardiac Diagnosis with Machine Learning: A Paradigm Shift in Cardiac Care," *Appl. Artif. Intell.*, vol. 36, no. 1, pp. 1–24, Jan. 2022, https://doi.org/10.1080/08839514.2022.2031816.

34. Z. Hoodbhoy, U. Jiwani, S. Sattar, R. Salam, B. Hasan, and J. K. Das, "Diagnostic Accuracy of Machine Learning Models to Identify Congenital Heart Disease: A Meta-Analysis," *Front. Artif. Intell.*, vol. 4, 2021, Accessed: Feb. 20, 2022. [Online]. Available: https://www.frontiersin.org/article/10.3389/frai.2021.708365

35. I. D. Mienye and Y. Sun, "Performance Analysis of Cost-sensitive Learning Methods with Application to Imbalanced Medical Data," *Inform. Med. Unlocked*, vol. 25, p. 100690, Jan. 2021, https://doi.org/10.1016/j.imu.2021.100690.

36. V. Jahmunah, E. Y. K. Ng, T. R. San, and U. R. Acharya, "Automated Detection of Coronary Artery Disease, Myocardial Infarction and Congestive Heart Failure Using GaborCNN Model with ECG Signals," *Comput. Biol. Med.*, vol. 134, p. 104457, Jul. 2021, https://doi.org/10.1016/j.compbiomed.2021.104457.

37. H. Serhal, N. Abdallah, J.-M. Marion, P. Chauvet, M. Oueidat, and A. Humeau-Heurtier, "Overview on Prediction, Detection, and Classification of Atrial Fibrillation Using Wavelets and AI on ECG," *Comput. Biol. Med.*, vol. 142, p. 105168, Mar. 2022, https://doi.org/10.1016/j.compbiomed.2021.105168.

38. S. M. Lauritsen et al., "Early Detection of Sepsis Utilizing Deep Learning on Electronic Health Record Event Sequences," *Artif. Intell. Med.*, vol. 104, p. 101820, Apr. 2020, https://doi.org/10.1016/j.artmed.2020.101820.

39. V. S. de Siqueira, M. M. Borges, R. G. Furtado, C. N. Dourado, and R. M. da Costa, "Artificial Intelligence Applied to Support Medical Decisions for the Automatic Analysis of Echocardiogram Images: A Systematic Review," *Artif. Intell. Med.*, vol. 120, p. 102165, Oct. 2021, https://doi.org/10.1016/j.artmed.2021.102165.

40. K. K. Agbele, P. K. Oriogun, A. G. Seluwa, and K. D. Aruleba, "Towards a Model for Enhancing ICT4 Development and Information Security in Healthcare System," in 2015 IEEE International Symposium on Technology and Society (ISTAS), Nov. 2015, pp. 1–6, https://doi.org/10.1109/ISTAS.2015.7439404.

41. N. Kagiyama, S. Shrestha, P. D. Farjo, and P. P. Sengupta, "Artificial Intelligence: Practical Primer for Clinical Research in Cardiovascular Disease," *J. Am. Heart Assoc.*, vol. 8, no. 17, p. e012788, Sep. 2019, https://doi.org/10.1161/JAHA.119.012788.

42. I. H. Sarker, "Machine Learning: Algorithms, Real-World Applications and Research Directions," *SN Comput. Sci.*, vol. 2, no. 3, p. 160, Mar. 2021, https://doi.org/10.1007/s42979-021-00592-x.

43. S. Uddin, A. Khan, M. E. Hossain, and M. A. Moni, "Comparing Different Supervised Machine Learning Algorithms for Disease Prediction," *BMC Med. Inform. Decis. Mak.*, vol. 19, no. 1, p. 281, Dec. 2019, https://doi.org/10.1186/s12911-019-1004-8.

44. L. R. Guarneros-Nolasco, N. A. Cruz-Ramos, G. Alor-Hernández, L. Rodríguez-Mazahua, and J. L. Sánchez-Cervantes, "Identifying the Main Risk Factors for Cardiovascular Diseases Prediction Using Machine Learning Algorithms," *Mathematics*, vol. 9, no. 20, Art. no. 20, Jan. 2021, https://doi.org/10.3390/math9202537.

45. K. M. Almustafa, "Prediction of Heart Disease and Classifiers' Sensitivity Analysis," *BMC Bioinformatics*, vol. 21, no. 1, p. 278, Jul. 2020, https://doi.org/10.1186/s12859-020-03626-y.

46. E. M. Senan, I. Abunadi, M. E. Jadhav, and S. M. Fati, "Score and Correlation Coefficient-Based Feature Selection for Predicting Heart Failure Diagnosis by Using Machine Learning Algorithms," *Comput. Math. Methods Med.*, vol. 2021, p. e8500314, Dec. 2021, https://doi.org/10.1155/2021/8500314.

47. A. Rahim, Y. Rasheed, F. Azam, M. W. Anwar, M. A. Rahim, and A. W. Muzaffar, "An Integrated Machine Learning Framework for Effective Prediction of Cardiovascular Diseases," *IEEE Access*, vol. 9, pp. 106575–106588, 2021, https://doi.org/10.1109/ACCESS.2021.3098688.

48. I. D. Mienye and Y. Sun, "Improved Heart Disease Prediction Using Particle Swarm Optimization Based Stacked Sparse Autoencoder," *Electronics*, vol. 10, no. 19, Art. no. 19, Jan. 2021, https://doi.org/10.3390/electronics10192347.

49. S. Mohan, C. Thirumalai, and G. Srivastava, "Effective Heart Disease Prediction Using Hybrid Machine Learning Techniques," *IEEE Access*, vol. 7, pp. 81542–81554, 2019, https://doi.org/10.1109/ACCESS.2019.2923707.

50. N. L. Fitriyani, M. Syafrudin, G. Alfian, and J. Rhee, "HDPM: An Effective Heart Disease Prediction Model for a Clinical Decision Support System," *IEEE Access*, vol. 8, pp. 133034–133050, 2020, https://doi.org/10.1109/ACCESS.2020.3010511.

51. P. Ghosh et al., "Efficient Prediction of Cardiovascular Disease Using Machine Learning Algorithms With Relief and LASSO Feature Selection Techniques," *IEEE Access*, vol. 9, pp. 19304–19326, 2021, https://doi.org/10.1109/ACCESS.2021.3053759.

52. I. D. Mienye, Y. Sun, and Z. Wang, "An Improved Ensemble Learning Approach for the Prediction of Heart Disease Risk," *Inform. Med. Unlocked*, vol. 20, p. 100402, Jan. 2020, https://doi.org/10.1016/j.imu.2020.100402.

53. A. Javeed, S. Zhou, L. Yongjian, I. Qasim, A. Noor, and R. Nour, "An Intelligent Learning System Based on Random Search Algorithm and Optimized Random Forest Model for Improved Heart Disease Detection," *IEEE Access*, vol. 7, pp. 180235–180243, 2019, https://doi.org/10.1109/ACCESS.2019.2952107.

54. K. Budholiya, S. K. Shrivastava, and V. Sharma, "An optimized XGBoost based diagnostic system for effective prediction of heart disease," *J. King Saud Univ. - Comput. Inf. Sci.*, vol. 34, no. 7, pp. 4514–4523, Jan., Oct. 2020, https://doi.org/10.1016/j.jksuci.2020.10.013.

55. S. P. Patro, G. S. Nayak, and N. Padhy, "Heart disease prediction by using novel optimization algorithm: A supervised learning prospective," *Inform. Med. Unlocked*, vol. 26, p. 100696, Jan. 2021, https://doi.org/10.1016/j.imu.2021.100696.

56. J. P. Li, A. U. Haq, S. U. Din, J. Khan, A. Khan, and A. Saboor, "Heart Disease Identification Method Using Machine Learning Classification in E-Healthcare," *IEEE Access*, vol. 8, pp. 107562–107582, 2020, https://doi.org/10.1109/ACCESS.2020.3001149.

57. S. A. Ali et al., "An Optimally Configured and Improved Deep Belief Network (OCI-DBN) Approach for Heart Disease Prediction Based on Ruzzo–Tompa and Stacked Genetic Algorithm," *IEEE Access*, vol. 8, pp. 65947–65958, 2020, https://doi.org/10.1109/ACCESS.2020.2985646.

58. L. Ali, A. Rahman, A. Khan, M. Zhou, A. Javeed, and J. A. Khan, "An Automated Diagnostic System for Heart Disease Prediction Based on χ^2 Statistical Model and Optimally Configured Deep Neural Network," *IEEE Access*, vol. 7, pp. 34938–34945, 2019, https://doi.org/10.1109/ACCESS.2019.2904800.

59. R. Valarmathi and T. Sheela, "Heart Disease Prediction Using Hyper Parameter Optimization (HPO) Tuning," *Biomed. Signal Process. Control*, vol. 70, p. 103033, Sep. 2021, https://doi.org/10.1016/j.bspc.2021.103033.

60. D. Deepika and N. Balaji, "Effective Heart Disease Prediction Using Novel MLP-EBMDA Approach," *Biomed. Signal Process. Control*, vol. 72, p. 103318, Feb. 2022, https://doi.org/10.1016/j.bspc.2021.103318.

61. S. I. Khan and A. S. M. L. Hoque, "SICE: An Improved Missing Data Imputation Technique," *J. Big Data*, vol. 7, no. 1, p. 37, Jun. 2020, https://doi.org/10.1186/s40537-020-00313-w.

62. M. S. Khan Inan, R. E. Ulfath, F. I. Alam, F. K. Bappee, and R. Hasan, "Improved Sampling and Feature Selection to Support Extreme Gradient Boosting For PCOS Diagnosis," in 2021 IEEE 11th Annual Computing and Communication Workshop and Conference (CCWC), Jan. 2021, pp. 1046–1050, https://doi.org/10.1109/CCWC51732.2021.9375994.

63. T. Le, M. T. Vo, B. Vo, M. Y. Lee, and S. W. Baik, "A Hybrid Approach Using Oversampling Technique and Cost-Sensitive Learning for Bankruptcy Prediction," *Complexity*, vol. 2019, p. e8460934, Aug. 2019, https://doi.org/10.1155/2019/8460934.

64. M. Krzywinski and N. Altman, "Classification and Regression Trees," *Nat. Methods*, vol. 14, no. 8, Art. no. 8, Aug. 2017, https://doi.org/10.1038/nmeth.4370.

65. J. S. Cramer, *The Origins of Logistic Regression*, Social Science Research Network, Rochester, NY, SSRN Scholarly Paper ID 360300, Dec. 2002, https://doi.org/10.2139/ssrn.360300.

66. C. Cortes and V. Vapnik, "Support-vector networks," *Mach. Learn.*, vol. 20, no. 3, pp. 273–297, Sep. 1995, https://doi.org/10.1007/BF00994018.

67. L. Breiman, "Random Forests," *Mach. Learn.*, vol. 45, no. 1, pp. 5–32, Oct. 2001, https://doi.org/10.1023/A:1010933404324.

68. T. Chen and C. Guestrin, "XGBoost: A Scalable Tree Boosting System," in Proceedings of the 22nd ACM SIGKDD International Conference on Knowledge Discovery and Data Mining, New York, Aug. 2016, pp. 785–794, https://doi.org/10.1145/2939672.2939785.

69. R. E. Schapire, "A Brief Introduction to Boosting," *IJCAI*, vol. 99, pp. 1401–1406, 1999.

70. M. Steurer, R. J. Hill, and N. Pfeifer, "Metrics for Evaluating the Performance of Machine Learning Based Automated Valuation Models," *J. Prop. Res.*, vol. 38, no. 2, pp. 99–129, Apr. 2021, https://doi.org/10.1080/09599916.2020.1858937.

71. I. D. Mienye, Y. Sun, and Z. Wang, "Prediction Performance of Improved Decision Tree-based Algorithms: A Review," *Procedia Manuf.*, vol. 35, pp. 698–703, Jan. 2019, https://doi.org/10.1016/j.promfg.2019.06.011.

72. S. Zian, S. A. Kareem, and K. D. Varathan, "An Empirical Evaluation of Stacked Ensembles With Different Meta-Learners in Imbalanced Classification," *IEEE Access*, vol. 9, pp. 87434–87452, 2021, https://doi.org/10.1109/ACCESS.2021.3088414.

73. L. Breiman, J. H. Friedman, R. A. Olshen, and C. J. Stone, *Classification and Regression Trees*, Wadsworth & Brooks, Monterey, 1983. /paper/Classification-and-Regression-Trees-Breiman-Friedman/8017699564136f93af21575810d557dba1ee6fc6 (accessed Aug. 05, 2020).

74. S. Sperandei, "Understanding Logistic Regression Analysis," *Biochem. Medica*, vol. 24, no. 1, pp. 12–18, Feb. 2014, https://doi.org/10.11613/BM.2014.003.

75. M. Kafai and K. Eshghi, "CROification: Accurate Kernel Classification with the Efficiency of Sparse Linear SVM," *IEEE Trans. Pattern Anal. Mach. Intell.*, vol. 41, no. 1, pp. 34–48, Jan. 2019, https://doi.org/10.1109/TPAMI.2017.2785313.

76. M.-S. Mushtaq and A. Mellouk, "2 - Methodologies for Subjective Video Streaming QoE Assessment," in *Quality of Experience Paradigm in Multimedia Services*, M.-S. Mushtaq and A. Mellouk, Eds. Elsevier, 2017, pp. 27–57, https://doi.org/10.1016/B978-1-78548-109-3.50002-3.

77. S. N. Singh, and M. Bhushan, "Monitoring and Analysis System using Machine Learning," in Proceedings of the 2022 IEEE VLSI Device Circuit and System (VLSI DCS), 2022, pp. 304–309, https://doi.org/10.1109/VLSIDCS53788.2022.9811433.

78. L. Cui, P. Chen, L. Wang, J. Li, and H. Ling, "Application of Extreme Gradient Boosting Based on Grey Relation Analysis for Prediction of Compressive Strength of Concrete," *Adv. Civ. Eng.*, vol. 2021, p. e8878396, Mar. 2021, https://doi.org/10.1155/2021/8878396.

79. F. Wang, Z. Li, F. He, R. Wang, W. Yu, and F. Nie, "Feature Learning Viewpoint of Adaboost and a New Algorithm," *IEEE Access*, vol. 7, pp. 149890–149899, 2019, https://doi.org/10.1109/ACCESS.2019.2947359.

80. S. Pal, N. Mishra, M. Bhushan, P. S. Kholiya, M. Rana, and A. Negi, "Deep Learning Techniques for Prediction and Diagnosis of Diabetes Mellitus," in Proceedings of the 2022 International Mobile and Embedded Technology

Conference (MECON), IEEE, 2022, pp. 588–593, https://doi.org/10.1109/MECON53876.2022.9752176.

81. I. D. Mienye, Y. Sun, and Z. Wang, "Improved Sparse Autoencoder Based Artificial Neural Network Approach for Prediction of Heart Disease," *Inform. Med. Unlocked*, vol. 18, p. 100307, Jan. 2020, https://doi.org/10.1016/j.imu.2020.100307.

82. D. J. Hand, P. Christen, and N. Kirielle, "F*: An Interpretable Transformation of the F-measure," *Mach. Learn.*, vol. 110, no. 3, pp. 451–456, Mar. 2021, https://doi.org/10.1007/s10994-021-05964-1.

83. R. Soleymani, E. Granger, and G. Fumera, "F-measure Curves: A Tool to Visualize Classifier Performance Under Imbalance," *Pattern Recognit.*, vol. 100, p. 107146, Apr. 2020, https://doi.org/10.1016/j.patcog.2019.107146.

84. A. Kulkarni, D. Chong, and F. A. Batarseh, "5 - Foundations of Data Imbalance and Solutions for a Data Democracy," in *Data Democracy*, F. A. Batarseh and R. Yang, Eds. Academic Press, 2020, pp. 83–106, https://doi.org/10.1016/B978-0-12-818366-3.00005-8.

85. I. D. Mienye, P. Kenneth Ainah, I. D. Emmanuel, and E. Esenogho, "Sparse Noise Minimization in Image Classification Using Genetic Algorithm and DenseNet," in 2021 Conference on Information Communications Technology and Society (ICTAS), Mar. 2021, pp. 103–108, https://doi.org/10.1109/ICTAS50802.2021.9395014.

86. M. Rana and M. Bhushan, "Advancements in Healthcare Services using Deep Learning Techniques," in Proceedings of the 2022 International Mobile and Embedded Technology Conference (MECON), 2022, pp. 157–161, https://doi.org/10.1109/MECON53876.2022.9752020.

87. G. Wang, K. W. Wong, and J. Lu, "AUC-Based Extreme Learning Machines for Supervised and Semi-Supervised Imbalanced Classification," *IEEE Trans. Syst. Man Cybern. Syst.*, vol. 51, no. 12, pp. 7919–7930, Dec. 2021, https://doi.org/10.1109/TSMC.2020.2982226.

Chapter 6

Immersive technologies in healthcare education

Mohammad Nasfikur R. Khan and Kari J. Lippert

CONTENTS

6.1 INTRODUCTION

Healthcare is undergoing rapid changes. According to Mantovani et al. (2003), healthcare doubles every six to eight years, and new medical treatments are developed every day [1]. In response to the rapid evolution of medical knowledge, new learning aids have been developed for medical practice and education. The last few years have witnessed the development of a lot of innovative technologies for education and training. In addition to virtual worlds and computer simulations, health professionals can also learn from virtual environments in three-dimensional and two-dimensional formats.

The recent development of technology has fundamentally altered the concept of teaching and learning. The American Heart Association (AHA) stresses the potential of immersive technology in improving resuscitation training by expanding learners' learning experiences [2]. As immersive

DOI: 10.1201/9781003286745-6

technology becomes more prevalent, users can become completely immersed in the background, fading the difference between the real and virtual worlds. On the whole, immersive technology refers to technologies such as VR, AR, MR, and XR [3].

Immersive technologies can be used to improve communication between those who have knowledge and information (clinicians/specialists, experts, and educators) and those seeking insight and understanding (patients/families, non-experts, learners). Besides, several studies show that immersive technology can enhance learning as well as promote cooperation and creativity among students in a broad range of fields, including medicine [4], training [5], and crisis management [6]. The simulation of surgical procedures, training, medical education, stroke rehabilitation, and other real-world applications in medicine are just a few examples.

In one study, Parham et al. (2019) created a low-cost VR surgical simulation to improve surgical skills. Through the use of an Oculus Rift headset and touch controller, surgical oncology simulation takes place in a virtual operating room modeled after a realistic hospital environment [7]. Tang et al. (2020) demonstrate that MR is a useful tool to assess students for learning design courses. A systematic approach and creativity were used to assess the effectiveness of their project. Testing was conducted before and after the project to evaluate the learning effects of the project. In addition, a comparison was conducted between MR and traditional materials in terms of effectiveness. In order to determine if the improvements were statistically significant, the researchers analyzed the results nonparametrically [8].

In one study, Sharon Fong Mei Toh and Kenneth N.K. Fong found that task-specific training was effective in promoting recovery of upper extremities after stroke in hemiparetic patients. A task-specific VR (TSVR) program was developed to examine how it was possible to enhance the recovery of hemiplegic upper extremities after stroke using a hierarchy of tasks implemented as part of a functional test for hemiplegic upper extremities. Additionally, VR applications were created to train medical practitioners to support stroke patients in a virtual environment [9].

Recently, Desselle et al. reviewed several current and emerging technologies in surgery, such as improved immersion, spatial awareness, and cognitive capabilities, which could be applied to learning, perioperative scenarios, and skill development. Moreover, VR and augmented reality provide better access to information, knowledge, and experiences, improving healthcare approaches and resulting in better outcomes for patients and the general public. Through the use of an MR machine, surgeons can recreate holographically the patient's vital signs and other information to assist them throughout the surgical process. Thus, immersive technology has become increasingly important in medical education and practice in the last 20 years [10].

Throughout the past decade, researchers have demonstrated that VR, AR, MR, and XR devices can be extremely useful for training medical professionals in a variety of ways and with a variety of applications. There are increasing numbers of applications for immersive technology in medical practice and education. However, there is insufficient research addressing trends, common applications, receivers, educational materials, assessment methods, and performance of immersive technology. As immersion technologies advance, the field of medicine and education has rapidly advanced, requiring new researchers to document their subject expertise and identify emerging trends. Accordingly, this research analyzes immersive technology studies from the past two decades.

The objective of this chapter is twofold. Initially, we will discuss immersive technology, and then we will look at how these technologies are being implemented in healthcare education. The structure of the paper appears as follows. The purpose of the chapter is outlined in section 6.1. Section 6.2 discusses research questions and research gaps, as well as how papers are selected for review. In section 6.3, we provide details about immersive technology and its applications in medical science. Section 6.4 outlines how immersive technologies can be used in general as well as in medical education. In section 6.5, we discuss the research gaps and propose solutions to resolve them. Section 6.6 concludes this chapter by addressing future possibilities.

6.2 BACKGROUND

Immersive technologies emerged from the video game industry. In this way, virtual environments can be created that are "real time" in which "players" can move around, interact, and experience the world. How a user interacts with or navigates the environment depends on the platform.

Immersive technologies provide humans with an excellent way to enhance reality. Through extensive use of immersive technologies, the digital and computational environment is evolving in such a way that the user finds himself immersed in a separate world that exists solely within gaming and imagination, even though there are no concerns or relationships between their imagination and the real world. It provides users with enhanced reality by displaying digital images of their real surroundings in a way that enhances their experience of it. By completely suffusing a user in a digitally created imaginative environment, these kinds of technologies are also excellent at creating a new reality by utterly cutting him off from the external world.

Immersive technologies are often used in education and training. Medical science, like medical education, has used immersive technologies for the last few years. In this section, we will discuss some research questions which will be answered in the next sections. Along with that, we will also discuss the current applications in the realm of medical education.

6.2.1 Research questions

For the best possible outcome of this research, we will try to find solutions for the research questions (RQ) mentioned next.

- RQ 1: Define VR, AR, MR, and XR.
- RQ 2: How is immersive technology being used in medical practice and education today?
- RQ 3: How do immersive technologies affect medical education and practice?
- RQ 4: How has medical education been adapted to support immersive technology-based learning?
- RQ 5: In medical practice and education, how have immersive technology applications been evaluated for their impact on learning?
- RQ 6: What is the impact of immersive technologies on medical education and practice students?

6.2.2 Reviews of VR/AR/MR/XR applications in the healthcare domain

According to the IEEE and Web of Science databases, 298 papers that relate to this topic were published after 2010 and as a result, are relevant to this topic. However, 143 of these articles were duplicates and, as such, have been removed. In the next step, the data were filtered according to the PRISMA guidelines [11] (Figure 6.1). During this process, 15 papers were deemed unsuitable based on their titles and abstracts, and 72 articles were evaluated according to their quality and availability. The systematic literature review managed to identify 68 publications that could be further analyzed. The process of selecting the articles was divided into four steps.

First, a search was conducted in March 2022 in two databases indexing peer-reviewed articles: IEEE and Web of Science. This search focused on the use of immersive technologies in medical science.

The next stage was to screen candidates based on the following criteria:

- There are only reviews included.
- The articles covered only concern medical-based higher education.
- Articles using AR/VR technologies are included.
- Articles about remote practices are included.

Following that, we checked the eligibility using these criteria:

- The full text of the articles is available in English.
- Multiple articles are reviewed in the article.
- Medical sciences are the subject of the article.
- The article discusses AR/VR technologies.

Review Process

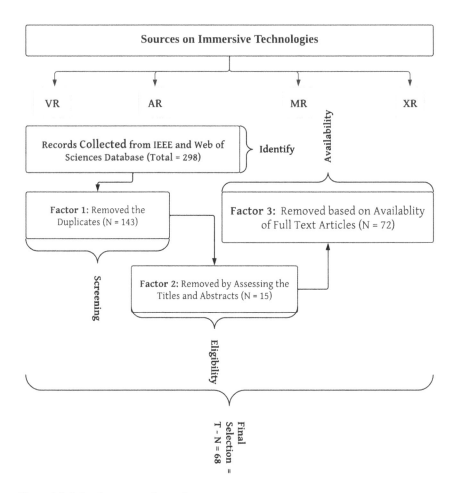

Figure 6.1 Selecting papers for review.

In the end, we evaluated the interventions that impacted one of two variables: full paper availability and quality.

For this stage, the following steps were considered.

- Development of digital materials related to medical sciences.
- Interactivity and feedback.
- Interaction and involvement in society.
- Remote practice, labs, and kinesthetic learning.

The next section discusses the basic concepts of VR, AR, MR, and XR, along with their real-world application.

6.3 IMMERSIVE TECHNOLOGIES

The four main forms of immersive technology are VR, AR, MR, and XR. These four technologies are discussed in this section, along with their major applications.

6.3.1 Virtual reality (VR)

Zhang et al. define VR as a three-dimensional spatial simulation generated by a computer system [12]. By wearing headgear and goggles coupled to sensors, participants are able to participate in a presumably real way. Sacks et al. describe VR as a technique for presenting customers with a virtual experience through computer-based operating systems [13]. A VR-based immersive system allows users to immerse themselves in an interactive environment by enabling them to inhabit a virtual environment. This imagined environment can be accessed by individuals through the use of technology.

According to Gadelha, VR technologies have significantly altered how teachers teach and students learn [14]. These technologies can assist teachers in shifting their attention from students to what they are teaching. The Multimedia Cone of Abstraction (MCoA) is modeled after Dale's Cone of Experience and illustrates how learners become active learners when they engage in meaningful virtual interactions [15]. In the CoE's principles, "Direct Purposeful Experiences" is the most abstract level. The use of VR was effective in replacing the Center of Excellence's foundation, which suggests that VR can provide highly realistic representations of objects that students might interact with and learn best from. If students are given the right conditions, including timely feedback and ample time to improve, they can comprehend concepts.

The students can practice what they have learned as many times as needed until they are able to accomplish the tasks using VR. The method also encourages people to keep working hard to improve. Furthermore, students may receive timely feedback on their current capability levels in a virtual learning environment. By using visual programming, a student will be able to create a customized virtual learning environment to begin mastering a skill or activity.

The number of studies that show that simulation training improves the knowledge and competency of healthcare educators has increased significantly [16]. Through VR, healthcare professionals can help students avoid scenarios that may negatively impact patients' outcomes. Several studies have demonstrated that VR allows medical students to develop the skills and confidence necessary for real-life situations, as well as provides a cost-effective method to practice simulated clinical scenarios repeatedly throughout their careers [17]. In consequence, VR offers young healthcare professionals the option of training without risking their lives, preparing for diagnosing illness indicators, and even performing difficult surgeries without necessarily endangering patients.

VR simulations allow medical professionals to develop key medical skills and gain professional information without using cadavers or animals. In this way, haptic (touch) perceptions need to be fine-tuned, but procedural, visual, and auditory perceptions can also be honed. In addition to endoscopic and laparoscopic surgeries, trainee surgeons can practice neurosurgery and epidural injections when they use the VR system. Vaughan et al. say that orthopedic VR training simulations offer surgeons a brilliant opportunity to develop their operations and decision-making skills in a safe, risk-free environment [18]. VR allows the training process to be conducted at high speeds without causing anxiety or risk. Furthermore, this technology is also beneficial to the medical industry as well as other applications. A medical solution can be implemented using the technology illustrated in Figure 6.2.

In order to provide accurate and relevant healthcare information to diverse patients experiencing an acute or chronic disease, education must be tailored to their individual needs. For stroke survivors and their primary caregivers, Thompson-Butel et al. designed guided, personalized VR instruction sessions to decrease recurrent strokes and enhance recovery. In their study, they examined how well VR sessions delivered post-stroke education [19]. According to the study, "various significant improvements in technical expertise in areas such as neurodevelopment and physiology, cognitive impairment, and stroke-specific instructions such as personalized stroke risk factors and acute therapy advantages" were achieved by VR sessions for the survivor and caregivers.

According to Roy et al. [20], dental education has reached a stage where VR simulations are commonly used. According to them, using VR technology to teach dental hygiene allows for a great deal of flexibility and self-learning. Due to this change, students can use VR devices to interact with their education in a variety of ways, including conducting simulations whenever and wherever they choose and storing and revisiting their work after completion. VR technology can also make learning more interesting and engaging for students by decreasing anxiety and monotony. In conclusion, due to recent advancements in VR technologies, trainees in all dentistry specialties may be able to experience pre-clinical experiences that are more effective and convincing.

6.3.2 Augmented reality (AR)

Currently, AR is one of the biggest technology trends, and it's only going to get bigger as mobile devices capable of displaying AR become more accessible around the world. In the most cited definition, AR involves combining virtual and real elements, interacting in real-time, and being mapped in three dimensions [21]. AR is contrasted with VR in the first condition;

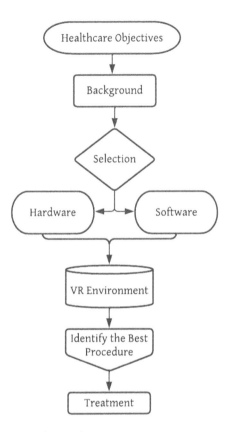

Figure 6.2 A VR process used in medicine.

computer-generated models in live-action movies are contrasted with it in the second, and annotation and overlays on video are contrasted with it in the third [21].

Milgram and Kishino [25] introduced the continuum that separates reality from VR. AR, MR, and enhanced virtuality were also positioned along that continuum. It has been suggested that the virtual and real worlds have varying intensities. By introducing this concept, the notion of diminished reality is introduced, in which objects in the real world are digitally removed [22].

In computer-mediated communication, the design and development are geared toward the achievement of specific communication outcomes. In this regard, it is useful to have a theory that predicts human communication behavior for designers and developers of mediating technologies. Though AR has been around since the 1980s, it remains in its developmental phase because of limitations related to technology, social acceptance, usability, finance, and time, as well as a lack of knowledge about what is possible

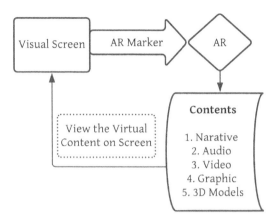

Figure 6.3 AR using markers.

with AR in education. Additionally, it includes three other fundamental criteria for an AR application, such as a virtual and real-world combination, real-time interactivity, and 3D registration [22].

A variety of devices can be used to view the AR virtual learning content, such as a head-mounted display (HMD), a computer with a web camera, a mobile or handheld device (HHD), or Kinect. According to a literature review done by [23], users and researchers are focused on mobile AR applications that can be used across all major domains. The benefit of mobile devices in the learning process is that they allow you to follow trends on the go. As illustrated in Figure 6.3, marker-based AR learning can be used to extract embedded virtual content from markers.

Figure 6.4 presents an example of how location-based AR can extract virtual content from real-world objects, buildings, and locations by using the Global Positioning System (GPS) and WiFi positioning system [24].

There have been several studies that demonstrate the ability to learn from markers based on AR, such as [23]. Students are more likely to stay on track and complete their learning when markers are used. According to a study conducted by [23] and [24], a learning AR approach is based on location. Bringing their devices along allows users to find and view virtual content via location-based AR. There are numerous problems that might result from the inadequate development of mobile-based AR applications, including the time required to recognize and render information, the inability to distinguish between reality and virtual, and the inability to interpret content. Three types of immersive technologies are illustrated in Figure 6.5 in one diagram to illustrate their relationship.

As technology becomes more prevalent, it enables all aspects of human existence to be improved, but the health sector will suffer the most. The crisis in healthcare calls for a rethinking of healthcare studies. The right use

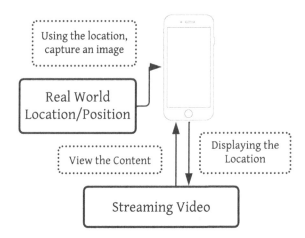

Figure 6.4 A portable device-based AR.

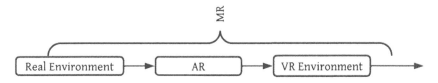

Figure 6.5 Relation between AR, VR, and MR.

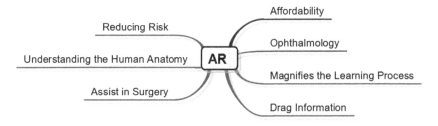

Figure 6.6 Utilization of AR in healthcare training.

of technology can make healthcare organizations more efficient. Using AR to deliver enhanced care to patients has proven to be efficient. AR will have a major impact on healthcare. It is due to the fact that AR works on sensors, displays, and embedded electronics. Figure 6.6 highlights the significance of AR in healthcare training.

6.3.3 Mixed reality (MR)

When the virtual world collides and interacts with the real world, it is called MR. Despite the popularity of AR and VR for training as well as gaming, MR is best suited to AI-driven training. The technology essentially lies between AR and augmented virtuality and requires a headset such as the HoloLens made by Microsoft in order to be experienced [25].

Medical professionals, technicians, and even medical professors can all benefit from MR and its expanding applications. The following are some areas where incorporating MR apps can produce incredible results:

- MR headsets provide real-time access to relevant medical data. A quick data feed can be critical in the event of an emergency so that doctors can take quick action.
- Hospitals will be able to offer patients hospital-level care with real-time data. As a result, patients will be more comfortable and hospital resources will be less burdened.
- By monitoring patients remotely, a large number of resources can be freed up to attend to more critical patients.
- MR can assist professionals in viewing 3D images more naturally. Better visualization of depth will allow for a better analysis of details.
- By utilizing MR, students can watch surgeries live and record them, thus allowing a great learning opportunity – as close to a real surgery as they can get without going to the operating theatre (OT). Furthermore, the recording can be used to delve into details and nuances of specific steps and techniques.
- By utilizing MR, information can be more easily stored, shared, and dissipated.
- The MR application also provides physicians with virtual surgery intelligence (VSI), which helps them explain the surgery to their patients and tell them what to expect in terms of complications.
- A surgeon can collaborate and connect via microphones and sensors using MR headset technology such as HoloLens, enabling remote surgery assistance. Remote assistance enables better execution.

6.3.4 Extended reality (XR)

Finally, there is also a new umbrella term called XR that encompasses all immersive technologies, including VR, AR, MR, and those yet to be invented. Through the fusion of the physical and virtual worlds or by creating a fully immersive environment, immersive technologies enhance our understanding of reality. XR will become mainstream within five years, as predicted by more than 60% of respondents in a recent survey. Examining the existing technologies can help us better understand XR [26].

The following section provides a review of the selected paper on medical education and training and its application in education.

6.4 IMMERSIVE TECHNOLOGIES IN EDUCATION

The use of immersive technology has broad appeal, thanks to its ability to create an engaging virtual environment that facilitates learning by leading students towards completing targeted tasks and enabling them to acquire a range of new skills. These tasks engage and captivate learners, according to Norris, Spicer, and Byrd [17]. These systems use head-mounted displays, headphones, and hand controllers to engage their multiple senses. In an immersive environment, people can develop new skills and learn new information by engaging multiple senses.

By eliminating distracting external factors from the classroom, VR allows educators and students to connect like never before. A study by Gadelha (2018) reveals that immersive technology has changed how teachers teach and how students learn. Therefore, it can be useful for facilitating the development of a student-centered approach rather than a teacher-centric one. The Multimedia Cone of Abstraction (MCOA), constructed by Dale based on his Cone of Experience (CoE), explains that learners hold more information when they are learning by doing [14]. According to the study by Baukal et al., students become active learners through engaging in a purposeful virtual environment in which they learn by doing specific tasks [27].

The "Direct Purposeful Experiences" (DPX) are being replaced by immersive devices, which is the least abstract level of the CoE, giving learners much more realistic simulations of things they can interact with and learn best by doing. It has been shown by Bloom (1974) that students master tasks or materials when they receive immediate feedback and have time to develop their skill set at their own pace. As students master the task through the use of immersive technology, no matter how many times they need to practice the process, they can practice what they have learned until it becomes second nature [28]. Further, it provides intrinsic motivation to practice successfully in their profession [29].

Rather than giving up on instructions, they are encouraged to keep practicing till they become proficient in a task. Additionally, students who participate in virtual learning environments are given immediate feedback on their performance. Creating a virtual learning environment tailored to their needs allows students to understand what they need to improve to develop a skill or to complete a task [17]. A user can experience potentially harmful, deadly, or risky situations through immersive technology without risking their safety.

Furthermore, immersive technology can be tailored to learners' needs by simulating countless scenarios to make sure that they are safe from hazards such as using medical devices or joining the military [17]. Creating these scenarios requires fewer natural and social resources than creating a real one, Zhang et al. say, even though it is possible to generate infinite virtual instructional scenarios using only imagination and knowledge [12].

The use of simulations in healthcare education is an effective method for improving knowledge acquisition and skills [30, 31]. The use of VR in medical education eliminates potential risks that could cause adverse outcomes. The use of VR technology is considered a cost-effective and interactive method to teach students the skills they will need in a real-life setting [32]. The use of VR means that medical learners can practice without worrying about making mistakes and facing grave consequences, as well as be better prepared to recognize symptoms of diseases and conduct complicated operations. Instead of cadavers and animals, VR simulations provide a realistic training environment for medical students, so they learn skills and acquire knowledge.

Furthermore, the immersive system allows trainees who have no experience with endoscopic surgery, laparoscopic surgery, neurosurgery, and epidural injections to practice surgical skills without being adversely affected by it. Vaughan et al. demonstrate that orthopedists can sharpen their operations and decision-making capabilities in a realistic, risk-free setting by using orthopedic immersive technology [18]. Suitable for practicing basic skills in orthopedics and other procedures, these simulations provide a suitable tool for surgeons with no prior surgical experience [18].

It may not be appropriate for traditional forms of education, such as verbal presentations and written materials, to be used in teaching complicated medical material to patients and caregivers [33]. Language proficiency, cultural background, socioeconomic status, level of education and understanding, and language or cognitive impairment should be considered in stroke cases in which risk factors and causes of stroke differ widely from individual to individual [19]. The goal is to provide stroke survivors with information that is accessible and relevant to their needs [34]. Using immersive technology is effective in the prevention of recurrent strokes and in the enhancement of rehabilitation following strokes when used in the delivery of post-stroke education. According to Thompson-Butel et al., the purpose of the study was to explore the use of VR in post-stroke education [19]. According to researchers, immersive technology-based education offers safe, personalized learning experiences for participants, who enjoyed the sessions and learned more about brain anatomy, physiology, damaged brain tissue, and stroke-specific information, such as risk factors and benefits of acute stroke treatment.

The current status and value of immersive technology-based simulations in dental education were studied by Roy, Bakr, and George [35]. Immersive devices are being used in dental education because they are a great way for self-learning and flexible instruction. Student participation is increased because of these devices. With immersive devices, users have the ability to practice simulations wherever and whenever they wish, assessing their performances after they have completed their training sessions. Further, immersive technology reduces classroom anxiety and boredom and boosts the learning process by making it more engaging. In total, immersive technology is a rapidly evolving technology that is transforming learning processes. Table 6.1 shows the outcome of several papers based on VR in medicine. Table 6.2 displays the results of using AR, MR, and XR in the field of medical sciences. Lastly, Table 6.3 demonstrates the outcome of modernized tools like virtual patients that were designed using immersive technologies.

6.4.1 Research gaps

An immersive training program that facilitates self-directed and personalized learning has several advantages, including but not limited to the creation of safe and reliable learning environments. The purpose of immersive technology in healthcare, argue Riener and Harders, is to enhance teaching and training through motivating and exciting realistic simulations [66]. A study has demonstrated that applying immersive technology-based simulation to clinical training improves learning outcomes impressively [67].

A study conducted by Gunn et al. compared the potential of immersive technology-based simulation to improve the technical skills of first-year students majoring in medical imaging and found that immersive technology-based simulation improved students' acquisition of technical skills more than the use of traditional laboratory-based simulations [43]. There are other limitations of the immersive system besides latency, including "the lag between actions taken by immersed patients and the response of the virtual environment" and "underestimation of perceived distance in virtual environments" when compared to real environments [68]. Both situations may prevent learning materials from being delivered effectively and the learning process itself from being efficient. The perception of educators' lack of technical skills may also hamper the usage of immersive technology. Immersive technology, for instance, is often seen as requiring a high level of technical expertise and skills to be used by students [69].

In addition, Sanchez-Cabrero et al. contend that immersive technology for learning is an area that has not been fully explored and needs to be explored more thoroughly [29]. There is a lack of scholarly documentation in the area of undergraduate medical education despite the popularity of immersive technologies in healthcare, Gunn et al. report [43]. To maximize the immersive system as a didactic tool, medical students must adopt immersive technology [70]. Therefore, the exploration of immersive technologies in medical education requires expanding current knowledge and a variety of research. Hence, this study reveals a gap in research since the acceptance of immersive technology among students and its usage in the medical sciences is still in doubt.

Table 6.1 The outcome of using VR

Author(s)	Outcome
Norris et al. [17] and Gamito et al. [36]	The authors discuss the advantages and disadvantages of VR safety training and explain the implications of this technology for professionals.
Baukal et al. [27], Ausburn et al. [37], Bloom et al. [28], and Krueger et al. [38]	These papers specifically focused on the use of multimedia-based immersive technologies in education.
Sánchez-Cabrero et al. [29], Khan et al. [30], and Bakar et al. [39]	These papers demonstrate how many times a student needs to practice until they master the task; it provides students with the opportunity to master what they have learned.
Thompson-Butel et al. [19] and Pottle et al. [40]	These papers suggest that factors affecting risk factors and causes of health issues vary greatly according to the individual, including language proficiency, cultural background, socioeconomic status, level of education, and cognitive and language impairments.
Calvert et al. [41] and Badaruddin et al. [42]	These papers found that immersive VR experiences could benefit students both cognitively and emotionally by providing new experiences.
Bracq et al. [31] and Vaughan et al. [18]	In these systematic reviews, the authors aim to evaluate the research results in VR for healthcare training, specifically about non-technical skills, using preferred reporting items for systematic reviews and meta-analyses.
Hoffmann et al. [33] and Roberts et al. [15]	In their research, the researchers concluded that traditional methods of educating patients and their primary caregivers, such as oral presentations and written materials, may not be appropriate.
Gunn et al. [43] and Gaggioli et al. [44]	The researchers compared immersive simulation to traditional laboratory-based simulation for improving student skills in medical imaging. They found that VR simulation improved students' ability to acquire skills more efficiently than traditional lab simulation.
Richa et al. [45], Negro et al. [46], and Riva et al. [47]	Based on these studies, immersive technology can provide powerful tools for personal development and change because it can support and enhance self-awareness and personal efficacy in its users.
Frolli et al. [48]	According to the results of this paper as well as previous preliminary data, VR can support the basic and complex skills of these individuals in a dynamic, effective, and promising way.
Zheng et al. [49]	These researchers developed CheerBrush, an interactive AR coaching system that helps children with autism spectrum disorder improve their toothbrushing skills.
Lege et al. [50]	They provide an overview of how VR is being used in classrooms and educational research through a literature review of papers published from 2017 to 2020. They conclude by making predictions for the future and suggesting possible research proposals.

Table 6.2 The outcome of using AR, MR, and XR

Author	Outcome
Doolani et al. [3]	According to this research, XR systems are increasingly being used to tackle various domains such as training, education, safety, etc. They also present a review of the current state-of-the-art of use of XR in training personnel in the field of manufacturing.
Barsom et al. [51], Kim et al. [52], Demir et al. [53], and Khor et al. [54]	In the light of these studies, AR, VR, and MR are rapidly becoming more and more affordable, accessible, and usable, which is why their application to healthcare is inevitable. These technologies were also incorporated into the surgical process.
Zheng et al. [49]	These researchers developed CheerBrush, an interactive AR coaching system that helps children with autism spectrum disorder improve their toothbrushing skills.
Lakshmiprabha et al. [55]	In an immersive and quick interaction manner, the proposed system helps children learn about new pictures or objects as well as the corresponding keywords or matching sentences. Use case-based tests show that the proposed AR/VR system works satisfactorily.
Desselle et al. [10] and Tang et al. [8]	The studies examine some of the current and emerging technologies and their potential applications in surgery using virtual and augmented reality.

Table 6.3 The outcome of using immersive tools

Authors	Outcome
Dafli et al. [56], Huang et al. [57], Kononowicz et al. [58], and Andrés et al. [59]	These papers discuss the concept of virtual patients, which possess numerous medical-based educational benefits but are costly to develop. Few medical schools can afford to create them.
Miller et al. [60]	The authors evaluate the effectiveness of VEs as an assessment and teaching tool based on the effects of this technical manipulation.
Newbutt et al. [61]	This paper intends to provide a few perspectives on immersive technologies, based on our extensive experience in utilizing and applying them to autistic groups during COVID-19.
Gadelha [14], King et al. [62], and Klopfer et al. [63]	These articles discuss the benefits of immersive technologies and how to judge the quality of immersive content.
Felnhofer et al. [64] and Ferrer-García et al. [65]	The results of these studies showed almost all virtual scenarios could elicit the desired emotional responses. There was no evidence that presence affected emotional reactions to virtual environments across all environments.

6.5 CONCLUSION

In this study, 68 research studies were reviewed to examine the use of immersive technologies in medical education. Using immersive technology-based applications increases the speed, accuracy, and retention of tasks, say students quoted in the articles.

The purpose of this section is to improve performance, productivity, and motivation in the courses, complete assignments efficiently, give better lectures, and make the educational process more efficient and effective. Researchers claim that incorporating immersive technologies will make it easier to divide tasks into virtual manageable ones, which will aid learning and enhance knowledge transfer. Further, researchers assert that immersive technology can bridge the knowledge gap between experts and novices, thus keeping them engaged and motivated.

In our review of articles, we found that the majority of those in the effort expectation sub-dimension stated that immersive applications are easy to learn, that these technologies and applications are easy to use, and that users are satisfied with the apps. Students can use immersive technology easily, therefore claiming it is simple to use. Their efforts to utilize it do not require a great deal of effort. It can be concluded from these results that immersive applications are easily usable [57].

The majority of articles that were analyzed in-depth in this review stated that immersive technology is easy to learn, users can easily use these technologies and applications, and users are satisfied with these applications. As a result, immersive technology can be said to be easy to use for students. This device requires little effort on their part in order to use it. Considering these results, we can conclude that immersive technology applications can be easily implemented [57].

Studies have found that students generally believed immersive technologies in medical education should be viewed as a priority by society and will be more respectable if they use them effectively. A survey of 350 people from the Republic of Korea conducted by Lee, Kim, and Choi revealed the same outcome: social relationships have a major effect on the desire to use immersive technologies [71]. These findings suggest that university students are highly inclined to accept and use immersive technologies in medical education [71]. The study by Sezer and Yilmaz finds that medical students are highly adept at using technology in their education. Immersive technology is an important component of medical education and lab exercises, and such studies are crucial to integrating it into those areas. There is a wide variety of instructional design techniques that can be used to integrate immersive technology. As part of its instructional design model, the ASSURE model can be used to create an appropriate learning environment in medical education [72]. In addition to learning challenging concepts through immersive technology in a medical curriculum, students can also practice burdensome tasks and learn subjects that may seem difficult through interactive and effective immersive learning experiences. As a result, students will perform more effectively, learn faster, and be more successful.

REFERENCES

1. Mantovani, F, et al. "Virtual reality training for health-care professionals." *Cyber Psychology & Behavior* vol. 6 (2003): 389–395. https://doi.org/10.1089/109493103322278772.
2. Gallagher, Anthony G, and Christopher U Cates. "Virtual reality training for the operating room and cardiac catheterization laboratory." *Lancet* vol. 364,9444 (2004): 1538–40. https://doi.org/10.1016/S0140-6736(04)17278-4.
3. Doolani, Sanika, Callen Wessels, Varun Kanal, Christos Sevastopoulos, Ashish Jaiswal, Harish Nambiappan, and Fillia Makedon. "A review of extended reality (XR) technologies for manufacturing training" *Technologies* vol. 8,4 (2020): 77. https://doi.org/10.3390/technologies8040077.
4. Zhao, H, H Huang, and S Lin. "Chemical approaches to angiogenesis in development and regeneration." *Methods in Cell Biology* vol. 134 (2016): 369–376. https://doi.org/10.1016/bs.mcb.2016.03.007.
5. Calvert, J, and R Abadia. "Impact of immersing university and high school students in educational linear narratives using virtual reality technology." *Computers and Education* vol. 159,159 (2020 Dec): 104005. https://doi.org/10.1016/j.compedu.2020.104005.
6. Kwok, JYY, JJ Lee, EPH Choi, PH Chau, and M Auyeung. "Stay mindfully active during the coronavirus pandemic: a feasibility study of a mHealth-delivered mindfulness yoga program for people with Parkinson's disease." *BMC Complement Medicine and Therapies* vol. 22,1 (2022): 37. Published 2022 Feb 7. https://doi.org/10.1186/s12906-022-03519-y.
7. Parham, LD, GF Clark, R Watling, and R Schaaf. "Occupational therapy interventions for children and youth with challenges in sensory integration and sensory processing: a clinic-based practice case example. *The American Journal of Occupational Therapy*, 73,1 (2019):7301395010p1–7301395010p9. https://doi.org/10.5014/ajot.2019.731002.
8. Tang YM, et al. "Evaluating the effectiveness of learning design with mixed reality (MR) in higher education." *Virtual Reality* vol. 24 (2020): 797–807. https://doi.org/10.1007/s10055-020-00427-9.
9. Toh, SFM, and KNK Fong. "Systematic review on the effectiveness of mirror therapy in training upper limb hemiparesis after stroke. *Hong Kong Journal of Occupational Therapy* vol. 22,2 (2012): 84–95. https://doi.org/10.1016/j.hkjot.2012.12.009.
10. Desselle MR, RA Brown, AR James, MJ Midwinter, SK Powell, and MA Woodruff. "Augmented and virtual reality in surgery." *Computing in Science & Engineering* vol. 22,3 (1 May-June 2020): 18–26. https://doi.org/10.1109/MCSE.2020.2972822.
11. Moher D, A Liberati, J Tetzlaff, DG Altman, and PRISMA Group. "Preferred reporting items for systematic reviews and meta-analyses: the PRISMA statement." *PLoS Med.* vol. 6,7 (2009):e1000097. https://doi.org/10.1371/journal.pmed.1000097.

12. Zhang, Juhua, et al. "LeNup: learning nucleosome positioning from DNA sequences with improved convolutional neural networks." *Bioinformatics* vol. 34,10 (2018): 1705–1712. https://doi.org/10.1093/bioinformatics/bty003.

13. Sacks, Rafael, Amotz Perlman, and Ronen Barak. "Construction safety training using immersive virtual reality." *Construction Management, and Economics* 31,9 (2013): 1005–1017. https://doi.org/10.1080/01446193.2013.828844.

14. Gadelha, Rene. "Revolutionizing education: the promise of virtual reality." *Childhood Education* vol. 94,1 (2018): 40–43. https://doi.org/10.1080/00094056.2018.1420362.

15. Roberts, Brent W, et al. "Patterns of mean-level change in personality traits across the life course: a meta-analysis of longitudinal studies." *Psychological bulletin* vol. 132,1 (2006): 1–25. https://doi.org/10.1037/0033-2909.132.1.1.

16. Johnson, Julie K, and Paul Barach. "Patient care handovers: what will it take to ensure quality and safety during times of transition." *The Medical Journal of Australia* vol. 190,S11 (2009): S110–2. https://doi.org/10.5694/j.1326-5377.2009.tb02614.x.

17. Norris, Michael W, Kristen Spicer, and Byrd Traci. "Virtual reality: the new pathway for effective safety training." *Professional Safety* vol. 64 (2019): 36–39.

18. Vaughan, Neil, et al. "A review of virtual reality-based training simulators for orthopedic surgery." *Medical Engineering & Physics* vol. 38,2 (2016): 59–71. https://doi.org/10.1016/j.medengphy.2015.11.021.

19. Thompson-Butel, Angelica G, et al. "The role of personalized virtual reality in education for patients post stroke-a qualitative case series." *Journal of Stroke and Cerebrovascular Diseases: The Official Journal of National Stroke Association* vol. 28,2 (2019): 450–457. https://doi.org/10.1016/j.jstrokecerebrovasdis.2018.10.018.

20. Roy, Arnab, et al. "Correction: the evolution of cost-efficiency in neural networks during recovery from traumatic brain injury." *PloS One* vol. 13,10 (12 Oct. 2018): e0206005. https://doi.org/10.1371/journal.pone.0206005.

21. Azuma, Ronald T.. "A survey of augmented reality." *Presence: Teleoperators & Virtual Environments* vol. 6,4 (1997): 355–385. https://doi.org/10.1162/pres.1997.6.4.355.

22. Boyd, N, J Hawkins, T Yang, and SA Valcourt *Augmented Reality: Telehealth Demonstration Application Practice and Experience in Advanced Research Computing*, 2020. https://doi.org/10.1145/3311790.3399629. Portland, OR, USA.

23. Riva, Giuseppe, et al. "Transforming experience: the potential of augmented reality and virtual reality for enhancing personal and clinical change." *Frontiers in Psychiatry* vol. 7 (30 Sep. 2016): 164. https://doi.org/10.3389/fpsyt.2016.00164.

24. Chytas, D, EO Johnson, M Piagkou, A Mazarakis, GC Babis, E Chronopoulos, VS Nikolaou, N Lazaridis, and K Natsis The role of augmented reality in Anatomical education: an overview. *Annals of Anatomy: Anatomischer Anzeiger*, 229 (2020): Article 151463. https://doi.org/10.1016/j.aanat.2020.151463.

25. Milgram, P and F Kishino "A taxonomy of mixed reality visual displays." *IEICE Transactions on Information and Systems* vol. E77-D (1994): 1321–1329. http://citeseerx.ist.psu.edu/viewdoc/summary?doi=10.1.1.102.4646.

26. Wiederhold, Brenda K, and Giuseppe Riva. "Positive technology supports the shift to preventive, integrative health." *Cyberpsychology, Behavior and Social Networking* vol. 15,2 (2012): 67–8. https://doi.org/10.1089/cyber.2011.1533.

27. Baukal, CE, FB Ausburn and LJ Ausburn "A proposed multimedia cone of abstraction: updating a classic instructional design theory." *Journal of Educational Technology* vol. 9,4 (2013): 15–24. Retrieved February 5, 2022, from https://www.learntechlib.org/p/194433/.

28. Bloom, BS. "Time and learning." *American Psychologist* vol. 29,9 (1974): 682–688. https://doi.org/10.1037/h0037632.

29. Sánchez-Cabrero, Roberto, et al. "Improvement of body satisfaction in older people: an experimental study." *Frontiers in Psychology* vol. 10 (12 Dec. 2019): 2823. https://doi.org/10.3389/fpsyg.2019.02823.

30. Khan, MNR, AK Shakir, SS Nadi, MZ Abedin "An android application for university-based academic solution for crisis situation." In: Shakya, S, VE Balas, S Kamolphiwong, KL Du (eds) *Sentimental Analysis and Deep Learning. Advances in Intelligent Systems and Computing*, vol 1408. Springer, Singapore, 2022. https://doi.org/10.1007/978-981-16-5157-1_51.

31. Bracq, Marie-Stéphanie, et al. "Virtual reality simulation in nontechnical skills training for healthcare professionals: a systematic review." *Simulation in Healthcare: Journal of the Society for Simulation in Healthcare* vol. 14,3 (2019): 188–194. https://doi.org/10.1097/SIH.0000000000000347.

32. King, Christopher L, et al. "A trial of a triple-drug treatment for lymphatic filariasis." *The New England Journal of Medicine* vol. 379,19 (2018): 1801–1810. https://doi.org/10.1056/NEJMoa1706854.

33. Hoffmann, Tammy, and Kryss McKenna. "Analysis of stroke patients' and carers' reading ability and the content and design of written materials: recommendations for improving written stroke information." *Patient Education and Counseling* vol. 60,3 (2006): 286–93. https://doi.org/10.1016/j.pec.2005.06.020.

34. Eames S, Hoffmann, T, Worrall L, and S Read. "Stroke patients' and carers' perception of barriers to accessing stroke information." *Topics in Stroke Rehabilitation* vol. 17,2 (2010): 69–78. https://doi.org/10.1310/tsr1702-69.

35. Roy, E, MM Bakr, and George R. "The need for virtual reality simulators in dental education: a review." *Saudi Dent J.* vol. 29,2 (2017):41–47. https://doi.org/10.1016/j.sdentj.2017.02.001.

36. Gamito, Pedro, et al. "Cognitive training on stroke patients via virtual reality-based serious games." *Disability and Rehabilitation* vol. 39,4 (2017): 385–388. https://doi.org/10.3109/09638288.2014.934925.

37. Ausburn, Lynna J., and Floyd B Ausburn "Effects of desktop virtual reality on learner performance and confidence in environment mastery: opening a line of inquiry." *Journal of STEM Teacher Education* vol. 45, 1 (2008): Article 6.

38. Krueger, MW, and S Wilson. "VIDEO PLACE: a report from the artificial reality laboratory." *Leonardo* vol. 18,3 (1985): 145–151. https://doi.org/10.2307/1578043.

39. Bakar, WAWA, MA Solehan, M Man, and IAA Sabri. "GAAR: gross anatomy using augmented reality mobile application." *International Journal of Advanced Computer Science and Applications* 12,5 (2021): 162–168.

40. Pottle, J. "Virtual reality and the transformation of medical education." *Future Healthcare Journal* 6,3 (2019): 181–185. https://doi.org/10.7861/fhj .2019-0036.

41. Calvert, J, and R Abadia "Impact of immersing university and high school students in educational linear narratives using virtual reality technology." *Computers & Education* vol. 159 (2020): Article 104005. https://doi.org/10 .1016/j.compedu.2020.104005.

42. Badarudeen, Sameer, and Sanjeev Sabharwal. "Assessing readability of patient education materials: current role in orthopedics." *Clinical Orthopedics and Related Research* vol. 468,10 (2010): 2572–80. https://doi.org/10.1007/ s11999-010-1380-y.

43. Gunn, T, L Jones, P Bridge, P Rowntree, and L Nissen "The use of virtual reality simulation to improve technical skills in the undergraduate medical imaging student." *Interactive Learning Environments* vol. 26,5 (2018): 613– 620. https://doi.org/10.1080/10494820.2017.1374981.

44. Gaggioli, A "An open research community for studying virtual reality experience." *Cyberpsychology, Behavior, and Social Networking* vol. 20,2 (2017): 138–139. https://doi.org/10.1089/cyber.2017.29063.csi.

45. Riches, Simon, et al. "Virtual reality relaxation for the general population: a systematic review." *Social Psychiatry and Psychiatric Epidemiology* vol. 56,10 (2021): 1707–1727. https://doi.org/10.1007/s00127-021-02110-z.

46. Negro Causa, Erica, et al. "new frontiers for cognitive assessment: an exploratory study of the potentiality of 360° technologies for memory evaluation." *Cyberpsychology, Behavior and Social Networking* vol. 22,1 (2019): 76–81. https://doi.org/10.1089/cyber.2017.0720.

47. Riva, Giuseppe, et al. "Transforming experience: the potential of augmented reality and virtual reality for enhancing personal and clinical change." *Frontiers in Psychiatry* vol. 7 (30 Sep. 2016): 164 https://doi.org/10.3389/ fpsyt.2016.00164.

48. Frolli, A, et al. "Children on the autism spectrum and the use of virtual reality for supporting social skills. *Children* vol. 9, no. 2 (2022): 181.

49. Z. Kevin Zheng, Nandan Sarkar, Amy Swanson, Amy Weitlauf, Zachary Warren, and Nilanjan Sarkar. 2021. "CheerBrush: a novel interactive augmented reality coaching system for toothbrushing skills in children with autism spectrum disorder." *ACM Transactions on Accessible Computing* vol. 14,4, Article 23 (December 2021), 20 pages. https://doi.org/10.1145 /3481642.

50. Lege, R, and E Bonner "Virtual reality in education: the promise, progress, and challenge." *The JALT CALL Journal* vol. 16, no. 3 (2020): 167–180. https://doi.org/10.29140/jaltcall.v16n3.388.

51. Barsom, EZ, M Graafland, and MP Schijven (2016). "A systematic review on the effectiveness of augmented reality applications in medical training. *Surgical Endoscopy*, vol. 30, no. 10): 4174–4183. https://doi.org/10.1007/ s00464-016-4800-6.

52. Kim, H, and J Ben-Othman, "Toward integrated virtual emotion system with AI applicability for secure CPS-enabled smart cities: AI-based research challenges and security issues." *IEEE Network* vol. 34,3 (May/June 2020): 30–36. https://doi.org/10.1109/MNET.011.1900299.

53. Demir, IE, GO Ceyhan, and H Friess "Surgery and the kings of medical science." *Langenbecks Archives of Surgery* vol. 406 (2021): 1669–1671. https://doi.org/10.1007/s00423-021-02242-5.

54. Khor, WS, B Baker, K Amin, A Chan, K Patel, and J Wong. "Augmented and virtual reality in the surgery-the digital surgical environment: applications, limitations, and legal pitfalls." *Annals of Translational Medicine* 4,23 (2016):454. https://doi.org/10.21037/atm.2016.12.23.

55. Lakshmiprabha, NS, A Santos, D Mladenov, and O Beltramello. "[Poster] An augmented and virtual reality system for training autistic children." In 2014 IEEE International Symposium on Mixed and Augmented Reality (ISMAR), 2014, pp. 277–278, https://doi.org/10.1109/ISMAR.2014.6948448.

56. Dafli, Eleni, et al. "Virtual patients on the semantic Web: a proof-of-application study." *Journal of Medical Internet Research* vol. 17,1 (22 Jan. 2015): e16. https://doi.org/10.2196/jmir.3933.

57. Huang, HM, SS Liaw, and CM Lai "Exploring learner acceptance of the use of virtual reality in medical education: a case study of desktop and projection-based display systems." *Interactive Learning Environments* vol. 24,1 (2016): 3–19. https://doi.org/10.1080/10494820.2013.817436.

58. Kononowicz, Andrzej A, et al. "Virtual patients--what are we talking about? A framework to classify the meanings of the term in healthcare education." *BMC Medical Education* vol. 15 (1 Feb. 2015): 11. https://doi.org/10.1186/s12909-015-0296-3.

59. Rodriguez-Andres, D, M Mendez-Lopez, MC Juan, and E Perez-Hernandez. "A virtual object-location task for children: gender and videogame experience influence navigation; age impacts memory and completion time." *Frontiers in Psychology* vol. 9 (2018): 451. Published 2018 Apr 4. https://doi.org/10.3389/fpsyg.2018.00451.

60. Miller, HL, and NL Bugnariu. "Level of immersion in virtual environments impacts the ability to assess and teach social skills in autism spectrum disorder." *Cyberpsychology, Behavior, and Social Networking* vol. 19,4 (2016): 246–256. https://doi.org/10.1089/cyber.2014.0682.

61. Newbutt, N, MM Schmidt, G Riva, and C Schmidt "The possibility and importance of immersive technologies during COVID-19 for autistic people." *Journal of Enabling Technologies* vol. 14,3 (2020): 187–199. https://doi.org/10.1108/JET-07-2020-0028.

62. King, D, S Tee, L Falconer, C Angell, D Holley, and A Mills. Virtual health education: scaling practice to transform student learning: using virtual reality learning environments in healthcare education to bridge the theory/practice gap and improve patient safety. *Nurse Education Today* vol. 71 (2018): 79. https://doi.org/10.1016/j.nedt.2018.08.002 PMID:30205259.

63. Klopfer, E., and Squire, K. "Environmental detectives: the development of an augmented reality platform for environmental simulations." *Educational Technology Research and Development* vol. 56,2 (2008): 203–228. https://doi.org/10.100711423-007-9037-6.

64. Felnhofer, Anna, et al. "Is virtual reality emotionally arousing? Investigating five emotion-inducing virtual park scenarios." *International Journal of Human-Computer Studies* vol. 82 (2015): 48–56.

65. Ferrer-García, Marta, et al. "A randomised controlled comparison of second-level treatment approaches for treatment-resistant adults with bulimia nervosa and binge eating disorder: assessing the benefits of virtual reality cue exposure therapy." *European Eating Disorders Review: The Journal of the Eating Disorders Association* vol. 25,6 (2017): 479–490. https://doi.org/10.1002/erv.2538.

66. Riener, R., and M. Harders (2012). "Introduction to virtual reality in medicine." In: *Virtual Reality in Medicine*, pp. 1–12. https://doi.org/10.1007/978-1-4471-4011-5

67. Seymour, N. "VR to OR: a review of the evidence that virtual reality simulation improves operating room performance." *World Journal of Surgery* vol. 32,2 (2008): 182–188. https://doi.org/10.100700268-007-9307-9 PMID:18060453

68. Morel, M, B Bideau, J Lardy, and R Kulpa. "Advantages and limitations of virtual reality for balance assessment and rehabilitation." *Neurophysiologie Clinique [Clinical Neurophysiology]* vol. 45,4–5 (2015): 315–326. https://doi.org/10.1016/j.neucli.2015.09.007 PMID:26527045.

69. Warburton, S.. Second Life in higher education: assessing the potential for and the barriers to deploying virtual worlds in learning and teaching. *British Journal of Educational Technology* vol. 40,3 (2009): 414–426. https://doi.org/10.1111/j.1467-8535.2009.00952.x

70. Huang, Grace, et al. "Virtual patient simulation at US and Canadian medical schools." *Academic Medicine: Journal of the Association of American Medical Colleges* vol. 82,5 (2007): 446–51. https://doi.org/10.1097/ACM.0b013e31803e8a0a.

71. Lee, Ju Ho, Booyeul Kim, and Junghee Choi. "How does learner-centered education affect teacher self-efficacy? The case of project-based learning in South Korea." *Teaching and Teacher Education* vol. 85 (2019): 45–57. https://doi.org/10.1016/j.tate.2019.05.005.

72. Sezer, B, FG KaraoğlanYılmaz, and R Yılmaz "Integrating technology into the classroom: The learner-centered instructional design." In: Proceedings of the 2nd World Conference on Educational and Instructional Studies –WCEIS. 2013.

Chapter 7

Implications of technological trends toward smart farming

S. Kripa, V. Jeyalakshmi, Masoud Daneshtalab,
and Manickavasagan Annamalai

CONTENTS

7.1 INTRODUCTION

7.1.1 Background

Rapid population growth has increased food production. Traditional procedures may not match demand. Smart farming is a feasible solution for reducing the demand–supply gap, along with traditional methods. Smart

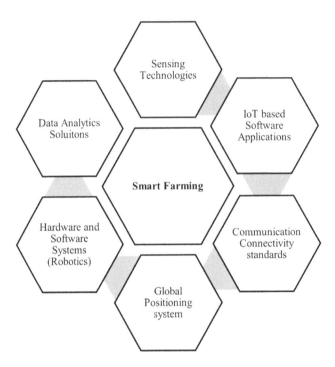

Figure 7.1 Smart farming technologies.

farming uses IoT, sensors, GPS, robotics, and AI on farms like the one in Figure 7.1 to increase agricultural output and quality while lowering labor. Soil, water, light, humidity, and temperature sensors are available to today's farmers. IoT application platforms use farm-specific software. Connectivity standards include cellular and LoRa. Location identifiers include GPS and satellite. Robotics include self-driving tractors and processing factories. Data analytics applications stand alone [1].

7.1.2 Motivation

First, it is necessary to comprehend traditional vs. smart farming. In traditional farming, fertilizer and pesticides must be physically applied across the entire field. Field and financial data are manually maintained, and the weather can't be predicted. Smart farming can solve these problems. Let's learn about smart farming. Smart farming [2] examines each farm to optimize crops and water, and satellite photography identifies farm zones. Smart systems record and analyze data. Precision agriculture gathers data before and after harvest by combining hardware (IoT) and software (software as a service). The data is well-organized, always available, and can be processed from anywhere in the world.

7.1.3 Major contribution

How do automation and robotics aid smart agriculture? In smart farming, IoT (Internet of Things) [3] refers to internet-connected sensing devices, unmanned aerial vehicles, and robotic systems that do analysis and gather data to boost productivity and reliability. Agri-bots, or agriculture automation and robotic technologies, are gaining popularity among farmers globally due to labor shortages [4]. Recent improvements in sensing systems and AI allow agri-bots to learn from their surroundings.

Semi-automated arm-mounted robots can assess weeds and apply insecticides, saving time and money. Robots can harvest and lift [5]. Heavy farming vehicles may be operated from home via phone screens, and GPS can track their location. Drones using cameras and sensors photograph, inspect, and evaluate farmland. Using computing systems, sensors, and GPS, they can be automatically operated or glided. UAV data can help with crop conditions, water management, spraying, sowing, field conditions, plant counts, and yield prediction. Maintaining market competitiveness requires low production costs. VLSI systems enable low-cost automation for all types of farming. Hence FPGA boards are utilized for water level sensing, atmospheric temperature sensing, atmospheric humidity sensing, insect detection in the field, and plant disease classification [6]. A commercial fruit calculation and production prediction system can help growers organize human labor and establish packing and stockpiling arrangements before sale, highlighting the necessity of accurate yield forecasting. Computer vision has played a huge role in smart agriculture by using AI deep learning and machine learning techniques [7]. Deep learning and computer vision are being used in smart agriculture.

7.1.4 Paper organization

This section provides an overview of the key ideas in early plant disease detection. Section 7.2 explains smart agriculture. Section 7.3 introduces IoT in smart agriculture. Section 7.4 describes smart farming's intelligent systems. Section 7.5 discusses measurement techniques like spectroscopy, image processing, and electronic noses in farming.

7.2 WHAT SMART AGRICULTURE CAN DO

Given the size of the agricultural sector, advanced technologies and alternatives are needed to ensure sustainability and reduce environmental damage. Advances in sensor and computer technology allow farmers to remotely monitor their fields. Wireless sensors are increasingly used to better monitor crops in real time. This makes detecting potentially harmful conditions easier. Modern agriculture uses smart equipment and kits for sowing, harvesting, transporting, and storing crops [8]. Robotic weeders and satellites are being used alongside tractors and farm equipment. Sensor nodes can be easily deployed and start collecting data, which can then be accessed online for real-time analysis. Sensing allows crop and location-specific agriculture by collecting accurate site data. Smart agriculture can now connect with IoT, machine vision imaging-based intelligent systems, and deep learning methodologies. IoT is a network of connected devices.

7.3 IOT IN SMART AGRICULTURE

Contrary to popular belief, modern agriculture is more data-driven, accurate, and intelligent than ever. Internet-of-Things (IoT) techniques have transformed nearly every business production, including "sustainable farming," which has shifted from analytical to quantitative methods. Smart agriculture [9] integrates IoT-connected sensing devices with traditional farming practices. Farm owners should visit agro-based locations regularly to assess crop health, according to conventional farming methods. IoT technology is starting to impact manufacturing, healthcare, telecommunications, power generation, and farmland to reduce inadequacies and improve performance across all sectors of the economy. Integrating sensing devices and the Internet of Things into sustainable farming can propel agriculture to unimaginable heights. Yield optimization, automation, resource optimization, climate, and weather effects are shown in Figure 7.2. IoT can improve soil analysis, water management, fertilizers, disease analysis and management, and yield monitoring by implementing smart agriculture methods.

Soil analysis: Soil testing identifies a region's nutrient composition. Nutritional deficits can be corrected if identified. Producers offer a variety of development tools and sensing systems to help farmers track

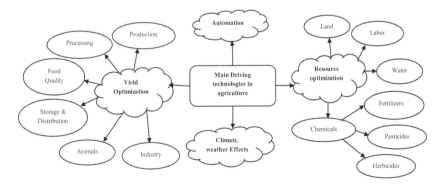

Figure 7.2 Main driving technologies in the agricultural industry.

soil health and, based on the information, suggest solutions to halt degradation. These systems monitor soil firmness, water-holding ability, and absorptivity, reducing corrosion, compaction, soil salinity, acidity, and pollutant levels (by reducing excess fertilizer use). AgroCare's Lab-in-a-Box soil analysis toolset is a whole in itself [10]. Drought reduces crop yield. This problem affects most of the world. Authors [11] used SMOS L2 modeling software to estimate Spain's Soil Water Deficit Index (SWDI) in 2014. To get the most accurate soil water variables, researchers compared them to the SWDI estimated from observations. The authors [12] plotted soil operating parameters using the MODIS sensor to predict soil degradation. Agri-bot is a seedling-focused sensor-based robotic system. The robot uses GPS to generate regional and global maps, while the onboard camera module is linked to a PC.

Water management: Traditional irrigation systems, such as surface irrigation, waste water; therefore, drip and sprinkler irrigation are prescribed to counter this issue. Internet of Things–based solutions and crop water stress index-based water management strategies are expected to increase crop yields [13]. Based on weather and satellite data, each location receives an irrigation index score used to determine water needs. Crop metrics optimize VRI (variable rate irrigation) and enhance water productivity.

Fertilizers: Organic or inorganic fertilizers provide essential nutrients for plant growth and reproduction. Vegetative growth requires nitrogen (N). Roots, flowers, and fruit maturation need phosphorus (P), while stem development and water movement need potassium (K) [14]. Unbalanced fertilizer uses cause subsoil nutrient mismatches and environmental change, as agricultural practices cause 80% of global deforestation. A node-MCU-based robot sprays fertilizer; an ultrasonic sensor detects obstacles [15]. Smart agriculture predicts the exact amount of nutrients needed, reducing the environmental impact of fertilizer use. The Normalized Difference Vegetation Index (NDVI) uses aerial and satellite photographs to examine plant nutrition [16].

Disease analysis and management: Infestations and pathogens cause 20–40% of global crop output losses each year, according to the FAO [17]. Modern disease and pest analysis relies on unprocessed photos taken across cultivated areas by field sensors, UAVs, or satellites [2]. Telemetry images cover large areas and are therefore cost-effective. Field sensors can collect environmental samples, crop growth, and insect conditions throughout agriculture. IoT-enabled automatic nets [18] can acquire, measure, and classify bug types, then upload the data to the cloud for study. Figure 7.3 shows smart agriculture's goals, utilities, and wireless sensors.

Yield monitoring: Yield tracking analyzes grain flow, water content, and planted grain production each season. It allows accurate crop yield and humidity assessments. Smart farming requires yield monitoring

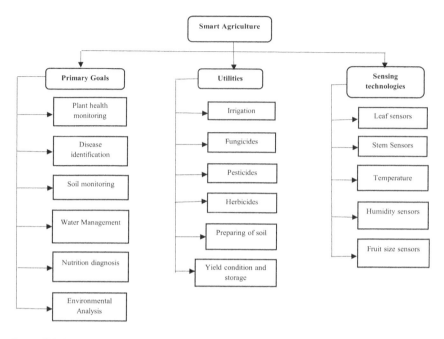

Figure 7.3 Services used in smart agriculture.

both during and before harvest. Installing a [19] yield tracker on any harvester combination and connecting it to the Farm RTX phone app displays true harvesting information and transfers it to the company's browser portal.

7.3.1 Major equipment and technologies

IoT solutions and technologies will help automate, manage, and control smart agriculture. Based on this knowledge, advanced instruments are being developed, such as robotic systems that can sow, irrigate, remove, pluck, cut, fertilize, sprinkle, package, and transport. This transformation is driven by technological advances, the threat of losing a low-cost workforce, and the desire for cheaper, more reliable food. Table 7.1 lists wireless sensors and their smart farming applications.

Table 7.2 illustrates some of the most important agriculture-related mobile apps. The author of [32] featured a few apps, software, and hardware that are helping to make the agricultural system more intelligent. The apps oversee gathering data for future analysis.

Precision agriculture relies on timely information sharing. Depending on accessibility, flexibility, and application requirements, a variety of communication channels and methods are used for this sustainable development goal.

Table 7.1 Wireless sensor uses in agriculture applications

Wireless sensors for agriculture	Purpose
Acoustic sensors	Pest observation and diagnosis, as well as classification of seed kinds according to their sound-absorbing spectrum
Field-programmable gate array (FPGA) sensors	Plant respiration, water management, and moisture are all monitored in real time
Optical sensors	Calculate the number of biological substances in the soil, the moisture and color of the soil, the presence and composition of minerals, and the amount of clay in the soil
Ultrasonic ranging sensors	Tank monitoring, spray distance measurement, weed detection
Optoelectronic sensors	Differentiate plant type, detect unwanted plants and herbicides
Airflow sensors	Measure the air permeability of the topsoil, the quantity of groundwater, as well as soil composition
Electrochemical sensors	Measure nutrient levels, salinity, and PH in the soil
Electromagnetic sensors	Nitrous oxide and biological content in the soil should be measured
Mass flow sensors	Yield monitoring
Soft water level–based (SWLB) sensors	Describe hydrological characteristics such as water level and flow
Light detection and ranging (LIDAR)	It is possible to use land modeling and categorization for a variety of purposes including assessing soil type, monitoring land degradation and losses, and yield prediction
Telematic sensors	Telecommunication between two places
Remote sensing	Assessing crop quality, forecast yield dates, identification of crops and pests, mapping of natural vegetation, and mapping of degradation are all part of the process

Table 7.2 Mobile apps related to smart agriculture

Application	Mobile apps
Water management	Pocket LAI [20], SW App [21], WISE [22], EVAPO [23]
Geographic information system (GIS)	PETEFA [24], EFarm [25]
Fertilizer and pest management, spraying applications, fungicide, and fertigation	Ecofert [26], Snap Card [27], Village Tree [28], Agro-DecisorEFC [29], cFertigUAL [30]
Crop health monitoring	BioLeaf [31]

Low-cost and low-power wireless sensing systems are integrated with Arduino and Raspberry Pi. Raspberry Pi was used to control a sensor-controlled irrigation valve. Lora and Raspberry Pi connected wirelessly to measure soil moisture. For smart farming management and problem-solving, the researchers used a Raspberry Pi and Arduino Uno board-based intelligent system with a microcontroller and mobile phones. FPGA is another controller board. The FPGA DE1 Altera Cyclone V board shows the potential for creating a humidity sensor for intelligent monitoring and water management decisions [33] (Figure 7.4).

7.4 INTELLIGENT SYSTEMS IN SMART AGRICULTURE

Intelligent systems include smart machines. Self-driving cars, drones, and voice and facial recognition are examples. An intelligent system collects, interprets, and acts on inputs. Instead of following rules, the system can discover data structure, identify patterns, and learn techniques and actions. The system gained artificial intelligence through data training and computational methods. Intelligence varies. Figure 7.5 shows an

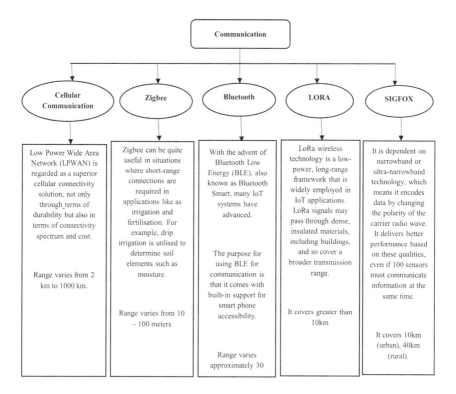

Figure 7.4 Communication technologies.

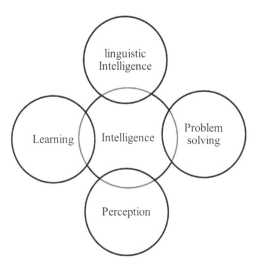

Figure 7.5 Composition of intelligence.

artificially intelligent machine with intelligence, perception, learning, and problem-solving.

7.4.1 Subsets of intelligent systems

Figure 7.6 shows AI subfields. Machine learning (ML) examines and explains data patterns to facilitate learning, reasoning, and decision-making without a human. Machine learning is the ability to submit large amounts of data to a predictive algorithm, which then provides data-driven recommendations and conclusions. The algorithm can use any adjustments to improve its judgment in the future.

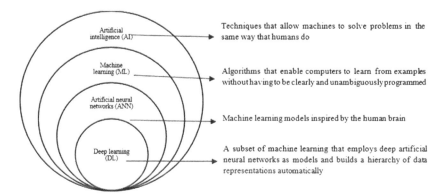

Figure 7.6 Subset of artificial intelligence.

7.4.1.1 Why artificial neural networks?

A neural network arranges algorithms to make trustworthy judgments on its own, while a machine learning model draws conclusions from data collection and processing. "Neural network" refers to a set of algorithms that stimulate brain function by establishing information relationships [34]. A neural network mimics the way a biological neuron learns. An artificial neural network (ANN) has three layers: input, hidden, and output. ANNs can be deep learning or convolutional. It's used in regression, classification, and image recognition.

7.4.1.2 What distinguishes deep learning from machine learning techniques?

Deep learning replicates how humans learn using AI and machine learning. ANNs are layered structures of algorithms used in deep learning applications with less human interaction and more data. Machine learning is a machine's ability to learn from pre-trained data and predict outcomes. Figure 7.7 compares machine and deep learning. Deep learning automatically extracts features from raw data, whereas machine learning requires manual selection. It uses artificial neural networks with many hidden layers, data, and processing power.

7.5 SMART MEASUREMENTS

Most automatic image recognition techniques use observable domain images, allowing for accurate and fast algorithms. As a result, many

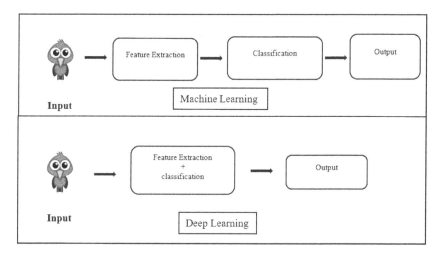

Figure 7.7 Machine learning and deep learning workflow.

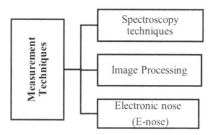

Figure 7.8 Smart ways of measurement.

systems for autonomous crop disease identification are described, including deep learning, probabilistic reasoning, and transfer learning (Figure 7.8). Electronic noses help assess smart farming quality metrics [35]. Infected crop leaves are common. If corrective measures aren't taken in time to stop the disease's spread, agricultural output and quality suffer. Figure 7.9 shows crop-damaging viruses, bacteria, and fungi.

7.5.1 Spectroscopic techniques

Rapid agricultural advances require non-invasive plant disease detection methods. Spectroscopy detects plant disease non-destructively. Spectroscopy examines UV, visible, and infrared interactions with materials. Absorption or emission spectra can show wavelength or frequency proportions. Visible, infrared, impedance, and fluorescence spectroscopy measure the amount of light that reaches a target to identify a pathogen (Figure 7.10).

Various researchers have reported results in Table 7.3 when using the VIS/IR, IS, and FS methods to identify plant disease. Non-invasive field diagnosis of plant diseases can be accomplished using spectroscopy techniques that rely heavily on frequency and spectral reflectance.

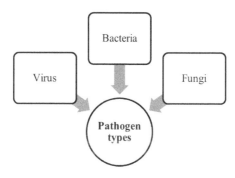

Figure 7.9 Disease types affecting plants.

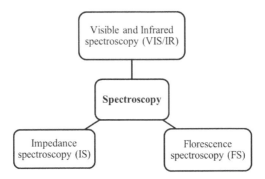

Figure 7.10 Types of spectroscopies.

7.5.2 Image processing

Image processing is essential for diagnosing leaf diseases. Plant diseases can affect food safety and crop production [50]. Detecting plant diseases is vital to agriculture's future. Manually monitoring plant diseases is difficult due to time constraints and disease complexity. Image-processing technologies are best if all other techniques fail. Figure 7.11 shows the computer vision and image processing pipeline.

ML and DL are AI algorithms. Machine learning algorithms can be used with quantifiable and organized data, and the programmer chooses the best algorithm for feature extraction and classification. Deep learning algorithms use unstructured data to retrieve the most important parts. Deep learning algorithms require a lot of data and processing power. Image processing algorithms recognize, estimate, and categorize plant diseases. Described image processing for plant disease diagnosis includes dataset collection/creation, color space identification, ROI segmentation, feature extraction, feature set optimization, classification approach, severity assessment, and result/classifier analysis. Specific methods are recommended for detecting plant diseases because they can affect any part. Leaf disease was diagnosed using image processing and AI [51]. The authors of [52] identified plant leaves by shape and color. Length, width, area, perimeter, and other leaf characteristics are used. The k-nearest neighbor classifier was accurate for 83.5% of 640 leaves from 32 plant species. Color histograms improved accuracy to 87.3%.

The authors of [53] used many visuals. Leaf dimensions, color, shape, and pattern indicate health. They trained with several combinations of the detected qualities. By combining the characteristics with SVM, plant species were categorized with 94.49% accuracy. The authors of [54] classified plant diseases. Using a genetic algorithm, they separated the infected area from the leaf and extracted textural data. When using minimal distance with k-means clustering, they achieved 86.54% accuracy, 93.65% with

Table 7.3 Detection of plant disease using different spectroscopic techniques

Plant type	Pathogen type	Spectroscopy	Wavelength range (nm)	Statistical approach	Cite
Wheat	Spot disease	VIS/NIR	360–900	Nearest neighbor classifier (KNN)	[36]
	Fusarium fungi	VIS/NIR	2,500–15,384	Principal component cluster analysis, partial least square, multiple linear regression	[37]
	Yellow rust	VIS/NIR	350–2,500	Regression analysis	[38]
	Powdery mildew	VIS/NIR	250–1,300	Analysis of variance and regression analysis	[39]
	Health leaf rust	FS	370–800	–	[40]
	Rust infection	FS	400–800	–	[41]
Tomato	Leaf minor damage	NIR spectroscopy	800–2,500	Regression analysis	[42]
Citrus	Huanglongbing (HLB)	VIS/NIR	350–2,500	Differential and regression analyses are both performed in steps. Discriminant analysis with quadratic coefficients	[43]
	HLB	FS	–	Naïve Bayes and decision tree	[44]
	HLB	Raman spectroscopy	785	Principal component analysis and linear discriminant analysis	[45]
	Citrus canker and HLB	FS	420–750	Support vector machine	[46]
Grape	Photo sanitary status	VIS/NIR	400–1,650	Partial least square- discriminant analysis	[47]
	Grapevine leafroll	VIS/NIR	400–2,500	Discriminant classifier	[48]
	Powdery mildew	FS	300–1,000	Analysis of variance	[49]

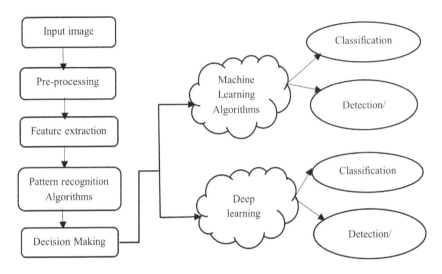

Figure 7.11 Image processing and computer vision pipeline.

their proposed technique, and 95.71% with the SVM classifier. One of the most well-known ANN studies led to transfer learning, which is popular in farming. Table 7.4 shows that deep learning is gaining popularity. CNN, AE, RNN, and RBM are common crop image categorization models. Deep learning has been studied for agricultural disease categorization and detection. A deep learning model based on AlexNet's architectures was developed and implemented in Raspberry Pi 3 [61] to detect plant illnesses using images of healthy or unhealthy plant leaves (Figure 7.12).

Table 7.4 Deep learning models for identifying leaf diseases

Crop type	Dataset	Model	Accuracy	References cited
Thirteen types of leaves	Plant village	Mobile-Net, RCNN	70.53%	[55]
Apple leaf	Plant village	Deep neural network (DNN), grasshopper optimization algorithm (GOA)	98.28%	[56]
Twelve types of leaves	Plant village	CNN-multichannel	93.67%	[57]
Fourteen types of leaves	Leaf disease dataset	Nine-layer-deep CNN	96.46%	[58]
Tomato	Own dataset	CNN, faster R-CNN	91.67%	[59]
Twenty-five types of crops	Open dataset	OverFeat, VGG 16, AlexNet	99.53%	[60]

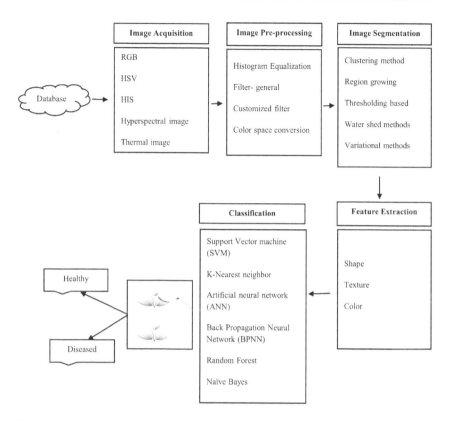

Figure 7.12 Various methods for assessing plant disease.

7.5.3 Electronic nose in food quality

The artificially intelligent nose, also known as the electronic nose, can be used to create pattern detection techniques like the random forest and support vector machine. Non-invasive and quick, the electronic nose diagnoses plant diseases [62]. In the food industry, quality evaluation is difficult to achieve food safety and consumer preferences. Food and agriculture quality can now be determined using volatile organic molecules with distinguishing characteristics. Electronic noses and tongues mimic the human nose and tongue to detect gases and chemicals [63]. Both e-nose and e-tongue have shown great potential and utility in improving food quality tests. e-Noses are gas sensor arrays. Chemical sensor arrays are "electronic tongues" (e-tongues).

7.5.3.1 How electronic nose (e-nose) works

Using the human nose to evaluate products before eating them and detect toxic gases is a useful strategy. Noses can rate smell, but not dangerous gases [64]. Figure 7.13 shows how human olfactory receptors inhale

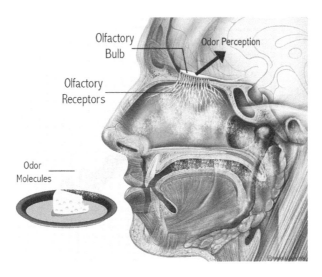

Figure 7.13 Human olfactory system.

volatile food compounds and send them to the olfactory bulb and brain for recognition.

An e-nose, a gas sensor array, fingerprints volatile components [65]. Artificial neural networks and other pattern-matching algorithms can use it to discriminate and classify. Figure 7.14 shows a computer-generated human nose.

7.5.3.2 e-Nose sensing system

Gas sensors are classified by Table 7.5 according to their detecting materials. When targeted molecules interact with sensor materials, they produce conductivity. The sensor's output voltage is monitored to evaluate

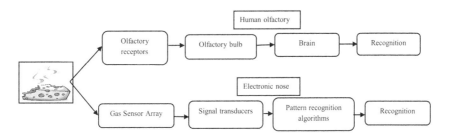

Figure 7.14 e-Nose concept with the olfactory system.

Table 7.5 Gas sensors coated with sensing materials

Gas sensors	Sensing materials	Disadvantages
Metal oxide semiconductor (MOS) sensors	Tin dioxides, zinc oxides, iron oxides, titanium dioxide, nickel oxide, and cobalt oxide are some of the metal oxides	Temperatures of 150 to 400° C are required for the devices to function. As a result, they use a lot of energy and take a long time to warm up before they can start taking measurements
Conducting polymers (CP) sensors	Poly-pyrrole, polyaniline, polythiophene	Another characteristic of conducting polymer sensor arrays is their sensitivity to moisture; similar to MOS sensors, they demand substantial working temperatures to assure that the chemical process between both the electrochemical sensors and the targeted gases takes place
SAW sensors (surface acoustic wave sensors) Quartz crystal microbalance (QCM)	Metal oxides, polymers, carbon nanotubes, graphene, nanocomposites	Complicated circuits, low signal-to-noise ratio, and humidity effect

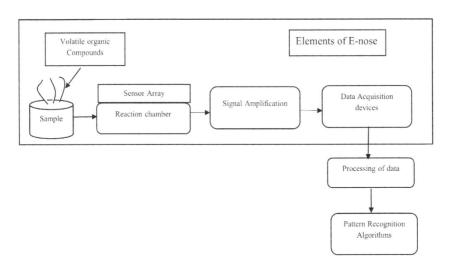

Figure 7.15 Elements of e-nose.

conductivity. The measured voltage pattern includes voltage peak, response speed, and recovery time.

Gas sensor arrays, reaction chambers, signal conditioning, and data acquisition (DAQ) devices are part of the system. Figure 7.15 depicts the structural elements that make up a typical e-nose setup in its entirety.

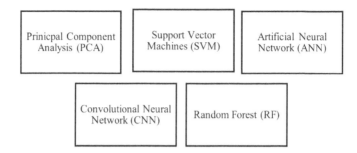

Figure 7.16 Pattern classifiers.

7.5.3.3 Pattern recognition algorithms

Figure 7.16 shows pattern classifiers. Pattern matching techniques group similar outputs into clusters indicating molecules from related food volatile components for sample detection.

7.6 IOT INTEGRATION WITH INTELLIGENT SYSTEMS IN SMART AGRICULTURE

IoT helps farmers detect crop diseases early, limiting disease spread and preserving productivity. Agricultural IoT apps boost production and reduce crop losses from disease. Table 7.6 shows that combining IoT devices and

Table 7.6 Studies on IoT applied with intelligent systems

Detection techniques and algorithms	Parameter evaluation	References cited
The Ride NN Cycling Neural Network, powered by SCA, is an Internet of Things automatic plant pathogens observation and detection system that uses the median filter and a revised optimizer	The accuracy of the Ride NN model based on SCA was 91.56%	[66]
GLCM, RFC, and k-means clustering are used in an IoT system	The overall accuracy of RFC-GLCM-based disease identification and classification was over 99.99%	[67]
SVM with k-means clustering in an IoT system	A text message is sent to the farmer right away	[65]
Rice Talk is a platform that uses an AI model and Internet of Things (IoT) devices	The overall forecast accuracy was 89.4%	[68]
Remote rice monitoring via the Internet of Things using deep learning and transfer learning	Environmental parameters are monitored in real-time	[69]
SVM-based IoT system	Analyses in real-time	[70]

image processing improves disease recognition. The authors of [71] used Node MCU to develop an Internet of Things system with SMS notifications, disease diagnosis, and insecticide applications.

7.7 SUMMARY

Plant diseases manifest differently on different plant parts. Infections are a major problem in agriculture. Classifying crop diseases early reduces disease severity and spread on farms. Modern techniques are evaluated for their effectiveness across multiple crops or crop categories. This chapter highlights considerations and future research directions after finding acceptable techniques. The survey would help researchers understand IoT applications in computer vision, intelligent systems, and crop diagnostics in agriculture. Smart farming uses spectroscopy and electronic noses to measure.

REFERENCES

1. Ayaz, M., Ammad-Uddin, M., Sharif, Z., Mansour, A. and Aggoune, E.H.M., 2019. Internet-of-Things (IoT)-based smart agriculture: Toward making the fields talk. *IEEE Access*, 7, pp.129551–129583.
2. Talaviya, T., Shah, D., Patel, N., Yagnik, H. and Shah, M., 2020. Implementation of artificial intelligence in agriculture for optimization of irrigation and application of pesticides and herbicides. *Artificial Intelligence in Agriculture*, 4, pp.58–73.
3. Rehman, A., Saba, T., Kashif, M., Fati, S.M., Bahaj, S.A. and Choudhary, H., 2022. A revisit of Internet of Things technologies for monitoring and control strategies in smart agriculture. *Agronomy*, 12(1), p.127.
4. Eli-Chukwu, N.C., 2019. Applications of artificial intelligence in agriculture: A review. *Engineering, Technology & Applied Science Research*, 9(4), pp.4377–4383.
5. Oliveira, L.F., Moreira, A.P. and Silva, M.F., 2021. Advances in agriculture robotics: A state-of-the-art review and challenges ahead. *Robotics*, 10(2), p.52.
6. Oukaira, A., Benelhaouare, A.Z., Kengne, E. and Lakhssassi, A., 2021. FPGA-embedded smart monitoring system for irrigation decisions based on soil moisture and temperature sensors. *Agronomy*, 11(9), p.1881.
7. Kakani, V., Nguyen, V.H., Kumar, B.P., Kim, H. and Pasupuleti, V.R., 2020. A critical review on computer vision and artificial intelligence in the food industry. *Journal of Agriculture and Food Research*, 2, p.100033.
8. Mois, G., Folea, S. and Sanislav, T., 2017. Analysis of three IoT-based wireless sensors for environmental monitoring. *IEEE Transactions on Instrumentation and Measurement*, 66(8), pp.2056–2064.
9. Mangla, M., Kumar, A., Mehta, V., Bhushan, M. and Mohanty, S.N.., *Real-Life Applications of the Internet of Things: Challenges, Applications, and Advances*, Apple Academic Press, 1st edn, pp. 536, 2022. https://doi.org/10.1201/9781003277460

10. Agro cares. [online]. Available: https://www.agrocares.com/products/lab-in -the-box/

11. Martínez-Fernández, J., González-Zamora, A., Sánchez, N., Gumuzzio, A. and Herrero-Jiménez, C.M., 2016. Satellite soil moisture for agricultural drought monitoring: Assessment of the SMOS derived Soil Water Deficit Index. *Remote Sensing of Environment*, *177*, pp. 277–286.

12. Vågen, T.G., Winowiecki, L.A., Tondoh, J.E., Desta, L.T. and Gumbricht, T., 2016. Mapping of soil properties and land degradation risk in Africa using MODIS reflectance. *Geoderma*, *263*, pp. 216–225.

13. Shi, X., Han, W., Zhao, T. and Tang, J., 2019. Decision support system for variable rate irrigation based on UAV multispectral remote sensing. *Sensors*, *19*(13), p.2880.

14. Plant nutrition. [online]. [Available] - https://vikaspedia.in/agriculture/crop -production/integrated-nutrient-management/what-is-plant-nutrition

15. Sharma, S. and Borse, R., 2016, September. Automatic agriculture spraying robot with smart decision-making. In *The International Symposium on Intelligent Systems Technologies and Applications* (pp. 743–758). Springer, Cham.

16. Benincasa, P., Antognelli, S., Brunetti, L., Fabbri, C.A., Natale, A., Sartoretti, V., Modeo, G., Guiducci, M., Tei, F. and Vizzari, M., 2018. Reliability of NDVI derived by high-resolution satellite and UAV compared to in-field methods for the evaluation of early crop N status and grain yield in wheat. *Experimental Agriculture*, *54*(4), pp.604–622.

17. Keeping plant pests and diseases at bay: Experts focus on global measures. [online]. Available FAO - News Article: Keeping plant pests and diseases at bay: experts focus on global measures

18. Semios Integrated Pest Management. [online]. Available: Insect Pest Management Solutions - Semios

19. Manfrini, L., Zibordi, M., Pierpaoli, E., Losciale, P., Morandi, B. and Grappadelli, L.C., 2016, October. Development of precision apple fruit growing techniques: Monitoring strategies for yield and high-quality fruit production. In I International Apple Symposium 1261 (pp. 191–198).

20. Orlando, F., Movedi, E., Coduto, D., Parisi, S., Brancadoro, L., Pagani, V., Guarneri, T. and Confalonieri, R., 2016. Estimating leaf area index (LAI) in vineyards using the PocketLAI smart-app. *Sensors*, *16*(12), p.2004.

21. Freebairn, D., Robinson, B., McClymont, D., Raine, S., Schmidt, E., Skowronski, V. and Eberhard, J., 2017, September. SoilWaterApp-monitoring soil water made easy. In Proceedings of the 18th Australian Society of Agronomy Conference.

22. Bartlett, A.C., Andales, A.A., Arabi, M. and Bauder, T.A., 2015. A smartphone app to extend the use of a cloud-based irrigation scheduling tool. *Computers and Electronics in Agriculture*, *111*, pp.127–130.

23. Júnior, W.M., Valeriano, T.T.B. and de Souza Rolim, G., 2019. EVAPO: A smartphone application to estimate potential evapotranspiration using cloud-gridded meteorological data from the NASA-POWER system. *Computers and Electronics in Agriculture*, *156*, pp.187–192.

24. Palomino, W., Morales, G., Huamán, S. and Telles, J., 2018, August. PETEFA: Geographic information system for precision agriculture. In 2018 IEEE XXV International Conference on Electronics, Electrical Engineering and Computing (INTERCON) (pp. 1–4). IEEE.

25. Yu, Q., Shi, Y., Tang, H., Yang, P., Xie, A., Liu, B. and Wu, W., 2017. Arm: A tool for better observing agricultural land systems. *Sensors*, *17*(3), p.453.

26. Bueno-Delgado, M.V., Molina-Martínez, J.M., Correoso-Campillo, R. and Pavón-Mariño, P., 2016. Ecofert: An Android application for the optimization of fertilizer cost in fertigation. *Computers and Electronics in Agriculture*, *121*, pp.32–42.

27. Suen, R.C.L., Chang, K.T., Wan, M.P.H., Ng, Y.C. and Tan, B.C., 2014. Interactive experiences designed for agricultural communities. In CHI'14 Extended Abstracts on Human Factors in Computing Systems (pp. 551–554).

28. Pérez-Castro, A., Sánchez-Molina, J.A., Castilla, M., Sánchez-Moreno, J., Moreno-Úbeda, J.C. and Magán, J.J., 2017. cFertigUAL: A fertigation management app for greenhouse vegetable crops. *Agricultural Water Management*, *183*, pp.186–193.

29. Machado, B.B., Orue, J.P., Arruda, M.S., Santos, C.V., Sarath, D.S., Goncalves, W.N., Silva, G.G., Pistori, H., Roel, A.R. and Rodrigues-Jr, J.F., 2016. Leaf: A professional mobile application to measure foliar damage caused by insect herbivory. *Computers and Electronics in Agriculture*, *129*, pp.44–55.

30. Vineela, T., NagaHarini, J., Kiranmai, C., Harshitha, G. and AdiLakshmi, B., 2018. IoT-based agriculture monitoring and smart irrigation system using raspberry pi. *International Research Journal of Engineering and Technology (IRJET)*, *5*(1).

31. Jindarat, S. and Wuttidittachotti, P., 2015, April. Smart farm monitoring using Raspberry Pi and Arduino. In 2015 International Conference on Computer, Communications, and Control Technology (I4CT) (pp. 284–288). IEEE.

32. Sinha, B.B. and Dhanalakshmi, R., 2022. Recent advancements and challenges of the Internet of Things in smart agriculture: A survey. *Future Generation Computer Systems*, *126*, pp.169–184.

33. Guo, X., 2021. Application of agricultural IoT technology based on 5 G network and FPGA. *Microprocessors and Microsystems*, *80*, p.103597.

34. Verma, K., Bhardwaj, S., Arya, R., Islam, M.S.U., Bhushan, M., Kumar, A. and Samant, P., 2019. Latest tools for data mining and machine learning. *International Journal of Innovative Technology and Exploring Engineering*, *8*(9S), pp. 18–23. https://doi.org/10.35940/ijitee.I1003.0789S19

35. Wilson, A.D., 2013. Diverse applications of electronic-nose technologies in agriculture and forestry. *Sensors*, *13*(2), pp.2295–2348.

36. Lasalle, A. and Muhammed, H.H., 2007. Measuring crop status using multivariate analysis of hyperspectral field reflectance with application to disease severity and plant density. *Precision Agriculture*, *8*(1), pp.37–47.

37. Abramovic, B., Jajic, I., Abramovic, B., Cosic, J. and Juric, V., 2007. Detection of deoxynivalenol in wheat by Fourier transform infrared spectroscopy. *Acta Chimica Slovenica*, *54*(4), p.859.

38. Huang, W., Lamb, D.W., Niu, Z., Zhang, Y., Liu, L. and Wang, J., 2007. Identification of yellow rust in wheat using in-situ spectral reflectance measurements and airborne hyperspectral imaging. *Precision Agriculture*, *8*(4), pp.187–197.

39. Bravo, C., Moshou, D., West, J., McCartney, A. and Ramon, H., 2003. Early disease detection in wheat fields using spectral reflectance. *Biosystems Engineering*, *84*(2), pp.137–145.

40. Römer, C., Bürling, K., Hunsche, M., Rumpf, T., Noga, G. and Plümer, L., 2011. Robust fitting of fluorescence spectra for pre-symptomatic wheat leaf rust detection with support vector machines. *Computers and Electronics in Agriculture*, 79(2), pp.180–188.

41. Lüdeker, W., Dahn, H.G. and Günther, K.P., 1996. Detection of fungal infection of plants by laser-induced fluorescence: An attempt to use remote sensing. *Journal of Plant Physiology*, 148(5), pp.579–585.

42. Xu, H.R., Ying, Y.B., Fu, X.P. and Zhu, S.P., 2007. Near-infrared spectroscopy in detecting leaf miner damage on tomato leaf. *Biosystems Engineering*, 96(4), pp.447–454.

43. Sankaran, S., Mishra, A., Maja, J.M. and Ehsani, R., 2011. Visible-near infrared spectroscopy for detection of Huanglongbing in citrus orchards. *Computers and Electronics in Agriculture*, 77(2), pp.127–134.

44. Sankaran, S. and Ehsani, R., 2012. Detection of huanglongbing disease in citrus using fluorescence spectroscopy. *Transactions of the ASABE*, 55(1), pp.313–320.

45. Pérez, M.R.V., Mendoza, M.G.G., Elías, M.G.R., González, F.J., Contreras, H.R.N. and Servín, C.C., 2016. Raman spectroscopy an option for the early detection of citrus Huanglongbing. *Applied Spectroscopy*, 70(5), pp.829–839.

46. Wetterich, C.B., de Oliveira Neves, R.F., Belasque, J. and Marcassa, L.G., 2016. Detection of citrus canker and Huanglongbing using fluorescence imaging spectroscopy and support vector machine technique. *Applied Optics*, 55(2), pp.400–407.

47. Beghi, R., Giovenzana, V., Brancadoro, L. and Guidetti, R., 2017. Rapid evaluation of grape phytosanitary status directly at the checkpoint station entering the winery by using visible/near-infrared spectroscopy. *Journal of Food Engineering*, 204, pp.46–54.

48. Naidu, R.A., Perry, E.M., Pierce, F.J. and Mekuria, T., 2009. The potential of spectral reflectance technique for the detection of Grapevine leafroll-associated virus-3 in two red-berried wine grape cultivars. *Computers and Electronics in Agriculture*, 66(1), pp.38–45.

49. Bélanger, M.C., Roger, J.M., Cartolaro, P., Viau, A.A. and Bellon-Maurel, V., 2008. Detection of powdery mildew in grapevine using remotely sensed UV-induced fluorescence. *International Journal of Remote Sensing*, 29(6), pp.1707–1724.

50. Pawar, S., Bhushan, M. and Wagh, M., 2020. The plant leaf disease diagnosis and spectral data analysis using machine learning: A review. *International Journal of Advanced Science and Technology*, 29(9s), pp. 3343–3359. http://sersc.org/journals/index.php/IJAST/article/view/15945

51. Orchi, H., Sadik, M. and Khaldoun, M., 2022. On using artificial intelligence and the internet of things for crop disease detection: A contemporary survey. *Agriculture*, 12(1), p.9.

52. Munisami, T., Ramsurn, M., Kishnah, S. and Pudaruth, S., 2015. Plant leaf recognition using shape features and color histogram with K-nearest neighbor classifiers. *Procedia Computer Science*, 58, pp.740–747.

53. Yigit, E., Sabanci, K., Toktas, A. and Kayabasi, A., 2019. A study on visual features of leaves in plant identification using artificial intelligence techniques. *Computers and Electronics in Agriculture*, 156, pp.369–377.

54. Singh, V. and Misra, A.K., 2017. Detection of plant leaf diseases using image segmentation and soft computing techniques. *Information Processing in Agriculture*, 4(1), pp.41–49.

55. Singh, D., Jain, N., Jain, P., Kayal, P., Kumawat, S. and Batra, N., 2020. PlantDoc: A dataset for visual plant disease detection. In Proceedings of the 7th ACM IKDD CoDS and 25th COMAD (pp. 249–253).

56. Al-bayati, J.S.H. and Üstündağ, B.B., 2020. Evolutionary feature optimization for plant leaf disease detection by deep neural networks. *International Journal of Computational Intelligence Systems*, 13(1), pp.12–23.

57. Arsenovic, M., Karanovic, M., Sladojevic, S., Anderla, A. and Stefanovic, D., 2019. Solving current limitations of deep learning-based approaches for plant disease detection. *Symmetry*, 11(7), p.939.

58. Geetharamani, G. and Pandian, A., 2019. Identification of plant leaf diseases using a nine-layer deep convolutional neural network. *Computers & Electrical Engineering*, 76, pp.323–338.

59. De Luna, R.G., Dadios, E.P. and Bandala, A.A., 2018, October. Automated image capturing system for deep learning-based tomato plant leaf disease detection and recognition. In TENCON 2018-2018 IEEE Region 10 Conference (pp. 1414–1419). IEEE.

60. Ferentinos, K.P., 2018. Deep learning models for plant disease detection and diagnosis. *Computers and Electronics in Agriculture*, 145, pp.311–318.

61. Alaeddine, H. and John, M., 2021, March. Deep batch-normalized ELU AlexNet for plant diseases classification. In 2021 18th International Multi-Conference on Systems, Signals & Devices (SSD) (pp. 17–22). IEEE.

62. Cui, S., Ling, P., Zhu, H. and Keener, H.M., 2018. Plant pest detection using an artificial nose system: A review. *Sensors*, 18(2), p.378.

63. Tan, J. and Xu, J., 2020. Applications of electronic nose (e-nose) and electronic tongue (e-tongue) in food quality-related properties determination: A review. *Artificial Intelligence in Agriculture*, 4, pp.104–115.

64. Brattoli, M., De Gennaro, G., De Pinto, V., Demarinis Loiotile, A., Lovascio, S. and Penza, M., 2011. Odor detection methods: Olfactometry and chemical sensors. *Sensors*, 11(5), pp.5290–5322.

65. Wojnowski, W., Majchrzak, T., Dymerski, T., Gębicki, J. and Namieśnik, J., 2017. Portable electronic nose based on electrochemical sensors for food quality assessment. *Sensors*, 17(12), p.2715.

66. Mishra, M., Choudhury, P. and Pati, B., 2021. Modified ride-NN optimizer for the IoT-based plant disease detection. *Journal of Ambient Intelligence and Humanized Computing*, 12, pp.691–703.

67. Devi, R.D., Nandhini, S.A., Hemalatha, R. and Radha, S., 2019, March. IoT enabled the efficient detection and classification of plant diseases for agricultural applications. In 2019 International Conference on Wireless Communications Signal Processing and Networking (WiSPNET) (pp. 447–451). IEEE.

68. Chen, W.L., Lin, Y.B., Ng, F.L., Liu, C.Y. and Lin, Y.W., 2019. RiceTalk: Rice blast detection using the internet of things and artificial intelligence technologies. *IEEE Internet of Things Journal*, 7(2), pp.1001–1010.

69. Win, T.T., 2018. *AI and IoT methods for plant disease detection in Myanmar* (Doctoral dissertation, Kobe Institute OF Computing. Master thesis, submitted to Markon lab department of information technology).

70. Truong, T., Dinh, A. and Wahid, K., 2017, April. An IoT environmental data collection system for fungal detection in crop fields. In 2017 IEEE 30th Canadian Conference on Electrical and Computer Engineering (CCECE) (pp. 1–4). IEEE.
71. Krishna, M., Sulthana, S.F., Sireesha, V., Prasanna, Y. and Sucharitha, V., 2019. Plant disease detection and pesticide spraying using dip and IoT. *Journal of Emerging Technologies and Innovative Research*, 6, pp.54–58.

Chapter 8

A smart sensing technology for monitoring marine environment conditions

Noorashikin Md Noor, Khairul Nizam Abdul Maulud, and Siti Norliyana Harun

CONTENTS

8.1 INTRODUCTION

Monitoring the marine environment has gotten much attention recently, owing to increased concern about climate change. The United Nations (UN) General Assembly approved "Transforming Our World: the 2030 Agenda for Sustainable Development" in September 2015, a global policy agenda for all governments and sectors to use as a roadmap for economic, social, and environmental sustainability growth. The 2030 Agenda is anchored by 17 Sustainable Development Goals (SDGs) and their indicators, which particularly call for the acquisition of new information and the utilization of a diverse variety of databases to enable implementation [1]. Indeed, Article 76 states, "We will promote transparent and accountable scaling-up of suitable public-private cooperation to maximize the value of a diverse range of data, including Earth Observation and geospatial information, while maintaining national ownership in supporting and tracking progress."

Hence, several marine environment monitoring programs have been designed using improved information and technology over the last few years [2]. The Internet of Things (IoT) has been applied to monitoring the marine environment. IoT is a continuous worldwide network architecture built on open and compatible communication protocols that give physical and virtual "things" identity, physical attributes, virtual personalities, and intelligent communication. The IoT has gained significant acceptance as a paradigm capable of altering our society and industry in recent years [3]. It can smoothly integrate numerous devices with sensors, identity, computing, connection, control, as well as communication systems. Wireless sensor networks (WSNs) are crucial elements of the IoT. They are composed of many dispersed sensors connected via wireless networks and used to monitor both physical and environmental factors.

WSNs, a part of the IoT, have been commonly deployed across a wide range of smart technology over the last two decades, consisting of smart cities, houses, and transportation [4]. Undoubtedly, similar IoT-based technology may monitor and protect the marine environment. As our community and economy have developed, scientists and intellectuals have shifted their focus to the marine environment. The IoT enables smart object control with substantially more robust data processing capabilities. In a marine environment monitoring system, sensors are used to assess and observe assorted chemical and physical aspects of the marine environment, such as water temperature, salinity, pH, and chlorophyll levels.

8.2 OVERVIEW OF IOT

Some of the IoT-based marine environment monitoring applications include water quality, wave, and ocean-sensing monitoring. Multiple IoT approaches, including designing, detecting, controlling, and communicating are used in different applications [5]. The IoT approach depends on hydrographic and oceanographic vessels. Examples of IoT-based monitoring applications are water quality, marine fish farm, coral reef, and wave and current monitoring systems. Temperature, turbidity, pH, and dissolved oxygen are measured in the water quality monitoring system, while the number of uneaten feed tracks of water quality is kept in the marine fish farm monitoring system [6]. Additionally, the habitat of the coral reef is monitored using the coral reef monitoring system while waves are measured to keep waterway routing safe in the wave and current monitoring system.

The IoT-based marine environment monitoring aims are to make the world "knowable, thinkable, and controllable," signifying that the IoT can observe and control the environment through gathering, assessing, and interpreting data. This would help in intelligent decision-making for the marine environment. The steps in designing layers for an IoT-based system are described in the following, as proposed by Antao et al. [7].

8.2.1 Perception and execution

The basic layer is the perception and execution layer. Sensors and controller units are incorporated to gather data and execute orders. This layer may consist of GPS detectors for marine environment monitoring, power storage devices, and water condition monitoring sensors.

8.2.2 Data transmission

The data transmission layer's main purpose is to convey different collected information to the following layer using the wireless network. Control actions done by applications are continuously sent by the earlier layer, enabling linked equipment to perform acquired actions (lowering or increasing temperature, relocating devices, or automatic fish feeding).

8.2.3 Preprocessing data

This layer would be essential to the design of the IoT system. Raw information can be kept and preprocessed in this location utilizing developed data mining tools. The data is collected or destroyed, cleansed, adapted, filtered, and distributed as required.

8.2.4 Application

The application layer responds to user requests for diverse programs by providing services. For example, it can provide water quality and condition information and the amount of fish waste in a farm. The layer's major objective is to provide a smart software program that meets users' needs. This involves tracking coral reefs, monitoring water quality and fish farms, and measuring tides across IoT-based marine environments.

8.2.5 The organizational layer

The business layer is responsible for overseeing the whole IoT system's operation, such as developing business models, control charts, and diagrams. It also observes and assesses the outcomes of the other four levels following business frameworks to provide services and ensure customers' confidentiality.

WSNs have gotten much press in recent years due to IoT-based marine environment concepts. A WSN is made up of a collection of linked sensor nodes that work cooperatively to analyze and obtain information about the marine environment [8]. Compared to typical sensors, these sensor nodes are often compact and affordable, with limited processing power. A sensor node is a unit embedded in a WSN that measures several physical parameters, like temperature, salinity, pH, and turbidity. The node comprises a control, transmission, and power unit with onboard storage. The power unit provides the energy supply. The data gathering and transmission procedures are controlled by the control unit. The data transmission unit synchronizes signals between a node and other nodes. It enables data exchange without going to the observation point, which is useful when such a sensor unit is installed inside a confined territory or at an otherwise inaccessible location, like deep under the sea [9].

WSNs serve as a foundation for advanced inventions involving the observation, analysis, and control of the physical world. WSN improvements have led to small-footprint, budget-cutting, and energy-saving multipurpose instruments that include sensors, data storage, and transmission units. These smart units have been effectively applied to various fascinating domains, including security, ecology, leisure, medicine, and the automotive sector, essential parts of smart applications [10]. WSNs function as links between the physical and the virtual, allowing the virtual world to observe and react to changes in the physical sector [11]. The two largest communication companies, Ericsson and Cisco, expect that by 20 years later, there will be 50 billion "things" connected to the internet, all sensing, controlling, or delivering information about the physical world. WSNs also provide novel solutions for the real-time monitoring of maritime ecosystems.

In a WSN, devices are classified into three categories of nodes: a sensor, a router, and a sink node [12]. Examples of sensor nodes include detection sensors that evaluate the physical properties of water, a communication module that transmits or receives data, and a power supply component. A router node may be linked to two sensor nodes, subject to the design chosen. The function of a sink node is to interface with the core network through a range of data routing protocols. Generally, a sensor node comprises five major components: one or more sensors that collect environmental data. The functions are managed by the central hub, which takes the form of a microprocessor. The design of a sensor is shown in Figure 8.1. A transmitter connects with the environment, while memory is utilized to keep data during the process. The battery provides energy to all components. To ensure a relatively long network lifespan, maximizing energy efficiency through a battery is critical. As a result of this requirement, data processing functions are frequently distributed across the network [13].

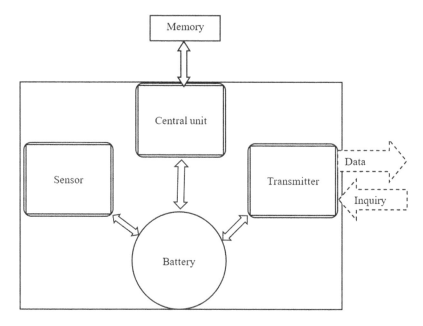

Figure 8.1 Design of a sensor node.

WSNs have particular requirements compared to other applications for IoT-based marine environment monitoring due to radio signal instabilities caused by weather and radio antenna oscillations and efficiency energy issues where low power consumption is crucial for long-flow and low maintenance costs [14]. This is especially important for expensive and challenging equipment to replace in far offshore locations.

WSNs enable high spatial and temporal scale issues to be met. In recent years, sensing technology has progressed to a mature degree in cost and accuracy, allowing for monitoring substantial geographical areas with high temporal frequency. However, the extensive use of instruments to collect data on large longitudinal scales has significant hurdles. Costly installation and operation of deployment equipment, together with sensor inaccuracy owing to circumstances including sensor drifting, lead to limited spatial variability of the majority of the marine zone [15, 16].

A large volume of data created by WSNs is too large to manage manually [17]. These massive amounts of data must be intelligently processed, indexed, and documented so that operators, scientists, and policymakers may better understand, access, and manage them. Current research shows that WSNs have their constraints, such as dependability concerns, the usage of passive systems, and data without context. Sensors are susceptible to noise, malfunction, and damage in aquatic environments, particularly marine conditions. Particles can block probes, especially optical-based sensors, resulting in noisy data that may not reflect the actual property of a water body. Sensors that

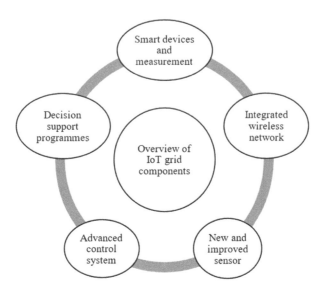

Figure 8.2 The IoT components in marine environment sensors.

are not working correctly can result in inaccurate data or coverage gaps. The smart sensor is a highly complicated combination and integration of numerous digital and non-digital technologies and systems from a technical component viewpoint. The fundamental component of IoT components is seen in Figure 8.2: i) new and improved sensor components, ii) smart devices and measurement, iii) integrated wireless network, iv) decision support programs, and v) advanced control system. Smart sensors do not have to be centralized but can have many control stations integrated highly.

8.3 CHARACTERISTICS OF SENSORS

The following characteristics should be considered when adapting the IoT-based marine monitoring system in harsh marine conditions [18]:

(i) Water resistance: water resistance is required for sensors and nodes.
(ii) Low consumption of energy: due to the enormous communication distances and constantly changing environment, additional procedures may be necessary to ensure data transmission reliability. Inconsistency between the transmitter and the receiver can be triggered by radio antenna oscillation, and poor weather conditions can also decrease radio transmission reliability.
(iii) Strong equipment tolerance: as the marine environment is severe and the weather is unpredictable (hurricane, high tides), the equipment used must be highly resistant.

(iv) Other concerns: owing to the difficulty of deployment and maintenance, the node and sensor must be well grounded, and equipment
must be constructed to withstand any vandalism.

8.4 PLATFORM FOR SENSORS

The technology used to monitor the oceans can be classified into two broad
categories: 1) the platform from which the measurement is made, such as
a research vessel, a static observatory, or an unmanned automated vehicle;
and 2) the sensor or method used to make the measurement, such as a
multi-beam sonar array, a seabed camera, or a chemical analysis of a physical sample. These categories have made remarkable strides, with the possibility of moving away from traditional operator-based solutions and toward
technology-based solutions. The following is a description of monitoring
platforms currently in use for marine monitoring with simplified details in
Table 8.1.

Table 8.1 List of platforms with sensors used in marine environment monitoring

Type of platform	Examples of sensors	Purpose	Restriction
Marine observation system with static point	Various sampling techniques including conductivity temperature and depth (CTD), video imaging, and sonar	Water quality and tide monitoring, biosensor mounting	Limited areas (not within shipping channels), expensive cost
Unmanned aerial vehicle (remotely piloted aircraft)	GPS, camera	Survey of commercial shoreline	Legal restrictions on flying patterns (up to a distance of one kilometer from the pilot, limitation power of batteries)
Mobile platform (subsurface floats, remotely operated and autonomous vehicles)	Video imaging, CTD, water samples collection, and acoustics	Mapping of seabed, Argo float for oceanographic measurement	Battery power should always be initiated and replenished
Satellite	Data exchange via autonomous platform, imaging using camera system	Water quality	Measurements can only be done on surface of sea, cloud cover may limit the ability, expensive

8.4.1 Marine observation system with static point

Globally, marine observation systems plus static points have been installed to collect in situ data on various physicochemical parameters. Fixed depth, fixed anchors, and seafloor rovers have all been deployed using equipment suitable for long navigation. Traditional platforms, for example, boats, have become less likely to solve temporal operations and exhibit a high degree of temporal changes. These platforms assess nitrogen, dissolved oxygen, chlorophyll, salinity, temperature, and turbidity. This information is used to determine the degree of eutrophication [19]. Additionally, these data have contributed to developing more comprehensive monitoring, model evaluation, satellite marine services, and ecosystem behavior research. Besides that, fixed-point moorings are used to monitor the tide pattern in enhancing flood forecasting models and risk assessments. For instance, WaveNet handles the United Kingdom's primary wave data archive, which helps engineers design coastal water barriers and offshore projects [20]. The fixed-point marine observation system can assess the marine temperature, salinity, and tide.

8.4.2 Subsurface floats

Subsurface floats are self-propelled devices that move in synchrony with the ocean to monitor it as it can be determined via deep-water acoustics or by developing floats to alter buoyancy and resurface. They can be observed by satellite. Floats have been developed to monitor the ocean's flow field. On the other hand, today's floats act as a platform for supplementary hydrographic assessments (oxygen, temperature, salinity), with data communicated back by satellite [21]. Worldwide coverage, constant direct data supply, ease of installation, cost-effectiveness, the ability to analyze big groups of floats, and vertical precision when sinking and resurfacing are all benefits of subsurface floats. The potential of misplacing them and the geographical location of measurements reliant on irregular motion are also potential downsides [22]. As an outcome, it may be challenging to focus findings on specified geographical processes or systems. Subsurface floats that are not recovered regularly must be subjected to restrictive inspection and calibration procedures. Due to the float's buoyancy control, this method does not allow complete water column sampling [23].

An example is Argo float, which revolutionized how oceans' internal workings are monitored, one of the most recognized subsurface float designs [21]. Since 1999, the Argo project has been operating globally, with over 5,000 profiled drifting floats monitoring salinity, temperature, and depth down to 2,000 m below the ocean. The ability of Argo floats to do biogeochemical measurements is also developing. Argo data have been used to investigate the properties, ocean circulation, dynamics, and ocean forecasting [24].

8.4.3 Remotely autonomous and operated vehicles (ROV)

ROV is often attached to a ship and used to collect data via a controller. The equipment transports data, enabling continuous and comprehensive activity. Monitoring was permitted in unknown locations and throughout the study [25]. They operate autonomously of a control center, allowing them to travel more ground. AUV size and power advancements enable missions to last weeks or months, with ranges of thousands of kilometers and depths of thousands of kilometers [26]. These developments have been put to the test to monitor the marine environment.

Submarine gliders are one of the ROVs for ocean monitoring. Gliders steer instead of drifting with the current as they run autonomously via a ship while connecting through a satellite for data transfer [27]. Gliders require very little energy, which keeps them operational for months. The internal batteries (which are often charged using photovoltaic cells) are utilized for routing and data exchange. They are faster than subsurface float, with speeds ranging between one and three knots [28]. They are, however, a good platform for ocean monitoring when running an operated boat is potentially risky due to their lower operating costs, durability, and long-term endurance. USVs can be equipped with water quality sensors, profiling of currents, and other sensors. Additionally, USVs' web-based navigation and operation system enables them to be re-tasked as required if an unexpected occurrence occurs.

8.4.4 Satellite

Earth observation (EO) data can considerably aid in marine monitoring of real-time data by providing system-wide perspectives on systems with high spatial rates. Furthermore, the data on ocean color progressively stipulates water quality measures at spatial and temporal scales that are becoming more important [29]. Concerns have been voiced about the applicability of EO products to officially directed monitoring operations due to intrinsic instability. However, the current invention of specialized algorithms has substantially aided satellite retrievals of turbidity, chlorophyll, and suspended particulate matter in the dense ocean [30]. Incorporating the EO data is critical in enhancing data collection for various marine monitoring, such as chlorophyll assessment and detecting the presence of harmful algal bloom [31, 32]. The data generated from satellites is commonly employed for mapping by monitoring parameters over time variables. Each year, satellites collect vast amounts of data, but only the relevant data is assessed locally by the satellite owner, namely, NASA, using appropriate tools like Python or Matlab.

8.4.5 Remotely piloted aircraft (RPA)

An RPA is an automobile that is relatively small and flies with various sensors, most commonly a camera system. They are classified as either rotary or fixed-wing aircraft, each with several characteristics [33]. These vessels remain outfitted with navigation, control, and data-collecting hardware and software [34]. RPAs are increasingly being employed as a component of statutory monitoring programs. Advances in camera technology and image processing will significantly boost their use to monitor coastal species such as reef and shellfish. RPAs can outperform traditional human-based intertidal survey methodologies in terms of data-collecting speed and coverage [35]. If a suitable equipment and sensors pair is supplied and the survey location is remotely feasible, these benefits can result in improved data collection at a cheaper cost.

8.5 TYPE OF SENSORS FOR DATA COLLECTION

Chemical, biogeochemical, physical, and biological characteristics are among the sensors available for marine monitoring [36]. The platforms on which the sensors can be placed are typically determined by their sensor systems which are often defined by their power usage and weight. Given recent advancements in lighter and more affordable electronic parts, a budget sensor for measuring factors including fluorescence, pH, salinity, and temperature has been designed, mainly for the marine environment [37, 38]. These can be implemented into monitoring programs if they have enough stability and sensitivity. With the growing number and range of sensors plus the quality of raw values generated, data sharing and sensor integration become more challenging. The following sections describe the types of sensors used in marine environment monitoring and a summary is shown in Table 8.2.

8.5.1 Acoustics

The seabed and water column are ensonified, and the reflected wave is analyzed using the acoustic technique. Such data can be used to create habitat mapping and geographical representations showing seabed structures, bathymetric features, and information on the population of biotas, such as fish and zooplankton. Numerous systems are available, ranging from smaller panels dragged or installed on poles to enormous boat displays with single or multiple beams. By directing a band of rays, a multibeam echo sounding (MBES) sonar may determine the seabed depth [39]. The cross-section of the seabed is joined when the ship sails forward, and it can be used to build a bathymetric model which considers ship motion and different depths of water caused by tides. By evaluating the strength of the

Table 8.2 List of techniques used in sensors for marine environmental monitoring

Sensor technique	Approach	Purpose	Restrictions
Acoustic	Mobile/fixed automated platform	Measurement of depth and monitoring of seabed	Specialized ship is needed, the need for storage of big data
Camera	Unmanned aerial vehicle, mobile/fixed automated platform, satellite	Monitoring of biodiversity, harmful algal bloom, and assessment of fish stock	High energy consumption, professional specialist is needed to analyze the image, the need for storage of big data
Satellite sensor	Embedded to satellite in space	Observation of ocean's tide and wind, current and oil spills, detection of ships	Expensive cost, expertise needed to analyze the data
Biosensors	Tagging to marine organism, mobile/fixed automated platform	Identification of marine species organism, phytoplankton, and zooplankton	The process of designing is complex and needs expert skills

returned signal, MBES can also provide some information on the type of seafloor.

Scan sonar is a deployed propeller sensor that delivers a cone-shaped ray further into the water to identify structures emerging from the seabed [40]. Single-beam echo sounders have been employed in fisheries acoustic metrics for evaluating systems in the water layer for some time. Due to the assertive aggregative behavior of many aquatic species and the subsequent uneven dispersion, trawling itself may give insufficient data on the location and population of the target species. Acoustic scatterers' distribution function, also known as resonance frequency, can estimate species diversity and distribution [41].

Recent improvements in marine acoustic technologies include the application of omnidirectional sonars (MBES), which have some advantages for fishery management research, including better monitoring of marine species near the seabed and a method for continuously resolving several locations at the same range by narrowing the sonar signal bandwidth and merging the different rays [42]. The omnidirectional multispectral sonar was designed to conduct investigations in the acoustic blackout spot in the sea bed as well as the location of the external sensors, which can be deployed on the ships [43]. Acoustic data from fisheries assessments can be used for spatial distribution and other metrics of the geographic population of a species.

8.5.2 Cameras

Seabed digital images and video are advantageous in support of various marine environment monitoring purposes. In conjunction with a sensor system that monitors the difference in a range of marine environments, high-definition (HD) cameras could be connected to remotely operated panels and launched into habitats where other sample collection techniques would be ineffective, including rocky corals or within sheltered locations populated by indigenous biodiversity. The real-time analysis could be utilized for a different purpose, including searching for specific parameters or stock assessment and identifying the existence of aimed local species plus visual proof of seabed alteration [44]. Sediment profile imagery (SPI) is a technique that employs cameras to investigate the point at which sediment mixes the waters in real time. Each survey creates high-resolution still images and clips on the diversity of species with habitats. At the moment, a specific data archive unit capable of storing seabed photographic data and supporting the processing of various information is needed [45].

8.5.3 Satellite sensors

The ocean color sensors embedded on assorted satellites can detect tiny volumes of infrared light (transmitted light) received by the ocean. This is a mean estimated at up to "one optical depth" from the top of the sea, which is the longest depth a satellite is able to view [46]. This depth ranges from 20 to 25 meters in the most visually transparent seas. NASA (National Aeronautics and Space Administration) operates OLCI (Ocean and Land Colour Instrument) and MODIS (Moderate Resolution Imaging Spectroradiometer), both sensors held by orbiting satellites observing the marine environment concurrently. Global coverage is provided in the apparent and near-infrared spectral zones (wavelength range of 400 to 800 nanometers, nm), with complete resolution down to 300 m, and revisit frequencies varying from every day to once per four days [47]. Notably, this information is openly accessible on the NASA and ESA websites. Ocean-color remote sensing is a valuable technique for large-scale environmental monitoring due to daily overpasses and comprehensive spectrum information. Cloud cover as well as weather conditions, sunlight, the world's geometry, and the optical properties of the ocean itself can all alter the data accuracy received from space. Increased uncertainty is associated with data from the polar zone, shorelines, and areas with a consistently large percentage of clouds. Calibration in situ is crucial for "ocean" EO data, and spectral data gathered in uncertain marine environments improves significantly from integrated algorithms [48, 49].

8.5.4 Biosensors

While physiochemical sensors are widely used and recognized in monitoring the marine environment, biosensors have not yet been developed to attain their maximum potential. Biosensors encompass various types of sensors and technically complex analysis devices. Complete organisms, particular compounds, for example, deoxyribonucleic acid (DNA), enzymes, and antibodies, are all examples of biological sensing elements. Numerous studies have been conducted on existing technology [50]. The studies demonstrate possible uses and combinations with platforms mentioned previously. However, several limitations include sensor durability, biological sensing elements accessibility, and a lack of commerce for marine applications. With remarkable progress in cell biology, the application of biology analysis and biosensors in a wide range of marine implementations, such as identifying harmful algal blooms or even threatened species, has become more cost-effective, paving the way for their incorporation into marine monitoring.

8.6 CHALLENGES IN APPLICATION

When compared to traditional sensors, sensor networks are a major advance. This, however, comes with new difficulties. Cost, power, maintenance, and data transmission capabilities limit the number of large-scale sensor networks deployed in an area, especially in an aquatic setting. Currently, there are only a few of these devices in use. Data errors and node failure are also common in sensing devices. Xu et al. [51] highlighted a number of scenarios that could cause a WSN to fail, including hardware or software failure, radio interference, battery depletion, or deliberate harm. In addition, another recessive failure is "data fault." Despite the fact that the sensor "works," it gives false data, leading to incorrect conclusions at the application stage. Previous research has revealed a significant issue that deserves additional investigation. Furthermore, sensor networks in aquatic environments provide particular difficulties. Devices, particularly sensing probes, are exposed to severe environments, requiring higher protection degrees. As WSNs frequently need to cover long distances and use attenuated data transmission channels, energy consumption is typically substantially greater in marine situations [52].

Sensor node movement must be taken into account. Sensor installation and maintenance costs in marine conditions are significantly greater than on land. Biofouling or unwanted microorganism growth on the surface of equipment is a serious problem in marine environment monitoring, restricting the time for the sensor to deploy [53]. Even though the sensor price is decreasing, the cost of establishing and maintaining such sensing systems remains considerable. Typically, raw sensor data lacks high-level information that is easily understandable and manipulable at the application level. The current status of research in WSNs is not domain-specific. New physical/chemical sensors, as well as anti-fouling solutions, are being developed on a continuous basis. However, recently, it has been demonstrated that adding new sensing modalities can significantly improve established WSNs. Vision sensing or sensors based on satellite have been provided in a variety of scenarios as a possible alternative sensing mode. Visual sensing is a useful sensing mode that may be used to supplement the use of in-situ sensor networks in a variety of projects [54]. Giving relevant information provides detailed images that can be used to verify in-situ measurements or manage WSNs. For instance, operators can search visual data from the time of the occurrence detected by an in-situ sensor to determine whether the incident was prompted by local activity. Visual sensors can also be used to generate in-situ sensor measurements or change the sample rate of in-situ sensors (adaptive sampling) to maximize in-situ sensor efficiency.

With billions of users worldwide and millions of images published daily, platforms for social media like Flickr, Google, Twitter, Tumblr, as well as Facebook have produced a new kind of WSN [55]. Compared to typical wireless sensor networks, social media establishes a "virtual WSN." Users' social media posts act as "sensor nodes," while the images and messages serve as "sensor measurements." Unlike standard WSN measurements, these sensor measurements are incredibly diverse and unreliable. Numerous initiatives have begun investigating how social media data could be utilized for surveillance purposes. Additionally, social media has been crucial in responding to environmental challenges. Ushahidi, a platform that allows cyber citizens to produce disaster-zone maps for rescuers, employed social network users to organize volunteers following the Haiti earthquake. Twitter was used at the time of the flood in Red River Valley, USA, through March and April 2009 [55]. Twitter is a social networking platform that allows users to send and receive short messages called "tweets." They concluded that the use of social media is associated with environmental risks.

Further, it has been revealed that by incorporating intelligence into sensor networks via cutting-edge computer engineering techniques, notably in the computational industry, existing WSNs could be considerably improved. According to Zhu [56], more effective but perhaps more widely available budgeted sensors could be employed for indicators to change the operational parameters of more complicated nodes. The crucial nodes can be triggered by data obtained from relatively incompetent sensors. These more advanced sensors can then validate or disprove the data collected by a less dependable sensor. It thus decreases the operating frequency of the more complicated sensor node, thereby lowering their energy consumption and increasing their overall efficiency while preserving high-resolution sensing. As data transmission, particularly over long distances, consumes a large amount of energy in WSNs, this can significantly reduce energy consumption. Integration of information is not a novel concept; it has been addressed in several domains in a variety of ways. In the scope of marine environmental monitoring, knowledge management refers to the process of collecting input from various sensors that provides the most comprehensive, precise picture of the observed marine ecology [57, 58].

As mentioned earlier, marine environment monitoring systems function in severe conditions, making replacement batteries expensive and complicated. As a result, they have an intelligent energy management system, specifically concerning energy harvesting. Battery-powered sensor nodes, capacitor-powered sensor nodes, fuel cell–powered sensor nodes, and fuel cells are well-known energy sources. Batteries are frequently used in sensor nodes, and they are present in more than half of the systems analyzed. However, using batteries in sensor nodes has several disadvantages, including the difficulty of recharging them, the possibility of power loss during usage, and environmental pollution [59]. As a result, it is necessary to consider alternative energy sources representing the node. Sustainable energy is a natural process that uses fuel cell technologies, such as the sun, tidal currents, and wind.

Energy consumption in the network typically increases rapidly as data rates increase. Considering battery degradation is unpredictable, the fast proliferation of IoT devices needs efficient battery technology. On the other hand, devices used to monitor the marine environment are diverse, each with its range of abilities and criteria [60]. Consequently, future WSNs will require a routing technique that is both cost-efficient and energy-efficient in time and area. Multilateral organizations' projects are multiplying as the scope of monitoring the marine environment develops. Depending on the project's objectives, different application platforms and methodologies have unique features that are incompatible.

Along with IoT communications protocols, it is vital to offer the industry specifications for IoT equipment used to monitor the marine environment at multiple government levels and marine environmental management organizations. As more than just a result, standardized platform development for monitoring the marine environment has various challenges, including the following: i) standardizing the equipment of the IoT, such as nodes and sensors [61–64], routers, and gateways; ii) standardizing the platform of the IoT, such as algorithms and network design; and iii) standardizing the transfer of IoT data, such as cloud and data archives.

8.7 CONCLUSION

Monitoring the marine environment has become increasingly popular in recent decades, with governments and academic institutions having made significant investments in research and development in this field. The IoT has been proven beneficial with the advanced information and communication technology of diverse marine environment monitoring technologies. Most systems and applications produced to date are for the sensing of oceans, according to a detailed assessment of several related projects. Fish farms, coral reefs, and wave and current activity have been carefully monitored. Numerous initiatives concentrated on a particular technology or equipment, such as vessels, energy efficiency, routing algorithms, data transfer systems, or data processing methods.

Energy management is typically approached from two perspectives: lesser energy usage and alternative energy sources. Energy usage can be reduced by designing nodes and implementing better network algorithms. Numerous researchers have examined alternate renewable energy sources such as solar, wind, and tides; however, this renewable power accounts for only approximately one-third of all current systems. Not only can IoT technology provide feedback to marine environment management organizations to speed up decision-making, but it might also allow remotely deployed equipment and automated vessels for tracking in-situ parameters in order to prevent marine disasters (thunderstorms, typhoons, oil spills). This is an area of study and technology that is constantly increasing. Several research concerns and possibilities were recognized in this study, including energy management, system platforms, technological standardization, and marine environmental monitoring measures.

Sensors capable of detecting critical physical and chemical factors (salinity, turbidity, chlorophyll, temperature) have contributed to this development, but so has basic knowledge of marine biology and ecological concepts. A shortage of sensors with sufficient spatial, temporal, and spectral resolution for ocean color sensing, and even a shortage of conceptual frameworks for understanding these data, constrain satellite monitoring of ocean areas. For instance, a satellite embedded with a salinity sensor can only monitor 200 kilometers of the shore, while at the moment, there seem to be no satellites tracking the salinity of the coastal sea surface. Additionally, wind products acquired from satellites are unreliable for shorelines. Indeed, only some satellites are able to supply the high-quality data required for dynamic research of coasts impacted by waves and prone to daily fluctuations. Multispectral images of the future may also comprehend the complications of shoreline waterways. In keeping with the open ocean coverage by satellite, a far more globalized and integrated strategy for coastlines should be favored. High-resolution coastal physical and biogeochemical model data should be supplied daily. Thus, oceanography provides an unparalleled opportunity to understand the ocean's sensitivity to climate change, particularly as the precision of climate models develops.

REFERENCES

1. Ntona M, Morgera E. Connecting SDG 14 with the other Sustainable Development Goals through marine spatial planning. *Mar Pol* 2018; 93: 214–222. https://doi.org/10.1016/j.marpol.2017.06.020
2. Popović T, Latinović N, Pešić A, Zečević Ž, Krstajić B, Djukanović S. Architecting an IoT-enabled platform for precision agriculture and ecological monitoring: A case study. *Comput Electron Agric* 2017; 140: 255–265. https://doi.org/10.1016/j.compag.2017.06.008

3. Hwang G, Lee J, Park J, Chang TW. Developing performance measurement system for Internet of Things and smart factory environment. *Internat J Prod Res* 2017; 55(9): 2590–2602. https://doi.org/10.1080/00207543.2016 .1245883

4. Tylecote A. Biotechnology as a new techno-economic paradigm that will help drive the world economy and mitigate climate change. *Res Pol* 2019; 48(4): 858–868. https://doi.org/10.1016/j.respol.2018.10.001

5. Yang JH, Yu L, Liu CT, Chang Y, Yang JY, Hsu TY, Hsiao SC. Monitoring coastal aquaculture devices in Taiwan with the radio frequency identification combination system. GISci *Rem Sens* 2021; 1–15. https://doi.org/10.1080 /15481603.2021.2016241

6. Noor NM, Das SK. Effects of elevated carbon dioxide on marine ecosystem and associated fishes. *Thalassas* 2019; 35(2): 421–429. https://doi.org/10 .1007/s41208-019-00161-3

7. Antao L, Pinto R, Reis J, Gonçalves G. Requirements for testing and validating the industrial internet of things. IEEE International Conference Soft Test Verificat Validat. 2018. (pp. 110–115). https://doi.org/10.1109/ICSTW.2018 .00036

8. Behera TM, Mohapatra SK, Samal UC, Khan MS, Daneshmand M, Gandomi AH. I-SEP: An improved routing protocol for heterogeneous WSN for IoT-based environmental monitoring. *IEEE Intern Things J* 2019; 7(1): 710–717. https://doi.org/10.1109/JIOT.2019.2940988

9. Song Y. Underwater acoustic sensor networks with cost efficiency for internet of underwater things. *IEEE Transact Indust Electron* 2020; 68(2): 1707–1716. https://doi.org/10.1109/TIE.2020.2970691

10. Ben-Daya M, Hassini E, Bahroun Z. Internet of things and supply chain management: a literature review. *Internat J Product Res* 2019; 57(15): 4719–4742. https://doi.org10.1080/00207543.2017.1402140

11. Yang H, Kumara S, Bukkapatnam ST, Tsung F. The internet of things for smart manufacturing: A review. *IISE Transact* 2019; 51(11): 1190–1216. https://doi.org/10.1080/24725854.2018.1555383

12. Prabakaran N, Kannan RJ. Sustainable life-span of WSN nodes using participatory devices in pervasive environment. *Microsyst Technol* 2017; 23(3): 651–657. https://link.springer.com/article/10.1007/s00542-016-3117-7

13. Akram SV, Singh R, AlZain MA, Gehlot A, Rashid M, Faragallah OS, Prashar D. Performance analysis of IoT and long-range radio-based sensor node and gateway architecture for solid waste management. *Sensors* 2021; 21(8): 2774. https://doi.org/10.3390/s21082774

14. Haseeb K, Ud Din I, Almogren A, Islam N. An energy efficient and secure IoT-based WSN framework: An application to smart agriculture. *Sensors* 2020; 20(7): 2081. https://doi.org/10.3390/s20072081

15. Mohtar WHMW, Maulud KNA, Muhammad NS, Sharil S, Yaseen ZM. Spatial and temporal risk quotient based river assessment for water resources management. *Environ Poll* 2019; 248: 133–144. https://doi.org/10.1016/j .envpol.2019.02.011

16. Marcelli M, Piermattei V, Gerin R, Brunetti F, Pietrosemoli E, Addo S, Crise A. Toward the widespread application of low-cost technologies in coastal ocean observing (Internet of Things for the Ocean). *Mediteran Mar Sci* 2021; 22(2): 255–269. http://dx.doi.org/10.12681/mms.25060

17. Jiang J, Wang H, Mu X, Guan S. Logistics industry monitoring system based on wireless sensor network platform. *Comput Commun* 2020; 155: 58–65. https://doi.org/10.1016/j.comcom.2020.03.016

18. Ahmad L, Nabi F. *Agriculture 5.0: Artificial Intelligence, IoT and Machine Learning.* CRC Press, 2021.

19. Jouhari M. Underwater wireless sensor networks: A survey on enabling technologies, localization protocols, and internet of underwater things. *IEEE Access* 2019; 7:96879–96899. https://doi.org/10.1109/ACCESS.2019.2928876

20. Yamamoto R, Song E, Kim JM. Parallel WaveGAN: A fast waveform generation model based on generative adversarial networks with multi-resolution spectrogram. *ICASSP* 2020; 6199–6203. https://doi.org/10.1109/ICASSP40776.2020.9053795

21. Wong AP, Wijffels SE, Riser SC, Pouliquen S, Hosoda S, Roemmich D, Park HM. Argo data 1999–2019: two million temperature-salinity profiles and subsurface velocity observations from a global array of profiling floats. *Front Mar Sci* 2020; 700–708. https://doi.org/10.3389/fmars.2020.00700

22. Kamarudin MKA, Nalado AM, Toriman ME, Juahir H, Umar R, Ismail A, Harith H. Evolution of river geomorphology to water quality impact using remote sensing and GIS technique. *Desalin Water Treat* 2019; 149: 258–273. http://dx.doi.org/10.5004/dwt.2019.23838

23. Chaffin JD, Kane DD, Johnson A. Effectiveness of a fixed-depth sensor deployed from a buoy to estimate water-column cyanobacterial biomass depends on wind speed. *J Environ Sci* 2020; 93: 23–29. https://doi.org/10.1016/j.jes.2020.03.003

24. Su J, Strutton PG, Schallenberg C. The subsurface biological structure of Southern Ocean eddies revealed by BGC-Argo floats. *J Mar Syst* 2021: 220; 103569. http://dx.doi.org/10.1016/j.jmarsys.2021.103569

25. Robert K, Huvenne VA, Georgiopoulou A, Jones DO, Marsh L, Carter G, Chaumillon L. New approaches to high-resolution mapping of marine vertical structures. *Sci Rep*, 2017; 7(1): 1–14. https://dx.doi.org/10.1038%2Fs41598-017-09382-z

26. Agarwala N. Monitoring the ocean environment using robotic systems: advancements, trends, and challenges. *Mar Techn Soc J* 2020; 54(5): 42–60. https://doi.org/10.4031/MTSJ.54.5.7

27. Cao J, Lu D, Li D, Zeng Z, Yao B, Lian L. Smartfloat: A multimodal underwater vehicle combining float and glider capabilities. *IEEE Access* 2019; 7: 77825–77838. https://doi.org/10.1109/ACCESS.2019.2922171

28. Bean TP, Greenwood N, Beckett R, Biermann L, Bignell JP, Brant JL, Righton D. A review of the tools used for marine monitoring in the UK: combining historic and contemporary methods with modeling and socioeconomics to fulfill legislative needs and scientific ambitions. *Front Mar Sci* 2017; 4: 263–267. https://doi.org/10.3389/fmars.2017.00263

29. Bracher A, Bouman HA, Brewin RJ, Bricaud A, Brotas V, Ciotti AM, Wolanin A. Obtaining phytoplankton diversity from ocean color: a scientific roadmap

for future development. *Front in Mar Sci* 2017; 4: 55. https://doi.org/10.3389/fmars.2017.00055

30. Saberioon M, Brom J, Nedbal V, Souček P, Císař P. Chlorophyll-a and total suspended solids retrieval and mapping using Sentinel-2A and machine learning for inland waters. *Ecol Indicat* 2020; 113: 106–112. http://dx.doi.org/10.1016/j.ecolind.2020.106236

31. Attila J, Kauppila P, Kallio KY, Alasalmi H, Keto V, Bruun E, Koponen S. Applicability of earth observation chlorophyll-a data in assessment of water status via MERIS: With implications for the use of OLCI sensors. *Rem Sens Environ* 2018; 212: 273–287. https://doi.org/10.1016/j.rse.2018.02.043

32. Eveleth R, Glover DM, Long MC, Lima ID, Chase AP, Doney SC. Assessing the skill of a high-resolution marine biophysical model using geostatistical analysis of mesoscale ocean chlorophyll variability from field observations and remote sensing. *Front Mar Sci* 2021; 8: 342–346. https://doi.org/10.3389/fmars.2021.612764

33. Rahman AA, Jaafar WSWM, Maulud KNA, Noor NM, Mohan M, Cardil A, Naba NI. Applications of drones in emerging economies: a case study of Malaysia. *IconSpace* 2019; 35–40. http://dx.doi.org/10.1109/IconSpace.2019.8905962

34. Berizzi F, Martorella M, Giusti E. *Radar imaging for maritime observation.* CRC Press, 2018.

35. Justino CI, Duarte AC, Rocha-Santos TA. Recent progress in biosensors for environmental monitoring: a review. *Sensors* 2017; 17(12): 2918.

36. Chai F, Johnson KS, Claustre H, Xing X, Wang Y, Boss E, Sutton A. Monitoring ocean biogeochemistry with autonomous platforms. *Nat Rev Earth Environ* 2020; 1(6): 315–326. http://dx.doi.org/10.1038/s43017-020-0053-

37. Yanes AR, Martinez P, Ahmad R. Towards automated aquaponics: A review on monitoring, IoT, and smart systems. *J Clean Prod* 2020; 263: 121–125. https://doi.org/10.1016/j.jclepro.2020.121571

38. Shin YH, Gutierrez-Wing MT, Choi JW. Recent progress in portable fluorescence sensors. *J Electrochem Soc* 2021; 168(1): 175–178. http://doi.org/10.1149/1945-7111/abd494

39. Li R, Li G, Hong WC, Reyes PI, Tang K, Yang K, Lu Y. Tunable surface acoustic wave device using semiconducting MgZnO and piezoelectric NiZnO dual-layer structure on glass. *Smart Mater Struct* 2018; 27(8): 85–88. http://dx.doi.org/10.1088/1361-665X/aad006

40. Lee S, Park B, Kim A. Deep learning based object detection via style-transferred underwater sonar images. *IFAC-PapersOnLine* 2019; 52(21):152–155. https://doi.org/10.1016/j.ifacol.2019.12.299

41. Yu Y, Zhao J, Gong Q, Huang C, Zheng G, Ma J. Real-time underwater maritime object detection in side-scan sonar images based on transformer-YOLOv5. *Rem Sens* 2021; 13(18): 35–40. https://doi.org/10.3390/rs13183555

42. Borith T, Bakhit S, Nasridinov A, Yoo KH. Prediction of machine inactivation status using statistical feature extraction and machine learning. *Appl Sci* 2020; 10(21): 74–77. https://doi.org/10.3390/app10217413

43. Ma J, Li H, Zhu J, Du W, Xu C, Wang X. Design and experiments of a portable seabed integrated detection sonar. *Sensors* 2021; 21(8): 26–33. https://doi.org/10.3390/s21082633

44. Hamouda AZ, Nassar MA, El-Gharabawy SM. Distinguish seabed objects utilizing different marine acoustic techniques. *Egypt J Petrol* 2021; 30(3): 45–51. https://doi.org/10.1016/j.ejpe.2021.07.002

45. Picardi G, Chellapurath M, Iacoponi S, Stefanni S, Laschi C, Calisti M. Bioinspired underwater legged robot for seabed exploration with low environmental disturbance. *Sci Robot* 2020; 5(42):15–18. https://doi.org/10.1126/scirobotics.aaz1012

46. Groom S, Sathyendranath S, Ban Y, Bernard S, Brewin R, Brotas V, Wang M. Satellite ocean colour: current status and future perspective. *Front Mar Sci* 2019; 6: 485–489. https://doi.org/10.3389/fmars.2019.00485

47. Hu C. Remote detection of marine debris using satellite observations in the visible and near infrared spectral range: Challenges and potentials. *Rem Sens Environ* 2021; 15: 259–262. https://doi.org/10.1016/j.rse.2021.112414

48. Nadzir MSM, Ashfold MJ, Khan MF, Robinson AD, Bolas C, Latif MT, Samah AA, Maulud KNA, Dal Sasso N. Spatial-temporal variations in surface ozone over Ushuaia and the Antarctic region: observations from in situ measurements, satellite data, and global models. *Environ Sci Pollut Res* 2018; 25(3): 2194–2210. https://doi.org/10.1007/s11356-017-0521-1

49. Bruno MF, Molfetta MG, Pratola L, Mossa M, Nutricato R, Morea A, Chiaradia M T. A combined approach of field data and earth observation for coastal risk assessment. *Sensors* 2019; 19(6): 139–142. https://doi.org/10.3390/s19061399

50. Turemis M, Silletti S, Pezzotti G, Sanchís J, Farré M, Giardi MT. Optical biosensor based on the microalga-paramecium symbiosis for improved marine monitoring. *Sens Actuators B Chem* 2018; 270: 424–432. https://doi.org/10.1016/j.snb.2018.04.111

51. Xu L, Collier R., O'Hare GM. A survey of clustering techniques in WSNs and consideration of the challenges of applying such to 5G IoT scenarios. *IEEE Internet Things J* 2017; 4(5): 1229–1249. https://doi.org/10.1109/JIOT.2017.2726014

52. Lavanya S, Prasanth A, Jayachitra S, Shenbagarajan A. A Tuned classification approach for efficient heterogeneous fault diagnosis in IoT-enabled WSN applications. *Measurement* 2021; 183: 109–113. https://doi.org/10.1016/J.MEASUREMENT.2021.109771

53. Hu C, Qi L, Xie Y, Zhang S, Barnes BB. Spectral characteristics of sea snot reflectance observed from satellites: Implications for remote sensing of marine debris. *Rem Sens Environ* 2022; 269: 112–115. http://doi.org/10.1016/j.rse.2021.112842

54. Kavanaugh MT, Bell T, Catlett D, Cimino MA, Doney SC, Klajbor W, Siegel DA. Satellite remote sensing and the marine biodiversity observation network. *Oceanogr* 2021; 34(2): 62–79. https://doi.org/10.5670/oceanog.2021.215

55. Nair MR, Ramya GR, Sivakumar PB. Usage and analysis of Twitter during 2015 Chennai flood towards disaster management. *Proced Comput Sci* 2017; 115: 350–358. https://doi.org/10.1016/j.procs.2017.09.089

56. Zhu, X. Complex event detection for commodity distribution Internet of Things model incorporating radio frequency identification and Wireless Sensor Network. *Fut Gen Comput Syst* 2021; 125: 100–111. https://doi.org/10.1016/j.future.2021.06.024

57. Mohd FA, Maulud KNA, Karim OA, Begum RA, Awang NA, Ahmad A, Mohtar WHMW. Comprehensive coastal vulnerability assessment and adaptation for Cherating-Pekan coast, Pahang, Malaysia. *Ocean Coast Manag* 2019; 182: 104–108. https://doi.org/10.1016/j.ocecoaman.2019.104948

58. Appolloni L, Buonocore E, Russo GF, Franzese PP. The use of remote sensing for monitoring posidonia oceanica and marine protected areas: a systemic review. *Ecol Quest* 2020; 31(2): 7–17. http://dx.doi.org/10.12775/EQ.2020.009

59. Onar OC. *Energy Harvesting: Solar, Wind, and Ocean Energy Conversion Systems*. CRC Press, 2017.

60. Jones KR, Klein CJ, Grantham HS, Possingham HP, Halpern BS, Burgess ND, Watson JE. Area requirements to safeguard Earth's marine species. *One Earth* 2020; 2(2): 188–196. https://doi.org/10.1016/j.oneear.2020.01.010

61. Sharma S, Nanda M, Goel R, Jain A, Bhushan M, Kumar A. Smart cities using internet of things: Recent trends and techniques. *International Journal of Innovative Technology and Exploring Engineering.* 2019; 8(9S): 24–28. https://doi.org/10.35940/ijitee.I1004.0789S19

62. Goel R, Jain A, Verma K, Bhushan M, Kumar A, Negi A. Mushrooming trends and technologies to aid visually impaired people. In 2020 International Conference on Emerging Trends in Information Technology and Engineering (ic-ETITE). 2020. (pp. 1–5). IEEE.

63. Samant P, Bhushan M, Kumar A, Arya R, Tiwari S, Bansal S. Condition monitoring of machinery: A case study. In 2021 6th International Conference on Signal Processing, Computing and Control (ISPCC). 2021. (pp. 501–505). https://doi.org/10.1109/ISPCC53510.2021.9609512.

64. Mangla M, Kumar A, Mehta V, Bhushan M, Mohanty SN. *Real-Life Applications of the Internet of Things: Challenges, Applications, and Advances*. Apple Academic Press, 1st Edn, pp. 536, 2022. https://doi.org/10.1201/9781003277460

Chapter 9

Managing agriculture pollution using life-cycle assessment and artificial intelligence methods

Siti Norliyana Harun, Marlia Mohd Hanafiah, and Noorashikin Md. Noor

CONTENTS

9.1 INTRODUCTION

The world's agricultural output is projected to increase by 60–110% by 2050, with a population of more than nine billion people predicted [1–3]. Over the past two decades, agriculture has evolved to include agricultural and livestock processing, production, marketing, and distribution. As a result, it plays an important role in long-term economic development as it provides a source of livelihood and national trade, creates more job opportunities, and provides raw materials for other manufacturing industries. As a result, long-term agricultural sustainability is crucial in ensuring food security and safety. As presented by the FAO [4], meeting the growing needs of the world's population requires adequate and affordable food through sustainable agricultural resources. In addition, global food security faces many challenges, including climate change, competition for land for biofuels, and declining soil quality; therefore, identifying sustainable strategies necessitates the incorporation of new approaches and information across multiple and diverse areas.

DOI: 10.1201/9781003286745-9

Digital tools such as the Internet of Things (IoT), artificial intelligence (AI), and cloud computing have been adopted by the agriculture sector in recent years. Furthermore, AI categories, for example, deep and machine learning, are frequently proposed to improve smart farming. Irrigation, weed control, nerve spraying, and other methods applied by robots and drones are just a few of the tools using AI in smart farming [5]. In addition, AI can reduce farmers' losses in the agricultural sector while improving productivity.

On the other hand, agricultural activities pose significant consequences to the environment, including air, soil, and water [6, 7]. The biggest challenge for the agricultural industry is to maintain food security and service delivery while minimizing environmental impact to ensure long-term environmental sustainability. In recent years, efforts have been made worldwide to improve agricultural practices toward a more environmentally friendly and sustainable sector, such as using fewer nutrients, pesticides, energy, and water in agricultural activities. LCA is among the most extensively utilized techniques in agriculture for evaluating the environmental performance of agricultural products, systems, and processes. LCA aids in the identification of "hot spots" across a product's or system's complete lifecycle that have led to adverse environmental effects, allowing for the development of alternative production methods [8–10].

Therefore, this chapter will discuss the following aspects: the benefit of artificial intelligence in the agricultural sector, environmental pollution management related to the agricultural sector, advantages of LCA–AI integration, and a conclusion.

9.2 BENEFITS OF ARTIFICIAL INTELLIGENCE IN AGRICULTURE

Year by year, AI has emerged. Indeed, even the term "AI" is ever-changing and has emerged over time. Several researchers have come up with the following definitions of AI:

> The ability of a system to visualize external information, learn from it, and apply what it has learned to achieve specific goals and functions by adapting it. [11]

> A study of the creation and analysis of intelligent machines. [12]

AI can change the way people think about agriculture by helping farmers to get the most important results with a little work while bringing in hundreds of additional benefits. Agriculture includes a variety of activities and phases, many of which are done manually. AI may assist with complex and common tasks in line with existing technologies. It can collect and analyze big data on a digital platform, identify the right strategy, and even take that action when combined with other technologies [13].

The agriculture industry might benefit from AI in the following ways.

9.2.1 IoT drives data analytics

The agricultural industry produces a lot of structured and unstructured data every day. Historical weather conditions, soil reports, current studies, rainfall, photographs, insect infestations, and more are all examples of this. Farm materials, drone images, and agricultural statistics create too much data for people to process.

Farmers can use AI to analyze climate, condition of the soil, use of water, and temperature collected on their farms to make wise business decisions, such as which crops are most viable in that year or which hybrid seeds reduce losses. Extensive data analysis can help improve irrigation, reduce greenhouse gas emissions (GHG), and determine the precise and sufficient needs of soil, light, food, and water for reproduction.

9.2.2 Drone-assistant technology

Drones can be used to capture photos and videos throughout the farm using AI and unmanned aircraft technologies. The amount of data generated by intelligent sensors and drones that provide real-time video and photography provides agricultural professionals with new data sets that they could not previously access. A combination of moisture, fertilizer, and natural nutrient data from the in-ground sensors can be used to investigate the growth trends of each plant over time [14]. Machine learning is ideal for integrating large data sets and providing recommendations for improving agricultural management.

Throughout the agricultural cycle, drones might be used in various ways. Consider the following examples:

i. Soil and field analysis: by submitting accurate 3D maps for early soil analysis, drones can assist with seed sowing and obtain information to control irrigation and nitrogen levels.
ii. Drones are able to scan the land, then spray the plants in real time to ensure uniform coverage. As a result, aerial spraying with drone assistance is five times faster than traditional approaches.
iii. Planting: drone planting technology has the potential to save up to 85% on planting costs [15]. These resources fire pods full of seeds and nutrients into the soil, providing all the nutrients needed for plant development.
iv. Irrigation: sensor drones (hyperspectral, multispectral, thermal sensors) may detect dry sections or sections needing improvement in a field as well as calculate the vegetation index.

v. Monitoring: drones may employ time-series visualizations to indicate crop growth and highlight productivity inefficiencies, enabling improved management.

vi. Plant health check: drone-mounted sensors can scan the plant using visible and near-infrared light to monitor plant health. The technology, carried by a drone, can help farmers monitor crop changes by detecting plant infections, showing their health, and informing farmers about plant diseases [16].

9.2.3 Weather prediction

A variety of environmental concerns, including climate change and others, represent the biggest threats to agricultural yields; however, AI-powered systems and data-driven farming use improved resource management to help farmers navigate changes in environmental circumstances.

9.2.4 Monitoring soil and crop health

With the assistance of developing technology and IoT sensors installed within agricultural soil, farmers might immediately analyze soil moisture levels and chemical compositions [17]. Farmers may use these implanted devices to get notifications when soil components like potassium, nitrogen, phosphorus, or moisture content fall below or above acceptable levels.

9.2.5 Artificial intelligence can assist with labor shortages

Non-driving tractors, smart irrigation and fertilizer systems, intelligent spraying, and AI-based harvesting robots can help farmers save money. Farm tools powered by AI are quicker, more complex, and more precise than any human farm worker [18].

9.2.6 Farm data analysis and pest monitoring

In the field, sensors might monitor when insects emerge and identify the bug species [19]. If it is a beneficial or neutral bug, it will depart and idle. However, if it is a harmful insect or pest, the information is sent to the cloud.

The benefits of AI applications in the agricultural sector have been summarized in Figure 9.1.

9.3 MANAGING ENVIRONMENTAL POLLUTION IN THE AGRICULTURAL SECTOR

Agricultural land occupies over five billion hectares, or 38% of the total land surface in the world [20]. The remaining two-thirds are used for farming animals in meadows and pastures, with about a third being utilized for

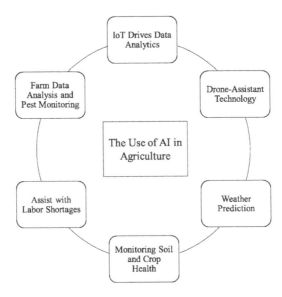

Figure 9.1 Summary of the use of AI in the agricultural sector.

crops. Agricultural activities have expanded significantly in recent years as the need for agricultural products has increased due to population and economic growth. Increased agricultural operations have led to increased environmental contamination, such as soil, water, and air pollution. As a result, assessing environmental implications throughout the life cycle process is critical for identifying hotspots and improving agricultural operations' environmental impact.

Life-cycle thinking (LCT) has increasingly been recognized as an important approach in addressing present challenges and research needs related to the long-term sustainability of food production and consumption programs. As a result, life-cycle approaches such as LCA [21], life-cycle costing (LCC), and social life-cycle assessment (sLCA) are increasingly being used to transform existing productivity and application patterns into sustainable ones. The LCA method has been extensively utilized worldwide for investigating the environmental performance of agricultural products or processes. From raw materials to production and disposal, LCA is a technique used to evaluate the environmental consequences, performances, and resources required across the whole life cycle (cradle to grave) of a product or system. The LCA is a generally accepted method developed by ISO 14040–ISO 14046. The LCA consists of four stages: the objective and scope statement, the life-cycle inventory analysis (LCI), the life-cycle impact assessment (LCIA), and also interpretation, as illustrated in Figure 9.2.

Various software has been developed to analyze LCA, such as SimaPro, OpenLCA, and GaBi. The software also provides extensive databases such

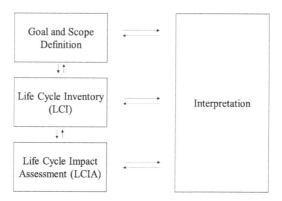

Figure 9.2 LCA framework. Source: Guinee [22].

as Ecoinvent and US Life Cycle Inventory Database (USLCI). A massive number of emission data is collected while conducting an LCA, such as energy and waste production, raw material production, etc. Those emissions often come in a variety of formats. For example, emissions from harvesting raw materials differ significantly from emissions produced from electricity generation. Hence, the multiple emissions with the same impact are combined into a single unit, corresponding to a single impact category in the life-cycle impact assessment (LCIA) phase [23]. Given the ReCiPe 2016 method created by Huijbregts et al. [24], there are 17 impact categories involved at the mid-point level. Figure 9.3 illustrates the 17 impact classifications based on damage assessment categories at end-point levels.

Given the importance of using the LCA method, many studies have reported using LCA in the agricultural system. For example, various studies compared two agricultural systems – organic and non-organic farming systems – such as [25–28]. In addition, various studies applied LCA in agricultural waste, such as [29–32]. On the other hand, previous LCA studies have been done focusing on bioenergy production using agricultural waste, such as Konur et al. [33], Zhang and Yu [34], Prasad et al. [35], and Aziz et al. [36].

LCA is a tool for environmental management that assists in comparing and enhancing the environmental practices of different systems as well as production [37–39]. In the LCA, inventory analysis is time-consuming due to in-depth information, which includes data collection and treatment. The integration of LCA with other test models allows for synergic and experimental analysis with more robust results, which improves the decision-making process. Therefore, AI has the potential to increase the amount of data and information handled on a regular basis in business operations, object planning, sensors, social networks, users, and analytics tools. AI collects accurate and important data, analyzes it, performs tasks, and solves problems. AI aids in the solving of problems in a variety of areas, including

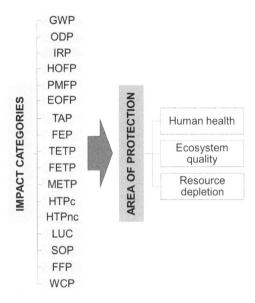

Figure 9.3 Impact classification using damage assessment categories. Source: Huijbregts et al. [24]. Note: GWP: global warming potential, ODP: stratospheric ozone depletion, IRP: ionizing radiation, HOFP: ozone formation referring to human health, PMFP: fine particulate matter formation, EOFP: ozone formation for terrestrial ecosystems, TAP: terrestrial acidification, FEP: freshwater eutrophication, TETP: terrestrial ecotoxicity, FETP: freshwater ecotoxicity, METP: marine ecotoxicity, HTPc: human carcinogenic toxicity, HTPnc: human non-carcinogenic toxicity, LOP: land use, SOP: mineral resource scarcity, FFP: fossil resource scarcity, WCP: water consumption.

observation in real time, environmental effect assessment, environmental modeling, and variable measurement plus status modeling, all of which provide crucial data for decision-making [40].

There has been an increasing interest in integrating systems LCA and AI methods recently to evaluate the agricultural sector's environmental performance level. Table 9.1 shows examples of LCA–AI integration in the agricultural industry. Based on Table 9.1, most of the AI technologies used are adaptive neuro-fuzzy inference systems (ANFIS) and AI networks (ANNs). ANFIS combines fuzzy logic with the neural network model, which integrates nodes and interactions [44]. ANFIS architecture contains multiple layers of five neurons to locate nodes due to the increasing time to calculate the number of rules [43]. According to Nabavi-Pelesaraei et al. [44], data collection methods or key component analysis (PCA) can reduce the number of conditions. Figure 9.4 illustrates the architecture of an ANFIS model.

ANNs are a nonlinear model that combines several processing nodes that receive inputs and outputs based on their weight and usage functions [43, 47]. According to a study by Ali Kaab et al. [43], both ANN and ANFIS

Table 9.1 Studies that combined LCA–AI in the agricultural sector

Author	Focus of study	Types of AI technologies
Romeiko et al. [41]	Impacts of corn output on global warming and eutrophication determined by comparing five machine learning approaches	Artificial neural network (ANN) Support vector machine regression (SVR) Linear regression (LR) Tree-based model which is a gradient-boosted regression tree (GBRT) Extreme gradient boosting (XGBoost)
Nabavi-Pelesaraei et al. [42]	Identifying the energy consumption, environmental consequences, and economic indicators of the process that transforms paddy into rice	Adaptive neuro-fuzzy inference system (ANFIS)
Kaab et al. [43]	Integrating LCA and AI to evaluate the output energy and environmental implications of the sugarcane production process	ANFIS ANN
Nabavi-Pelesaraei et al. [44]	Determining the output energy and environmental effects of paddy cultivation by LCA and AI	ANFIS ANN
Khoshnevisan et al. [45]	Contrasting the energy use and environmental implications between two systems of rice production	ANFIS

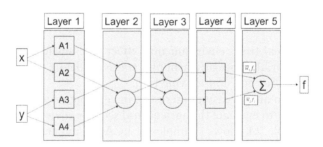

Figure 9.4 The architecture of ANFIS. Source: Kablan et al. [46].

models accurately predict the environmental impact and power generation in their research.

9.4 ADVANTAGES OF LCA–AI INTEGRATION

LCA is a quantitative approach that requires data quality for accuracy. LCA is exposed and sensitive to uncertainties. Thus, the data sources should be defined clearly and specifically during the life-cycle inventory phase. In addition, it is essential to make proper considerations when selecting data sources. Generally, all inputs and outputs of product-related processes should be identified at all levels. The type of machinery used at the farm level and the travel distance to carry farm products to the factory are two examples of data-gathering strategies. On the other hand, improper data collecting procedures may lead to inaccuracies, which can significantly impact the LCI findings [48]. For instance, data on actual materials and energy use are more reliable than questionnaire responses.

Sensitivity and uncertainty are two attributes that directly affect LCA's output quality and outcome. According to Hujbregts [49], uncertainty can be divided into six types (Figure 9.5). The parameter uncertainty relates to data shortage in a collection. The data shortage about a certain process, materials, and emissions is related to the calculating techniques which have inherent flaws. Model variability is related to choices of both functionality and methods which might have an impact on the final outcome: spatial variability is caused by the spreading feature of environmental consequences that could lead to inappropriate LCA results; temporal variability is related to the data inventories for emissions and impacts related to the differences in inputs and emissions that might generate variability [50].

Bjorcklund [51] modified the first draft proposed by Hujbregts [49] by dividing the parameter variability into data clauses: accuracy, spaces, and unstructured include new categories of uncertainty such as epistemological uncertainty, errors, and degree of uncertainty. Each stage in the LCA process has a potential bias, and the result will be a combination of all the

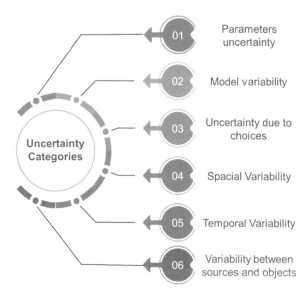

Figure 9.5 Six categories of uncertainty in LCA. Source: Huijbregts [49].

previous mistakes. As a result, it is important to determine the source of uncertainty for ease of assessment [52, 53]. Thus, analyzing LCA statistics is important to ensure data quality and eliminate bias. Therefore, LCA may be integrated with analytical algorithms such as ANN and ANFIS to close the gap between conceptual data and ultimate environmental effects [54, 55].

9.5 CONCLUSION

The agricultural sector has faced many challenges due to its impact on the environment contributing to climate change and food supply disruption. Advanced AI technology has been applied to the agricultural sector in terms of automation and assistance in farm management. In addition to focusing on increasing productivity, pollution from agricultural activities has also been a major focus on supporting the Sustainable Development Goals (SDGs), in particular, SDG 2 (end hunger, achieving food security plus enhancing nutrition) and SDG 13 (require immediate steps to address climate change and its consequences).

One of the most crucial aspects of agriculture sector management for long-term sustainability is decision-making. LCA is well suited as a decision-making tool for providing scientific and comprehensive answers to environmental impact decisions. However, uncertainty must be addressed for direct, fair, and transparent results during the LCA process. Therefore, integrating the LCA approach with other concepts and approaches such as AI is necessary to strengthen and ultimately increase its effectiveness in sustainable decision-making. AI systems can maximize the quantity of data handled on a regular basis in business operations, object planning, sensors, social networks, users, and analytics tools. AI collects accurate and useful data, analyzes it, performs tasks, and solves problems.

AI helps solve problems in numerous sectors of society, especially environmental issues such as impacts on the environment, real-time observation and monitoring, parameter measurement, and simulation. Those data and information could help in decision-making. In addition, AI technologies such as ANNs and ANFIS are well-known methods that can be used to predict the outcome of complex systems. Therefore, the integration of LCA–AI can create machine learning models that allow for a robust decision-making process.

REFERENCES

1. Rockström J, Williams J, Daily G, Noble A, Matthews N, Gordon L, Wetterstrand H, DeClerck F, Shah M, Steduto P, de Fraiture C. Sustainable intensification of agriculture for human prosperity and global sustainability. *Ambio* 2017; 46(1):4–17. https://doi.org/10.1007/s13280-016-0793-6

2. Krishna KL, Silver O, Malende WF, Anuradha K. Internet of Things application for implementation of smart agriculture system. In 2017 International Conference on I-SMAC (IoT in Social, Mobile, Analytics and Cloud) 2017; 54–59. https://doi.org/10.1109/I-SMAC.2017.8058236

3. Tangermann S. *Agriculture: Food Security and Trade Liberalization. The World Trade System: Trends and Challenges.* MIT Press. 2016.

4. FAO. *The Future of Food and Agriculture: Trends and Challenges.* FAO. 2017; ISBN 9789251095515.

5. Talaviya T, Shah D, Patel N, Yagnik H, Shah M. Implementation of AI in agriculture for optimization of irrigation and application of pesticides and herbicides. *AI in Agriculture* 2020; 4:58–73.https://doi.org/10.1016/j.aiia.2020.04.002

6. Van der Werf HM, Knudsen MT, Cederberg C. Towards better representation of organic agriculture in life cycle assessment. *Nature Sustainability* 2020; 3(6):419–425. https://doi.org/10.1038/s41893-020-0489-6

7. McLellan EL, Cassman KG, Eagle AJ, Woodbury PB, Sela S, Tonitto C, Marjerison RD, van Es HM. The nitrogen balancing act: tracking the environmental performance of food production. *Bioscience* 2018; 68(3):194–203. https://doi.org/10.1093/biosci/bix164

8. Mungkung, R., Dangsiri, S. and Gheewala, S.H. Development of a low-carbon, healthy and innovative value-added riceberry rice product through life cycle design. *Clean Technologies and Environmental Policy* 2021; 1–11. https://doi.org/10.1007/s10098-021-02101-3

9. Müller, L.J., Kätelhön, A., Bachmann, M., Zimmermann, A., Sternberg, A. and Bardow, A. A guideline for life cycle assessment of carbon capture and utilization. *Frontiers in Energy Research* 2020; 8:15. https://doi.org/10.3389/fenrg.2020.00015

10. Goossens, Y., Geeraerd, A., Keulemans, W., Annaert, B., Mathijs, E., De Tavernier, J. Life cycle assessment (LCA) for apple orchard production systems including low and high productive years in conventional, integrated and organic farms. *Agriculture System* 2017; 153:81–93. https://doi.org/10.1016/j.agsy.2017.01.007

11. Kaplan, A. and Haenlein, M. Siri, Siri, in my hand: Who's the fairest in the land? On the interpretations, illustrations, and implications of artificial intelligence. *Business Horizons* 2019; 62(1):15–25. https://doi.org/10.1016/j.bushor.2018.08.004

12. Poole DL, Mackworth AK. *AI: Foundations of Computational Agents.* Cambridge University Press. 2010.

13. Sharma, S., Nanda, M., Goel, R., Jain, A., Bhushan, M., Kumar, A. Smart cities using internet of things: Recent trends and techniques. *The International Journal of Innovative Technology and Exploring Engineering* 2019; 8(9):24–28. http://dx.doi.org/10.35940/ijitee.I1004.0789S19

14. Mangla, M., Kumar, A., Mehta, V., Bhushan, M., and Mohanty, S. N. *Real-Life Applications of the Internet of Things: Challenges, Applications, and Advances.* Apple Academic Press. 2022. https://doi.org/10.1201/9781003277460

15. Ahirwar, S., Swarnkar, R., Bhukya, S., Namwade, G. Application of drone in agriculture. *International Journal of Current Microbiology and Applied Sciences* 2019; 8(01):2500–2505. https://doi.org/10.20546/ijcmas.2019.801.264

16. Pawar, S, Bhushan, M, Wagh, M. The plant leaf disease diagnosis and spectral data analysis using machine learning-A review. *International Journal of Advanced Science and Technology* 2020; 29(9s):3343–3359.

17. Sahoo RN. Sensor-based monitoring of soil and crop health for enhancing input use efficiency. In *Food, Energy, and Water Nexus*. Springer 2022; 129–147. https://doi.org/10.1007/978-3-030-85728-8_7

18. Vadlamudi S How artificial intelligence improves agricultural productivity and sustainability: A global thematic analysis. *Asia Pacific Journal of Energy and Environment* 2019; 6(2):91–100. https://doi.org/10.18034/apjee.v6i2.542

19. Bhat SA, Huang NF. Big data and AI revolution in precision agriculture: Survey and challenges. *IEEE Access* 2021; 9:110209–110222. https://doi.org/10.1109/ACCESS.2021.3102227

20. FAO. *State of Food and Agriculture Report "Climate change Agriculture and Food Security"*. FAO 2016. Rome http://www.fao.org/3/a-i6030e.pdf.

21. ISO International Organization for Standardization. *14044: Environmental Managements: Lifecycle Assessments – Requirements and Guidelines*. International Organization for Standardization. 2006.

22. Guinée JB. Handbook on life cycle assessment operational guide to the ISO standards. *The International Journal of Life Cycle Assessment* 2002; 7(5):311.

23. Aziz NIHA, Hanafiah MM. Application of life cycle assessment for desalination: Progress, challenges and future directions. *Environmental Pollution* 2021; 268(B):115948. https://doi.org/10.1016/j.envpol.2020.115948

24. Huijbregts M, Steinmann Z, Elshout P, Stam G, Verones F, Vieira M, Hollander A, Zijp M, Van Zelm R. *Recipe 2016: A Harmonized Life Cycle Impact Assessment Method at Midpoint and Endpoint Level Report I: Characterization*. 2016. https://doi.org/10.1007/s11367-016-1246-y

25. Harun SN, Hanafiah MM, Aziz NIHA. An LCA-based environmental performance of rice production for developing a sustainable agri-food system in Malaysia. *Environmental Management* 2021; 67(1):146–161. https://doi.org/10.1007/s00267-020-01365-7

26. Boone L, Roldán-Ruiz I, Muylle H, Dewulf J. Environmental sustainability of conventional and organic farming: Accounting for ecosystem services in life cycle assessment. *Science of the Total Environment* 2019; 695:133841. https://doi.org/10.1016/j.scitotenv.2019.133841

27. Tricase C, Lamonaca E, Ingrao C, Bacenetti J, Giudice AL. A comparative life cycle assessment between organic and conventional barley cultivation for sustainable agriculture pathways. *Journal of Cleaner Production* 2018; 172:3747–3759. https://doi.org/10.1016/j.jclepro.2017.07.008

28. Zhu Z, Jia Z, Peng L, Chen Q, He L, Jiang Y, Ge S. Life cycle assessment of conventional and organic apple production systems in China. *Journal of Cleaner Production* 2018; 201:156–168. https://doi.org/10.1016/j.jclepro.2018.08.032

29. Deng J. *LCA of Three Thermal Treatment Methods of Agricultural Waste*. Master's thesis, Lappeenranta-Lahti University of Technology (LUT). 2020.

30. Vega GC. *Environmental Sustainability Assessment of Advanced Agricultural Waste Technologies and Agricultural Territories*. 2020.

31. Shang X, Song S, Yang J. Comparative environmental evaluation of straw resources by LCA in China. *Advances in Materials Science and Engineering* 2020. https://doi.org/10.1155/2020/4781805

32. Hanafiah MM, Ali MYM, Aziz NIHA, John A. Biogas production from agrowaste and effluents. *Acta Chemica Malaysia* 2017; 1(1):13–15. https://doi.org/10.26480/acmy.01.2017.13.15

33. Konur O. Palm oil-based biodiesel fuels: A review of the research. *Biodiesel Fuels Based on Edible and Nonedible Feedstocks, Wastes, and Algae*2021; 477–496.

34. Zhang C, Xu Y. Economic analysis of large-scale farm biogas power generation system considering environmental benefits based on LCA: A case study in China. *Journal of Cleaner Production* 2020; 258:120985. https://doi.org/10.1016/j.jclepro.2020.120985

35. Prasad S, Singh A, Korres NE, Rathore D, Sevda S, Pant D. Sustainable utilization of crop residues for energy generation: A life cycle assessment (LCA) perspective. *Bioresource Technology* 2020; 303:122964. https://doi.org/10.1016/j.biortech.2020.122964

36. Aziz NIHA, Hanafiah MM. Life cycle analysis of biogas production from anaerobic digestion of palm oil mill effluent. *Renewable Energy* 2020; 145:847–857. https://doi.org/10.1016/j.renene.2019.06.084

37. Bong PXH, Malek MA, Mardi NH, Hanafiah MM. Cradle-to-gate water-related impacts on production of traditional food products in Malaysia. *Sustainability* 2020; 12(13):5274. https://doi.org/10.3390/su12135274

38. Aziz NIHA, Hanafiah MM, Ali MYM. Sustainable biogas production from agrowaste and effluents: A promising step for small-scale industry income. *Renewable Energy* 2019; 132: 363–369. https://doi.org/10.1016/j.renene.2018.07.149

39. Hanafiah MM, Leuven RSEW, Sommerwerk N, Tockner K, Huijbregts MAJ. Including the introduction of exotic species in life cycle impact assessment: the case of inland shipping. *Environmental Science & Technology* 2013; 47:13934–13940. https://doi.org/10.1021/es403870z

40. De Jesus JO, Oliveira-Esquerre K, Medeiros DL. Integration of AI and life cycle assessment methods. *In IOP Conference Series: Materials Science and Engineering* 2021; 1196(1):012028). IOP Publishing. https://doi.org/10.1088/1757-899X/1196/1/012028

41. Romeiko XX, Guo Z, Pang Y, Lee EK, Zhang X. Comparing machine learning approaches for predicting spatially explicit life cycle global warming and eutrophication impacts from corn production. *Sustainability* 2020; 12(4):1481. https://doi.org/10.3390/su12041481

42. Nabavi-Pelesaraei A, Rafiee S, Mohtasebi SS, Hosseinzadeh-Bandbafha H, Chau KW. Comprehensive model of energy, environmental impacts and economic in rice milling factories by coupling adaptive neuro-fuzzy inference system and life cycle assessment. *Journal of Cleaner Production* 2019; 217:742–756. https://doi.org/10.1016/j.jclepro.2019.01.228

43. Kaab A, Sharifi M, Mobli H, Nabavi-Pelesaraei A, Chau KW. Combined life cycle assessment and AI for prediction of output energy and environmental impacts of sugarcane production. *Science of the Total Environment* 2019; 664:1005–1019. https://doi.org/10.1016/j.scitotenv.2019.02.004

44. Nabavi-Pelesaraei A, Rafiee S, Mohtasebi SS, Hosseinzadeh-Bandbafha H, Chau KW. Integration of AI methods and life cycle assessment to predict energy output and environmental impacts of paddy production. *Science of the Total Environment* 2018; 631:1279–1294. https://doi.org/10.1016/j.scitotenv .2018.03.088

45. Khoshnevisan B, Rajaeifar MA, Clark S, Shamahirband S, Anuar NB, Shuib NLM, Gani A. Evaluation of traditional and consolidated rice farms in Guilan Province, Iran, using life cycle assessment and fuzzy modeling. *Science of the Total Environment* 2014; 481:242–251. https://doi.org/10.1016/j.scitotenv .2014.02.052

46. Kablan A, Ng WL. Intraday high-frequency FX trading with adaptive neuro-fuzzy inference systems. *International Journal of Financial Markets and Derivatives* 2011; 2(1–2):68–87.

47. Bhojani SH, Bhatt N. Wheat crop yield prediction using new activation functions in neural network. *Neural Computing & Applications* 2020; 32(17). https://doi.org/10.1007/s00521-020-04797-8

48. Alyaseri I, Zhou J. Handling uncertainties inherited in life cycle inventory and life cycle impact assessment method for improved life cycle assessment of wastewater sludge treatment. *Heliyon* 2019; 5(11):02793. https://doi.org/10 .1016/j.heliyon.2019.e02793

49. Huijbregts MA. Application of uncertainty and variability in LCA. *The International Journal of Life Cycle Assessment* 1998; 3(5):273–280. https:// doi.org/10.1007/BF02979835

50. Chang D, Lee CKM, Chen CH. Review of life cycle assessment towards sustainable product development. *Journal of Cleaner Production* 2014; 83:48–60. https://doi.org/10.1016/j.jclepro.2014.07.050

51. Björklund AE. Survey of approaches to improve reliability in LCA. *The International Journal of Life Cycle Assessment* 2002; 7(2):64–72. https://doi .org/10.1007/BF02978849

52. Igos E, Benetto E, Meyer R, Baustert P, Othoniel B. How to treat uncertainties in life cycle assessment studies?. *The International Journal of Life Cycle Assessment* 2019; 24(4):794–807. https://doi.org/10.1007/s11367-018 -1477-1

53. Ziyadi M, Al-Qadi IL. Model uncertainty analysis using data analytics for life-cycle assessment (LCA) applications. *The International Journal of Life Cycle Assessment* 2019; 24(5):945–959. https://doi.org/10.1007/s11367-018 -1528-7

54. Culaba AB, Mayol AP, San Juan JLG, Vinoya CL, Concepcion II RS, Bandala AA, Vicerra RRP, Ubando AT, Chen WH, Chang JS. Smart sustainable biorefineries for lignocellulosic biomass. *Bioresource Technology* 2022; 344:126215. https://doi.org/10.1016/j.biortech.2021.126215

55. Iddio E, Wang L, Thomas Y, McMorrow G, Denzer A. Energy efficient operation and modeling for greenhouses: A literature review. *Renewable and Sustainable Energy Reviews* 2020; 117:109480. https://doi.org/10.1016/j.rser .2019.109480

Ensemble techniques for effective prediction of crop selection in the Coastal Andhra deltaic region

A. Vanathi, S. Rama Sree and K. Swaroopa

CONTENTS

DOI: 10.1201/9781003286745-10

10.1 INTRODUCTION

Agriculture is the backbone of every developing nation and is considered the key role and foremost culture practiced from ancient times. Agriculture, farmers, farming, and food are important every day and in everyone's life, all because of the single reason that all living things need food to survive and energy to do work. Without food, no one could survive. And there are a lot of people in India; with a population of 1.4 billion, it is equal to 17.7% of the world's total population [1]. Agriculture not only provides food to people but also provides a great contribution to the Indian economy. Agriculture is not the occupation of a single person as a farmer but a livelihood for all citizens throughout the country and the world. The survey says that more than 70% of people in rural areas have farming as their main occupation and they completely rely on agriculture.

10.1.1 Agriculture in India

In India, the agriculture sector is crucial as it creates numerous job opportunities and a very large industry, which plays a key role in increasing the opportunities for employment in the nation. Agriculture is a predominant sector of the Indian economy, as it contributes about 17% to the total GDP and provides employment to over 60% of the population [2]. As India is known for its diversity, the nature of the soil, weather conditions, geographical areas, and farming techniques also vary from one region to another in the country. Due to this, the country has a variety of crops grown, which are used for the country's own needs as well as the needs of the world. The primary crops grown in India are rice, wheat, and pulses.

Agriculture has been the main source of income in India for a very long time, and with its other sectors, it is still the most important source of income in India. Farmers are the hardest-working people in the world. They don't do farming as a job but as a kind of holy work. Seventy percent of rural households still rely mostly on farming for their income, with 82% of farmers being small and marginal [2].

One-quarter of the global production came from developing countries like the Republic of India. As a consumer, they took a little more than that, accounting for 27% of world consumption. As an importer, they took 14% of the world pulse market. There are a lot of fruits and vegetables grown there: 10.9% of the world's fruit and vegetable production comes from there. It is also the second-largest rice producer. Rice is the most important crop in our country, which has been democratic for a long time. The country is second in the world when it comes to making rice. Rice is grown and cultivated in most of the states of India, but the southern states of Andhra Pradesh, Tamil Nadu, Telangana, Karnataka, and Kerala make up most of the country's rice crop. Rice covers about 34% of the country's cropped land. Rice is the most important food crop in the country, and it makes up 42% of all food crops grown there.

Indian farmers and crop growers still have a lot of work to do, even though our country has been producing the most in the world for a long time. As the Indian economy has become more diverse and grown, agriculture's share of GDP has steadily dropped from 1951 to 2011 [2]. With food production, India has reached self-sufficiency. But India is still home to more than 190 million people who aren't getting enough food.

10.1.2 Agriculture in Andhra Pradesh

Andhra Pradesh (AP) lies in the southeastern coastal part of India, and with a population of 5.27 crores (as of 2021), it is one of the most populous states and stands in tenth position in the country with an annual growth rate varying from 2.1 to 2.4% [3]. AP is the fourth largest state in the Republic of India with respect to area, with about 27.5 million hectares in area, and farming has been the chief source of income. Andhra Pradesh is a prominent exporter of many agricultural products. With its highest contribution to the production of rice in the nation, it is called the "Rice Bowl of India" and stands as the largest producer of rice in the country [3].

The state has 26 districts, and it is mainly divided into two areas: Coastal Andhra and Rayalaseema. AP has a tropical climate with moderate diffusion to subtropical weather. The region Rayalaseema, which is in the southmost part of the state, has a climatic condition of arid to semiarid, and the coastal region has humid to semi-humid conditions [3].

The main parameter for agriculture is rainfall. The main sources of rainfall in AP are induced by the northeast, northwest, and southwest monsoons. As per the statistical data, the annual rainfall of the state is 925 mm [3]. The southwest monsoon from June to September is the principal source of rainfall, contributing 68.5% of the overall rainfall of AP. Then the northeast follows from the months of October to December with a contribution of 22.3%. The other 9.2% of the rainfall is from the months of summer and winter [3].

The second factor that plays a vital role in farming is soil type and nutrient values. AP state has a variety of soils ranging from poor coastal sands to highly fertile deltaic alluviums. The coastal region is mixed up with these soil types and the other region Rayalaseema has the red soil type which occupies 66% of the area under cultivation.

The Godavari region, which covers the major deltaic region of Coastal Andhra, is found to be rich in alluvial soil, the same as the Prakasam district Krishna River deltaic region too. Both cover 5% of the cultivated area of AP [3]. The coastal region sands have only 3%, while the other 2% is covered by laterite soils in the state.

The rivers in AP are also a major advantage for the state's contribution to agriculture. The state has the advantage of having rivers that flow towards the east in the main regions of AP. Those rivers rich in copious supplies are brought from the Western and Eastern Ghats and the Deccan Plateau up to the Bay of Bengal [3]. The state contains almost 40 rivers rich in various minerals and nutrients that flow throughout the state. Out of these 40, the most important rivers that contribute mainly to state agriculture are the Godavari and the Krishna in the coastal part, the Vamsadhara in the northeastern part of the state, and the Pennar in the Rayalaseema region. The remaining rivers are minor coastal rivers.

The crops that are cultivated in the state are rice, chili, sugarcane, cotton, tobacco, mango, and pepper [4]. Recently, crops used for vegetable oil production such as sunflower and peanuts have gained favor. Based on the climate for agriculture, the state is divided into six zones, as shown in Figure 10.1. They are the Godavari zone, Krishna zone, north coastal zone, southern zone, scarce rainfall zone, and high-altitude zone.

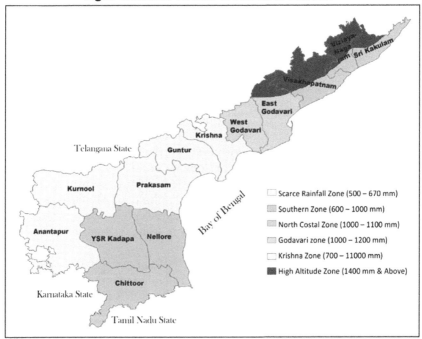

Figure 10.1 Agro-climatic zones – AP. Source: http://sap.ipni.net/article/andhra -pradesh#, accessed on 28 January 2022.

The Godavari zone is a predominantly agricultural district, and it is famous for it, contributing about 10% of the total food production of Andhra Pradesh [4]. It is the most prosperous district in the state and is the second richest district in India. The major crop grown is paddy. Other crops grown are maize, oil seeds, sugarcane, and pulses such as black gram and green gram. This Godavari zone is rich in red clayey soil, the coastal area with sandy and lateritic soil, and the deltaic region of Godavari with rich alluvial soil, which is suitable for all crops.

10.1.3 Essential nutrients for production of crops

Soil is a principal source of nutrients needed by crops for growth. For farming, based on the soil nutrient value, the crops grown are varied. To meet crop needs throughout the growing season, soil fertility must be consistently high. There are 15 mineral nutrients in the soil. It is classified into six macronutrients and nine micronutrients. Under macronutrients, three primary nutrients are present, named nitrogen (N), phosphorous (P), and potassium (K), and all these three together are called NPK. And three more secondary nutrients in the macro category are sulfur (S), magnesium (Mg), and calcium (Ca). There are nine micronutrients like iron, manganese, zinc, copper, boron, and so on. The requirement of nutrients for each crop should depend on the specific guidelines given by the regional agriculture department, environmental factors such as soil type and weather conditions, and the nutrients applied. Using biological nitrogen fixation, residues of plants (remains of past harvests), organic matter as manures, and fertilizers can also be used to provide nutrients as a supplement, but it should be within limited usage. The excessive usage of fertilizers degrades the natural nutrients present in the cultivated land.

Alluvial soil in the deltaic region and the coastal regions is fertile by nature. The river brings plenty of nutrients and minerals from various places. But due to the absence of organic farming and excessive use of fertilizer, the agricultural land is made unfertile and the natural soil nutrients are reduced gradually.

10.1.4 Challenges in agriculture

Agriculture is a complex, uncertain, unpredictable, and individual business. Even though agriculture is the backbone of our nation, losses in farming affect the individual farmer alone. There are plenty of challenges for the farmers; they must meet uncertain changes and the needs of the environment and the consumers as well as the expectations of regulators and various industries based on farming, food processors, and retailers. There is always a threat from climatic change, which creates more pressure on farmers. There is uncertainty due to the failure of rainfall, soil erosion, and diversified consumers who have changing tastes in food. The fertilizers used for farming also pose challenges for farmers; over-usage of fertilizers spoils the natural nutrients present in the soil. Pests can create new diseases and the diverse ways to control them creates a hectic task for farmers. From sowing to harvesting, farmers face numerous challenges and overheads. Because of this, some farmers struggle a lot.

The following challenges are faced by the farmers:

- Natural disasters like cyclones, heavy downpours of rainfall, draught, etc.
- Most of them are uneducated and unable to adapt to modern technologies.
- Staying resilient against global economic factors.
- The present generation considers farming low-scale and disgusting.
- Due to technological change, consumers' expectations also vary and this involves looking for new species or varieties of items.
- Most of the farmers are below the poverty line and depend on farming for day-to-day needs, so are unable to invest more in farm productivity.

The farmers, due to the unpredictable climatic changes, debts taken from various financial sources, and failure to return them due to the aforementioned challenges, lose their hope in the future and are forced to attempt suicide. AP has one of the highest rates of farmer suicide. Because each farm is different, modern agriculture doesn't always work the same way. There are different landscapes, soils, available technology, and yields in each one. So, this chapter as crop advisor helps the farmer society to understand the new technologies and provides knowledge on the appropriate selection of crops based on the soil nutrients and meteorological parameters.

10.1.5 Data mining techniques in agriculture

Data mining is a technique that is applied to the repository of huge and enormous data. Nowadays there is a great demand for data mining techniques. With the revolution in technology increasing, various categories of data are generated. Old forecasting methods are not that effective. Data mining is a powerful tool; the techniques are mostly used for prediction, clustering, decision trees, relevance analysis, and so on. The present days are uncertain and so there is a need for techniques to predict the future. This prediction helps us to overcome future consequences. Data mining techniques are used for various applications like military, medical, banking, e-commerce, finances, stocks, and so on. Machine learning and ensemble techniques are used for the prediction of crop selection. This application is provided for the farmers of the deltaic and coastal regions of AP, which helps the farmers to go for some additional crops suitable for that region. Thereby the farmer can gain knowledge about various crops beyond rice to grow and gain yield.

Farmers can recognize crop losses and prevent them from occurring in the future if they have detailed information on crop output. Instead of planting the same crop year after year, farmers should experiment with different crops based on soil type and weather conditions. This would help them expand and profit more. Crop selection and yield prediction are major agricultural problems that must be dealt with carefully. Every single farmer is constantly interested in knowing how much produce he may expect based on his expectations. The traditional method of predicting crop yields was to look at a farmer's experience with a particular kind of crop. Weather conditions, pests, and the timing of harvest operations are all crucial factors in determining agricultural productivity. Accurate information regarding the history of crop selection and yield is a main source of information that is used to make important decisions about risk management in agriculture.

10.1.6 Organization of the chapter

Section 10.2 discusses relevant research on different learning approaches for crop prediction, including machine learning and deep learning. The machine learning and ensemble strategies are covered in detail in section 10.3. The experimental analysis is presented in section 10.4. Section 10.5 provides the findings of several crop forecast strategies that have been tested. Section 10.6 brings the chapter to a close by defining the most effective strategy for crop prediction.

10.2 RELATED WORK

In developing countries where technology is not that applicable for agriculture, most people involved in agriculture predict the suitable crop yield based on their experience with production. This section presents a detailed survey of techniques used for prediction in the agriculture field.

Ghosh and Koley presented an article on the prediction of soil fertility in which they used backpropagation neural networks to predict the fertility of the soil and essential nutrients needed for plants [5]. The authors applied the dataset to backpropagation neural network (BPN) and artificial neural network (ANN) methods. The paper also concluded that BPN shows an incredibly significant accuracy in soil fertility prediction.

Prasad published a study on the prediction of agricultural production increases using meteorological factors and the use of the vegetation index [6]. There are several elements that influence crop yield [6], including rainfall, surface temperature, soil moisture, and vegetation index. The primary crops, paddy and wheat, are selected for the testing process. Rice and wheat crop yields were evaluated in this article, which looked at the key states of India and compared the major factors of each state. When used in prediction mode, the experiential equation and its corresponding coefficient, which is dependent on past satellite and meteorological data, are proven to be an extremely promising approach to predicting crop production.

Using an ensemble algorithmic model with a voting approach, Pudumalar published a study in which the K-nearest neighbor, naive Bayes, random tree, and CHAID are used as a learner to suggest a crop for the site-specific parameters with good accuracy and efficiency [7]. The quick miner tool [7] was utilized in this manner. The learner who receives the greatest number of votes will have the greatest accuracy. According to this research, the forecast is 88% accurate.

Maya Gopal and Bhargavi assess the most important characteristics for reliable crop yield prediction and recommend improvements [8]. Random forest (RF), K-nearest neighbor, support vector regression, and artificial neural network are some of the machine learning techniques that have been developed for improved accuracy [8]. According to the findings of the experiment, the RF algorithm achieves the maximum accuracy in terms of its error analysis values for all the various feature subsets while utilizing the identical training agricultural data as the other algorithms. Based on the overall performance, the random forest (RF VarImp) is identified as the superior prediction method, with forward feature selection (FFS) providing the highest accuracy and precision.

Suruliandi et al.'s paper has stated that selecting appropriate attributes for the right crops is a vital role in the prediction of crops and it is undertaken by feature selection techniques. The dataset is an agricultural dataset with 16 attributes, which includes the soil characteristics and environmental factors, collected from the Agricultural Department of Tamil Nadu [9]. The accuracy and error rate by considering a few attributes from the data set is computed using random forest, KNN, decision tree, naive Bayes, SVM, and bagging. The experimentation results show that the bagging classifier with selection techniques like SFFS, RFE, etc. has given good accuracy with a 70% training and 30% testing data splitting range, and RFE with the bagging method provided better results compared to the remaining methods.

Bali and Singla have done research by considering the agricultural lands in Punjab and wheat crop prediction [10]. This paper shows that deep learning methods are more efficient than machine learning methods. The recurrent neural network (RNN) model is used in this paper. The models like ANN, random forest, and multivariate linear regression are used for comparison with the RNN method. The results presented in the paper show that RNN gives more accurate prediction than the other models.

Oikonomidis et al. used the XGBoostML algorithm, deep neural networks (DNN), convolutional neural networks (CNN), CNN-XGBoost, CNN-recurrent neural networks (RNN), and CNN-long short-term memory (LSTM) for prediction using a soybean dataset with 395 parameters which include soil and temperature values [11]. The hybrid combination of the CNN-DNN model performed better than the other models, and the second one in terms of less execution time was the XGBoost model, which performed well compared to the other DL-based models.

Keerthana et al. provide the top ten important crops that, when the characteristics of location and weather conditions are taken into consideration, answer the bulk of the consequences [12]. The ensemble algorithm is used to anticipate the outcome with a higher accuracy rate than the individual algorithms. Taking this into consideration, it can be stated that the ensemble of decision tree regressors combined with the AdaBoost regressors produced the highest accuracy.

According to Kedlaya and colleagues, the data set was gathered from the Karnataka area. The varied datasets containing horticultural data with factors such as rainfall, temperature, slope, humidity, and soil moisture are analyzed using a variety of machine learning algorithms [13]. Datasets are analyzed using Xarray functions, and a pattern matching approach is utilized to get the crop depending on area and season. According to the testing findings, the decision tree classifier outperforms the naive Bayes, K-nearest neighbor, CHAID, random tree, association rule mining, linear regression, and artificial neural network in terms of accuracy.

Ismael et al. researched the comparison of several classification algorithms used for agricultural production prediction and discussed and evaluated the results. According to the error levels and accuracy [14], the algorithms are compared. The decision tree, naive Bayes, random forest, support vector machine, and K-nearest neighbor algorithms were also evaluated for the comparisons. The article concludes that SVM delivers the highest accuracy for agricultural yield prediction.

Van Klompenburg et al. did a systematic study of various ML algorithms for crop yield, crop to be grown, and seasonal crops to be grown. Nearly 50 ML papers and 30 DL papers were taken, and an exhaustive study was done [11]. The authors concluded that most of the experiments are done with convolutional neural networks (CNN); long short-term memory (LSTM) and deep neural networks (DNN) are two more deep learning methods that are commonly employed.

Garanayak et al. suggested a system for crop recommendations. In this paper various regression algorithms like decision tree, linear regression, SVM, RF, and polynomial regression algorithms are used for crop prediction [15]. In this, five crops – rice, ragi, potato, gram, and onion – are considered, and area and crop production are used as meteorological parameters. Finally, the results say that major voting (MV) with combination techniques achieve a greater accuracy in the crop and yield prediction of those five crops.

Kalimuthu et al. suggested the machine learning algorithm naive Bayes, which is a supervised learning algorithm [16]. Seed data for the crops, temperature, moisture content, humidity, and so on are some of the things that are taken into account when making a prediction. These things, along with the right parameters, help the crops grow well.

The related work shows that a single algorithm has been used for prediction. Moreover, if multiple algorithms are used then the data considered for prediction will be of a single dataset like datasets consisting only of soil parameters or weather parameters, and hence the prediction is based on soil strength or on weather conditions. This might not guarantee higher accuracy in prediction as there are multiple machine learning algorithms for predictive learning.

The aforementioned works have their own pros and cons. The general observations from the studies cited are the following:

- A single algorithm does not guarantee the proper prediction.
- Multiple prediction models for the same purpose result in more time and cost.
- Farmers might face the risk of market failure or production problems if the prediction is not up to the mark.
- This approach is less effective in comparison to the proposed system.

10.3 LEARNING METHODS

Learning is particularly important in data mining. The system must learn using some algorithm, and then it is used for the predictions. In this section machine learning algorithms and ensemble algorithms are discussed, which are used in this proposed crop prediction application.

10.3.1 Machine learning

Machine learning is the trending technology that is mostly used by multidisciplinary researchers for predictions using past historical data. There is a lot of information from the past that machine learning algorithms use as training data. It is an important process to check the quality of data [17–24] used for machine learning algorithms. This data is used to build a mathematical model that helps make predictions or decisions without having to be explicitly programmed [25]. An example, direct experience, or instruction can be used to start the process of learning. This helps people look for patterns in data and make better decisions in the future based on what they have seen. It can be used in real time to learn from data after it has been trained. The training process and automation are part of machine learning. In machine learning, there are three types of algorithms: supervised learning, unsupervised learning, and reinforcement learning [26]. Here, machine learning models like discriminant analysis and classification trees are built and used to predict what crops will grow.

Discriminant analysis is a way to look at data when the criterion or the dependent variable is a group and the predictor is a single number [27]. The goal of discriminant analysis is to produce discriminant functions that are nothing more than the linear combination of independent variables that will be able to tell the diverse types of the dependent variable in a perfect way. It allows the researcher to see if there are big differences between the groups in terms of the predictor variables. It also looks at how well the classification is done.

10.3.1.1 Classification tree

Classification using trees, which are also called decision trees, is one way to use machine learning to make predictions. The goal is to build a model that predicts the value of a target variable based on several other variables. This is a simple representation for classifying examples.

10.3.1.2 K-nearest neighbor algorithm

One of the simplest machine learning algorithms, based on the supervised learning method, is K-nearest neighbour. The K-NN algorithm [28] makes the assumption that the new case and the existing cases are comparable, and it places the new instance in the category that is most like the existing categories.

10.3.2 Ensemble methods

Ensemble methods [29] are a type of method that uses a group of people to accomplish a task. A machine learning strategy known as ensemble learning is one that involves combining numerous base models in order to build one best prediction model. In order to achieve greater prediction performance than could be gained from any of the constituent learning algorithms alone [30], ensemble approaches employ many learning algorithms in combination. When used in conjunction with other approaches, ensemble methods assist to increase the resilience and generalizability of the model.

Max voting, averaging, and weighted averaging are simple ensemble techniques, whereas the advanced methods are stacking, blending, random space, bagging, boosting, etc. [31–33]. The ensemble techniques random space, bagging, and boosting are used for the experimental work.

10.3.2.1 Random space

The random space ensemble constructs individual classifiers by selecting feature subspaces at random from a pool of feature subspaces. This is accomplished by the use of the algorithm "subspace." In random subspace [34], the feature subspaces are selected at random from the original feature space, and individual classifiers are constructed solely based on the qualities from the original training set in order to maximize accuracy. For the final prediction, the outputs from multiple separate classifiers are merged using uniform majority voting to provide the final result.

10.3.2.2 Bagging

Bagging (or bootstrap aggregating) is a way to get a good idea of the distribution of a set of things by looking at these smaller groups (bags) [35, 36]. The number of subsets that are made for bagging may not be as big as the original set, but they could be. The algorithm called "bag" is used to try new things.

10.3.2.3 AdaBoosting

Adaptive boosting, or AdaBoost, is one of the simplest ways to boost your score. In most cases, decision trees are used to make a model [37]. A series of models are made, each one correcting the mistakes in the previous model. Weight is added to the observations that were wrongly predicted, and then the model that comes after works to predict these values correctly. It is common in this experiment to use the algorithm "AdaBoostM2."

10.4 EXPERIMENTAL ANALYSIS

10.4.1 Dataset

The idea is to implement machine learning and ensemble algorithms for predicting the suitable crop to be grown using the real environmental data from the deltaic region of Coastal Andhra Pradesh. However, due to the unavailability of complete data for the deltaic regions, the data publicly available is used. The dataset that is used in this chapter is taken from the publicly available Kaggle repository dataset. The dataset is termed "Crop Advisor." The dataset includes 2,499 instances and eight parameters, of which 299 instances have missing values for the parameters. Therefore, the dataset is considered after taking away the instances of missing values. Finally, the dataset with 2,200 instances is considered, leaving the instances with missing values. The eight parameters are nitrogen, phosphorus, potassium, and pH as soil attributes, temperature, humidity, and rainfall as weather attributes, and suitable crop to be grown.

The value of nitrogen varies from 0 to 140 CCF, phosphorous varies from 5 to 145, potassium ranges from 5 to 205, temperature varies from 8.83 to 43.68 degrees centigrade, humidity varies from 14.26 to 99.98, pH ranges from 3.5 to 9.94, and rainfall amount ranges from 20.21 to 298.56 mm. The suitable crop based on the aforementioned parameters is identified as any one of the following: apple, banana, black gram, chickpea, coconut, coffee, cotton, grapes, jute, kidney beans, lentils, maize, mango, moth beans, musk melon, mung bean, orange, pigeon peas, pomegranate, papaya, rice, and watermelon.

10.4.2 Process flow

The experimentation for predicting the right crop to be grown under the given conditions is carried out in five steps. The process flow diagram of crop prediction is shown in Figure 10.2.

10.4.2.1 Step 1: Selection of suitable dataset for crop prediction

The resultant dataset named "Crop Advisor dataset," with 2,200 instances and eight parameters, after removing the instances with missing parameters, is used for experimentation of predicting and advising the suitable crop to be grown under certain environmental conditions.

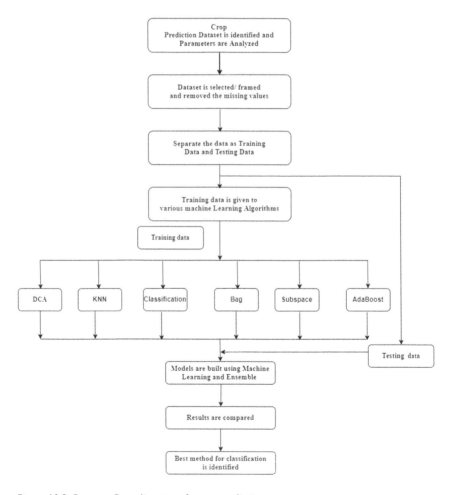

Figure 10.2 Process flow diagram of crop prediction.

10.4.2.2 Step 2: Identification of training data and testing data

The task of framing the training and testing datasets is very crucial for experimentation using machine learning techniques. Generally, 70:30, 75:25, 80:20, or 60:40 can be used for generating the training and testing datasets. For this experimentation, from the Crop Advisor dataset, 1,760 randomly selected instances (80% of the total dataset) are used as training data and 440 instances (20% of the total dataset) are used as testing data.

10.4.2.3 Step 3: Build the crop advisor models

To build the Crop Advisor models, three machine learning algorithms and three ensemble algorithms are used. The training data with 1,760 instances and the first seven parameters are used as input and the eighth parameter is used as output for building the models. Three models for crop prediction are developed using the machine learning algorithms discriminant analysis, classification tree, and k-nearest neighbor, and the other three models are developed using the ensemble algorithms subspace, bag, and AdaBoost.

10.4.2.4 Step 4: Test the models

The already trained and built six Crop Advisor models are now tested using the testing data of 440 instances. The test data is passed as input to the models and the predicted values are compared with the actual values in the test dataset. The training data and the total dataset values can also be passed to the models to identify their performance in predicting the suitable crop.

10.4.2.5 Step 5: Comparison of models

The accuracy of the models is firstly observed for the total dataset, training data, and testing data to identify the best model. The other metrics used for comparing all the six developed models are precision, recall, and F1-score. The best model for classification is identified based on all of the evaluation metrics.

10.4.3 Performance metrics

The performance metrics used for identifying the best Crop Advisor model are accuracy, precision, recall, and F1-score.

10.4.3.1 Accuracy

Accuracy is the number of correct predictions divided by the number of predictions.

$$ac = (T1 + T0) / (T1 + T0 + F1 + F0) \tag{10.1}$$

Those are the things that are true positive (T1) and true negative (T0). Those are the things that are false positive (F1), false negative (F0), and so on.

10.4.3.2 Precision

It is the precision of a thing that was supposed to be good but was actually good. It's also called a "good predicted value" (PPV). Precision is shown as Pr.

$$Pr = T1 / (T1 + F1) \tag{10.2}$$

10.4.3.3 Recall

This is the percentage of positive results out of the number of samples that were positive. Under another name, sensitivity refers to how well you can remember things. It is called rc.

$$rc = T1 / (T1 + FO) \tag{10.3}$$

10.4.3.4 F1-score

It's called the F1-score because it's the sum of precision and recall.

$$F1\text{-Score} = 2 \left[\frac{(pr + rc)}{(pr + rc)} \right] \tag{10.4}$$

10.4.4 Experimentation

The experimentation of developing the Crop Advisor models for classification is carried out in MATLAB. Three models using machine learning algorithms – discriminant analysis, classification tree, and K-nearest neighbor – are developed. Three other models are developed using the ensemble algorithms subspace, bag, and AdaBoost. The MATLAB functions are used for generating the models. The functions "fitcdiscr," "fitctree," and "fitcknn" are used for creating the three machine learning models – discriminant analysis model, classification tree, and K-nearest neighbor classification model respectively. For creating the ensemble model subspace, the function "fitensemble" with the aggregation method as subspace, the number of weak learners as 420, and weak-learner as discriminant are used. To create the ensemble model bag, the function "fitcensemble" with the aggregation method as bag, number of learning cycles as 150, and learner as "tree" with method surrogate as "on" is used. To create the ensemble model AdaBoost, the function "fitcensemble" with the aggregation method as AdaBoostM2, MaxNum Splits as 11 are used. All six models are developed based on the training data. The training dataset is formed by randomly picking up 80% of the records from the total dataset, and the other 20% is the testing dataset.

10.5 RESULTS AND DISCUSSION

The experimentation is conducted in five iterations by varying the training and testing datasets. The accuracy is measured in all five iterations for the total dataset, training dataset, and testing dataset separately. In all the iterations, the model having the highest accuracy is observed. Based on the number of times the model achieved highest accuracy, it is noticed that the ensemble model using "bag" achieved the highest accuracy for the total dataset, training data, and testing data in the majority of the iterations when compared to the other five models. After all five iterations are completed, it is observed that the ensemble model "bag" has given the highest accuracy in all the iterations for the total dataset, training data, and testing data. The accuracy of the models for different iterations is shown in Table 10.1, Table 10.2, and Table 10.3. The number of items in which each model obtained the highest accuracy is also represented in Tables 10.1, 10.2, and 10.3 under the highest accuracy count (HAC). For one iteration of randomly picked training and testing data using 80:20, the performance metrics like accuracy, precision, recall, and F1-score for all the Crop Advisor models are presented in Table 10.4. It is observed that the ensemble model "bag" has achieved an accuracy of 99.99%.

Figure 10.3 shows a comparison of six learning models by varying the number of iterations from one to five using the total dataset and the

Table 10.1 Total dataset accuracy

Models/ iteration	Discriminant analysis	Classification tree	K-nearest neighbors	Subspace	Bag	AdaBoost
1	96.86	99.64	99.73	91.32	99.86	99.86
2	96.59	99.50	99.27	92.32	99.95	99.91
3	96.73	99.55	99.50	91.55	99.82	99.82
4	96.68	99.55	99.50	90.05	100.00	99.91
5	96.73	99.68	99.77	91.23	99.86	99.86
HAC	0	0	0	0	5	3

Table 10.2 Training dataset accuracy

Models/ iteration	Discriminant analysis	Classification tree	K-nearest neighbors	Subspace	Bag	AdaBoost
1	96.99	99.72	100.00	91.70	100.00	100.00
2	96.53	99.66	100.00	92.27	100.00	100.00
3	96.65	99.77	100.00	91.25	100.00	100.00
4	96.76	99.66	100.00	90.11	100.00	100.00
5	97.10	99.77	100.00	91.48	100.00	100.00
HAC	0	0	5	0	5	5

Table 10.3 Testing dataset accuracy

Models/ iteration	Discriminant analysis	Classification tree	K-nearest neighbors	Subspace	Bag	AdaBoost
I	96.36	99.32	98.64	89.77	99.32	99.32
2	96.82	98.86	96.36	92.50	99.77	99.55
3	97.05	98.64	97.50	92.73	99.09	99.09
4	96.36	99.09	97.50	89.77	100.00	99.55
5	95.23	99.32	98.86	90.23	99.32	99.32
HAC	0	2	0	0	5	3

Table 10.4 Performance metric analysis

Models/ metrics	Discriminant analysis	Classification tree	K-nearest neighbor	Subspace	Bag	AdaBoost
Accuracy	96.77	99.55	99.55	92.09	99.91	99.86
Precision	97.03	97.03	99.57	92.48	99.91	99.86
Recall	96.77	96.77	99.55	92.09	99.91	99.86
FI-score	96.90	96.90	99.56	92.28	99.91	99.86

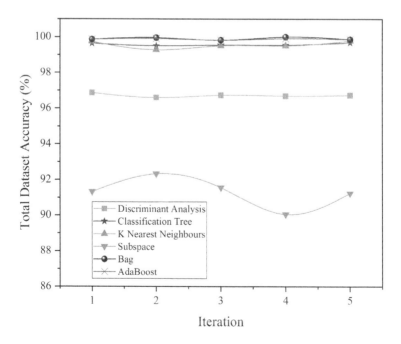

Figure 10.3 Comparison of accuracy of six models.

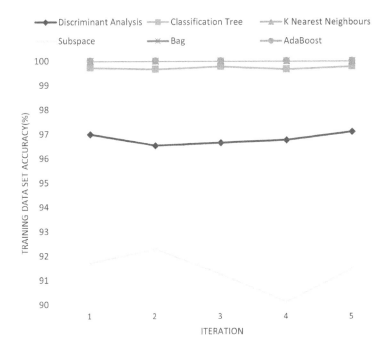

Figure 10.4 Accuracy of six models with number of iterations for training dataset.

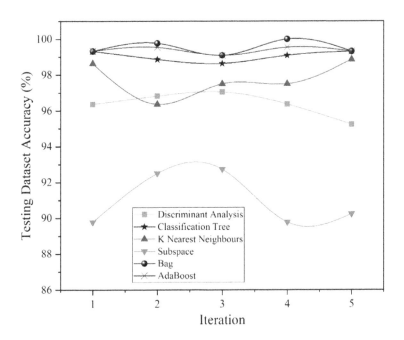

Figure 10.5 A.ccuracy of six models with number of iterations for testing dataset.

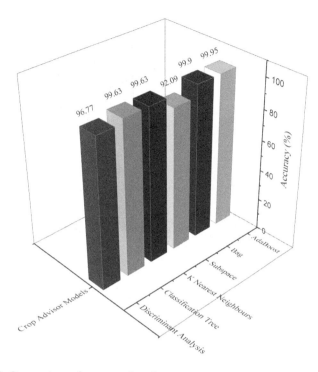

Figure 10.6 Comparison of accuracy for all.

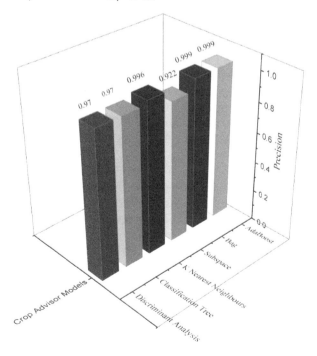

Figure 10.7 Comparison of precision for all six models.

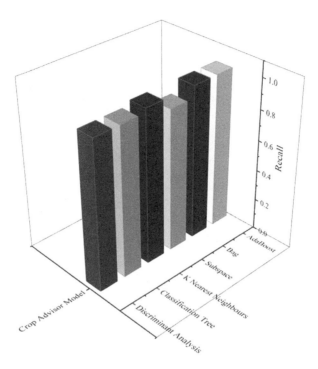

Figure 10.8 Comparison of recall.

accuracy obtained for each iteration. The resultant graph shows for all five iterations the "bag" algorithm has maximum accuracy and for three iterations "AdaBoost" has the maximum accuracy.

Figure 10.4 shows a comparison of six learning models by varying the number of iterations from one to five using the training dataset and the accuracy obtained for each iteration. The resultant graph shows for all five iterations "K-NN," "bag," and "Adaboost" algorithms have maximum accuracy.

Figure 10.5 shows a comparison of six learning models by varying the number of iterations from one to five using the testing dataset and the accuracy obtained for each iteration. The resultant graph shows for all five iterations the "bag" algorithm has maximum accuracy and for three iterations "AdaBoost" has the maximum accuracy.

Figure 10.6 shows the comparison of all six models based on the accuracy obtained. The "bag" algorithm has higher accuracy than the other models. Figure 10.7 shows the comparison of the metric precision of all six learning models. The "bag" algorithm has higher precision than the other models.

Figure 10.8 shows the comparison of the metric recall of all six learning models. The "bag" algorithm has a higher value for recall than the other

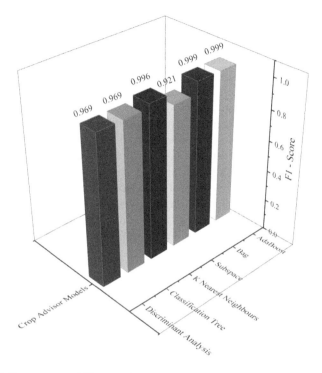

Figure 10.9 Comparison of F1-score for all six models.

models. Figure 10.9 shows the comparison of the metric F1-score of all six learning models. The "bag" algorithm has a higher value for F1-score than the other models.

10.6 CONCLUSION

Agriculture is the backbone of the Republic of India and it contributes a lot to the country's economy. At the same time, the farmer and his timeless work should be paid correctly. The designed model "Crop Advisor" predicts the most suitable crop for a particular land based on soil and weather parameters such as nitrogen, potassium, phosphorus, pH, temperature, humidity, and rainfall. The parameters are based on the dataset collected from Kaggle. The system takes the required input from the user. This all-input data applies to machine learning predictive algorithms and ensemble algorithms to identify the patterns among the data and then process it as per the input conditions.

Using MATLAB, the training dataset is given to the six models of machine learning and ensemble techniques. Then the testing data is given to the models and the results are compared based on the four performance metrics. From the experimentation results, it is clearly shown that the ensemble algorithm "bag" has the highest value in terms of the performance metrics such as accuracy, precision, recall, and F1-score. The Crop Advisor model predicts the crops to be grown on the basis of soil and weather parameters given by the user according to their preference. The Crop Advisor model using the "bag" algorithm can now be used using the real environmental data of the coastal deltaic region of AP for predicting the suitable crop to be grown by which the crop yield would be improved. This would provide an extensive prediction on the basis of geographical and environmental conditions which improves the economic status of the farmers in the deltaic region. The work can further be extended and used with the real environmental data collected from any other geographical region.

REFERENCES

1. https://www.worldometers.info/world-population/india-population/
2. https://www.fao.org/india/fao-in-india/india-at-a-glanc
3. https://www.ihs.org.in/apstateprofile/apagriculturalprofile1.htm
4. http://sap.ipni.net/article/andhra-pradesh#
5. Koley, Santanu. "Machine learning for soil fertility and plant nutrient management using back propagation neural networks." *Shivnath Ghosh, SantanuKoley (2014) "Machine Learning for Soil Fertility and Plant Nutrient Management using Back Propagation Neural Networks" International Journal on Recent and Innovation Trends in Computing and Communication* 2.2 (2014): 292–297.
6. Prasad, A. K., et al. "Use of vegetation index and meteorological parameters for the prediction of crop yield in India." *International Journal of Remote Sensing* 28.23 (2007): 5207–5235.
7. Pudumalar, S., Ramanujam, E., Rajashree, R. H., Kavya, C., Kiruthika, T., and Nisha, J. "Crop recommendation system for precision agriculture." In 2016 Eighth International Conference on Advanced Computing (ICoAC) (2017, January). (pp. 32–36). IEEE.
8. Maya Gopal, P. S. "Performance evaluation of best feature subsets for crop yield prediction using machine learning algorithms." *Applied Artificial Intelligence* 33.7 (2019): 621–642.
9. Suruliandi, A., G. Mariammal, and S. P. Raja. "Crop prediction based on soil and environmental characteristics using feature selection techniques." *Mathematical and Computer Modelling of Dynamical Systems* 27.1 (2021): 117–140.
10. Bali, Nishu, and Anshu Singla. "Deep learning based wheat crop yield prediction model in Punjab region of North India." *Applied Artificial Intelligence* 35.15 (2021): 1–25.

11. Oikonomidis, Alexandros, Cagatay Catal, and Ayalew Kassahun. "Hybrid deep learning-based models for crop yield prediction." *Applied Artificial Intelligence* 36.1 (2022): 1–18.

12. Keerthana, Mummaleti, et al. "An ensemble algorithm for crop yield prediction." In Third International Conference on Intelligent Communication Technologies and Virtual Mobile Networks (ICICV) (2021). IEEE.

13. Kedlaya, Aishwarya, et al. "An efficient algorithm for predicting crop using historical data and pattern matching technique." *Global Transitions Proceedings* 2.2 (2021):294–298.

14. Ismael, Halbast Rashid, Adnan Mohsin Abdulazeez, and Dathar A. Hasan. "Comparative study for classification algorithms performance in crop yields prediction systems." *Qubahan Academic Journal* 1.2 (2021): 119–124.

15. Garanayak, Mamata, et al. "Agricultural recommendation system for crops using different machine learning regression methods." *International Journal of Agricultural and Environmental Information Systems (IJAEIS)* 12.1 (2021): 1–20.

16. Kalimuthu, M., Vaishnavi, P., and Kishore, M. "Crop prediction using machine learning." Third International Conference on Smart Systems and Inventive Technology (ICSSIT) (2020, August): 926–932.

17. Bhushan, M., Kumar, A., Samant, P., Bansal, S., Tiwari, S., and Negi, A. "Identifying quality attributes of FODA and DSSA methods in domain analysis using a case study." In 2021 10th International Conference on System Modeling & Advancement in Research Trends (SMART) (2021): pp. 562–567. https://doi.org/10.1109/SMART52563.2021.9676289.

18. Bhushan, M., Duarte, J. Á. G., Samant, P., Kumar, A., and Negi, A. "Classifying and resolving software product line redundancies using an ontological first-order logic rule-based method." *Expert Systems with Applications* 168 (2021): 114167. https://doi.org/10.1016/j.eswa.2020.114167

19. Bhushan, M., Goel, S., and Kumar, A. "Improving quality of software product line by analysing inconsistencies in feature models using an ontological rule-based approach." *Expert Systems* 35.3 (2018): e12256. https://doi.org /10.1111/exsy.12256

20. Bhushan, M., Goel, S., and Kaur, K. "Analyzing inconsistencies in software product lines using an ontological rule-based approach." *Journal of Systems and Software* 137 (2018): 605–617. https://doi.org/10.1016/j.jss.2017.06.002

21. Bhushan, M., Negi, A., Samant, P., Goel, S., and Kumar, A. "A classification and systematic review of product line feature model defects." *Software Quality Journal* 28.4 (2020): 1507–1550. https://doi.org/10.1007/s11219 -020-09522-1

22. Megha, Negi, A., and Kaur, K.. "Method to resolve software product line errors." In International Conference on Information, Communication and Computing Technology, Springer (2017): pp. 258–268. https://doi.org/10 .1007/978-981-10-6544-6_24

23. Bhushan, M., Goel, S., Kumar, A., and Negi, A. "Managing software product line using an ontological rule-based framework." In 2017 International Conference on Infocom Technologies and Unmanned Systems (Trends and Future Directions) (ICTUS), (2017): 376–382. IEEE. https://doi.org/10.1109/ ICTUS.2017.8286036

24. Bhushan, M., and Goel, S. "Improving software product line using an onto-logical approach." *Sādhanā* 41.12 (2016): 1381–1391. https://doi.org/10.1007/s12046- 016-0571-y

25. Balducci, Fabrizio, Donato Impedovo, and Giuseppe Pirlo. "Machine learning applications on agricultural datasets for smart farm enhancement." *Machines* 6.3 (2018): 38.

26. Verma, K., S. Bhardwaj, R. Arya, M.S.U. Islam, M. Bhushan, A. Kumar, and P. Samant. "Latest tools for data mining and machine learning." *International Journal of Innovative Technology and Exploring Engineering* 8.9S (2019): 18–23. https://doi.org/10.35940/ijitee.I1003.0789S19

27. Ramayah, T., et al. "Discriminant analysis: An illustrated example." *African Journal of Business Management* 4.9 (2010): 1654–1667.

28. Pal, S., N. Mishra, M. Bhushan, P. S. Kholiya, M. Rana, and A. Negi. "Deep learning techniques for prediction and diagnosis of diabetes mellitus," In 2022 International Mobile and Embedded Technology Conference (MECON), IEEE, (2022): pp. 588–593. https://doi.org/10.1109/MECON53876.2022.9752176.

29. Guo, Gongde, et al. "KNN model-based approach in classification." In *OTM Confederated International Conferences" On the Move to Meaningful Internet Systems."* Springer, Berlin, Heidelberg (2003).

30. Dietterich, Thomas G. "Ensemble methods in machine learning." In International Workshop on Multiple Classifier Systems. Springer, Berlin, Heidelberg, (2000).

31. Hamza, Mounir, and Denis Larocque. "An empirical comparison of ensemble methods based on classification trees." *Journal of Statistical Computation and Simulation* 75.8 (2005): 629–643.

32. Ren, Ye, Le Zhang, and Ponnuthurai N. Suganthan. "Ensemble classification and regression-recent developments, applications and future directions." *IEEE Computational Intelligence Magazine* 11.1 (2016): 41–53.

33. Bauer, Eric, and Ron Kohavi. "An empirical comparison of voting classification algorithms: Bagging, boosting, and variants." *Machine Learning* 36.1 (1999): 105–139.

34. Kuncheva, Ludmila I., and Catrin O. Plumpton. "Choosing parameters for random subspace ensembles for fMRI classification." International Workshop on Multiple Classifier Systems. Springer, Berlin, Heidelberg, (2010).

35. Dutta, Ritaban, et al. "Dynamic cattle behavioural classification using supervised ensemble classifiers." *Computers and Electronics in Agriculture* 111 (2015): 18–28.

36. Shahhosseini, Mohsen, Guiping Hu, and Sotirios V. Archontoulis. "Forecasting corn yield with machine learning ensembles." *Frontiers in Plant Science* 11 (2020): 1120.

37. Peerlinck, Amy, John Sheppard, and Jacob Senecal. "Adaboost with neural networks for yield and protein prediction in precision agriculture." In International Joint Conference on Neural Networks (IJCNN) (2019). IEEE.

Chapter 11

Artificial intelligence-based quality inference for food processing industry applications

Ninja Begum, Shagufta Rizwana, and Manuj Kumar Hazarika

CONTENTS

11.1 INTRODUCTION

Agriculture 4.0 alludes to the industry's next big trend focusing more on the digitalization of agriculture. By 2025, the population is expected to surpass eight billion people, and by 2050, it will be about ten billion. [1]. This in turn will result in a rapid demand for basic human needs, particularly food and agriculture. With urbanization, growth in education, and a rise in income, this demand for quantitative and qualitative food will reach its peak. To meet these demands, world food production needs to increase by 60–70%. [2]. With this motive, agriculture 4.0 or the fourth agricultural revolution has come up with meeting the demands on demographics. And to overcome such a huge demand for agricultural productivity, the adoption of emerging technologies in the agri-food sector becomes a must. Digitalization in agriculture is a smart solution in this regard, maximizing agricultural productivity from farm to fork. This has already been dubbed the "Digital Agricultural Revolution" [3] by the United Nations Food and Agriculture Organization, which combines cutting-edge technology such as the Internet of Things (IoT), big data, artificial intelligence (AI), and cloud computing [4]. These technologies have made several breakthroughs in several fields of study and thus have been deployed in agriculture 4.0. In the

DOI: 10.1201/9781003286745-11

223

field of food, these technologies are implemented by the combination of AI with sensors, robots, spectroscopy, thermal images, etc. AI is making machine intelligence equivalent to human intelligence. AI techniques like machine learning and deep learning have been able to make an outstanding performance in handling huge data and making decisions, matching or even beating human intelligence. AI techniques have been able to solve problems related to identification, classification, and quality analysis non-destructively and in less time. AI techniques solve problems both at the farm as well as industry level on the basis of data and data gathered from sensing devices or cameras. RGB photos, RGB depth images (RGB-D), spectral images, and a variety of other types of data can be used. This chapter explains the importance and applications of AI in the agri-food sector in conjugation with non-destructive techniques. The non-destructive techniques discussed here include NIR spectroscopy, hyperspectral imaging, thermal imaging, and e-nose/e-tongue. Data in the form of spectra or signals is generated out of these techniques and is then fed into the AI-based models for feature extraction and classification. Thus, the integration of AI with non-destructive techniques will be a good solution in food industries in solving manual problems that are tedious to humans.

11.2 FOOD QUALITY AND SAFETY

Food quality and safety are of utmost concern when it comes to health and well-being. Production of high-quality safe agro-food has become a challenge in the coming years. This urge for qualitative and quantitative food intensifies more with the rapid increase in urbanization. Hence it has become a major concern on both industry and farm levels. Quality includes all the attributes mostly preferred by consumers. "Quality" is thus a broad area, comprising different stages of production. Quality has to be monitored starting from farm to fork. Food quality includes all the attributes like shape, size, color, texture, and flavor, including its nutritional content. It must meet the consumer's demand. Second, food safety refers to all of the risks that cause food to be harmful to human health. A safe food must be free of toxic components which are threatening to the health of consumers. The government has been paying continuous attention in this regard. The government has made several policies to ensure food quality by enforcing food safety standards for manufacturers and producers of food items. These policies have been made mandatory for the protection of consumers. This attention is needed globally both in the case of import and export markets. But to detect the contaminations or spoilage rapidly and without much human intervention, smart farming technologies have to be endorsed. This is where computer vision technologies can help the cause. AI-based solutions are setting the gold standard in solving this problem of automatic detection. A product may be attractive in appearance but may be contaminated with undetected pathogens, chemicals, or metals. Here AI coupled with sensors can be very helpful, as shown in Figure 11.1.

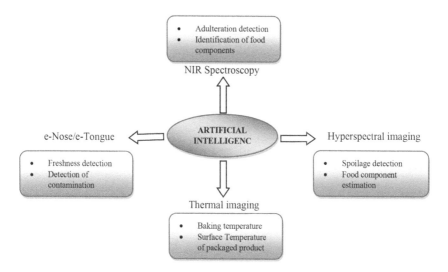

Figure 11.1 AI coupled with non-destructive techniques in food.

11.2.1 Artificial intelligence in food quality and safety

The importance and application of AI, particularly machine learning and deep learning, in the food and agriculture sector will be covered in this chapter. Various operations involved during food processing starting from food handling to application in industry are discussed here. AI plays a critical role in the overall processing unit task. Some AI applications in food and agriculture are demonstrated in Figure 11.2.

Automation is completely based on AI. In this chapter, machine learning and deep learning will be discussed as AI methodologies. Because of their ability to deal with real-world challenges, machine learning and deep learning are gaining popularity. Data can be recognized and predictions can be made using machine learning and deep learning algorithms [5]. Machine learning techniques have been able to achieve outstanding results in all fields of study making their way toward industrial applications [6]. Currently, deep learning is becoming the most widespread in the AI community by outperforming its predecessors. The effectiveness of deep learning is due to its ability to extract features automatically from a large amount of raw data. Hence it becomes one of the most widespread techniques in executing virtuoso performance in solving complex cognitive problems, on par with human intelligence [7]. Deep learning algorithms are multi-layered and are inspired by the human brain, in which the first layers extract features while the last layers are responsible for classification. Convolutional neural network (CNN) in particular has gained more popularity in the field of agriculture and food in image classification and recognition. At the farm level, deep learning techniques have made contributions

AI in Agri Farm
- Disease/Pest detection
- Maturity detection
- Spoilage Detection
- Crop quality assessment

AI in Food Industry
- Sorting/grading
- Drying
- Quality Control
- Packaging
- Dietary assessment

Figure 11.2 AI in food and agriculture.

to the maturity detection of fruits and vegetables, spoilage detection of agricultural products, disease detection in farm produce, etc. and during processing, deep learning techniques are applied during all stages of production right from material handling to packaging [8]. Deep learning finds application in all unit operations including sorting, grading, detection of foreign materials, etc. Some of the applications are listed in Table 11.1.

Table 11.1 Applications of AI in food

AI technique	Non-destructive technique	Application	Reference
Machine learning models	NIR	Quality evaluation of meat, fish, fruits, and vegetables	[9]
Deep learning CNN	NIR	Powdery food evaluation and its mixing proportions	[10]
Deep learning	Hyperspectral	Composition of food nutrients: basically carbohydrates, proteins, and fats of foods	[11]
Deep learning	Thermal imaging	Quality such as defects, shape, size, and maturity grading of mangoes	[12]
Machine learning	e-Nose	Classification of different coffee	[13]
Deep learning, CNN	e-Tongue	Classifying pu-erh tea	[14]

Hence it is seen that AI-based systems play a significant role in agricultural product handling and during food production. AI is able to make such significant performance because of data which is RGB images, spectral images, or signals acquired from non-destructive sources like NIR spectroscopy, hyperspectral imaging, thermal imaging, or e-nose/e-tongue [15].

11.3 NON-DESTRUCTIVE TECHNIQUES

Non-destructive techniques are in favor of minimizing food waste. It helps maintain food quality and safety. Non-destructive techniques allow the analysis of a product without causing much damage to it and reducing wastage. Thus, it surpasses the traditional technique of detection and assessment of components in food. The usefulness of non-destructive techniques comes from the fact that they allow simultaneous assessment of chemical as well as physical properties of food without the food being destroyed. Another important advantage is that non-destructive techniques give us qualitative and quantitative data simultaneously without separate analyses [16]. Some of the studies performed using non-destructive techniques for the detection of agro-food products and their quality assessment are listed in Table 11.1. Hence non-destructive techniques will be one among the most popular preferred methods for assessing the quality of agro-food products coupled with imaging systems like RGB images or spectral images as shown in Figure 11.3. Non-destructive techniques in combination with computer vision are better alternatives to laborious chemical analysis for quality evaluation of food with high accuracy [17]. Some of the most common non-destructive techniques, their principles, and their applications in the quality evaluation of agricultural products are listed in Table 11.2.

11.3.1 Near infrared

Near-infrared (NIR) spectra are electromagnetic frequencies in the region of 780–2,500 nm. Near-infrared spectroscopy (NIRS) is usually preferred for its non-destructive nature and can easily generate spectra from solid samples (both solid and liquid) without any initial treatment. The rapidness of this method has made speedy characterization possible without any use of chemicals, thus making it a reagent-free methodology when calibrated against the primary reference method [22]. The principle behind molecular spectroscopy is the fundamental vibration of molecules due to combination and overtones bonds resulting in absorption or reflection of light. The bonds which are recognized in the infrared region are OH, CH, CO, NH, and so on. NIR absorption bands are also very wide and highly overlapped [23]. The absorption of light is based on the vibration of atoms in the molecules. In contrast to other spectral ranges, NIR spectra offer an advantage in food analysis since they can provide a succession of absorptions of

Table 11.2 Application of non-destructive techniques in food

Technique	Principle	Application	Reference
NIR	Vibration of molecular bonds when light of range 750–2,500 nm falls, generating spectrum of reflectance/absorbance	Storage quality of fruits, classifying food products, etc.	[18]
Hyperspectral imaging	With relatively narrow band passes, measure the intensity of light diffusely reflected from a surface at one or more wavelengths. Capture spectral and spatial information about an object at the same time	Online detection of food quality, mostly in a non-destructive way	[19]
Thermal imaging	Emission of IR radiation subjected to temperature above the absolute zero	Bakery, meat, and fish products	[20]
e-Nose/e-tongue	Uses sensors to detect volatile compounds and convert them into electrical signals	Tea, coffee, wine, meat, fish, etc.	[21]

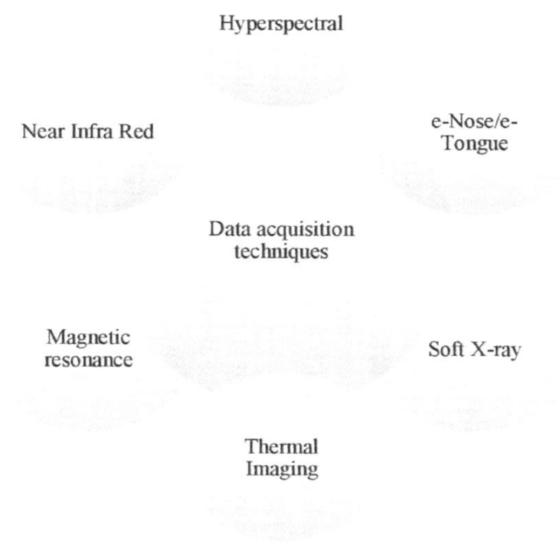

Hyperspectral

e-Nose/e-Tongue

Near Infra Red

Data acquisition techniques

Soft X-ray

Magnetic resonance

Thermal Imaging

Figure 11.3 Non-destructive data acquisition techniques.

varying intensities over a wavelength range while still conveying the same chemical information [24]. Compared to other non-destructive techniques NIR is cost-effective, involves simple instrumentation, and is thus preferred more in process analysis [16].

At present times, there are advancements in the technologies for instrumentation, and they have resulted in the manufacturing of portable spectrophotometers that are able to give spectral data without time consumption, making them better for rapid analysis [25]. They use machine learning as a calibrating tool to map a link of near-infrared spectroscopy-based measurements into desirable extrinsic factors of analysis for quality that uses our smartphones as visualizing media for output. In this study, we plan to briefly discuss such applications of machine learning as an enabler for calibration and validation tools of NIR spectroscopy. This will surely give us insight into how we can apply ML techniques combined with NIR for providing better solutions for the food industry in quality analysis and in process monitoring. Brief details about portable NIR sensors are given in Table 11.3.

AI techniques used for spectra calibration are machine learning. Deep learning models like convolutional neural networks (CNNs: form weight-sharing architecture for visual data), recurrent neural networks (RNNs: feedback recurrent for time-series data), and long short-term memories (LSTMs: handling lags for time series data) have proven to be highly reliable methods for sequence learning, recognition of visual data, and subdivision of tasks to classify plants and for understanding physiology by using images of the plants [32]. Basically, we can describe machine learning as a part of AI, which learns from data and enables the computer to perform different tasks based on the data. It is different from conventional programming where we define the method and get an output; it is rather generating the method from the output (data). The property of the data points is called features [33]. ML processes involve the methods shown in Figure 11.4 [34].

A number of applications of AI, specifically deep learning and machine learning in spectroscopy, adulteration, identification, proximate evaluation, storage quality, process monitoring, and post-harvest analysis are discussed

Table 11.3 Brief details about portable NIR sensors

S. no.	Application/study	Wavelength (nm)	Reference
2	Dry matter and soluble solid content	310–1,100	[26]
3	Segregation of seedlings for postharvest fruit phenotypes	400–1,100	[27]
5	Internal flesh browning in apples	302–1,150	[28]
7	Fruit maturity	310–1,100	[29]
8	Physical and chemical assessment of mandarin	1600–2,400	[30]
9	Allergens in food using smartphone	1350–2,150	[31]

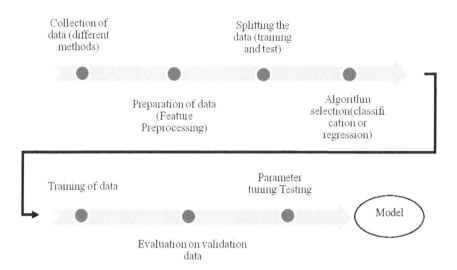

Figure 11.4 Steps involved in machine learning.

in Table 11.4. Support vector machine (SVM), artificial neural network (ANN), k-nearest neighbor (KNN), and random forest (RF) classifiers are the most extensively used machine learning approaches [44].

11.3.2 Hyperspectral imaging

Hyperspectral imaging (HSI) is different from conventional imaging which just assigns the primary colors (RGB) to each pixel; instead, it uses a wide-range spectrum of light. In hyperspectral imaging, each pixel contains spectral data, which adds a third dimension to the two-dimensional spectral data, referred to as hypercube data. In hyperspectral data, the spectral range can extend beyond the UV-visible range to the infrared range. Now, the advancement of technology and different data handling software being made so easily available has given opportunities for creating viable and efficient solutions, be they military or agricultural. his application has made promising progress in the field of analytical technology [45]. Here, the application of machine learning, a type of AI, plays a big role in mapping the data.

The capacity to integrate both spectroscopic and imaging techniques to evaluate different components directly at the same time, as well as localize the spatial distribution of such components within the evaluated product, is the main advantage of hyperspectral imaging systems. HSI is better compared to NIR spectroscopy for generating more accurate and detailed information. This makes it very appropriate for the application of HSI in the food and agro-sector, where certain targeted regions need to be specified. Some of the applications of hyperspectral imaging in food coupled with AI are listed in Table 11.5.

Table 11.4 Applications of NIR in food coupled with AI

Food	Technique	AI-based technique	Application	Reference
Milk	NIR	Feed-forward MLP-ANN	Classify milk on geo origin	[35]
Tea		BP-ANN	Classification of tea varieties	[36]
Prawn		LS-SVM	Adulterants present in prawn	[37]
Food powder		CNN	Classified eight food powders	[38]
Cereals and pulses		SVM and PLS-DA	Identifying barley, chickpea, and sorghum	[39]
Eggs		ANN	Monitor egg's freshness and determine the egg storage time	[40]
Pork		LDA, k-NN, and SVM	Storage time of pork and its spoilage	[41]
Spanish wine		LDA, SIMCA, and SVM	Distinguish Spanish wine based on polyphenolic profile	[42]
Chicken		SVM	Identification and classification of chicken constituents	[43]

Table 11.5 Applications of hyperspectral in food coupled with AI

Food	Technique	AI technique	Application	Reference
Red berry	Hyperspectral imaging	SVM	Bruise detection in red berry	[46]
Lamb/beef/pork		SVM and CNN	Adulteration	[47]
Strawberry		ANN	Strawberry firmness detection	[48]
Eggs		K-means algorithm	Omega-3 fatty acids detection in designer eggs	[49]

11.3.3 Thermal imaging

Thermal imaging is a discipline of remote sensing that involves the collection, processing, and interpretation of data largely in the thermal infrared spectrum. In this method, infrared radiation produced by an item is recorded using an infrared detector. The infrared ray (IR) is an electromagnetic spectrum band of invisible light with wavelengths ranging from 0.75 to 100 m [50]. Thermal infrared cameras are provided with sensors that inherit the capacity to detect infrared radiation. The sensor receives the IR radiations and converts them into electrical signals, and the resultant output is in the form of an infrared thermal image. The thermal images are thermograms, which are two-dimensional temperature data. Thermograms allow us to see temperature distribution and gradients in all areas without having to touch the photographed item directly. To properly employ thermal imaging techniques, one must first understand the purpose of the thermal camera and the data it provides in the generated thermal infrared pictures.

The theory of infrared imaging is that thermal images are pseudo-images that are obtained when an object emits IR radiations from its surface upon exposure to temperature gradients. For a body to emit such radiations it has to be exposed to a temperature above absolute zero (–273.15° C or –459° F). At above absolute zero temperature, the body emits IR radiation in the range of 0.75 to 1,000 μm of the electromagnetic spectrum. The IR radiations within this range are further divided into five regions on the basis of increasing wavelength and decreasing frequency. Near-infrared, short-wave infrared, mid-wave infrared, long-wave infrared, and extreme infrared are the five types [51].

Figure 11.5, shows a thermal imaging system used basically in industries for food quality evaluation. The thermal imaging setup comprises two basic components: (1) a thermal camera and (2) a control and display unit [52]. The thermal camera is the core component with optical units and a thermal detector, which absorbs infrared radiation emitted by an object and converts it into electrical signals [53]. The control and display unit consists of signal processing and image processing tools. The signal processing unit converts the received electrical signals in the form of thermal records and displays them in the display unit. Thus, this system produces an image by detecting temperature at different levels of infrared light, recognizing them and converting them to electrical signals. The essence of the thermal imaging

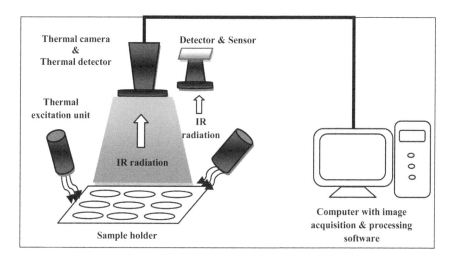

Figure 11.5 Thermal imaging system.

Table 11.6 Applications of thermal imaging in food coupled with AI

Food	Technique	AI technique	Application	Reference
Microwave oven	Thermal imaging	Deep learning	Classifies both solid and liquid foods and recommends the target temperature with 93% accuracy	[54]
Fruit	Thermal imaging	Deep convolutional neural network	Quality evaluation	[55]
Apples	Thermal imaging	ANN	Compares packaging and estimates surface temperature over a pallet of apples	[56]

system comes from the fact that it helps in non-invasive quality evaluation without contacting the food product. Here AI techniques play an important role in extracting features out of the thermograms thus produced and classifying them accordingly. AI-based techniques thus outperform humans in the segmentation and detection of large thermogram data making it feasible for both farm and industry applications. AI techniques have proven to be an efficient tool in data handling, analysis, and decision-making. An intelligent system based on either machine learning or deep learning helps recognize patterns from thermograms of food products and classify them accordingly. The steps in classification include data acquisition, data augmentation, feature extraction, and classification. AI technique, specifically deep learning, is gaining more attention because of its automatic feature extraction ability. The works of several researchers that involve AI techniques in handling thermal images of food are discussed in Table 11.6.

11.3.4 e-Nose and e-tongue

e-Nose and e-tongue are novel technologies that sense and evaluate food quality. They assess food quality using a collection of gas or chemical sensors. E-nose and e-tongue mimic the human nose and tongue respectively when it comes to sensing food. In conjunction with AI techniques like machine learning and deep learning, both e-nose and e-tongue have demonstrated amazing results and value in the sector of food and agriculture.

e-Nose is basically a sensor that has the capacity to sense volatile gases, simulating a human nose. This sensor is basically gas sensitive and gives fingerprint response to specific volatile chemical substances simulating the olfactory function of the human nose. Thus, it can also be termed as an "artificial olfaction sensor."

e-Noses are engineered to identify and classify aroma mixtures. This technology is made up of a number of sensors that respond to the volatile chemical substances present in the sample. The sensors act as receptors to the volatile compounds and transmit them to electrical signals. Pattern recognition algorithms identify and describe these signals, allowing for identification and categorization. The most popular e-nose sensors are metal-oxide-semiconductor (MOS), conducting polymers (CP), quartz crystal microbalance (QCM), and surface acoustic wave (SAW). By aggregating comparable emissions into clusters representing components from food-released volatiles, an e-nose system paired with pattern-recognition algorithms may recognize distinct sample kinds. Signals in the form of data are fed to the pattern-recognition model based on either machine learning or deep learning. These models help in the identification and classification of the input signals and make predictions out of them. Gas sensor arrays, reaction chambers, valves, air pumps for sampling and cleaning, control devices, and data acquisition (DAQ) devices make up an electronic nose system as shown in Figure 11.6. Some of its potential applications for food are shown in Table 11.7.

e-Tongue, on the other hand, is a group of chemical sensors that mimics the human tongue in sensing taste. Unlike e-nose, e-tongue makes use of non-specific or low selective potentiometric chemical sensors which have the potentiality of cross-sensitivity with a number of different components in a mixture. The e-tongue system comprises a liquid autosampler, chemical sensor, acquisition system, and data processing system. One of the major components of an e-tongue sensor is the lipid membrane which is used as an element recognition unit. This membrane recognizes taste-relevant substances and converts them to electric potential charge. This recognition capability of the membrane is independent of thickness. For efficient use,

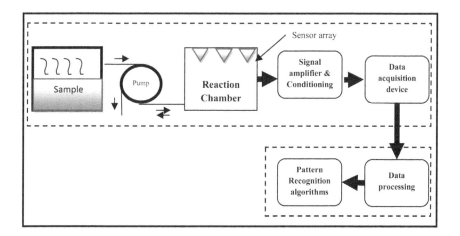

Figure 11.6 e-Nose working system.

Table 11.7 Applications of e-nose in food coupled with AI

Food	Technique	AI-based technique	Application	Reference
Beer	e-Nose	CNN–SVM	Automatic extraction of beer olfactory information and its classification	[57]
Tea/coffee	e-Nose	KNN, LDA	Grading	[58, 59]
Pork	e-Nose	SVM	Prediction of TVC in chilled pork	[60]
Essential oils	e-Nose	LDA, SVM	Identify and classify different volatile essential oils	[61]
Beverage	e-Nose	PCA, MLPNN	Classification of beverages such as blackcurrant, mango, and orange juice	[62]
Fruits	e-Nose	ANN	Fruit maturity	[63]

Table 11.8 Applications of e-tongue in food coupled with AI

Food	Technique	AI-based technique	Application	Reference
Orange juice/ Chinese vinegar	e-Tongue	RF, ANN, SVM	To recognize the type as well as brand of the two beverages	[64]
Olive oils	e-Tongue	SVM	Characterize five types of virgin olive oils based on geographic area	[65]
Argan oil	e-Tongue	PCA, SVM, and discriminant factor analysis	Detect adulteration in argan oil as an indicator of quality	[66]
Cherry tomato juices	e-Tongue	SVM, PCA, PCR	Detect adulteration in cherry tomato juices	[67]

this membrane must be durable and highly reproducible upon repetitive use. Thus, this system involves detecting phenolic compounds and predicting sensory attributes like sweet, sour, bitter, fruity, and caramel. The results obtained out of e-tongue give information on taste characteristics such as sourness, bitterness, and astringency for foodstuffs. Applicability of e-tongue is mostly found in the beverage industry such as beers, wine, tea, coffee, etc. as listed in Table 11.8.

11.4 CONCLUSION

The chapter briefly explains how, with the demand in food supply and expansion of food industries, a need for safe food from farm to fork is so crucial. So, the increase in analysis of food products' quality is indispensable. However, conventional biochemical analysis is less efficient when it comes to cost and time. The advancement of technology has given many opportunities for integrating AI with analytical techniques. On a physics front, the application of light and its analytical power has developed much over the years. This chapter gives a glimpse of the commonly used spectral and imaging techniques for providing various agricultural and food industry solutions. Overall, we have discussed NIR, hyperspectral imaging, thermal imaging, and e-nose/e-tongue and their principle and applications. In addition, the AI techniques machine learning and deep learning are thoroughly discussed in an elementary manner.

REFERENCES

1. Araújo, S. O., Peres, R. S., Barata, J., Lidon, F., & Ramalho, J. C. (2021). Characterizing the agriculture 4.0 landscape: Emerging trends, challenges and opportunities. *Agronomy, 11*(4), 667.
2. Food and Agriculture Organization. (2016). *The State of Food and Agriculture. Climate Change, Agriculture and Food Security.* Food and Agriculture Organization of the United Nations.
3. Trendov, N. M., Varas, S., & Zeng, M. *Digital Technologies in Agriculture and Rural Areas: Status Report*; Licence: cc by-nc-sa 3.0 igo: Rome, Italy, 2019.
4. Rose, D. C., & Chilvers, J. (2018). Agriculture 4.0: Broadening responsible innovation in an era of smart farming. *Frontiers in Sustainable Food Systems, 2*, 87.
5. Begum, N., & Hazarika, M. K. (2022). Artificial intelligence in agri-food systems: An introduction. In *Internet of Things and Analytics for Agriculture, Volume 3* (pp. 45–63). Springer.
6. Verma, K., Bhardwaj, S., Arya, R., Islam, M. S. U., Bhushan, M., Kumar, A., & Samant, P. (2019). Latest tools for data mining and machine learning, *International Journal of Innovative Technology and Exploring Engineering, 8*(9S), 18–23. https://doi.org/10.35940/ijitee.I1003.0789S19
7. Kiourt, C., Pavlidis, G., & Markantonatou, S. (2020). Deep learning approaches in food recognition. In *Machine Learning Paradigms* (pp. 83–108). Springer.
8. Pawar, S., Bhushan, M., & Wagh, M. (2020) The plant leaf disease diagnosis and spectral data analysis using machine learning: A review. *International Journal of Advanced Science and Technology, 29*(9s), 3343–3359. http://sersc .org/journals/index.php/IJAST/article/view/15945
9. Lee, S., Gyoon, T., Hoe, J., Han, J., Young, J., & Young, J. (2017). NIR spectroscopic sensing for point-of-need freshness assessment of meat, fish, vegetables and fruits. *Sensing for Agriculture and Food Quality and Safety IX, 10217*, 51–57. https://doi.org/10.1117/12.2261803.
10. Zhou, L., Tan, L., Zhang, C., Zhao, N., He, Y., & Qiu, Z. (2022). A portable NIR-system for mixture powdery food analysis using deep learning. *LWT, 153*, 112456.

11. Ahn, D., Choi, J. Y., Kim, H. C., Cho, J. S., Moon, K. D., & Park, T. (2019). Estimating the composition of food nutrients from hyperspectral signals based on deep neural networks. *Sensors, 19*(7), 1560.

12. Bhole, V., & Kumar, A. (2020, October). Mango quality grading using deep learning technique: Perspectives from agriculture and food industry. In Proceedings of the 21st Annual Conference on Information Technology Education (pp. 180–186).

13. Singh, S., Hines, E. L., & Gardner, J. W. (1996). Fuzzy neural computing of coffee and tainted-water data from an electronic nose. *Sensors and Actuators B: Chemical, 30*(3), 185–190.

14. Yang, Z., Miao, N., Zhang, X., Li, Q., Wang, Z., Li, C., ... & Lan, Y. (2021). Employment of an electronic tongue combined with deep learning and transfer learning for discriminating the storage time of Pu-erh tea. *Food Control, 121*, 107608.

15. Zhu, R., Yu, D., Ji, S., & Lu, M. (2019). Matching RGB and infrared remote sensing images with densely-connected convolutional neural networks. *Remote Sensing, 11*(23), 2836.

16. El-Mesery, H. S., Mao, H., & Abomohra, A. E. F. (2019). Applications of non-destructive technologies for agricultural and food products quality inspection. *Sensors, 19*(4), 846.

17. Quelal-Vásconez, M. A., Lerma-García, M. J., Pérez-Esteve, É., Arnau-Bonachera, A., Barat, J. M., & Talens, P. (2019). Fast detection of cocoa shell in cocoa powders by near infrared spectroscopy and multivariate analysis. *Food Control [Internet], 99*(December 2018), 68–72. Available from: https://doi.org/10.1016/j.foodcont.2018.12.028

18. Ortiz, A., Sánchez, M., García-Torres, S., León, L., López-Parra, M. M., Barraso, C., & Tejerina, D. (2022). Feasibility of near infrared spectroscopy to classify lamb hamburgers according to the presence and percentage of cherry as a natural ingredient. *Applied Food Research, 2*(1), 100069.

19. Yao, K., Sun, J., Chen, C., Xu, M., Zhou, X., Cao, Y., & Tian, Y. (2022). Non-destructive detection of egg qualities based on hyperspectral imaging. *Journal of Food Engineering, 325*, 111024.

20. Usamentiaga, R., Venegas, P., Guerediaga, J., Vega, L., Molleda, J., & Bulnes, F. G. (2014). Infrared thermography for temperature measurement and non-destructive testing. *Sensors, 14*(7), 12305–12348.

21. Tan, J., & Xu, J. (2020). Applications of electronic nose (e-nose) and electronic tongue (e-tongue) in food quality-related properties determination: A review. *Artificial Intelligence in Agriculture, 4*, 104–115.

22. Blanco, M., & Villarroya, I. (2002). NIR spectroscopy: A rapid-response analytical tool. *Trends in Analytical Chemistry, 21*(4), 240–250.

23. Stuart, B. (2004). *Infrared Spectroscopy: Fundamentals and Applications.* John Wiley and Sons, Ltd.

24. Osborne, B. G. (2006). Near-infrared spectroscopy in food analysis. *Encyclopedia of Analytical Chemistry*, 1–14. https://doi.org/10.1002/9780470027318.a1

25. Guillemain, A., Dégardin, K., & Roggo, Y. (2016). Performance of handheld spectrophotometers for detection of counterfeit tablets. *Talanta [Internet].* (December 21), 1–20. Available from: https://doi.org/10.1016/j.talanta.2016.12.063

26. Goke, A. (2018). Postharvest dry matter and soluble and bartlett pear using near-infrared spectroscopy. *Am Soc Hortic Sci.*, 53(5):669–680.

27. Li, M., Qian, Z., Shi, B., Medlicott, J., & East, A. (2018). Postharvest biology and technology evaluating the performance of a consumer scale SCiO ™ molecular sensor to predict quality of horticultural products, *Postharvest Biology and Technology*, 145(March), 183–192.

28. Khatiwada, B. P., Subedi, P. P., Hayes, C. (2016). LCCC, Walsh KB. Postharvest biology and technology assessment of internal flesh browning in intact apple using visible-short wave near infrared spectroscopy. *Postharvest Biol Technol [Internet]*, 120, 103–111. Available from: https://doi.org/10 .1016/j.postharvbio.2016.06.001

29. Antonucci, F., & Pallottino, F. (2011). Non-destructive estimation of mandarin maturity status through portable VIS-NIR spectrophotometer. *Food Bioprocess Technol.*, 4, 809–813.

30. Sánchez, M., Haba, M. De, & Pérez-marín, D. (2013). Internal and external quality assessment of mandarins on-tree and at harvest using a portable NIR spectrophotometer. *Comput Electron Agric.*, 92, 66–74.

31. Grifantini, K. (2016) Knowing what you eat: Researchers are looking for ways to help people cope with food allergies. *IEEE Pulse*, 7(5), 31–34. https:// doi.org/10.1109/MPUL.2016.2592239

32. Taghavi Namin, S., Esmaeilzadeh, M., Najafi, M., Brown, T. B., & Borevitz, J. O. (2018). Deep phenotyping: Deep learning for temporal phenotype/genotype classification. *Plant Methods [Internet]*, 14(1), 1–14. Available from: https://doi.org/10.1186/s13007-018-0333-4

33. Bishop, C. (2006). *Pattern Recognition and Machine Learning.* Springer Science and Business Media.

34. Harrington P. (2012). *Machine Learning in Action.* Manning Publications Co.

35. Behkami, S., Zain, S. M., Gholami, M., Khir, M. F. A. (2019). Classification of cow milk using artificial neural network developed from the spectral data of single- and three-detector spectrophotometers. *Food Chemistry*, 294(February), 309–315.

36. He, Y., Li, X., & Deng, X. (2007). Discrimination of varieties of tea using near infrared spectroscopy by principal component analysis and BP model. *Journal of Food Engineering*, 79(May), 1238–1242.

37. Wu, D., Shi, H., He, Y., Yu, X., & Bao, Y. (2013). Potential of hyperspectral imaging and multivariate analysis for rapid and non-invasive detection of gelatin adulteration in prawn. *Journal of Food Engineering*, 119, 680–686.

38. You, H., Kim, H., Joo, D-K., Lee, S. M., Kim, J., & SC. (2019). Classification of food powders with open set portable VIS-NIR Spectrometer. In International Conference on Artificial Intelligence in Information and Communication (ICAIIC). Toronto: IEEE. pp. 423–426.

39. Kosmowski, F., & Worku T. (2018). Evaluation of a miniaturized NIR spectrometer for cultivar identification: The case of barley, chickpea and sorghum in Ethiopia. *PLOSONE*, 13(3), 1–17.

40. Coronel-reyes, J., Ramirez-morales, I., Fernandez-blanco, E., Rivero, D., & Pazos, A. (2018). Determination of egg storage time at room temperature using a low-cost NIR spectrometer and machine learning techniques. *Comput Electron Agric [Internet]*, 145(December 2017), 1–10. Available from: https:// doi.org/10.1016/j.compag.2017.12.030

41. Chen, Q., Cai, J., Wan, X., & Zhao, J. (2011). LWT: Food science and technology application of linear / non-linear classi fi cation algorithms in discrimination of pork storage time using Fourier transform near infrared (FT-NIR) spectroscopy. *LWT - Food Sci Technology [Internet]*, *44*(10), 2053–2058. Available from: https://doi.org/10.1016/j.lwt.2011.05.015

42. Jiménez-carvelo, A. M., González-casado, A, Bagur-gonzález, M. G., & Cuadros-rodríguez, L. (2019). Alternative data mining / machine learning methods for the analytical evaluation of food quality and authenticity: A review. *Food Research International [Internet]*, *122*(March), 25–39. Available from: https://doi.org/10.1016/j.foodres.2019.03.063

43. Geronimo, B. C., Mastelini, S. M., Carvalho, R. H., Júnior, S. B., Barbin, D. F., Shimokomaki, M., & Ida, E. I. (2019). Computer vision system and near-infrared spectroscopy for identification and classification of chicken with wooden breast, and physicochemical and technological characterization. *Infrared Physics & Technology*, *96*, 303–310.

44. Arvind, C. S., & Senthilnath, J. (2019). Autonomous RL: Autonomous vehicle obstacle avoidance in a dynamic environment using MLP-SARSA reinforcement learning. In 2019 IEEE 5th Int Conf Mechatronics Syst Robot ICMSR 2019, vol. 2019, pp.120–124.

45. Chang, C. I. (2003). *Hyperspectral Imaging: Techniques for Spectral Detection and Classification* (Vol. 1). Springer Science & Business Media.

46. Liu, Q., Wei, K., Xiao, H., Tu, S., Sun, K., Sun, Y., Pan, L., & Tu, K. (2019). Near-infrared hyperspectral imaging rapidly detects the decay of postharvest strawberry based on water-soluble sugar analysis. *Food Analytical Methods*, *12*, 936–946.

47. Al-Sarayreh, M., Reis, M. M., Yan, Q. W., & Klette, R. (2018). Deep spectral-spatial features of snap shot hyperspectral images for redmeat classification. In 2018 International Conference on Image and Vision Computing New Zealand (IVCNZ), Auckland, New Zealand, pp 1–6.

48. Sun, D. W. (Ed.). (2016). *Computer Vision Technology for Food Quality Evaluation*. Academic Press.

49. Abdel-Nour, N., & Ngadi, M. (2011). Detection of omega-3 fatty acid in designer eggs using hyperspectral imaging. *International Journal of Food Sciences and Nutrition*, *62*(4), 418–422.

50. Holst, G. C. (2000). *Common Sense Approach to Thermal Imaging* (Vol. 1). SPIE Optical Engineering Press.

51. Gowen, A. A., Tiwari, B. K., Cullen, P. J., McDonnell, K., & O'Donnell, C. P. (2010). Applications of thermal imaging in food quality and safety assessment. *Trends in Food Science & Technology*, *21*(4), 190–200.

52. ElMasry, G., ElGamal, R., Mandour, N., Gou, P., Al-Rejaie, S., Belin, E., & Rousseau, D. (2020). Emerging thermal imaging techniques for seed quality evaluation: Principles and applications. *Food Research International*, *131*, 109025.

53. Vadivambal, R., & Jayas, D. S. (2011). Applications of thermal imaging in agriculture and food industry: A review. *Food and Bioprocess Technology*, *4*(2), 186–199.

54. Khan, T. (2020). An intelligent microwave oven with thermal imaging and temperature recommendation using deep learning. *Applied System Innovation*, *3*(1), 13.

55. Melesse, T. Y., Bollo, M., Di Pasquale, V., Centro, F., & Riemma, S. (2022). Machine learning-based digital twin for monitoring fruit quality evolution. *Procedia Computer Science, 200*, 13–20.

56. Badia-Melis, R., Qian, J. P., Fan, B. L., Hoyos-Echevarria, P., Ruiz-García, L., & Yang, X. T. (2016). Artificial neural networks and thermal image for temperature prediction in apples. *Food and Bioprocess Technology, 9*(7), 1089–1099.

57. Shi, Y., Gong, F., Wang, M., Liu, J., Wu, Y., & Men, H. (2019). A deep feature mining method of electronic nose sensor data for identifying beer olfactory information. *Journal of Food Engineering, 263*, 437–445.

58. Dai, Y., Zhi, R., Zhao, L., Gao, H., Shi, B., & Wang, H. (2015). Longjing tea quality classification by fusion of features collected from E-nose. *Chemometrics and Intelligent Laboratory Systems, 144*, 63–70.

59. Dong, W., Zhao, J., Hu, R., Dong, Y., & Tan, L. (2017). Differentiation of Chinese robusta coffees according to species, using a combined electronic nose and tongue, with the aid of chemometrics. *Food Chemistry, 229*, 743–751.

60. Wang, D., Wang, X., Liu, T., & Liu, Y. (2012). Prediction of total viable counts on chilled pork using an electronic nose combined with support vector machine. *Meat Science, 90*(2), 373–377.

61. Rasekh, M., Karami, H., Wilson, A. D., & Gancarz, M. (2021). Classification and identification of essential oils from herbs and fruits based on a MOS electronic-nose technology. *Chemosensors, 9*(6), 142.

62. Mamat, M., Samad, S. A., & Hannan, M. A. (2011). An electronic nose for reliable measurement and correct classification of beverages. *Sensors, 11*(6), 6435–6453.

63. Kasbe, M. S., Deshmukh, S. L., Mujawar, T. H., Bachuwar, V. D., Deshmukh, L. P., & Shaligram, A. D. (2015). An electronic nose with LabVIEW using SnO2 Based Gas Sensors: Application to test freshness of the fruits. *International Journal of Scientific & Engineering Research, 6*(4), 1977.

64. Liu, M., Wang, M., Wang, J., & Li, D. (2013). Comparison of random forest, support vector machine and back propagation neural network for electronic tongue data classification: Application to the recognition of orange beverage and Chinese vinegar. *Sensors and Actuators B: Chemical, 177*, 970–980.

65. Haddi, Z., Alami, H., El Bari, N., Tounsi, M., Barhoumi, H., Maaref, A., ... & Bouchikhi, B. E. N. A. C. H. I. R. (2013). Electronic nose and tongue combination for improved classification of Moroccan virgin olive oil profiles. *Food Research International, 54*(2), 1488–1498.

66. Joshi, R., Cho, B. K., Joshi, R., Lohumi, S., Faqeerzada, M. A., Amanah, H. Z., ... & Lee, H. (2019). Raman spectroscopic analysis to detect olive oil mixtures in argan oil. *Korean Journal of Agricultural Science, 46*(1), 183–194.

67. Hong, X., & Wang, J. (2014). Detection of adulteration in cherry tomato juices based on electronic nose and tongue: Comparison of different data fusion approaches. *Journal of Food Engineering, 126*, 89–97.

Chapter 12

A study on intelligent systems and their influence on smarter defense service

P.R. Anisha, C. Kishor Kumar Reddy,
and Nhu Gia Nguyen

CONTENTS

12.1 INTRODUCTION

Defense is the activity undertaken to defend or guard anyone or anything against a vicious attack. Countries need to keep themselves alert to any external or internal attacks, risks, or threats. This very reason makes it highly significant for the nation to allow a substantial part of its budget for defense needs.

DOI: 10.1201/9781003286745-12
                                                          241

The forces that defend a country are made available with highly developed arms and ammunition. The armed forces need to be ready in terms of preparedness, trained, well-equipped, and vigilant in technology to face any unpredicted or predicted situations. Quite a few defense tasks get simplified with the use of technology. Innovative ideas in this field help in the rapid and effective development of technology in defense service. Such technology includes certain types, which are military or defensive by nature. Lack of proper training might result in destructive use of the technology. Defense technology is meant chiefly for military purposes and not used for civilian purposes. Further, technologies intended for civilians have been in use for defense purposes [1].

Defense technology is not a tiny topic. It can cover a wide range of imperative matters. The technology used for defense reasons is specifically researched and developed by professional engineers and scientists. The defense forces are using these technologies in combating enemies. Modern defense technology is created and influenced in a big way by innovative ideas. It is necessary to have vital knowledge in such development to generate result-oriented creative ideas.

Artificial intelligence has made its way into most civilian industries. Besides transforming the way an individual or a business works, it has become a crucial part of modern warfare [2]. Computerized reasoning (artificial intelligence), likewise named the modern insurgency 4.0, has been taking major steps in logical and mechanical development across differing fields. It can make critical changes to most regular citizen exercises and military activities. Achieving military prevalence has been possible just for a couple of nations like the US, China, and Russia, who keep up with a huge military. Being a double-use innovation, simulated intelligence might have fascinating ramifications for the appropriation of military power from here on out. The chance of simulated intelligence-guided headways has opened the extent of a weapons contest where the customary military capacities will matter considerably less over time. Accordingly, central powers driving the non-military-personnel man-made intelligence tech additionally have vast scope to go after solid power. In this light, India is unable to enter the computer-based intelligence race in defense in the near future.

In spite of the fact that there is a wide agreement on artificial intelligence, i.e., doing undertakings that people can perform through a PC or carefully controlled robots, there are assorted feelings about how artificial intelligence is utilized productively to accomplish the abovementioned. Though data science is the new jargon being used widely, the fact is it cannot be separated from artificial intelligence. As an add-on, machine learning is one of the tools that has contributed to creating AI-based technologies, robotics, autonomous locomotives, natural language processing (NLP), and a lot more. Defense systems supported by AI can handle humongous data both effectively and efficiently. Likewise, methods have worked on poise, self-guideline, and self-realization because of their unrivaled processing and dynamic capacities [3].

12.2 ARTIFICIAL INTELLIGENCE AND ITS CURRENT STATUS

AI is an intellect displayed by the computer system on par with the natural intelligence of humans and other living beings. Given the intricacy involved in applying man-made intelligence in both military and regular citizen circles, a functioning meaning of man-made intelligence is yet to be characterized. Nobody generally chooses the aim, even among computer researchers and specialists. All things considered, an overall depiction of artificial intelligence is the capacity of a machine to perform assignments that normally require the human mind, for example, visual insight, discourse acknowledgment, and independent direction [4]. Figure 12.1 depicts the pictorial representation of the patterns of AI.

12.2.1 AI as a growing technology

AI is a technology that helps a computer system perform a task such as decision-making, speech recognition, and visual perception that requires human intelligence [5]. In general terms, AI emulates the human brain to reason, learn, predict, infer, judge, and initiate actions. AI works hand in hand with machine learning and deep learning. The best way to understand the three is their interrelationship, which can be visualized via a concentric circle. AI is

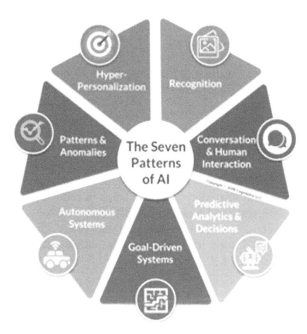

Figure 12.1 All applications of artificial intelligence fall into seven common patterns.

the largest, followed by machine learning and finally deep learning. AI is a technique that mimics the human brain and its intelligence. Machine learning is a subset of AI that focuses on building computer programs that can be used to generate outcomes based on training the existing data and drawing new data from it [6]. Deep learning is a subset of machine learning used to compose new algorithms that permit the software to train on its own by using neural networks imitating how neurons support the human brain.

12.2.2 AI-built technologies

Robotic process automation (RPA) [7], decision management, machine learning, speech recognition, text analysis, biometrics, and natural language processing are some of the technologies proliferating. The AlphaGo program is based on an artificial neural network developed by Google. Facebook has also announced new algorithms. IBM Watson is a cognitive system that integrates data with machine learning algorithms. Microsoft uses many intelligent algorithms that support the development of Android and various Windows applications. The Baidu search engine used by China makes use of different AI technologies that brings global research talent under one roof.

12.2.3 Fear of AI

The smarter one grows, the sooner the roots are lost. Similarly, there is increasing insecurity that the intense use of artificially intelligent machines shall take over and end civilization. The main problem of developing such technologies is the lack of proper understanding of the usage of the technology built. Ultimately resulting in the abuse of the technology, misuse of the same can lead to more massive destruction than constructive use.

12.3 ARTIFICIAL INTELLIGENCE AND ITS USAGE IN DEFENSE

AI has rapidly become the field of interest in the defense community. It facilitates making military decisions and helps in reducing human casualties and combat forces, and much more. Effective decision-making plays a crucial role in wartime, for which intelligent data processing plays an essential task. AI acts as a boon for intelligent computing and decision-making to achieve this. Figure 12.2 shows the use of AI in military applications.

12.3.1 Training

Training and simulation are multidisciplinary fields that use framework and programming standards to build models that can assist troopers with preparing

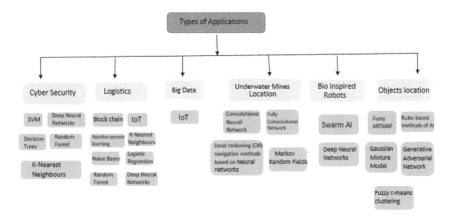

Figure 12.2 Taxonomy proposed in the overview of military applications.

different battle frameworks sent during military tasks. The US Navy and Army forces have previously started a few sensors reenactment programs.

Further, augmented and virtual reality techniques can make functional, practical, and dynamic recreations for the purpose of preparing. The support strategies improve battle preparation for both virtual specialists and human warriors [8].

12.3.2 Surveillance

Using geospatial analysis with AI, intelligent information could be identified from automatic identification systems and radar. If any suspicious or illegal activity is observed, soon the departments shall be alerted for necessary action or preventive measures. To strengthen the strategy, AI with IoT and computer vision shall act as fuel for classifying and identifying any such threats or misconduct [9].

12.3.3 Artillery

AI technology has proved its presence in developing new-age weapons embedded with AI technology. Missiles with sophisticated AI technology hold the capability to analyze and target attack zones without human intervention.

12.3.4 Cyberattacks

Besides air, water, and land, now cyberspace is considered the fourth war front. A malicious network could affect the security of the whole region. To safeguard defense establishments from unauthorized intrusions, defense services use machine learning techniques. Classification methods turned out to be fruitful in accurately identifying such attacks.

12.3.5 Cognitive radio and cognitive electronic warfare

Artificial intelligence can be utilized in the advancement of cognitive radio with dynamic range across the board to improve correspondence while chasing after hostiles, abilities in electronic mental fighting through AI to learn, and quickly devising countermeasures for foe frameworks. As the electromagnetic range turns out to be always complicated and challenging, the presentation of artificial intelligence will be essential to accomplishing improvement [10].

12.3.6 Computational military reasoning (tactical artificial intelligence)

Computational military reasoning is a computer that uses artificial intelligence to make battlefield decisions. This tactical analysis of the battlefield by AI acts as a support to set coherent orders called COA (course of action) to solve human-level military problems. The COA exploits the position of the enemy found during battlefield analysis.

12.3.7 Intelligent and autonomous unmanned weapon systems

Man-made intelligence is utilized to foster clever and independent weapons frameworks, including uncrewed flying, surface and submerged vehicles, military mechanical technology, and voyage rockets. This kind of weapon framework can use artificial intelligence to consequently seek after, recognize, and annihilate adversary targets and is frequently made out of data assortment, and the board information base frameworks help to make choices [10].

12.3.8 Information processing, intelligent analysis, and data fusion using AI

Artificial intelligence successfully processes sensor information and crude knowledge, fusing keen detecting and robotization of multi-sensor information combinations to improve situational mindfulness. Additionally, the presentation of deep learning calculations into the examination interaction for satellite symbolism could essentially work on the velocity of handling: simulated intelligence helped data handling and insight investigation [10].

12.4 PRACTICAL USE OF AI IN MILITARY APPLICATIONS

AI paves its way in attack analysis, communication, transport, logistics, and many military applications [11]. The Artificial Intelligence Exploration (AIE) program initiated by DARPA (Defense Advanced Research Project

Agency) has shown gigantic interest in applications fabricated utilizing AI [12]. The European Defense Agency uses AI in processing a large amount of data in their defense service [13].

12.4.1 Application of neural networks in object location

Strategies such as air patrols, drones, satellite imagery, radar stations, and maritime patrols are used to locate a point on the sea. For example, CleanSeaNet, a European satellite article and pollution detecting system created by EMSA, is used to monitor a location on the sea [14]. The AIS system, also known as an automatic identification system, has become popular in providing a lot of marine traffic information but is not always used to process a large amount of data. Therefore many AI procedures are laid out to screen and illuminate any irregularity. Fuzzy ARTMAP is one of the AIS methods used popularly [15]. The fuzzy ARTMAP combines adaptive resonance theory (ART), which uses unsupervised learning techniques and fuzzy logic elements. The network operation algorithm learns new patterns by maintaining the previously learned ones [16]. On-time updates of significant events and action towards non-essential events will be held. The ART network includes two layers and a reset module as in Figure 12.3. Layer 1, named the comparison field, takes in normalized input data, processes the data, and moves it to layer 2 along with its suitable weights. Further, layer 2, named the recognition field, works on the WTA (winner takes all) principle per which the most elevated result of the info vector and weight is viewed as the best match and turns into the hotspot for new examples. The reset module checks if the new unit is capable of learning based on the prototype vector, called the vigilance test. Figure 12.3 gives a pictorial representation of adaptive resonance theory structure [17].

12.4.2 Location of underwater mines using deep convolution neural network

Submarines stand as the more considerable risk for the ships traveling over the sea or oceans. Numerous countermeasures and attacks are used to neutralize the threat caused by submarines [18, 19]. The need for such countermeasures is to allow the free movement of naval forces. To achieve this, unmanned airborne vehicles (UAVs), unmanned undersea vehicles (UUVs), and autonomous underwater vehicles (AUVs) were developed. UAVs are utilized as optoelectronic heads by the military for perception and reconnaissance. Unmanned combat air vehicles (UCAVs) comprise equipped robots intended to lead battle activities. Sonars that create seabed maps based on data collected are used as underwater drones. All such vehicles utilized for gathering data from submerged regions are fabricated and kept up with by

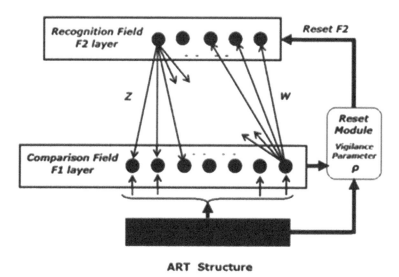

ART Structure

Figure 12.3 Adaptive resonance theory structure.

the Monterey Bay Aquarium Research Institute (MBARI) [20]. The AUV uses a deep convolution neural network to capture photographs to differentiate the mines from other objects.

12.4.3 Application of neural networks in cybersecurity

With each passing year, hacker attacks keep increasing. Reports show that most commercial, public, defense, and government organizations succeed in this threat [21]. An intrusion detection system (IDS) is used to detect incidents, analyze network traffic, and accordingly send notifications [22]. But this system is comparatively slow and expensive to implement, giving rise to the use of artificial intelligence algorithms. One such supportive AI algorithm is the support vector machine which is expected to be seen as a hyperplane in N-dimensional space to classify the data points [23].

AI can deal with immense measures of military information proficiently. It expands the discretion, self-guideline, and self-incitation abilities of war frameworks, utilizing qualities like processing and navigation. Table 12.1 shows the list of countries that have announced their defense strategies using AI. The rising utilization of cloud-based administrations by militaries has additionally animated the market's development. In addition, the inaccessibility of organized information is a limitation of the market. Besides, the rising functional proficiency of independent frameworks would give worthwhile open doors to the market [24]. Figure 12.4 gives a graphical representation of AI being used globally for military operations.

Table 12.1 List of states that have announced their AI national strategy

No.	Year	State	National strategy title
1	2017	UAE	UAE Strategy of Artificial Intelligence
2	2017	China	A Next Generation Artificial Intelligence Development
3	2017	Finland	Finland Age of Artificial Intelligence
4	2017	Japan	Artificial Intelligence Technology Strategy
5	2017	Singapore	AI Singapore
6	2017	Canada	Pan-Canada AI Strategy
7	2018	Denmark	Strategy for Denmark's Digital Growth
8	2018	Kenya	Blockchain and Artificial Intelligence Task Force
9	2018	Taiwan	Taiwan AI Action Plan
10	2018	France	France Strategy of AI
11	2018	Italy	Artificial Intelligence at the Service of Citizens
12	2018	EU Commission	EU Commission Communication on Artificial Intelligence for Europe
13	2018	Tunisia	National AI Strategy
14	2018	UK	Industrial Strategy: Artificial Intelligence Sector Deal
15	2018	Australia	Australia Technology and Science Growth Plan
16	2018	South Korea	Artificial Intelligence R&D Strategy
17	2018	Sweden	National Approach for Artificial Intelligence
18	2018	India	National Strategy for Artificial Intelligence
19	2018	Mexico	Towards an AI Strategy in Mexico: Harnessing the AI Revolution
20	2018	Germany	Key Points for a Federal Government Strategy on AI
21	2018	South Korea	Artificial Intelligence R&D Strategy
22	2019	US	Accelerating America Leadership in Artificial Intelligence

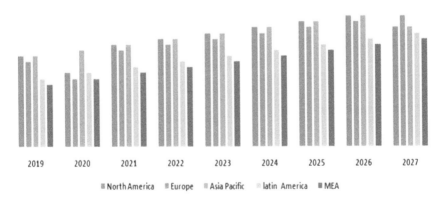

Figure 12.4 Global use of artificial intelligence in military operations.

12.5 CHALLENGES OF USING AI IN DEFENSE OPERATIONS

The use of AI in defense is categorized into three major parts by the Defense Academy as shown in Figure 12.5: 1) sustainment and support use, 2) adversarial and non-kinetic use, and 3) adversarial and kinetic use. The sustainment and support use refers to the deployment of AI in back-office tasks that even include logistical distribution of any kind of resources provided to the defense. It also includes using AI to secure the infrastructure and maintain huge security on the communication system as well. The adversarial and non-kinetic use refers to making use of AI not just for counterattacks but to also maintain active cyber defense and cyber-operations and to curb cyberattacks. The adversarial and kinetic use integrates intelligent systems with combat operations; this ranges from identifying targets to providing aid to autonomous weapon systems [25].

From an industry point of view, adapting to new technology has always been a troublesome action. As it is important to assess the impact of including new technology, it depends not just on cost but on many other relevant aspects like operational ones, which include training, ease of use, etc., technical aspects in terms of complexity, performance, computational burden, security, etc., and support in terms of associated logistics, industrial maintenance, etc. Figure 12.6 shows the potential impact of AI and the need for technology upgradation in control and command systems.

The three motivations behind the utilization of AI in the defense area are more ethically problematic, as one action for sustainment and backing uses

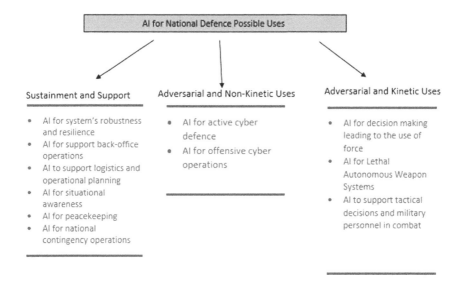

Figure 12.5 The three purposes of AI in defense.

Function	Description	Timeframe	Notes
Classification	Determination Of the type/class Of the target	Near term	Conventional solutions have shown their limits. AI-based solutions may provide better performance.
Threat Assessment	Determination of The threat level Of a target	Near term	Need to manage different situations based on context (e.g. peacetime, crisis). Importance of real data for various situations.
Generation of 'Smart' Red Forces	Training and Wargaming	Near term	Creation of novel situations
Analysis/ understand-ing of the situation and Determination of the Action	Situational Awareness And decision support/ Making to support the Human operator	Medium-term	Very broad class, to be implemented and verified on increasingly complex scenarios
Management/ Use of resources	Support for mission planning	Medium-term	Problems with many variables and constraints are generally solved with heuristic techniques
Damage/Kill Assessment	Evaluation of damage Inflicted to the enemy	Near term	Not much real data is available, more work should be dedicated towards reliable automatic solutions

Figure 12.6 Impact of AI on command and control operations.

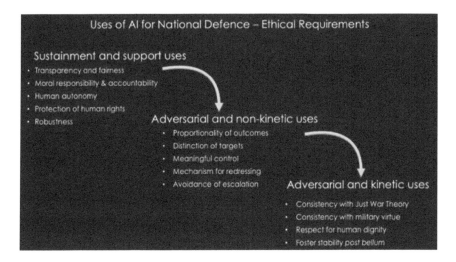

Figure 12.7 AI and its ethical requirements in defense service.

can be used for antagonistic and dynamic purposes. This is on the grounds that close to the ethical problems connected with the utilization of AI (for example straightforwardness and reasonableness), one likewise needs to consider the moral issues connected with adversarial, whether non-kinetic or kinetic, uses of this innovation and its problematic and disastrous effect. Figure 12.7 shows the use of AI and its ethical requirements [25].

Some of the difficulties of involving AI in the military are that commercial AI-embedded applications may generate undesirable outcomes in a military context. Similarly, substantial regional effects are to be considered when deploying AI technology, as its utility and adversarial use might vary based on the geographical conditions of a place. AI algorithms also require memory and processing capacity to execute data from time to time, which increases its complexity. This is typically tough to scale with military devices or with the existing IT infrastructure. If further done, it needs time-to-time training, which adds a capital burden besides the other training activities.

AI systems are a new technology, prone to producing incorrect, surprising, or deliberately misleading results and outputs designed with malicious intent to fool the AI. Even highly trained military operators aren't versed in machine learning; therefore, modifying systems in the field is not a plausible option. The latest technological breakthroughs have led to the innovation of alleged "standoff" weapons or at least armed gadgets that may be launched at a distance sufficient to allow attacking personnel to protective shoot from the target area. Surrogate warfare, that is, the process of outsourcing military functions to auxiliaries, mercenaries, pirates, and contractors, isn't new; however, these new innovations are questioning the fundamental compromises made between delegation and control, bringing up new issues by enabling unmanned platforms to be operated from a distance, initially for observation and reconnaissance, then, at that point, for discipline and execution missions. Despite being not the first machine to be used as an intermediary in warfare (cruise missiles previously served the same purpose), the new weapons likewise give an astounding level of caution (low visibility, domestically as well) and deniability, particularly before the global local area.

Presently some of them are readily available on business markets and comparatively easy to use, breaking away from the conventional imposing business model of states over weaponry and utilization of power and making new "spaces" for new kinds of warfare. They have previously been utilized in (counter-)terrorism and (counter-)insurgency operations abroad, however, could undoubtedly be sent in metropolitan conditions – and possibly stacked with chemical, biological, or radiological specialists. In reality, access and expectation are essential in each of these cases, bringing the boundary down to utilizing and expanding the horizons of their application.

As far as it matters for them, the cyberspace-based weapons – when utilized for damage (cyberattacks) and disruption (disinformation and destabilization crusades) as opposed to reconnaissance – go considerably further in pressuring and disturbing while at the same time protecting prudence and deniability, as they function in an entirely man-made imperfectly directed climate that is dependent upon innovation to work. Although many specialists consider digital warfare from a thin perspective an outlandish situation, digital weapons can accomplish impacts similar to fighting without involving direct physical violence. Digital weapons, unlike atomic weapons, are not deterrence weapons but are used in real-time and even continuous warfare. They can be used by states, their intermediaries, and privateers without geographical or, on the other hand, jurisdictional limitations. It is hard to attribute blame and risky to retaliate [26].

In today's media sphere, the views of good and bad, triumph and rout (so-called "audience effects") are located in a transnational global public sphere, creating different battlefields [27]. They are molded and united at lightning speed. Even though social media have not traditionally been associated with militarization, servicemen use them, making them susceptible to antagonistic missions. "Open-source warfare" is the name of this new game [28], in which individual residents and purchasers frequently go about as more or less unwitting auxiliaries. Unlike cyber-enabled sabotage, which requires significant skill but generally little labor, digitally empowered disruption has fewer complexities to configure yet depends on a minimum amount of clients to scale. The blend of this multitude of advancements in a thorough technique with strategic varieties has been conceptualized as "hybrid" warfare – or, when it stays beneath the degree of outfitted struggle, just malicious activity [29].

As the defense administrations move to bridle this innovation, its prosperity might pivot part of the way on something not specialized: beating the huge gaps in trust around AI. That trust gap separates humans and machines, but also humans and governments, the private area, and the public authority, and government and government. Working through these gaps is crucial for integrating artificial intelligence into national defense. The trust gap is nothing new to a technologist, as it's common for new advances to confront human–machine trust difficulties. Yet, AI and autonomy will require us to reckon with the human–machine relationship much more profoundly than we have done so far. There is a fundamental difference between the ways humans and machines learn, and that is at the heart of this challenge. For instance, machine learning regularly depends on pattern detection enabled by ingesting tremendous measures of information, as opposed to the inferential thinking that distinguishes human intelligence. In addition, AI is typically not set up to explain its reason to skeptics and ensure they have reached the correct conclusion. Humans struggle to gain complete trust in new creations until they have a demonstrated history of safety, which is part of the normal process of technology adoption. Yet this issue is acutely complex in the military, where a commander or even the computer itself may have to decide whether or not to send troops into battle based on the information provided by an AI-enabled system. While there are many challenges here, the arrangements are basically specialized and center on working on innovation and fostering a superior human–machine interface.

12.6 CONCLUSION

AI is here to stay, and it will revolutionize the known norms. It is challenging the traditional ways we have approached and operated upon information and transforming how systems are designed. In today's world, AI is mainly evolutionary, and the defense system is impacted by it predominantly. Therefore, it is imperative to screen, research, investigate, explore, and experiment with advancements in the field of AI to best deploy it. Because the basic idea of military tasks and ML is susceptible to noise intrusions and is vulnerable to adversarial attacks, applying ML to the military is not straightforward. Understanding and explaining the reasoning behind decision-making processes in strategic applications is essential; ML solutions have to be carefully designed and built, and it must be figured out how to procure the trust of creators and end clients. The specificities of AI expect that the combination of these innovations happens solely after every one of the vital confirmations is made and effectively passed. As AI becomes more involved in such countless parts of our day-to-day innovation experience, so will it become progressively necessary in our public safety devices. Although the most significant technological promise may still be years in the making, right now is an ideal opportunity to build a system for viable administration of this innovation and trust in its deployment.

REFERENCES

1. Artificial Intelligence in Defence Technology. https://www.innefu.com/blog/artificial-intelligence-in-Defence-technology
2. What Are the Scope and Challenges of Using AI in Military. https://thegoodai.co/2020/11/01/what-are-the-scope-and-challenges-of-using-ai-in-military-operations/
3. Artificial Intelligence in Military Operations: Where Does. https://www.medianama.com/2019/08/223-artificial-intelligence-in-military-operations-where-does-india-stand/
4. Bhushan, M., Iyer, S., Kumar, A., Choudhury, T., and Negi, A. *Artificial Intelligence for Smart Cities and Villages: Advanced Technologies, Development, and Challenges*, Bentham Science Publishers, 2022.
5. What Is Artificial Intelligence (AI) in Technology? – SJCSKS. https://www.sjcsks.org/what-is-artificial-intelligence-ai-in-technology/
6. Verma, K., Bhardwaj, S., Arya, R., Islam, M. S. U., Bhushan, M., Kumar, A., and Samant, P. Latest Tools for Data Mining and Machine Learning. *International Journal of Innovative Technology and Exploring Engineering* 2019, 8 9S, 18–23. https://doi.org/10.35940/ijitee.I1003.0789S19.
7. Kholiya, P. S, Kapoor, A., Rana, M., Bhushan, M. Intelligent Process Automation: The Future of Digital Transformation. In Proceedings of the 10th International Conference on System Modeling & Advancement in Research Trends (SMART), 2021; pp. 185–190. https://doi.org/10.1109/SMART52563.2021.9676222.
8. Future Wars Artificial Intelligence in Military Operations. https://futurewars.rspanwar.net/artificial-intelligence-in-military-operations-an-overview-part-i/
9. What Are the Scope and Challenges of Using AI in Military. https://analyticsindiamag.com/what-are-the-scope-and-challenges-of-using-ai-in-military-operations/
10. Military Applications of Artificial Intelligence – Centre. https://archive.claws.in/1878/military-applications-of-artificial-intelligence-deepak-kumar-gupta.html
11. Svenmarck, P., Luotsinen, L., Nilsson, M., Schubert, J. Possibilities and Challenges for Artificial Intelligence in Military Applications. In Proceedings of the NATO Big Data and Artificial Intelligence for Military Decision Making Specialists' Meeting, Bordeaux, France, 31 May 2018.
12. DARPA – Accelerating the Exploration of Promising Artificial Intelligence Concepts. Available online: https://www.darpa.mil/ news-events/2018-07-20a (accessed on 25 January 2021).
13. Sanchez, S.L. Artificial Intelligence (AI) Enabled Cyber Defence. Available online: https://www.eda.europa.eu/webzine/issue1 4/cover-story/artificial-intelligence-(ai)-enabled-cyber-Defence (accessed on 25 January 2021).
14. MSA – European Maritime Safety Agency. Available online: http://www.emsa.europa.eu/ (accessed on 25 January 2021).
15. Rhodes, B.J., Bomberger, N.A., Seibert, M., Waxman, A.M. Maritime Situation Monitoring and Awareness Using Learning Mechanisms. In Proceedings of the MILCOM 2005-2005 IEEE Military Communications Conference, Atlantic City, NJ, USA, 17–20 October 2005; pp. 646–652. [CrossRef]

16. Al Salam, M. Adaptive Resonance Theory Neural Networks. Available online: https://www.academia.edu/38067953/Adaptive_ Resonance_Theory_ Neural_Networks (accessed on 25 January 2021).
17. Mao, Z., Massaquoi, S.G. Dynamics of winner-take-all competition in recurrent neural networks with lateral inhibition. *IEEE Trans. Neural Netw.* 2007, 18, 55–69. [CrossRef]
18. The Future of Mine Countermeasures. Available online: https://fas.org/man/ dod-101/sys/ship/weaps/docs/mcmfuture.htm (accessed on 25 January 2021).
19. THALES. The Future of Mine Warfare: A Quicker, Safer Approach. Available online: https://www.thalesgroup.com/en/unitedkingdom/news/future-mine -warfare-quicker-safer-approach (accessed on january 2021).
20. MBARI – Autonomous Underwater Vehicles. Available online: https://www .mbari.org/at-sea/vehicles/autonomousunderwater-vehicles/ (accessed on 25 January 2021).
21. Center for Strategies & International Studies – Significant Cyber Incidents. Available online: https://www.csis.org/programs/ technology-policy-program /significant-cyber-incidents (accessed on 25 January 2021).
22. Pratt, M.K. What Is an Intrusion Detection System? How an IDS Spots Threats. Available online: https://www.csoonline.com/ article/3255632/what -is-an-intrusion-detection-system-how-an-ids-spots-threats.html   (accessed on 25 January 2021).
23. Ghanem, K., Aparicio-Navarro, F.J., Kyriakopoulos, K.G., Lambotharan, S., Chambers, J.A. Support Vector Machine for Network Intrusion and Cyber-Attack Detection. In Proceedings of the 2017 Sensor Signal Processing for Defence Conference (SSPD), London, UK, 6–7 December 2017; pp. 1–5. [CrossRef]
24. Aritificial Intelligence in Radiology: Siemens Healthineers. https://www.sie-mens-lhealthineers.com/medical-imaging/digital-transformation-of-radiol-ogy/ai-in-radiology
25. Taddeo, Mariarosaria, McNeish, David, Blanchard, Alexander, Edgar, Elizabeth. Ethical Principles for Artificial Intelligence in National Defence. *Philos. Technol.* 2021, 34, 1–23. https://doi.org/10.1007/s13347 -021-00482-3.
26. Thomas Rid. *Cyber War Will Not Take Place*, Hurst & Co., 2013 and 2017. See also Antonio Missiroli, "The Dark Side of the Web: Cyber as a Threat", *European Foreign Affairs Review*, vol.24, no.2, 2019, 135–152.
27. Emile Simpson. *War from the Ground Up: Twenty-First Century Combat as Politics*, Columbia University Press, 2012.
28. John Robb. *Brave New War*, John Wiley & Sons, 2007. See also Peter W. Singer, Emerson T. Brooking, Like War: The Weaponization of Social Media, Boston-New York, Houghton Mifflin Harcourt, 2018.
29. For an overview see Antonio Missiroli. From Hybrid Warfare to "Cybrid" Campaigns: The New Normal? NDC Policy Brief, no. 19, September 2019.

Chapter 13

Steam turbine controller using fuzzy logic

Abhay Krishan and Sachin Umrao

CONTENTS

13.1 INTRODUCTION

Steam turbine controller technology allows the turbine to function in a safe and reliable way. Steam turbines are energy converters. They have input energy from steam and convert it into torque, as output. The transmitted energy is the function of the temperature and the pressure. The safety system of the turbine helps keep the machines' functions from operating improperly. It reduces the risk of the turbine overspeeding and monitors all the turbine's critical

DOI: 10.1201/9781003286745-13

257

parameters and turbine trips. The process system controls the steam turbine operation. The steam control is controlled, which can be mechanical/hydraulic and electrical. An electro-hydraulic control system has flexibility for the use of electronic circuits. The advanced control usually operates the high-pressure and low-pressure valves and the electro-hydraulic turbine controls. The controller chooses the set point to sense the shaft speed and compare the actual speed. For the difference of their speeds, a signal is sent by the controller to the actuator, which changes the speed to balance the two signals [1–3].

Steam turbine stability is linked with good quality control and increased reliability and efficiency. Adequate speed control means fewer speed problems to overcome; speed fluctuations result in manual control, which is an inefficient operation with more risk of machine and process trips. It takes longer to start and machine trips start. The system variables "temperature" and "pressure" have a range of "states," such as "cold," "warm," "hot," "very hot," "low," and "high." Arranging their states in an appropriate manner is a bit tricky.

Temperature is the degree of hotness and coldness of the body. Temperature is an important factor for turbine safety and efficiency. The turbine inlet improves the engine's efficiency; it produces the same/more power with the same amount of fuel. The temperature conditions, the exit at the high-pressure compressor, and the inlet of the pressure turbine are high. For the hot temperatures, the failure of the compressor blade damages serious components. Turbine steam inlet pressure affects turbine performance. If the design efficiency is retained, the steam inlet pressure is maintained. The inlet pressure steam being low reduces turbine efficiency and the steam consumption increases.

The state "fuzzy" changes from one state to another. Fuzzy logic (FL) has well-defined discrete numeric values. Fuzzy logic control is the most thriving and important control technology to develop advanced process control and system design [4, 5]. Fuzzy systems have large applications in engineering and sciences. The present work is associated with a steam turbine controller to develop a suitable rule-based processing system that allows one to know the performance of parameters, temperature, and pressure. Villages have suitable space to preserve renewable sources of energy. These particular spaces allow the development of such a type of controller that requires a renewable source of energy and these controllers function to complete the processes to work in smart villages. In smart villages, people are allowed to work with such a type of controller in order to have a power backup for the village and for running power projects.

13.1.1 Description of technology at block level

Figure 13.1 represents the block diagram of the fuzzy controller. It consists of the following four elements:

1. A rule-base (if–then rules) from an FL expert on linguistic variable quantification.

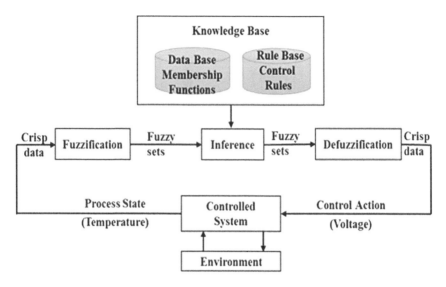

Figure 13.1 Block diagram of a fuzzy controller.

2. An inference engine that emulates the expert's decision for interpreting and applying knowledge.
3. A fuzzification interface that represents the inputs of the information into a controller, which allows starting the rules and implementing them.
4. A defuzzification interface that represents the inference conclusions.

13.1.2 Practical realization of fuzzy controller

This block diagram consists of a thermally insulated chamber consisting of a fan and bulb as a pressure and temperature source operated through power supplies. FP-RTD-122/FP-AO-200 acts as a sensor. This device is connected to the PC through a standard RS-232 serial link. With the help of a computer, a fuzzy logic toolkit controls the variables with the support of MATLAB. The working diagram of the fuzzy controller is shown in Figure 13.2.

Several researchers have worked on the fuzzy logic controller (FLC) during the last few years. Lamkhade et al. [6] evaluated the FLC to improve the performance in comparison to the proportional integral (PI) controller; regarding water level control, fuzzy gives effective output, which overcomes the limitations of the proportional integral (PI) controller. Thao et al. [7] presented a control strategy to determine the active power reference voltage. That controls the converters, the output active power delivering to the grid, forcing the grid-frequency into an appropriate desired range. Rodzman et al. [8] implemented ranking

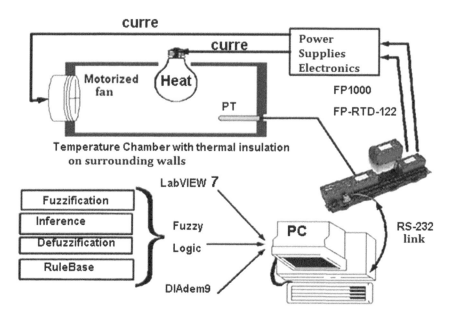

Figure 13.2 Working of a fuzzy controller.

as the information retrieval system, the classification of text documents to yield a score that allowed an addition in the ranking function and improved the rank finally. Najmurrokhman et al. [9] developed a hexapod mobile robot using its speed as the variable. The distance between the root and the obstacle allows the movement of the robot. It implements a triangular membership function for implementation. Swethamarai et al. [10] designed a car driver model for three degrees of freedom. It minimizes driver body acceleration, utilizing the fuzzy proportional integral derivative (FPID) model that produces better results than the proportional integral derivative (PID). Bajpai et al. [11] proposed a text mining application, which categorizes the text according to user sentiments and the orientations according to the product review. Saidi et al. [12] utilized two FLC algorithms and implemented a speed regulator of a doubly fed induction machine using two non-linear control techniques. Unde et al. [13] implemented a closed-loop FLC to generate solar power. It improved the efficiency of the system for a three non-linear phase system, which minimizes the total harmonic distortion using a closed-loop FLC. Oleiwi et al. [14] presented a new controller design for the avoidance of collision in mobile robots. Nguyen et al. [15] compared the PI and the proportional derivative (PD) which provides different scenarios for a fuzzy rule-base and showed the superiority of the PI-type FLC over the PD-like in a control problem. Rawat et al. [16] compared the frequency changes with the tie-line power fluctuations and variations in area control errors for the test system. It is not suitable for the variation in control frequency. In this, an improved FLC allowed for unknown dynamic obstacles in their environment using onboard sensor information.

In the next section of the chapter, there is a description of the methodology that is used to implement the chapter, including FLC input and the output functions' implementation details. In the third section, there are details about the results that show the details output for the chapter and some useful points outcomes. In the last section, there is a conclusion of the chapter related to the useful data, detailing desired rules that are useful for the implementation of the future aspects of the chapter.

13.2 DESCRIPTION OF METHODOLOGY USED FOR IMPLEMENTATION

Fuzzy logic control is the most thriving and important control method to develop advanced process control and system design. In the fuzzy control design methodology, there is a set of rules and then a fuzzy controller to emulate the decision-making process [17–24].

The fuzzy logic toolbox allows us to do several things: create and edit fuzzy inference systems, which is a unique type of method of fuzzy inference. FL starts as a fuzzy set. A fuzzy set has a defined boundary, only with a partial degree of membership elements. FL is a multi-valued logic (0 to 1). A membership function (MF) is the input space with a value between 0 and 1 [25]. Each MF is represented by a triangular or straight-line segment.

13.2.1 Choosing fuzzy controller inputs and outputs

Temperature and pressure are two input variables, and the turbine throttle setting is an output variable. The fuzzy set mappings are shown in Figure 13.3. Fuzzy control system input variables are mapped as "fuzzy sets."

13.2.2 Linguistic descriptions

The linguistic description is split into several parts. The linguistic variables and values express the views about the control decision and the fuzzy controller inputs and outputs choices.

13.2.3 Rules

The rule set includes four rules which are as follows:

Rule 1: IF temperature IS cool AND pressure IS weak,
    THEN throttle is P3.

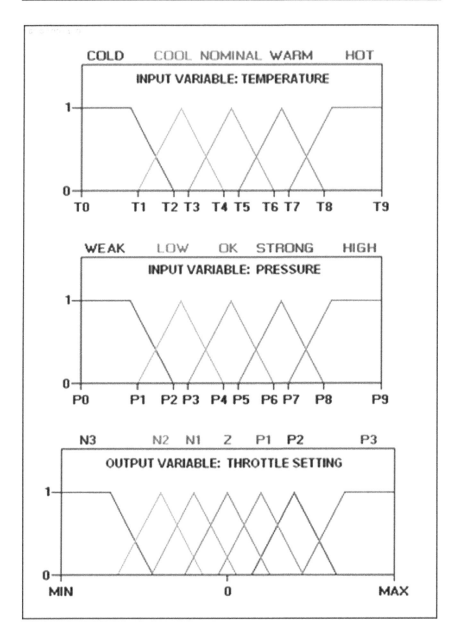

Figure 13.3 Graph showing fuzzy set mappings of the input variable.

Rule 2: IF temperature IS cool AND pressure IS low,
  THEN throttle is P2.

Rule 3: IF temperature IS cool AND pressure IS okay,
  THEN throttle is Z.

Rule 4: IF temperature IS cool AND pressure IS strong,
  THEN throttle is N2

13.2.4 Rule-bases

The rules will be written for turbine control with as many cases as possible; there are at most $5^2 = 25$ possible rules, with linguistic values for all of them.

13.2.5 Operations

Figure 13.4 represents the operations of logical operators of two fuzzy sets A and B, the union of these sets, the intersection of these sets, and the negation of set A.

13.2.6 Fuzzy quantification of knowledge

This is the knowledge about how it is possible to control the plant. Next, we implement FL to fully vary the linguistic rule. The fuzzy controller automates the control rules expert.

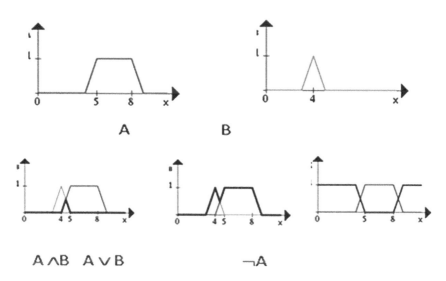

Figure 13.4 Operations of logical operators.

Implication methods: the implication was introduced for the evaluation of individual rules. A few of the types are:

- Mamdani type: Mamdani's proposed implication method.
- Lusing Larson type: the output MF is scaled instead of truncated.
- Sugeno type: the output MFs are a constant type or linear relation with input functions.

13.2.7 Defuzzification methods

Defuzzification is the conversion of fuzzy output to crisp output. A few important methods of defuzzification are center of area (COA), height, mean of maxima (MOM), and Sugeno.

13.3 FUZZY LOGIC CONTROLLER

A fuzzy rule-based system has a set of rules. An inference rules system, as shown in Figure 13.5, implements a simple logic using the FL:

The throttle valve parameters are defined as follows:

N3/N2/N1: large/medium/small negative.
Z: Zero.
P3/P2/P1: large/medium/small positive.

Practically, the controller allows the inputs that map into the membership functions, or it may be truth values. The mappings are fed to the fuzzy rules.

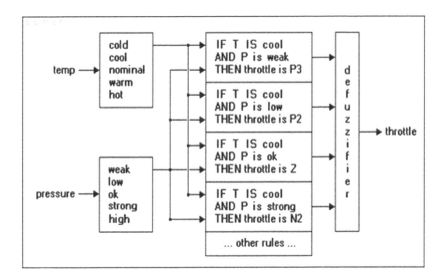

Figure 13.5 A rule-based system.

An AND relationship of the mappings is specified as the rule by the two input functions; their combined truth value is used as the minimum of the two, or if an OR is specified, the maximum of the two. The selection of an appropriate output state is done and the truth level of the premise is assigned a membership value. These truth values are then de-fuzzified [26–28]. These rule-based applications allow us to get useful information regarding how to interpret a steam turbine controller in smart villages. The smart village users know this rule allows them to generate a suitable turbine controller, which has maximum efficient work for the smart village progress.

13.3.1 Problems encountered and their solutions

Figure 13.6 and Figure 13.7 present the output controller and the throttle output defuzzification, respectively.

13.3.2 Deciding the input variables

The pressure and temperature are input variables and with these two variables, the throttle is to be controlled.

13.3.3 Deciding membership functions

The problem arises in selecting membership functions for temperature, pressure, and throttle.

For temperature, the MFs are: cold, warm, hot
For pressure, the MFs are: weak, strong, high
And for throttle, the settings are: N3, N2, N1, Z, P1, P2, P3

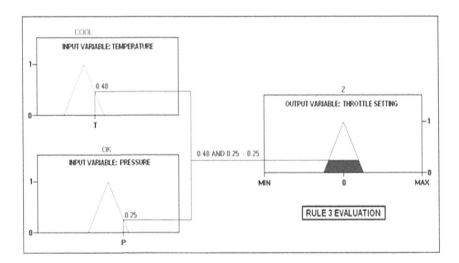

Figure 13.6 Output of the controller.

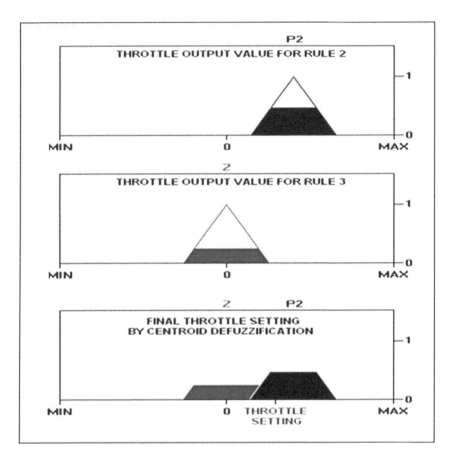

Figure 13.7 Throttle output of controller according to distinct rules.

13.3.4 Deciding range

Ranges of membership functions must satisfy the practical conditions of operation of the turbine.

13.4 DECIDING THE TYPE OF FUNCTION

Take a trapezoidal function. These are the primary tools to design and append fuzzy inference systems in the fuzzy logic toolbox [29–31]. They are:

- FIS editor: It is required for high-level system issues including input and output variables.
- Membership function editor: Each variable has the shapes of all the membership functions linked.

- Rule editor: It edits the list of rules for the system behavior.
- Rule viewer: It acts as a diagnostic for active rules or individual membership.
- Surface viewer: The surface viewer builds a system output, allowing it to show one of the outputs related to any one or two of the inputs.

13.5 RESULTS AND DISCUSSIONS

The MATLAB/fuzzy logic toolbox's salient features have been reviewed for application in steam turbine controllers. PID controller output values vary with tuning process control parameters (K_P, K_I, and K_D). The optimal parameters have a minimization of overshooting, oscillations, and steady-state errors. The set points are the fuzzy membership functions, which are tuned with a ramp function. The fuzzy sets input/output partition into five membership functions, which correspond to five linguistic variables. The FLC performed a faster response than the PID controller in a transient state and has been settled down without any type of overshoot and any oscillation in a steady state. Robustness is the most important against possible disturbances in control action. Table 13.1 represents the FLC's better characteristics of response in comparison to the PID controller.

The evaluations can be further made with the set point variations by the use of the step function. The step function followed by the FLC is better in terms of speed than the PID controller with reduced overshoot and oscillation.

13.6 CONCLUDING REMARKS

The developed FL-based steam turbine controller eliminates the need for mathematical modeling as required in a PID controller-based system. The FLC is designed for temperature and pressure control. The FLC-evaluated performance is compared with the PID controller.

During the term that had been given for finishing the project, a fuzzy controller had been produced and finished according to specification, with controlling action according to a set of rules. The steam turbine is well

Table 13.1 The response characteristics of the proposed system

Characteristics	FLC (ramp/step function)	PID
Overshoot	0.001%/0.001%	11.7%
Steady-state errors	0/0.2	0.7
Oscillations	Fast grow/grow oscillations	Slow decay

controlled and should be able to perform according to conditions. The suitable condition of the controller allows the smart village people to take benefit from the steam turbine controller. A well-known fact about the steam turbine controller is that it can have the benefits of getting power backup in case of a power failure and yielding a large amount of power generation, which allows it to work on several industrial projects in the smart village. A smart village always retains power for emergency purposes. The rule base and its specifications allow the smart village people to use the controller to get power and also allow them to get some more natural resource experiments in order to develop more efficient types of controller for future aspects.

CONFLICT OF INTEREST

The authors declare that they have no conflicts of interest.

REFERENCES

1. M. Dulau and D. Bica, "Simulation of speed steam turbine control system," in 7th International Conference Interdisciplinarity in Engineering (INTER-ENG 2013) Procedia Technology. 12, 2014, pp. 716–722.
2. M. Azubalis, V. Azubalis, A. Jonaitis, and R. Ponelis, "Identification of model parameters of steam turbine and governor," *Oil Shale*, vol. 26, pp. 716–722, 2009.
3. T. Inoue and H. Amano, "A thermal power plant model for dynamic simulation of load frequency control," in 2006 IEEE PES Power Systems Conference and Exposition. IEEE, 2006, pp. 1442–1447.
4. A. Kaufmann and A. Bonaert, "Introduction to the theory of fuzzy subsets vol. 1: Fundamental theoretical elements," *IEEE Transactions on Systems, Man, and Cybernetics*, vol. 7, pp. 495–496, 1977.
5. F. Farbiz, M. B. Menhaj, S. A. Motamedi, and M. T. Hagan, "A new fuzzy logic filter for image enhancement," *IEEE Transactions on Systems, Man, and Cybernetics, Part B (Cybernetics)*, vol. 30, pp. 110–119, 2000.
6. P. N. Lamkhade, B. Parvat, and C. Kadu, "Design and implementation of fuzzy logic controller for level control," in 2015 International Conference on Energy Systems and Applications. IEEE, 2015, pp. 475–479.
7. N. G. M. Thao and K. Uchida, "A control strategy based on fuzzy logic for three-phase grid-connected photovoltaic system with supporting grid-frequency regulation," *Journal of Automation and Control Engineering*, vol. 4, pp. 96–103, 2016.
8. S. B. bin Rodzman, N. K. Ismail, N. Abd Rahman, and Z. M. Nor, "The implementation of fuzzy logic controller for defining the ranking function on malay text corpus," in 2017 IEEE Conference on Big Data and Analytics (ICBDA). IEEE, 2017, pp. 93–98.

9. A. Najmurrokhman, G. I. Sofyan, E. C. Djamal, A. Munir, B. H. Wibowo et al., "Design and implementation of fuzzy logic controller for a class of hexapod mobile robot," in 2018 Electrical Power, Electronics, Communications, Controls and Informatics Seminar (EECCIS). IEEE, 2018, pp. 269–273.

10. A. Bajpai and V. S. Kushwah, "Importance of fuzzy logic and application areas in engineering research," *International Journal of Recent Technology and Engineering (IJRTE)*, vol. 7, pp. 1467–1471, 2019.

11. P. Swethamarai and P. Lakshmi, "Design and implementation of fuzzy-pid controller for an active quarter car driver model to minimize driver body acceleration," in 2019 IEEE International Systems Conference (SysCon). IEEE, 2019, pp. 1–6.

12. A. Saidi, F. Naceri, L. Youb, M. Cernat, and L. G. Pesquer, "Two types of fuzzy logic controllers for the speed control of the doubly-fed induction machine," *Advances in Electrical and Computer Engineering*, vol. 20, pp. 65–74, 2020.

13. M. Unde, K. Deokar, M. Hans, and S. Kawthe, "Closed-loop design of fuzzy logic controller in solar power generation," in 2020 Fourth International Conference on Inventive Systems and Control (ICISC). IEEE, 2020, pp. 215–219.

14. B. K. Oleiwi, A. Mahfuz, and H. Roth, "Application of fuzzy logic for collision avoidance of mobile robots in dynamic-indoor environments," in 2021 2nd International Conference on Robotics, Electrical and Signal Processing Techniques (ICREST). IEEE, 2021, pp. 131–136.

15. N-K. Nguyen and D-T.Nguyen, "A comparative study on PI- and PD-type fuzzy logic control strategies," *International Journal of Engineering Trends and Technology (IJETT)*, vol. 69 (7), pp. 101–108, 2021.

16. S. Rawat, B. Jha, M.K. Panda, and J. Kanti, "Interval type-2 fuzzy logic control-based frequency control of hybrid power system using DMGS of PI controller,"*Applied Science*, vol. 11, p. 01217, 2021.

17. L. Zhang, M. Xiao, J. Ma, and H. Song, "Edge detection by adaptive neuro-fuzzy inference system," in 2009 2nd International Congress on Image and Signal Processing. IEEE, 2009, pp. 1–4.

18. M. Bhushan and S. Goel, "Improving software product line using an ontological approach," *Sādhanā*, vol. 41 (12), pp. 1381–1391, 2016. https://doi.org/10.1007/s12046-016-0571-y

19. A. Negi Megha, and K. Kaur, "Method to resolve software product line errors," in International Conference on Information, Communication and Computing Technology. Springer, 2017, pp. 258–268. doi: https://doi.org/10.1007/978-981-10-6544-6_24

20. M. Bhushan, S. Goel, A. Kumar, and A. Negi, "Managing software product line using an ontological rule-based framework," in 2017 International Conference on Infocom Technologies and Unmanned Systems (Trends and Future Directions)(ICTUS). IEEE, 2017, pp. 376–382. https://doi.org/10.1109/ICTUS.2017.8286036

21. M. Bhushan, S. Goel, and A. Kumar, "Improving quality of software product line by analysing inconsistencies in feature models using an ontological rule-based approach," *Expert Systems*, vol. 35, (3), p. e12256, 2018. https://doi.org/10.1111/exsy.12256

22. M. Bhushan, S. Goel, and K. Kaur, "Analyzing inconsistencies in software product lines using an ontological rule-based approach," *Journal of Systems and Software*, vol. 137, pp. 605–617, 2018. https://doi.org/10.1016/j.jss.2017.06.002

23. M. Bhushan, A. Negi, P. Samant, S. Goel, and A. Kumar, "A classification and systematic review of product line feature model defects," *Software Quality Journal*, vol. 284 (3), pp. 1507–1550, 2020. https://doi.org/10.1007/s11219-020-09522-1

24. M. Bhushan, J. ´A. G. Duarte, P. Samant, A. Kumar, and A. Negi, "Classifying and resolving software product line redundancies using an ontological first-order logic rule based method," *Expert Systems with Applications*, vol. 168, p. 114167, 2021. https://doi.org/10.1016/j.eswa.2020.114167

25. E. B. Kumar and M. Sundaresan, "Edge detection using trapezoidal membership function based on fuzzy's mamdani inference system," in 2014 International Conference on Computing for Sustainable Global Development (INDIACom). IEEE, 2014, pp. 515–518.

26. R. Din, "Intellectual matlab medical images classification on graphic processors," *UPB Science Bulletin, Series C*, vol. 75, (2), 2013.

27. A. Krishnamurthy, S. Samsi, and V. Gadepally, *Parallel MATLAB Techniques*. Ohio Supercomputer Center and Ohio State University, 2009.

28. J. Kepner, *Parallel MATLAB for Multicore and Multinode Computers*. SIAM, 2009.

29. K. Yadav, A. Mittal, M. Ansari, and V. Vishwarup, "Parallel implementation of similarity measures on gpu architecture using cuda," *Indian Journal of Computer Science and Engineering*, vol. 3, pp. 1–9, 2012.

30. M. Hajarian, A. Shahbahrami, and F. Hoseini, "A parallel solution for the 0–1 knapsack problem using firefly algorithm," in 2016 1st Conference on Swarm Intelligence and Evolutionary Computation (CSIEC). IEEE, 2016, pp. 25–30.

31. M. K. Shah, "Performance analysis of Sobel edge detection filter on gpu using cuda & opengl," *International Journal for Research in Applied Science and Engineering Technology (IJRASET)*, vol. 1, pp. 22–26, 2013.

Chapter 14

Speech recognition for Indian-accent English using a transformer model

P. Teja, Anjali Gupta, Sakshi, and Mathang Peddi

CONTENTS

DOI: 10.1201/9781003286745-14

14.1 INTRODUCTION

Speech recognition is the technology that enables a machine to identify spoken language and convert it into readable text [1]. Simple speech recognition applications have a small vocabulary of terms and phrases and identify words accurately only if the speech lacks noise and exhibits clarity. With continuous developments and the evolution of technology, this technology is widely used in critical applications such as the medical and legal industries. Voice biometry is a sector that allows organizations to create a digital profile of a person's voice by examining a set of specific characteristics such as tone, dynamics, pitch, intensity, and dominant frequencies. Applications like these require extremely high-accuracy speech recognition systems, with lives at stake leaving no room for errors.

However, there arise certain complications in this technology due to the complexities involved with speech such as the domain of speech, characteristics of the speaker, style, and external environment. Speaker characteristics vary due to the accent of the speaker which may vary significantly from person to person and from region to region. Commonly used speech recognition models generally fail to predict text for accented speech with accuracy.

Another complication arises due to the inability of the software to understand the complexities of the English language, with every sector having its own lexicon and phrases, and if these are not part of regular English, the program may be unsuccessful in the efficient transcription of speech to written English [2]. The program may also experience accuracy drops when multiple speakers are present and being recorded. The effect of these complications gets magnified in regions with English as a non-native language like India.

This chapter aims at tackling these complications by training a transformer model using data collected from Indian engineering college lectures and newspaper read speech, read by people from various cities like Bangalore, Mumbai, Delhi, Kolkata, etc. The results of this chapter will help form the pipeline for bigger systems like technological conferences where subtitles for speech would be needed and obtaining transcriptions in native Indian languages where transcriptions for English can be generated by this model and then converted to the native language.

14.2 PROBLEM STATEMENT

It is very difficult to find a speech recognition system that could recognize Indian-accent English and that could easily pick up the words when the audio file is given. So, to solve this problem, a deep learning speech recognition model is built that can generate transcripts for Indian-accent English when fed to an audio file that contains a pure Indian accent in it.

This will help users to retrieve transcripts for technological seminars/conferences, which can be used for language translation from English to other languages like Hindi, Telugu, and Bengali. The limitations of this chapter include focusing only on technical terms from computer science and electrical engineering domains, excluding other domains such as organic chemistry, biotechnology, and mechanical engineering, which have further complications due to the complexities of the subjects and lack of datasets for the same. Another limitation may include inaccuracies due to extreme noise in the provided audio input.

The aim here is to create a completely free-of-cost web application using an API service where the user enters his credentials and the credentials are encrypted and stored in a database using encryption techniques like elliptic curve cryptography and hashing techniques. Here, the user uploads a raw audio or video file and then can get the transcripts of that particular file that he has uploaded. This chapter intends to take audio input from users/videos/technological forums and transform it into text with minimal latency and delays using deep learning models. This chapter involves a variety of compromises. The quality of the dataset used determines the way the deep learning model gets trained and what the precision of its performance is. This poses a problem in terms of the right selection of the dataset. Also, there is a risk that the model may not work well on datasets that are extremely different from the dataset that the model is trained on.

This also poses a lot of challenges. The data might contain noise and disturbances, so these have to be removed to get better accuracy. There are many words with the same pronunciation but with different spelling, so this has to be taken care of. Accent recognition has been regarded as a more difficult challenge than language recognition since accents of the same language are more similar. This also requires building a speaker-independent framework because the model is being trained on the IIT Madras lectures, which may only have two to three speakers, but this model must work for any speaker.

14.3 PROPOSED METHODOLOGY

The data consists of audio recordings of Indian-accent English. To determine the efficiency of this model, the audio files dataset was split into training and validation data. The MFCC features were extracted and the output was a matrix consisting of feature vectors. This input was then passed on to the model for training, and then the model was tested on the validation data for accuracy. After checking the model's accuracy, it was saved as a .pth file and deployed to the cloud using an API and monitored. Figure 14.1 represents the flow chart containing different steps to execute and deploy the transformer model.

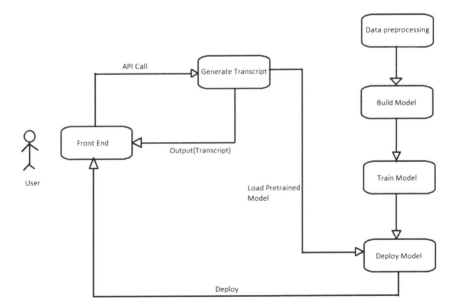

Figure 14.1 Flow chart representing system design.

When the user visits the website, he/she has an option of login and signup. If the user is new, then the user can sign up and then log in to the website [3]. Once the user gives his username and password, elliptic curve cryptography is used where the password is hashed using the SHA256 algorithm and saved in the database. So when the user tries to log in, the password is first hashed and verified with the database and if the credentials are valid then the user logs in.

The user visits the website and gives input in the form of audio recordings on the front end. The front end is able to find out incorrect input audio files in different formats other than .wav files and asks the user to input these audio files in the specified format. The input data does basic validation and is fed to the pre-trained deep learning model which predicts the outcome and generates the text. This text is then sent to the front and the transcript is displayed on the website

When the user visits the website, he has an option to log in or sign up. If he is a new user, then he has to first sign up and then log in to the website. Once the user gives his username and password, then elliptic curve cryptography is used and the password is hashed using the SHA256 algorithm and saved in the database.

14.4 DATA OVERVIEW

The dataset used comprises Indian English read-speech and lecture-speech data along with the corresponding transcripts. It covers general genres like politics, sports, entertainment, etc. The read speech text data was crawled from newspapers and read by volunteers. The lecture speech data was obtained from the computer science and electrical lectures of the National Programme on Technology-Enhanced Learning (NPTEL).

Speech data includes audio segments of variable lengths from as short as one minute to as long as one hour [4]. Along with raw speech, the dataset includes text files – segments, spk2utt, text, utt2dur, utt2spk, wav, lexicon, nonsilence_phones, optional_silence, and silence_phones. These files contain information about the audio files, the transcripts from various parts of each audio file, and the phonetics of the English language. Each audio file has been divided into various sub-parts or segments of smaller durations up to 30 seconds, for each of which the transcripts have been given in the dataset.

14.4.1 Text files

The text files provided in the dataset include:

1. segments: This file contains details regarding the audio segments, the audio file from which the audio segment is taken, and the beginning time and the end time of that part in the audio file in seconds.

2. spk2utt: This file lists all audio segments belonging to each audio file.
3. text: This is the main file that maps the transcripts to each audio segment.
4. utt2dur: This file lists the duration of each audio segment with the segment name.
5. utt2spk: This file maps each segment to its corresponding audio file.
6. wav: This file maps the audio file name to its exact path in the dataset directory.

14.4.2 Data preprocessing

The information contained in the text files was condensed to form a CSV file that contains the audio segments, the corresponding audio file from which the segment was obtained, the destination path of that segment in the dataset directory, the duration of each segment, and the start and end time of each segment.

The audio files were split into corresponding segments using the FFmpeg library and stored at destination paths indicated in the CSV file. As a result, a dataset with 167,930 segments is obtained with lengths ranging from 0.2 to 29.54 seconds and their corresponding transcripts.

14.5 TECHNOLOGIES USED

14.5.1 Transformers

The transformer is a deep architecture that makes use of attention to remarkably improve the performance of NLP translation models. While processing a part of the input, attention allows the model to focus on other parts in the input that are closely linked to that part. Figure 14.2 represents the architecture of the transformer model.

It can process all the sentences in the sequence parallelly, thus significantly speeding up computation, and it computes dependencies between adjacent parts of input audio and parts that are far apart too.

Transformers have an advantage over using RNNs/LSTMs/GRUs, as using the latter makes it hard to deal with long-range dependencies between parts of input audio spread far apart. On the other hand, the sequence-to-sequence models involve a single-context vector being passed from encoder to decoder, which is a bottleneck, making it challenging to deal with long sentences, and making transformers the preferred model.

14.5.2 Attention

In attention, all the hidden states of the encoder are passed to the decode. Each hidden state of the encoder is most related to a certain part of the

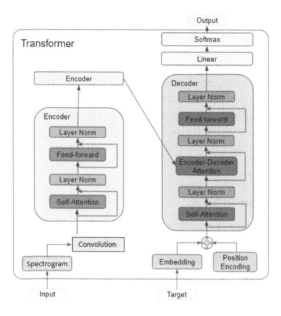

Figure 14.2 Transformer architecture [5].

input audio in the input sentence. At time step t, each hidden state is given a score. Then, each hidden state is multiplied by its score, which is obtained using the softmax function, thus giving less importance to hidden states with low scores, and paying more attention to the hidden states with high scores. This makes it extremely useful to capture the complexities involved in transcribing the complex input speech file. Figure 14.3 represents the encoder and decoder of the attention model.

14.5.3 Elliptic curve cryptography (ECC)

The elliptic curve cryptosystems are a family of encryption systems. The general mathematical equation of the curve used in ECC is of the form

$$y^2 = x^3 + a * x + b \tag{14.1}$$

Figure 14.4 is a mirror image of the x-axis. For example, for a = 1, b = 0, c = 1. The curve will be y = x ^ 3 + 7.

This algorithm uses smaller key lengths of 256-bits size for the same security level. ECC also provides the generation of keys very fast, and key agreement and signatures are also faster than RSA, making it ideal for the encryption of passwords on the backend. Figure 14.5 represents the comparison between the security level of RSA and ECC with an increase in the number of bits.

14.5.4 Keys in ECC

The length of the private key used in ECC is generally 256 bits. Then, the private key is calculated as the summation of ASCII values of the username and password entered by the user.

ECC also has a constant point which is called a generator point and is represented as G [9]. The private key is obtained by the multiplication of the public key and generator point. Here, the multiplication is different from the actual multiplication done in algebra. The public key is visible to all whereas the generator point and the private key are hidden in the code itself.

14.5.5 Addition in ECC

The ECC addition works as shown in Figure 14.6, i.e., C = A + B [10]. The third point cannot be obtained if two points are vertically collinear. C + X = ∞ (infinity). Figure 14.6 represents the addition of points P and Q to get point R.

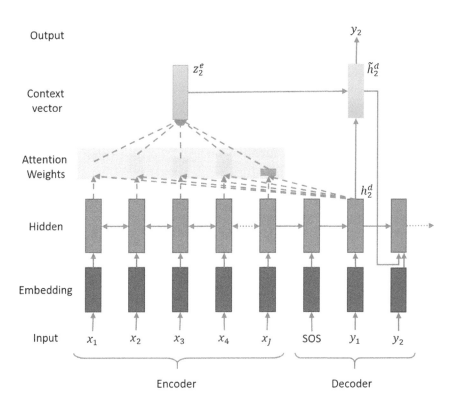

Figure 14.3 Working of attention module [6].

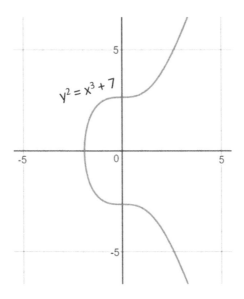

Figure 14.4 Curve y ^ 2 = x^ 3 + a * x + b [7].

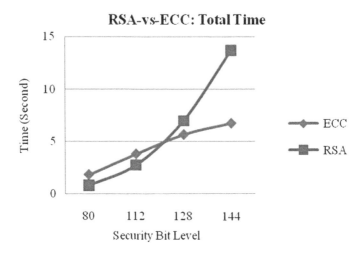

Figure 14.5 Security level of RSA and ECC with varying key length [8].

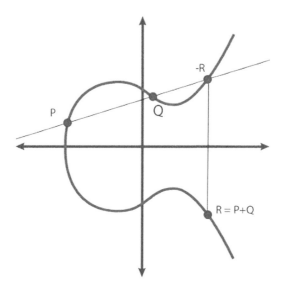

Figure 14.6 Addition in ECC.

14.5.6 Multiplication in ECC

When A and B are equal, C = 2A is obtained. Similarly, 3A is obtained by adding points 2A and A. Thus, nA can be computed.

14.6 LITERATURE SURVEY

In this chapter, the current knowledge of the field is presented and substantial findings are reviewed that help shape, inform, and reform our study.

14.6.1 "SpecAugment: a simple data augmentation method for automatic speech recognition"

This paper was written by Daniel S. Park, William Chan, Yu Zhang, Chung-Cheng Chiu, Barret Zoph, Ekin D. Cubuk, and Quoc V. Le from Google Brain.

14.6.1.1 Augmentation policy

This involves taking input as the log mel spectrogram of the audio directly, which helps the network extract and learn useful features. Figure 14.7 depicts four different spectrograms obtained after doing changes like no augmentation, time warp, frequency masking, and time masking to the input.

These augmentations help the learned features to withstand distortions along the time axis, handle the partial losses along the frequency axis, and

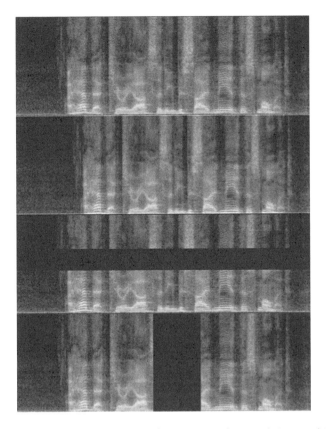

Figure 14.7 No augmentation, time-warp, frequency masking, and time masking applied to base input [11].

also partial loss of small parts of speech. Augmentation is done by techniques of time warping, frequency masking, and time masking.

Time warping is applied on the log mel spectrogram wherein a randomly chosen point along the horizontal axis from time step W to τ – W is to be shifted along that line by a distance w either to the right or left [12].

Frequency masking is done by applying a mask over "f" consecutive mel frequency channels in the range [f0, f0 + f]. f0 is chosen from the range [0, ν – f). ν is the number of mel frequency channels. f is taken from a uniform distribution from 0 to F.

14.6.1.2 Learning rate schedules

A learning rate schedule is used wherein the learning rate is increased, held constant, and then decayed exponentially till it becomes 0.01 fraction of its maximum value. After this, the learning rate is kept constant.

14.6.1.3 Results

Time warping did contribute but does not provide a major improvement in performance. Label smoothing introduced instability to training, which became more conspicuous while the learning rate was being decayed. The use of augmentation converted an overfitting problem into an under-fitting problem.

14.6.2 "Speech recognition using deep neural networks: a systematic review"

14.6.2.1 Machine learning techniques

This paper mainly describes what exactly speech recognition is, what its practical applications are, and how the computations are performed. Speech recognition is an application of artificial intelligence and uses ML and DL techniques to train the model and validate it. Figure 14.8 represents the different stages involved in making a machine learning model.

Machine learning can be categorized as supervised, unsupervised, deep learning, and reinforcement learning, but deep learning is mainly useful for speech recognition tasks. Recurrent neural networks (RNNs) are the ones that are most commonly used for the sequence-to-sequence modeling and speech recognition tasks.

14.6.2.2 Generative models

In the past, researchers mainly used generative models like Gaussian mixture models and hidden Markov models for training, and these were widely used in speech recognition tasks. But these were not able to solve complex problems, necessitating the implementation of deep neural networks; as they were discriminative, they were able to catch the signal easily and were also able to remove noise and disturbance with the help of many hidden layers.

14.6.2.3 Deep neural networks

Introducing hidden layers with a vast number of neurons into a deep neural network has proven to greatly increase its modeling abilities and therefore

Figure 14.8 Different stages of machine learning.

bring about a considerable amount of almost optimal outputs; however, it involves extremely large computation power during the training process.

14.6.2.4 Conclusion

Most of the signal processing techniques were dependent on the traditional models which were ideally suited for basic and constrained problems as their limited capabilities could trigger issues in complex, real-world problems.

14.6.3 "Deep learning: from speech recognition to language and multimodal processing"

This paper was written by Li Deng in 2016 [22].

14.6.3.1 Introduction

The central subject of this study is to show the recent trend of how DL has intensely transfigured the field of ASR and its applications. Text semantic analysis and multimodal processing also have the power to fathom some complex and difficult ASR issues which pose special challenges to DL innovation.

14.6.3.2 From deep generative models to DL models

Analogous to the advancement of these probabilistic models, another form of deep generative models represented image pixels as the observation data called deep belief networks (DBNs). Deep neural networks also showed excellent performance but were very expensive to train as they required fast computing-based GPUs to train and the training time for these neural networks was very high.

14.6.3.3 Advanced architectures

When the output of a CNN is fed into the LSTM model, then fed into a fully connected deep neural network, it is known as the convolutional long short-term deep neural network (CLDNN). It leverages complementary modeling capabilities of three types of neural nets and is demonstrated to be more effective than each of the neural net types.

14.6.3.4 Summary

Large-scale ASR is the first and most compelling successful case of DL in recent times, accepted across the board by both industry and academia. Apart from ASR, deep learning is having a significant effect on image recognition, voice synthesis, and spoken language analysis.

14.6.4 "Speech commands: a dataset for limited vocabulary-speech recognition"

This paper was written by Pete Warden from Google Brain in April 2018.

14.6.4.1 Abstract

This research paper is mainly focused on designing the speech recognition system from a raw audio dataset sample. This dataset has only limited data to train and run the model. At the end of this research paper, there are some results that define the accuracy of the model that has been designed.

14.6.4.2 Introduction

In this paper, they make a prototype for the speech recognition model and the main goal is to recognize a spoken word from only a set of 20 words.

14.6.4.3 Conclusion

The primary objective of this research paper is to demonstrate the form of various models on the same dataset and to determine the model with the highest accuracy. This paper helps us differentiate the types of models available thus helping us to decide which speech recognition model is more suitable for our dataset.

14.6.5 "A neural attention model for speech command recognition"

This paper is by Douglas Coimbra de Andradea, Sabato Leob, Martin Loesener Da Silva Vianac, and Christoph Bernkopfc from the Laboratory of Voice, Speech, and Singing at the Federal University of the State of Rio de Janeiro, Adecco Italia SPA, GSK Vaccines Srl, and CCERN.

14.6.5.1 Abstract

This research paper is about making a speech recognition model using convolutional recurrent neural networks (CRNN) [35]. This model gets almost 94 % accuracy with Google's speech recognition dataset V1 and almost 94.5% accuracy on Google's speech recognition dataset V2 with only a few parameters.

14.6.5.2 Introduction

Many technological giants like Google, Apple, and Microsoft give service to users via speech recognition. To make this possible, they have to build a model in such a way that it can recognize the speech and understand the

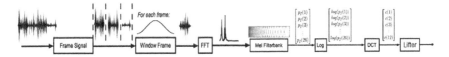

Figure 14.9 Waveform, mel-frequency spectrogram [13].

context of it. Figure 14.9 depicts how raw audio is converted to MFCCs using Fourier transform methods.

14.6.5.3 Neural network implementation

A python module called Keras is used to implement the model along with Kapre, which directly converts the raw audio file to MFCCs directly with an inbuilt function.

14.6.5.4 Conclusion

The following results are obtained:

Google speech dataset V1: 94% average accuracy.
Google speech dataset V2: 94.5% average accuracy.

Figure 14.10 depicts the flow chart of how an input audio file is taken and generated with transcripts with the help of MFCC and the attention layer.

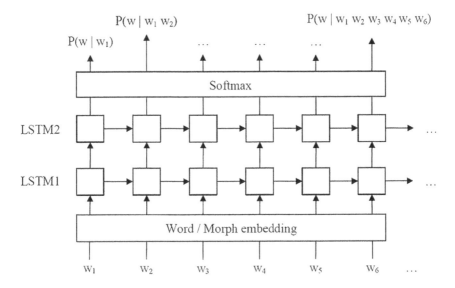

Figure 14.10 Generation of transcripts using LSTM [14].

14.6.6 "Automatic speech recognition using different neural network architectures – a survey"

This is a survey chapter by K.R. Lekshmi and Elizabeth Sherly that explains using different neural network architectures like CNNs, RNNs, and DNNs [15].

14.6.6.1 Convolutional neural network (CNN)

A feed-forward artificial neural network with convolutional and pooling layers is called a convolutional neural network. The following survey takes into account 40MFSC characteristics, first and second derivatives, and a context window of 15 frames for each speech frame. Figure 14.11 represents the architecture of the convolutional neural network.

14.6.6.2 Recurrent neural network (RNN)

RNNs are networks that perform the same task for each element of a sequence, with the result relying on the prior computations. LSTM is a form of RNN that can learn long-term dependencies and also deals with vanishing and exploding gradient problems. Figure 14.12 represents how an RNN is unfolded as time passes.

The lowest error rate can be brought about with the use of a discriminative sequence transcription method with RNN – they are connectionist temporal classification (CTC) and sequence transduction.

14.6.7 Towards end-to-end speech recognition with recurrent neural networks

This chapter has shown that an RNN can do character-level speech transcription with little preprocessing and no explicit phonetic representation. The deep bidirectional LSTM recurrent neural network architecture is used to build this system. Figure 14.13 depicts the frame-level character probabilities with training errors with different phonetic representations.

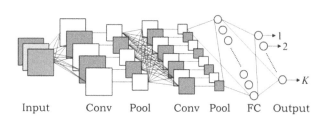

Figure 14.11 Convolutional neural network architecture [16].

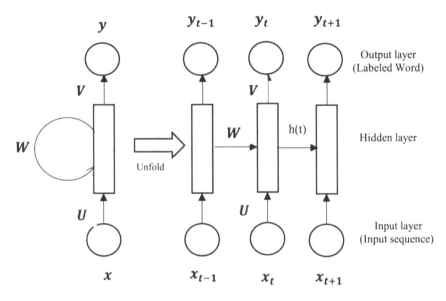

Figure 14.12 A recurrent neural network and the unfolding in time of computation [17].

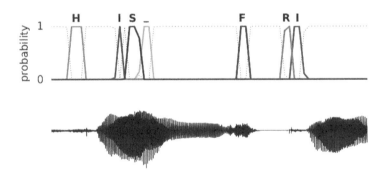

Figure 14.13 Frame-level character probabilities emitted by the CTC layer, along with the corresponding training errors, while processing an utterance [18].

With no prior linguistic information, the system achieves a word error rate of 27.3% on the *Wall Street Journal* corpus, 21.9% with simply a lexicon of authorized terms, and 8.2% with a trigram language model.

14.7 IMPLEMENTATION

The transformer is a deep architecture that makes use of attention. While processing a part of the input, attention allows the model to focus on other parts in the input that are closely linked to that part.

14.7.1 Input audio processing

Spectrograms are extracted from the input audio file. Then, the spectrogram is passed through three convolutional layers that are used to capture the temporal and spatial dependencies. They also help to downsample the input to a smaller size, without losing important features which are essential for getting a good prediction. Figure 14.14 represents the architecture of the transformer model.

14.7.2 Encoder

A self-attention layer incorporated into the encoder helps it look at other parts of the input audio when it encodes a specific input part. Multi-head attention entails doing numerous computations simultaneously, each of which is referred to as an attention head. It aids the transformer in encoding various relationships and nuances for each input component. Figure 14.15 represents the architecture of the encoder in a transformer model.

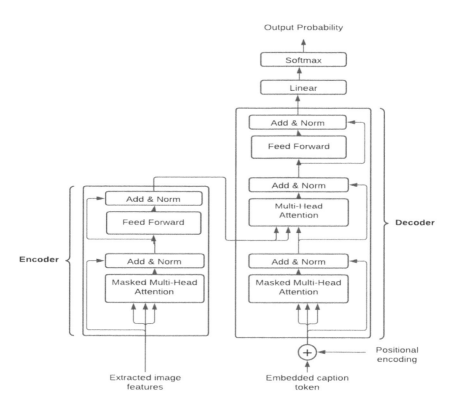

Figure 14.14 Transformer model [19].

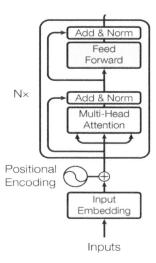

Figure 14.15 Encoder architecture [20].

14.7.3 Target sentence encoding

Token embeddings are used to obtain vector representations of fixed dimensions for each word while position embeddings capture word order; without them, the representation is bag-of-words. These representations are added element by element to produce a single representation for target tokens to be passed to the decoder.

14.7.4 Decoder

In the decoder, self-attention captures the interactions between a target word with the various other target words, while encoder-decoder attention captures the interactions between each target word and the input part as it receives both representations, i.e., the target sequence from the decoder self-attention and the input sequence from the encoder. Figure 14.16 represents the decoder architecture in the transformer model.

14.8 RESULTS AND CONCLUSIONS

For the NPTEL dataset containing audio files and its transcripts, a transformer model consisting of an encoder stack and a decoder stack has been used. This model is significantly more complex and is able to predict sentences more accurately. As shown in Figure 14.17, a front-end user interface has been developed to take the user's input and generate the transcribed output.

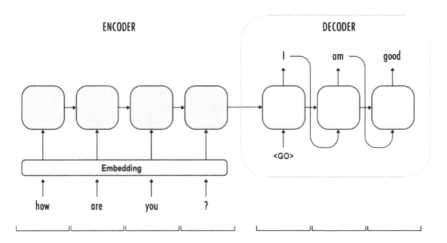

Figure 14.16 Decoder architecture [21].

Here, an audio file can be given as input to the front end, which is then sent to the back end after validation. If the user provides the audio input file in formats other than .wav format, then the front end is easily able to identify incorrect input audio files and hence prompts the user to input these audio files in the specified format. Table 14.1 represents the training loss and validation loss for different numbers of epochs.

The front end has been integrated with the back end and the input data is fed to the pre-trained deep learning model which predicts the desired output and generates the text for that audio file. The model at the backend

Figure 14.17 Transcripted text for the uploaded audio.

Table 14.1 Final model output and loss

Epochs	Training loss	Validation loss
97/100	0.3490	0.4115
98/100	0.3490	0.4104
99/100	0.3491	0.4091
100/100	0.3495	0.4073

predicts using the saved model file (.pth) and the predicted output is displayed on the front end.

As seen in Table 14.1, the model is trained for 100 epochs and by the end of 100 epochs the training loss is reduced to 0.3, and validation loss comes down to 0.4 implying that the target sentence matches closely with the prediction of the model.

From the graph in Figure 14.18, the blue line represents the final training loss which came out to be 0.3495 and the orange line represents the final validation loss which turned out to be 0.4073. The final word error rate came out to be 13.2 which is almost 87% accuracy.

In future endeavors, this model can be extended to transcribe lectures and audio/videos of other complex domains like chemistry, biology, physics, mechanical engineering, and civil engineering.

This model can also be extended to accommodate other different accents of English along with other languages as well. Further features like highlighting text in correspondence with the audio/video and removal of noise can be added.

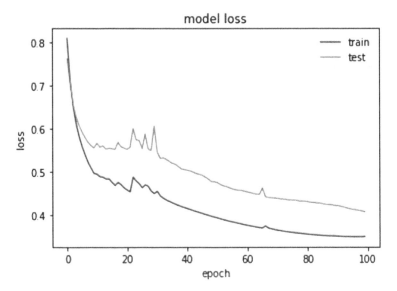

Figure 14.18 Final training loss and validation loss.

REFERENCES

1. Nalavade, Archana, Anita Bai, and Megha Bhushan. "Deep learning techniques and models for improving machine reading comprehension system." *International Journal of Advanced Science and Technology* 29, no. 04 (2020): 9692–9710. http://sersc.org/journals/index.php/IJAST/article/view/32996
2. Saon, George, and Michael Picheny. "Recent advances in conversational speech recognition using convolutional and recurrent neural networks." *IBM Journal of Research and Development* 61, no. 4/5 (2017): 1:1–1:10. doi: 10.1147/JRD.2017.2701178
3. Dong, Mai Trung, and Xianwei Zhou. "Fog computing: Comprehensive approach for security data theft attack using elliptic curve cryptography and decoy technology." *Open Access Library Journal* 3, no. 09 (2016): 1.
4. Povey, Daniel, Arnab Ghoshal, Gilles Boulianne, Lukáš Burget, Ondrej Glembek, Nagendra Goel, Mirko Hannemann, Petr Motlíček, Yanmin Qian, Petr Schwarz, Jan Silovský, Georg Stemmer, and Karel Vesel. "The Kaldi speech recognition toolkit." IEEE 2011 Workshop on Automatic Speech Recognition and Understanding.
5. Wolf, T., L. Debut, V. Sanh, J. Chaumond, C. Delangue, A. Moi, P. Cistac, T. Rault, R. Louf, M. Funtowicz, and J. Davison. "Huggingface's transformers: State-of-the-art natural language processing." *arXiv preprint arXiv:1910.03771.* 2019 Oct 9.
6. Ahmed, M., S. Islam, A.K.M. Islam, and S. Shatabda. "An ensemble 1D-CNN-LSTM-GRU model with data augmentation for speech emotion recognition." *arXiv preprint arXiv:2112.05666* (2021).
7. Blake, Ian, Gerald Seroussi, Gadiel Seroussi, and Nigel Smart. *Elliptic Curves in Cryptography.* Vol. 265. Cambridge University Press, 1999.
8. Avanzi R. "Another look at square roots and traces (and quadratic equations) in fields of even characteristic." *Cryptology ePrint Archive* (2007).
9. Vanstone, S.A.. "Elliptic curve cryptosystem: The answer to strong, fast public-key cryptography for securing constrained environments." *Information Security Technical Report* 2, no. 2 (1997): 78–87.
10. Sinha, Rounak, Hemant Kumar Srivastava, and Sumita Gupta. "Performance based comparison study of RSA and elliptic curve cryptography." *International Journal of Scientific & Engineering Research* 4, no. 5 (2013): 720–725.
11. Vaswani, A., N. Shazeer, N. Parmar, J. Uszkoreit, L. Jones, A.N. Gomez, Ł. Kaiser, and I. Polosukhin "Attention is all you need." *Advances in Neural Information Processing Systems* 30 (2017).
12. Mousavi, S., F. Afghah, and U.R. Acharya. SleepEEGNet: Automated sleep stage scoring with sequence to sequence deep learning approach. *PloS One* 14, no. 5 (2019): e0216456.
13. Deng, Jia, Wei Dong, Richard Socher, Li-Jia Li, Kai Li, and Li Fei-Fei. "Imagenet: A large-scale hierarchical image database." In 2009 IEEE Conference on Computer Vision and Pattern Recognition, pp. 248–255. IEEE, 2009.
14. Park, D.S., W. Chan, Y. Zhang, C.C. Chiu, B. Zoph, E.D. Cubuk, and Q.V. Le "Specaugment: A simple data augmentation method for automatic speech recognition." *arXiv preprint arXiv:1904.08779* (2019 Apr 18).

15. de Andrade, D.C., S. Leo, and M.L. Viana, C. Bernkopf "A neural attention model for speech command recognition. *arXiv preprint arXiv:1808.08929* (2018 Aug 27).

16. Wang, C.Y., H.Y.M. Liao, Y.H. Wu, P.Y. Chen, J.W. Hsieh, and I.H. Yeh. "CSPNet: A new backbone that can enhance learning capability of CNN." In Proceedings of the IEEE/CVF Conference on Computer Vision and Pattern Recognition Workshops, pp. 390–391. 2020.

17. Lekshmi, K.R., and S. Elizabeth. "Automatic speech recognition using different neural network architectures: A survey." *International Journal of Computer Science and Information Technologies* 7, no.6 (2016): 2422–2427.

18. Peng, Y., A. Jiang, and Q. Lu, Automated music making with recurrent neural network. *Computer Science & Information Technology*, 19, no. 13 (2019) 183–188.

19. Vaessen, P.T.M. "Transformer model for high frequencies." *IEEE Transactions on Power Delivery* 3, no. 4 (1988): 1761–1768.

20. Rush, Alexander M., Sumit Chopra, and Jason Weston. "A neural attention model for abstractive sentence summarization." arXiv preprint arXiv:1509.00685 (2015).

21. Ma, Yu-Fei, Lie Lu, Hong-Jiang Zhang, and Mingjing Li. "A user attention model for video summarization." In Proceedings of the tenth ACM international conference on Multimedia, pp. 533–542. 2002.

22. Deng, Li. "Deep learning: from speech recognition to language and multimodal processing." *APSIPA Transactions on Signal and Information Processing* 5 (2016): e1. doi:10.1017/atsip.2015.22

Chapter 15

Stock market prediction using sentiment analysis with **LSTM and RFR**

Monica Madan and Ashima Rani

CONTENTS

15.1 INTRODUCTION

Predicting the stock market accurately is crucial for business decision-makers in the financial domain. Successful prediction of stock prices can result in a good amount of profit for investors. It is particularly difficult because of the uncertainty of its nature, including market fluctuations due to a variety of dependent or indirect variables that influence stock values in the market.

Researchers have been quite motivated to achieve good accuracy for stock market prediction as it has a direct impact on the decision-making of any

DOI: 10.1201/9781003286745-15

organization. They have achieved great results. Stock market prediction has been handled as a time series using the classic time-series approach. Many new approaches in machine learning [1] and deep learning are being used now for the prediction of stock prices [2]. It has been handled in two ways by authors using machine learning. One way is to predict movement, i.e., up or down, and treat it as a classification problem [3]. The other approach is to treat it as a regression problem and to be able to predict the price for the following day.

The stock market is greatly affected by the current political situation and by other factors in the country at various levels. The news headlines and social media reflect such factors impacting the stock market directly or implicitly and can help account for the random factors affecting the financial markets. Thus, they are important contributors to prediction [4].

In this chapter, a comparative study and prediction of stock prices are done. First, classic time series analysis is applied to data using the statistical model, autoregressive integrated moving average (ARIMA), to forecast. Next, the regression approach is applied after including sentiment analysis from news headlines. The BSE closing prices are predicted using the latest deep learning technique, LSTM for sequential data analysis, and finally, the results are compared with the robust, strong approach of ensemble using RFR that utilizes techniques different than deep learning.

15.2 BACKGROUND STUDY

It is very important for any business or financial decision to have a stronghold on the market. It can be clearly seen that extensive work has been done by researchers in this area of predicting stock market prices accurately. This illustrates its importance not only to a financial institution but to all the stakeholders. A variety of approaches taken by researchers is discussed briefly. Moreover, a short overview is provided for the models that are used to work on stock price prediction in this chapter along with some of the previous works done in these areas individually.

15.2.1 Literature review

To begin with, the early statistical approaches for time-series analysis are still quite popular and are used widely for short-term predictions. The models used are moving average, ARIMA, etc. The ARIMA model was used by Adebiyi et al. [5] on the New York Stock Exchange (NYSE) index and Nigeria Stock Exchange (NSE) and the author concluded that ARIMA has enough potential to predict stock prices for the short term. Gooijer et al. [2] have presented an extensive summary of the work done towards forecasting for a time range of 25 years which offers a good starting point to study the prediction techniques in financial markets. Similarly, Shah et al. [6] provided an outline of the machine learning algorithms applied to the stock data for prediction. They suggested a three-tier architecture with one layer using machine learning algorithms and the other two layers constituting the text analysis of news and financial reports. Support vector machine (SVM) [7] appeared to be a popular choice. Das et al. [8] concluded that SVM performed better. Shen et al. [9] further worked for both long-term movement and price prediction using SVM. Ren et al. [10] used sentiment analysis along with SVM. Later, as deep learning techniques evolved, Mehtab et al. [11] applied a convolution neural network (CNN) and compared the results by applying many machine learning algorithms on NIFTY 50 and National Stock Exchange of India data for predicting both the index movement and the price. Selvamuthu et al. [12] worked with an artificial neural network (ANN) on the Indian Stock Market data. Vijh et al. [13] compared ANN with random forest with quiet competitive results; they found ANN outperforming those two. Nikou et al. [14] compared results by applying machine and deep learning models to the data from Morgan Stanley Capital International (MSCI) and concluded that LSTM worked best.

Having stated in brief the background about the work done in this area of the stock market forecast, this chapter expands on the individual areas and provides short descriptions of the algorithms utilized here for the BSE data followed by brief writing about literature studies in these respective directions.

15.2.2 Time series

A time series is where data is recorded as per a time interval. Thus, a time series represents the variation or patterns in data according to a time interval and can be used to represent any data that varies over time hourly, daily, or monthly. In this case, the time series would be the closing stock price for the BSE per day. A common and relevant model for the analysis of time series is the ARIMA model [15, 5]. It was introduced in 1970 by Box and Jenkins and is good for short-term forecasts. It is a statistical model used for both seasonal and non-seasonal time series [16]. ARIMA can be broken up into three main components: AR, I, and MA.

AR: autoregression, I: integrated, and MA: moving average

An autoregressive is a model where values earlier in time are the inputs for further evaluation. Integrated is about the number of times differencing is needed to make the time series stationary. Moving average reflects the lags in forecast error. The three parameters ARIMA (p, d, and q) essentially represent these aforementioned features.

p = number of autoregressive terms, d = number of non-seasonal differences, and q = number of lagged forecast errors.

15.2.3 Deep learning – LSTM

One of the models used in deep learning for analyzing sequential data is LSTM. It was introduced by Hochreiter and Schmidhuber [17]. LSTMs have connections to themselves that provide feedback; that is, information

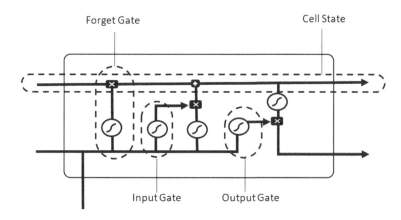

Figure 15.1 LSTM [20].

about its own state is given as input after every time "t." This helps it to consider the long and short patterns or context while processing. LSTM is quite popular and is used extensively in processing sequential data such as time series and text.

Among the deep learning strategies, LSTM not only was found a suitable choice [18], but also presented good accuracy and performed best in handling the predictions in contrast to all other deep learning models that were compared [19]. Figure 15.1 shows a general structure of an LSTM. LSTMs have been found to be useful for time series and are quite a popular choice among researchers.

A few recent papers have been compiled in a tabular form for an easy comparative overview as done in Table 15.1. It displays a list of different variations of LSTM used by the researchers for the stock market problem in chronological order, along with other details. It can be observed that the combination of LSTM with attention mechanism and CNN is a common choice along with others. Table 15.2 depicts the performance achieved by some of these models based on the common metrics for the ones used by the corresponding authors. It can be seen from this table based on R^2 values that the attention mechanism gives better outcomes.

15.2.4 Random forest

An ensemble connects multiple algorithms to achieve better results. The ensemble has its advantages to offer, such as performance and robustness. A random forest, introduced by Leo Breiman [31], is an ensemble model and can be used for both regression and classification. It uses multiple decision trees and uses bootstrap and aggregation, also known as bagging. For classification, majority voting can be taken. Whereas, for regression, the average of the results can be taken for the overall outcome. Ensembles are the

Table 15.1 Comparison of different approaches with LSTM

Authors	Year	LSTM approach	SA	Data source
Althelaya et al. [21]	2018	Bidirectional (BiLSTM)	No	S&P 500
Li et al. [22]	2018	Multi-input (MI-LSTM)	No	China Stock Market
Pawar et al. [23]	2019	Deep (DLSTM), LSTMP, DLSTMP	No	S&P 500
Jin et al. [24]	2020	Empirical mode decomposition (EMD) and attention mechanism (AM), S_EMDAM, S_AM	Yes	NASDAQ: American Association of Professional Landmen (AAPL)
Lu et al. [25]	2020	CNN-BiLSTM-AM	No	Shanghai Composite Index
Lu et al. [26]	2020	CNN LSTM	No	China Stock Market
Ding et al. [27]	2020	Network LSTM predicting multiple prices simultaneously	No	DJIA, London Financial Times Stock Exchange (FTSE), Tokyo (Nikkei), the Taiwan Stock Exchange
Jing et al. [28]	2021	Hybrid CNN-LSTM	Yes	Shanghai Stock Exchange (SSE)
Lin et al. [29]	2021	Complete ensemble empirical mode decomposition with adaptive noise (CEEMDAN)	No	S&P500 and China Securities
Dami et al. [30]	2021	LSTM and feature engineering technique using an autoencoder	No	Tehran Stock Exchange

Table 15.2 Comparing results by authors on various versions of LSTM

Model	R2	MAE	RMSE	MSE	MAPE
DLSTM	NA	NA	NA	3.1464e−04	NA
CNN LSTM	0.9646	27.564	39.688	NA	NA
CNN-BiLSTM-AM	0.9804	21.952	31.694	NA	NA
LST autoencoder	NA	0.034	NA	NA	NA
S_EMDAM_LSTM, S_AM_LSTM	0.973262 0.977388	2.64963 2.396121	3.475939 3.196534	1.82 1.65	NA
Hybrid CNN-LSTM	NA	NA	NA	NA	0.0449
CEEMDAN-LSTM	NA	16.3634	20.8811	436.0208	0.0060
Bi LSTM	0.96	0.05242	0.060	NA	NA

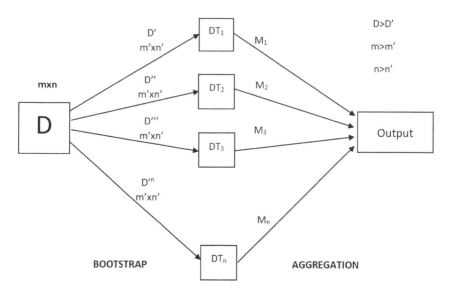

Figure 15.2 Ensemble technique [32].

best-performing predicting models. Figure 15.2 represents a general ensemble concept. Figure 15.3 depicts the general structure of a decision tree.

Random forest has been used to forecast the movement of the stock market, such as upwards or downwards. It has also been used for regression to predict stock market prices. In literature, more of its usage in movement prediction can be seen [33], mostly in comparative studies contrasting it with multiple

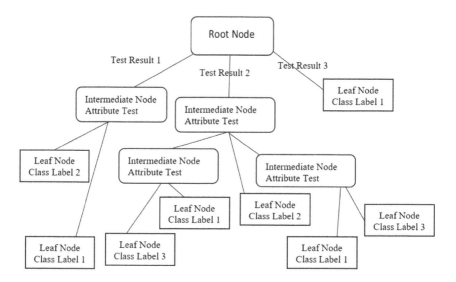

Figure 15.3 A sample decision tree for multiclass classification.

machine learning algorithms. It was discovered that not many authors have written about random forest as the strongest model available for stock market prediction. Nti et al. [34] presented an all-inclusive evaluation of ensembles for the prediction of the stock market, along with random forest, and they worked with multiple indicators, homogeneous and heterogeneous ensembles, and presented extensive comparisons using several techniques. In this chapter, random forest is applied to the data, and as per current understanding, very few authors would have mentioned work done explicitly with sentiment analysis and RFR.

15.2.5 Sentiment analysis

Sentiment analysis in natural language processing (NLP) aims at finding emotion reflected in certain textual data. The result thus obtained representing the emotion can be categorical such as positive, negative, or neutral, or can be numeric depicting intensity or polarity. It can be used for text classification, representing opinions, and filtering. There are many ways to approach this problem. A rule-based approach using lexicons can be used, machine learning algorithms treating it as a classification problem can be applied, or a hybrid approach can be taken for the same.

When it comes to the lexicon-based approach, Valence Aware Dictionary for Sentiment Reasoning (VADER) is one of the models for the analysis of the sentiment of a given text. It talks about the intensity of the sentiment along with the polarity of the feelings. VADER is a pre-trained dictionary of words used for sentiment analysis and especially suits well for social media and news slang.

Sentiment analysis and its usage for the stock market have been proven by researchers. The sentiment analysis from the social media or newspaper headlines helps understand the investor's sentiment and thus can support predicting the stock market more accurately. Sentiment analysis itself is a broad area of research. Mao et al. [35] worked on the S&P500 data to correlate it with Twitter data and concluded a strong correlation with many stock indicators. Mohan et al. [36] predicted stock prices using deep learning models and sentiment analysis of news articles and mentioned that the results suggest a good relationship. Souma et al. [37] applied enhanced deep learning methods for sentiment analysis on newspaper articles and confirmed their usability for the stock market. Atzeni et al. [38] worked on fine-grained sentiment analysis on news headlines and financial blogs from multiple sources comparing different algorithms.

15.3 METHODOLOGY

Two very strong approaches are chosen here, deep learning LSTM and ensemble RFR, to work on this prediction problem. Input from sentiment analysis from the newspaper headlines using VADER is added to handle the uncertainties due to the random factors. The classic approach of univariate time-series processing using the traditional ARIMA model is worked upon as well.

15.3.1 Data source

Data is taken from the Yahoo Finance website for the BSE. The data is current-date data from 1997, for approximately 20 years, with around 6,000 rows of daily opening, high, low, and closing prices along with volume. Approximately 20 features were taken including the moving averages for weekly, biweekly, monthly, quarterly basis, etc. to read the periodic sequences and patterns. Along with this were the closing stock prices for the previous day and sentiment scores based on news headlines. The news headlines data source was the *Times of India* News Headlines dataset from https://datverse.harvard.edu.

15.3.2 Evaluation criteria

The evaluation parameters used here are the same as popularly used by authors and are listed below in equations 15.1–15.4.

MSE is quite commonly used to evaluate regression models.

$$\text{MSE} = \frac{1}{n} \sum_{i=1}^{n} \left(\widehat{y_1} - y_i \right)^2 \tag{15.1}$$

MAE is the average of the absolute difference between the predicted and actual values.

$$\text{MAE} = \frac{1}{n} \sum_{i=1}^{n} \left| \widehat{y_1} - y_i \right| \tag{15.2}$$

The value R^2, the coefficient of determination, reflects the scattering of the points around the regression line.

$$R^2 = 1 - \frac{SS_{RES}}{SS_{TOT}} = 1 - \frac{\sum_{i=0}^{n} \left(y_i - \hat{y}_i \right)^2}{\sum_{i=0}^{n} \left(y_i - \bar{y} \right)^2} \tag{15.3}$$

RMSE is the square root of MSE.

$$RMSE = \sqrt{\sum_{i=0}^{n} \frac{\left(\hat{y}_i - y_i \right)^2}{n}} \tag{15.4}$$

n is the number of observations.
$y^1, y^2, \ldots y_n$ are observed or actual values.
$\hat{y}_1, \hat{y}_2, \ldots \hat{y}_n$ are the predicted values.
$\bar{y}$ is the mean value.

15.4 APPROACH AND IMPLEMENTATION

This prediction problem is treated here as regression and moving forward with the implementation details.

15.4.1 Data preprocessing

The data is imported using the "yfinance" package using the ticker object. The ticker is used as the name of the object that has the daily information, in this case for BSE. The closing price is considered the best indicator for understanding stocks.

ARIMA is a univariate processing of data. The deep learning and ensemble methods being multivariate, the following preprocessing of the data was done for them. The moving average for various periods was added, such as monthly, quarterly, etc., to capture the sequences and patterns over this period (moving averages for four, 16, 28, 40, and 52 weeks along with ten-day and 50-day average windows). Moving averages help to smoothen out the noise and prevent overfitting. The close price was shifted to one day back. The data as such did not show nulls or other inconsistencies. The rows where nulls were introduced due to moving averages were removed. The data was then divided into train, test, and unseen data sets (15% unseen, 20% test data). The shuffled data was used. The data was scaled using a "Min–Max" scaler.

15.4.2 Visualization

The visualization of data is one of the very important aspects of analysis, especially time series data. Figure 15.4 shows the time series. It helps in understanding the trends and features of the series. Similarly, the results were also visualized and displayed in the coming sections.

15.4.3 Time series analysis

Analysis based on the time series is a univariate analysis based on the closing price only. For the BSE data, based on the visualization, any cycles or seasonality were not seen in this data. Irregularity could be noticed. The moving average or the average using a window of a particular period is quite often used to filter out the random fluctuations or noise from a time series to be able to view a smoother trend. Visualization of the 90-day window moving average and standard deviation revealed the trend of the stock market time series as upward for the past few years. The standard deviation over the same window showed an almost flat trend with a few fluctuations. The same can be visualized in Figure 15.5.

This (upward trend) reveals that the time series has an increasing moving average and is not stationary. The Dickey-Fuller test also confirmed nonstationary time series with a p-value of 0.996. The Dickey-Fuller test checks a time series for the null hypothesis that a unit root is present in a non-stationary

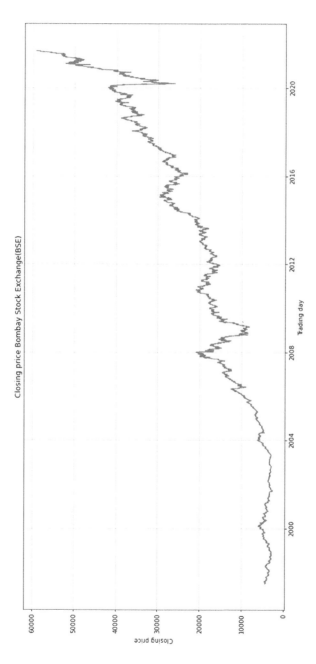

Figure 15.4 BSE data time series visualization.

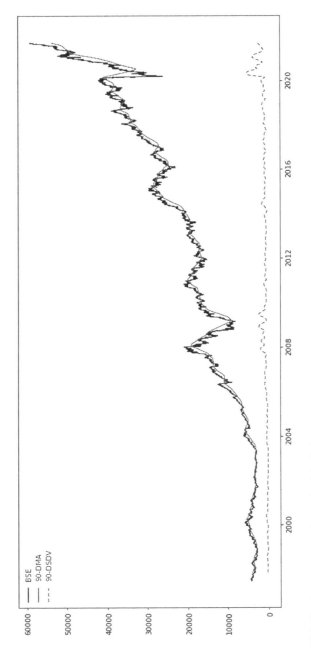

Figure 15.5 Moving average and standard deviation.

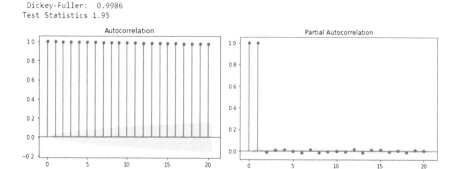

Time Series Analysis Plots
Dickey-Fuller: 0.9986
Test Statistics 1.95

Figure 15.6 Dickey-Fuller test, ACF, and PACF.

autoregressive model. It is a statistical test that verifies if a time series is stationary. The trend observed and a stationary standard deviation make it suitable for applying a non-seasonal ARIMA model in the absence of seasonality [39]. This involves the plotting of the ACF and PACF as shown in Figure 15.6. The autocorrelation graph or ACF represents the relation of the series with itself "t" time period back (lag) and similarly, the PACF is a measure of the correlation directly without considering the other terms in between.

For further analysis, the time series was converted to stationary by taking the difference of its previous day value, thus making it a stationary series. The Dickey-Fuller p-value of 0 reinstated that the time series is stationary. Figure 15.7 shows the stationary time series. Figure 15.8 shows the new ACF and PACF of the stationary series.

To be able to use ARIMA, the values for p, d, and q parameters had to be identified. These values for p, d, and q were derived as 2, 1, and 0. They can be derived by plotting the ACF and PACF as shown in Figure 15.6: the gradual downward slope in ACF with the sharp dip in PACF, where the intercept in the PACF is at 2, and the fact that one differentiation was enough to achieve a stationary time series. The same parameters were arrived at and confirmed by using auto ARIMA. The auto ARIMA trying to find the best fit of the three parameters can be seen in Figure 15.9.

Figure 15.10 depicts residuals for the regression in detail after fitting the auto ARIMA model. The residuals are the difference between predicted and observed values. The normal Q–Q plot (quantile vs quantile plot) here shows normal distributions of residuals as the line is mostly flat diagonal. The correlogram shows no autocorrelation pattern. The standardized residual graph shows constant variance and no pattern. The histogram again shows a normal distribution among the residuals. Table 15.3 shows the results obtained by the ARIMA model. The details of the results and predictions of stock prices are shown. The forecast thus obtained is visualized in Figure 15.11. ARIMA outputs can be seen in detail in Figure 15.12.

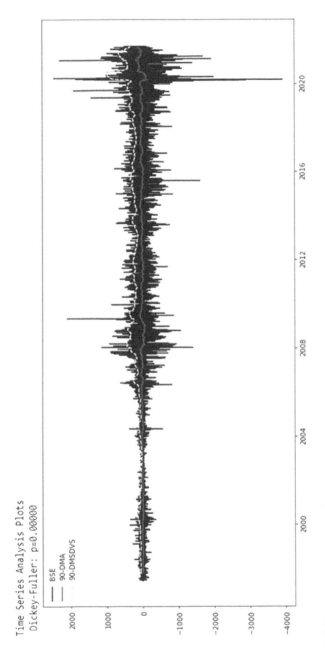

Figure 15.7 The stationary time series.

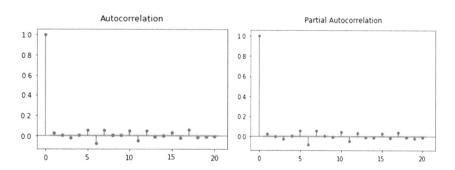

Figure 15.8 ACF and PACF for stationary time series.

```
Performing stepwise search to minimize aic
 ARIMA(0,1,0)(0,0,0)[0] intercept   : AIC=-29795.763, Time=2.60 sec
 ARIMA(1,1,0)(0,0,0)[0] intercept   : AIC=-29823.600, Time=2.41 sec
 ARIMA(0,1,1)(0,0,0)[0] intercept   : AIC=-29826.137, Time=3.60 sec
 ARIMA(0,1,0)(0,0,0)[0]             : AIC=-29793.774, Time=0.74 sec
 ARIMA(1,1,1)(0,0,0)[0] intercept   : AIC=-29829.017, Time=3.32 sec
 ARIMA(2,1,1)(0,0,0)[0] intercept   : AIC=-29829.705, Time=9.11 sec
 ARIMA(2,1,0)(0,0,0)[0] intercept   : AIC=-29831.677, Time=2.08 sec
 ARIMA(3,1,0)(0,0,0)[0] intercept   : AIC=-29829.710, Time=1.54 sec
 ARIMA(3,1,1)(0,0,0)[0] intercept   : AIC=-29827.713, Time=6.01 sec
 ARIMA(2,1,0)(0,0,0)[0]             : AIC=-29829.935, Time=0.66 sec

Best model:  ARIMA(2,1,0)(0,0,0)[0] intercept
Total fit time: 32.153 seconds
```

Figure 15.9 Auto ARIMA finding the values of p, d, and q.

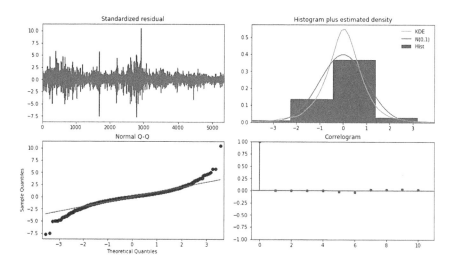

Figure 15.10 Detailed visualization of the residuals.

Table 15.3 The results obtained by ARIMA

Metrics	Result
MAPE	0.00909421045502504
MAE	0.09595934351344888
MSE	0.01802650204684007
RMSE	0.1342628096191945

Figure 15.11 Time series prediction results.

```
ARIMA Model Results
===================================================================
Dep. Variable:            D.Close   No. Observations:          5342
Model:             ARIMA(2, 1, 0)   Log Likelihood        14878.603
Method:                   css-mle   S.D. of innovations       0.015
Date:           Sun, 29 Aug 2021    AIC                  -29749.207
Time:                    23:51:44   BIC                  -29722.873
Sample:                         1   HQIC                 -29740.008

=====================================================================
                 coef    std err          z      P>|z|      [0.025      0.975]
---------------------------------------------------------------------
const          0.0004      0.000      1.926      0.054    -7.2e-06       0.001
ar.L1.D.Close  0.0779      0.014      5.700      0.000       0.051       0.105
ar.L2.D.Close -0.0435      0.014     -3.181      0.001      -0.070      -0.017
                                   Roots
=====================================================================
                 Real        Imaginary         Modulus        Frequency
---------------------------------------------------------------------
AR.1           0.8960         -4.7113j          4.7958          -0.2201
AR.2           0.8960         +4.7113j          4.7958           0.2201
---------------------------------------------------------------------
```

Figure 15.12 Result details from ARIMA.

15.4.4 Sentiment analysis

VADER was used for sentiment analysis of news headlines. First, all the news headlines for the day were combined into one paragraph as shown in Figure 15.13 along with fixing the publish date format. Then, the scores were calculated. While negative, neutral, and positive scores are not assigned values less than zero, the compound score (normalized sum) lies between −1 and 1 and a score toward 1 represents positivity. The results are depicted in Figure 15.14. The results were then added to the finance dataset for further analysis.

15.4.5 LSTM

Adding outcomes of the sentiment analysis to the normalized data from Yahoo Finance, further processing was done using LSTM. The structure of LSTM is mentioned in the following with dropout layers to avoid overfitting as depicted in Figure 15.15. Table 15.4 shows the results obtained by the LSTM. Parameters included activation function "tanh," loss function "mse," optimizer "Adam," and batch size as eight and with ten epochs.

	publish_date	headline_category	headline_text
0	2001-01-02	unknown	Status quo will not be disturbed at Ayodhya; s...
1	2001-01-02	unknown	Fissures in Hurriyat over Pak visit
2	2001-01-02	unknown	America's unwanted heading for India?
3	2001-01-02	unknown	For bigwigs; it is destination Goa
4	2001-01-02	unknown	Extra buses to clear tourist traffic

Figure 15.13 News headline data.

Date	Close	Compound	Negative	Neutral	Positive
2001-01-02	4018.879883	-0.9621	0.119	0.817	0.064
2001-01-03	4060.020020	0.6322	0.084	0.817	0.098
2001-01-04	4115.370117	0.6648	0.077	0.843	0.080
2001-01-05	4183.729980	0.9253	0.104	0.744	0.152
2001-01-08	4120.430176	-0.9638	0.119	0.855	0.026

Figure 15.14 Results from sentiment analysis.

```
Shape of Training set X: (2676, 20, 1)
Shape of Test set X: (669, 20, 1)
Model: "sequential"
```

Layer (type)	Output Shape	Param #
lstm (LSTM)	(None, 20, 100)	40800
dropout (Dropout)	(None, 20, 100)	0
lstm_1 (LSTM)	(None, 20, 100)	80400
dropout_1 (Dropout)	(None, 20, 100)	0
lstm_2 (LSTM)	(None, 100)	80400
dropout_2 (Dropout)	(None, 100)	0
dense (Dense)	(None, 1)	101

```
Total params: 201,701
```

Figure 15.15 The LSTM.

Table 15.4 Results obtained for LSTM

Metrics	Test data	Unseen data
R2	0.9740718779522495	0.9610500617009163
MAE	0.0691608136085114	0.0752821526804841
MSE	0.00767708240581539I	0.00731I762524243813
RMSE	0.08761896145136275	0.08550884471353716

The details of the ten epochs along with the loss and the overall loss are presented in Figure 15.16 and Figure 15.17.

15.4.6 RFR

The following results were obtained with RFR while using the following parameters.

Random number seed (random_state) = 42; number of trees in the forest (n_estimators) = 500; in case of regression here the splitting criteria (criterion) = "mse"; maximum height for a tree (max_depth) = 30; min_samples_leaf = 2; min_samples_split = 5; parallel runs (n_jobs) = 1.

```
Epoch 1/10
268/268 [==============================] - 12s 27ms/step - loss: 0.0206 - val_loss: 0.0050 ETA:
0s - loss: 0.02
Epoch 2/10
268/268 [==============================] - 6s 23ms/step - loss: 0.0061 - val_loss: 0.0050
Epoch 3/10
268/268 [==============================] - 11s 43ms/step - loss: 0.0058 - val_loss: 0.0046
Epoch 4/10
268/268 [==============================] - 6s 23ms/step - loss: 0.0051 - val_loss: 0.0054
Epoch 5/10
268/268 [==============================] - 8s 29ms/step - loss: 0.0055 - val_loss: 0.0080
Epoch 6/10
268/268 [==============================] - 6s 23ms/step - loss: 0.0044 - val_loss: 0.0078
Epoch 7/10
268/268 [==============================] - 6s 24ms/step - loss: 0.0047 - val_loss: 0.0028
Epoch 8/10
268/268 [==============================] - 10s 37ms/step - loss: 0.0039 - val_loss: 0.0054
Epoch 9/10
268/268 [==============================] - 8s 31ms/step - loss: 0.0039 - val_loss: 0.0025
Epoch 10/10
268/268 [==============================] - 13s 50ms/step - loss: 0.0033 - val_loss: 0.0026
```

Figure 15.16 Details of the epochs.

```
2676/2676 [==============================] - 30s 11ms/step - loss: 0.0028
669/669 [==============================] - 12s 18ms/step - loss: 0.0077
Train Loss = 0.0028
Test Loss = 0.0077
```

Figure 15.17 The overall loss.

Table 15.5 Results obtained for RFR

Metrics	Test data	Unseen data
R2	0.9987590685622808	0.9851712107139378
MAE	0.012807010958478622	0.03369416760954001
MSE	0.00036742857387791057	0.002783690822542039
RMSE	0.01916842648414080	0.05276069391641887

Table 15.5 shows the results obtained by the RFR. Visualization of the results obtained by RFR is displayed in Figure 15.18.

15.5 RESULTS

In this section, a comparison is done for the results obtained and since LSTM and RFR use the same dataset, therefore, they are focused upon here. Figure 15.19 shows a comparative visualization of the results using the predicted values from random forest [40, 41] and LSTM and the outcome is that the RFR outperformed LSTM in every aspect. They both performed

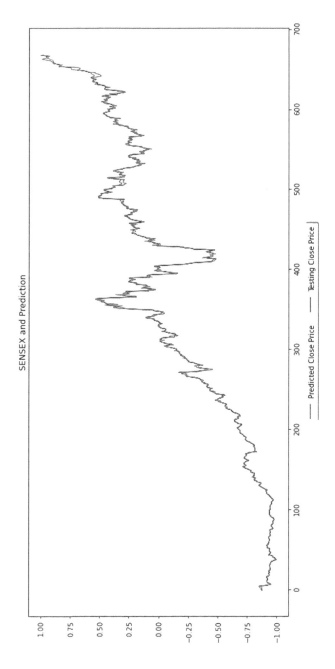

Figure 15.18 Visualizing the results obtained from RFR.

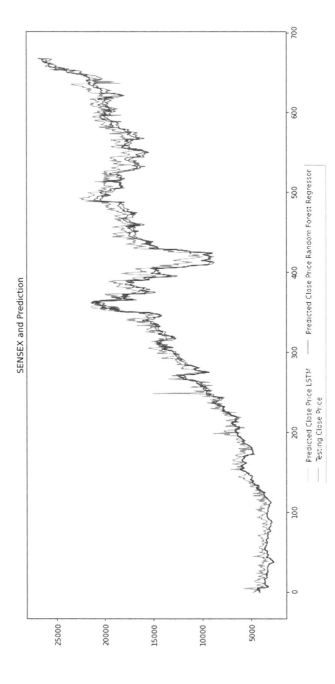

Figure 15.19 Visualizing the prediction of prices by LSTM, RFR with the actual prices.

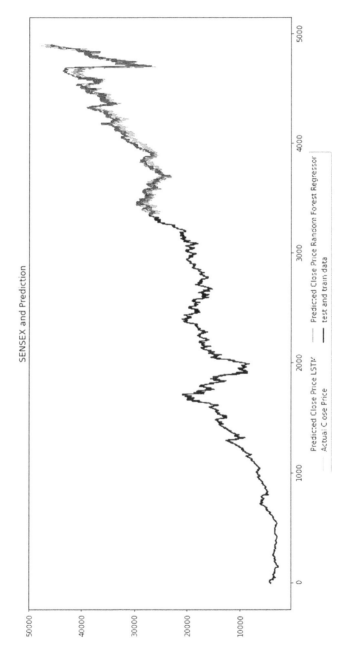

Figure 15.20 Unseen data prediction and visualization of the results.

Table 15.6 Comparing the results for unseen data

Metrics	LSTM	RFR
R2	0.9610500617009163	0.9851712107139378
MAE	0.0752821526804841	0.03369416760954001
MSE	0.007311762524243813	0.002783690822542039
RMSE	0.08550884471353716	0.05276069391641887

better than ARIMA as can be seen from MAE, MSE, and RMSE scores in Table 15.3. Predictions were made on unseen data as well and Figure 15.20 displays the forecasted results in it. The result is mostly similar in terms of performance with a slight change in the values where metrics for the unseen are only a little toward the lower side. Table 15.6 shows the comparison of unseen data results. The RFR and sentiment analysis, so far, has been a lesser-used combination and with fewer mentions explicitly in the text, while LSTM is a widely used model with a lot of variations.

15.6 CONCLUSION

Both the deep learning (LSTM) and ensemble (RFR) are quite capable of giving good prediction results with sentiment analysis as shown, also when compared to the traditional ARIMA model. The ensemble technique shows slightly better results in terms of R^2 values and also with much reduced MSE and MAE values, making it a preferable choice along with being a robust model. There are many upcoming models with attention mechanisms that can be employed for stock market prediction as far as regression is concerned. While VADER has worked well, various other techniques can be explored for sentiment analysis in detail and such combinations can be studied for their results in future works.

REFERENCES

1. K. Verma, S. Bhardwaj, R. Arya, M. S. U. Islam, M. Bhushan, A. Kumar, and P. Samant, "Latest tools for data mining and machine learning," *International Journal of Innovative Technology and Exploring Engineering*, vol. 8, no. 9S, pp. 18–23, 2019. doi: 10.35940/ijitee.I1003.0789S19
2. J. G. de Gooijer and R. J. Hyndman, "25 years of time series forecasting," *International Journal of Forecasting*, vol. 22, no. 3, pp. 443–473, 2006. doi: 10.1016/j.ijforecast.2006.01.001.
3. O. Bustos and A. Pomares-Quimbaya, "Stock market movement forecast: A systematic review," *Expert Systems with Applications*, vol. 156. Elsevier Ltd, Oct. 15, 2020, p. 113464. doi: 10.1016/j.eswa.2020.

4. D. Shah, H. Isah, and F. Zulkernine, "Predicting the effects of news sentiments on the stock market," in Proceedings - 2018 IEEE International Conference on Big Data, Big Data 2018, Jan. 2019, pp. 4705–4708. doi: 10.1109/BigData.2018.8621884.

5. A. A. Adebiyi, A. O. Adewumi, and C. K. Ayo, "Stock price prediction using the ARIMA model," in Proceedings - UKSim-AMSS 16th International Conference on Computer Modelling and Simulation, UKSim 2014, 2014, pp. 106–112. doi: 10.1109/UKSim.2014.67.

6. V. H. Shah, "Machine Learning Techniques for Stock Prediction," *Foundations of Machine Learning*, vol. 1, no. 1, pp. 6–12.

7. A. J. Smola, B. Sch¨olkopf, and S. Sch¨olkopf, *A Tutorial on Support Vector Regression* *, Kluwer Academic Publishers, 2004.

8. S. P. Das and S. Padhy, "Support vector machines for prediction of futures prices in Indian stock market," *International Journal of Computer Applications*, vol. 41, no. 3, 2012.

9. S. Shen, H. Jiang, and T. Zhang, "Stock market forecasting using machine learning algorithms," Accessed: Mar. 10, 2022. [Online]. Available: https://citeseerx.ist.psu.edu/viewdoc/download?doi=10.1.1.278.6139&rep=rep1&type=pdf

10. R. Ren, D. D. Wu, and D. D. Wu, "Forecasting stock market movement direction using sentiment analysis and support vector machine," *IEEE Systems Journal*, vol. 13, no. 1, pp. 760–770, Mar. 2019. doi: 10.1109/JSYST.2018.2794462.

11. S. Mehtab and J. Sen, "Stock price prediction using convolutional neural networks on a multivariate timeseries." 2020. arXiv preprint arXiv:2001.09769

12. D. Selvamuthu, V. Kumar, and A. Mishra, "Indian stock market prediction using artificial neural networks on tick data," *Financial Innovation*, vol. 5, no. 1, pp. 1–12, Dec. 2019. doi: 10.1186/s40854-019-0131-7.

13. M. Vijh, D. Chandola, V. A. Tikkiwal, and A. Kumar, "Stock closing price prediction using machine learning techniques," in *Procedia Computer Science*, vol. 167, pp. 599–606, 2020. doi: 10.1016/j.procs.2020.03.326.

14. M. Nikou, G. Mansourfar, and J. Bagherzadeh, "Stock price prediction using DEEP learning algorithm and its comparison with machine learning algorithms," *Intelligent Systems in Accounting, Finance and Management*, vol. 26, no. 4, pp. 164–174, Oct. 2019. doi: 10.1002/isaf.1459.

15. D. A. Dickey and W. A. Fuller, "Distribution of the estimators for autoregressive time series with a unit root," *Journal of the American Statistical Association*, vol. 74, no. 366a, pp. 427–431, Jun. 1979. doi: 10.1080/01621459.1979.10482531.

16. G. E. P. Box, G. M. Jenkins, G. C. Reinsel, and G. M. Ljung, "Time series analysis." Accessed: Jan. 29, 2022. [Online]. Available: http://www.ru.ac.bd/stat/wp-content/uploads/sites/25/2019/03/504_05_Box_Time-Series-Analysis-Forecasting-and-Control-2015.pdf

17. S. Hochreiter and J. Urgen Schmidhuber, "Long short-term memory." *Neural Computation*, vol. 9, no. 8, pp. 1735–1780, Nov 1997.

18. D. Shah, W. Campbell, and F. H. Zulkernine, "A Comparative Study of LSTM and DNN for Stock Market Forecasting," in Proceedings - 2018 IEEE International Conference on Big Data, Big Data 2018, Jan. 2019, pp. 4148–4155. doi: 10.1109/BigData.2018.8622462.

19. M. Nabipour, P. Nayyeri, H. Jabani, A. Mosavi, E. Salwana, and S. Shahab, "Deep learning for stock market prediction," *Entropy*, vol. 22, no. 8, Aug. 2020. doi: 10.3390/E22080840.

20. M. Phi, "Illustrated guide to LSTM's and GRU's: A step by step explanation," https://towardsdatascience.com/, Sep. 24, 2018. https://towardsdatascience.com/illustrated-guide-to-lstms-and-gru-s-a-step-by-step-explanation-44e9eb85bf21 (accessed Feb. 08, 2022).

21. K. A. Althelaya, E. S. M. El-Alfy, and S. Mohammed, "Evaluation of bidirectional LSTM for short and long-term stock market prediction," in 2018 9th International Conference on Information and Communication Systems, ICICS 2018, May 2018, vol. 2018-January, pp. 151–156. doi: 10.1109/IACS.2018.8355458.

22. H. Li, Y. Shen, and Y. Zhu, "Stock price prediction using attention-based multi-input LSTM," 2018.

23. K. Pawar, R. S. Jalem, and V. Tiwari, "Stock market price prediction using LSTM RNN," in *Advances in Intelligent Systems and Computing*, vol. 841, pp. 493–503, 2019. doi: 10.1007/978-981-13-2285-3_58.

24. Z. Jin, Y. Yang, and Y. Liu, "Stock closing price prediction based on sentiment analysis and LSTM," *Neural Computing and Applications*, vol. 32, no. 13, pp. 9713–9729, Jul. 2020. doi: 10.1007/s00521-019-04504-2.

25. W. Lu, J. Li, J. Wang, and L. Qin, "A CNN-BiLSTM-AM method for stock price prediction," in *Neural Computing and Applications*. Springer Science and Business Media Deutschland GmbH, 2020. doi: 10.1007/s00521-020-05532-z.

26. W. Lu, J. Li, Y. Li, A. Sun, and J. Wang, "A CNN-LSTM-based model to forecast stock prices," *Complexity*, vol. 2020, Article ID 6622927, 10 pages, 2020. doi: 10.1155/2020/6622927.

27. G. Ding and L. Qin, "Study on the prediction of stock price based on the associated network model of LSTM," *International Journal of Machine Learning and Cybernetics*, vol. 11, no. 6, pp. 1307–1317, Jun. 2020. doi: 10.1007/s13042-019-01041-1.

28. N. Jing, Z. Wu, and H. Wang, "A hybrid model integrating deep learning with investor sentiment analysis for stock price prediction," *Expert Systems with Applications*, vol. 178, Sep. 2021. doi: 10.1016/j.eswa.2021.115019.

29. Y. Lin, Y. Yan, J. Xu, Y. Liao, and F. Ma, "Forecasting stock index price using the CEEMDAN-LSTM model," *North American Journal of Economics and Finance*, vol. 57, Jul. 2021. doi: 10.1016/j.najef.2021.101421.

30. S. Dami and M. Esterabi, "Predicting stock returns of Tehran exchange using LSTM neural network and feature engineering technique," *Multimedia Tools and Applications*, vol. 80, no. 13, pp. 19947–19970, May 2021. doi: 10.1007/s11042-021-10778-3.

31. L. Breiman, "Random forests," *Machine learning*, vol. 45, no. 1, pp. 5–32. Oct 2001. https://link.springer.com/content/pdf/10.1023/A:1010933404324.pdf.

32. A. Dutta, "Random forest regression in python," https://www.geeksforgeeks.org/, Jan. 18, 2022. https://www.geeksforgeeks.org/random-forest-regression-in-python/ (accessed Feb. 08, 2022).

33. L. Khaidem, S. Saha, and S. R. Dey, "Predicting the direction of stock market prices using random forest," 2016. arXiv preprint arXiv:1605.00003

34. I. K. Nti, A. F. Adekoya, and B. A. Weyori, "A comprehensive evaluation of ensemble learning for stock-market prediction," *Journal of Big Data*, vol. 7, no. 1, Dec. 2020. doi: 10.1186/s40537-020-00299-5.

35. Y. Mao, W. Wei, B. Wang, and B. Liu, "Correlating S&P 500 stocks with Twitter data," in Proceedings of the 1st ACM International Workshop on Hot Topics on Interdisciplinary Social Networks Research, HotSocial 2012, 2012, pp. 69–72. doi: 10.1145/2392622.2392634.

36. S. Mohan, S. Mullapudi, S. Sammeta, P. Vijayvergia, and D. C. Anastasiu, "Stock price prediction using news sentiment analysis," in Proceedings - 5th IEEE International Conference on Big Data Service and Applications, Big Data Service 2019, Workshop on Big Data in Water Resources, Environment, and Hydraulic Engineering and Workshop on Medical, Healthcare, Using Big Data Technologies, Apr. 2019, pp. 205–208. doi: 10.1109/BigDataService.2019.00035.

37. W. Souma, I. Vodenska, and H. Aoyama, "Enhanced news sentiment analysis using deep learning methods," *Journal of Computational Social Science*, vol. 2, no. 1, pp. 33–46, Jan. 2019. doi: 10.1007/s42001-019-00035-x.

38. M. Atzeni, A. Dridi, and D. Reforgiato Recupero, "Fine-grained sentiment analysis on financial microblogs and news headlines," *Communications in Computer and Information Science*, vol. 769, pp. 124–128, 2017. doi: 10.1007/978-3-319-69146-6_11.

39. R. Nau, "Notes on nonseasonal ARIMA models," Fuqua School of Business, Duke University, 2014.

40. U. Verma, C. Garg, M. Bhushan, P. Samant, A. Kumar, and A. Negi, "Prediction of students' academic performance using Machine Learning Techniques," in Proceedings of the 2022 International Mobile and Embedded Technology Conference (MECON), IEEE, 10–11 March, 2022, pp. 151–156. doi: 10.1109/MECON53876.2022.9751956.

41. S. Kedia and M. Bhushan, "Prediction of mortality from heart failure using machine learning," in Proceedings of the 2nd International Conference on Emerging Frontiers in Electrical and Electronic Technologies (ICEFEET), 2022, pp. 1–6, doi: 10.1109/ICEFEET51821.2022.9848348.

Chapter 16

A systematic and exhaustive analysis of intelligent software effort estimation models

S. Rama Sree, S. N. S. V. S. C. Ramesh, A. Vanathi, and V. Ravi Kishore

CONTENTS

DOI: 10.1201/9781003286745-16

16.1 INTRODUCTION

Nowadays, software has become a vital part of human life. Any activity carried out in a person's life directly or indirectly includes some kind of software or another. Hence software development has become a very crucial task for software companies. In software development, the most challenging component is determining the amount of time and effort that is necessary early in the software development life cycle (SDLC). For any software to be successful, the initial estimates must be more accurate [1]. Over-estimates or under-estimates both lead to unsuccessful software projects. Estimations can be for size or time or cost or effort. The main concentration in this chapter is on effort estimation. The activity of predicting or estimating the amount of work required to construct a software system is referred to as software effort estimation or software development effort estimation [2]. However, mistakes are more common in software effort estimation because the data taken is not precise, clear, or complete in the initial stages. The traditional reports convey that the majority of the projects are unsuccessful because of poor estimates. Hence, more accurate estimation is very necessary for a successful project. Estimations can be done based on the metrics such as size, function points, use cases, user stories, etc. The popular estimation methods are algorithmic models, expert systems, and soft computing techniques. The conventional approaches for software effort estimation include the algorithmic models and the expertise models. The recent developments are the soft computing techniques.

16.1.1 Algorithmic models

The algorithmic models depend on a mathematical formula for software effort estimation. Several algorithmic models exist in the literature, where each model has its own pros and cons for estimation. A few of the algorithmic models [3] used for estimations are the software life cycle management model (SLIM), the Jensen model, the constructive cost model (COCOMO), etc. The majority of these models are proprietary in nature and cannot be used freely. The COCOMO model proposed by Boehm in the 1980s [4] was more popular and has been the basis for several estimation models. This model worked well for software effort estimation initially. Basic, intermediate, and detailed COCOMO are the three types of COCOMO. The basic COCOMO takes only the size parameter into count for effort estimation. The intermediate COCOMO uses 15 cost drivers along with size for effort estimation. The detailed COCOMO presents the phase-wise development effort using the 15 cost drivers along with size. However, the estimations by COCOMO were not so accurate. Later, several models were proposed to overcome the limitations of COCOMO [5].

16.1.2 Expert systems

The expert systems or expertise models are used for effort estimation when the empirical data is unavailable. These models include expert judgment [6] and the Delphi approach [7]. In expert systems, the estimates are just based on the expertise of the experts used for estimation. Though these approaches are suited to some extent, they do still have their own limitations and there is an extreme need for accurate estimation. The result is the soft computing techniques, artificial intelligence techniques, or machine learning (ML) techniques applied for effort estimation.

16.1.3 Soft computing techniques

The literature shows that the software development effort estimates are more accurate when artificial intelligence is applied for the estimation. Several soft computing techniques or machine learning techniques [8] are used for this purpose. Initially, backpropagation neural networks (BPNN) and feedforward neural networks (FFNN) were used for effort estimations, and later on, genetic programming (GP), fuzzy logic (FL), particle swarm optimization (PSO), neuro-fuzzy inference systems (NFIS), support vector machines (SVM), and naïve Bayes were used to improve the accuracy. The estimation models are further fine-tuned to give better results using ensemble techniques like AdaBoost, subspace, bagging, etc. All of these techniques are developed year after year, changing the datasets, parameters, methods, etc. in order to increase the accuracy of the effort estimate. Section 16.2 provides a quick overview of the work done to estimate software effort using different machine learning or AI approaches.

16.1.4 Major contributions

The main aim of this study is to describe the number of standard publications on the topic of software effort estimation using AI techniques. The number of publications per year, per source, per language, per country, per author, per type, etc. along with the number of citations per author, per co-author, per organization, etc. are also presented. The primary idea is to showcase the work done till now for accurate estimations using various AI techniques and thereby provide guidance for future researchers to aim for better accuracies. The models developed for this purpose of estimations can also be deployed for use by public or software industries which further helps to improve the economic status of individuals or companies.

16.1.5 Organization of the chapter

The organization of this chapter is as follows. A brief introduction to the topic was given in section 16.1. Section 16.2 presents the literature survey on the usage of AI techniques for software effort estimation. In section 16.3, the detailed analysis of research using the Scopus database was presented. In section 16.4, an exhaustive study using the statistical analysis approach and network analysis approach was presented. The directions to people for future research on the topic of estimations and the usage of AI techniques for other related topics were presented in section 16.5, followed by the conclusions in section 16.6.

16.2 LITERATURE SURVEY

In the initial article of study [9], two methods of machine learning, CARTX and backpropagation, are developed for estimating the effort from the data acquired from the past. These strategies appear to be competitive with classic estimators such as SLIM, COCOMO, and function points, according to the experiments. In the work carried out for effort estimation [10], effort estimation using function points was carried out by using neural networks and regression models based on a dataset of 299 projects. It was observed that regression models performed poorly for this dataset. In another experimentation work, connectionist models were used effectively for estimation, using a small dataset [11]. A comparative study was done on various OO software cost estimation methodologies [12]. The next-generation software estimating framework was discussed by Ross [13]. A comparative study was also carried out based on the NNs and regression models for effort estimation [14].

A multilayer FFNN is trained using the backpropagation algorithm, which is shown to be suitable for effort estimation using a dataset of 650 projects [15][16]. The outspread basis function neural organizations created have shown promising outcomes for programming exertion assessment [17]. Enhanced effort estimation was done using the multi-layered FFNN [18]. The BPNN for software effort estimation is designed to improve the COCOMO performance [19]. The software effort estimation model by using Taguchi's orthogonal arrays and NN was experimented on for optimized learning. A feedforward deep neural network algorithm (FFDNN) is also proposed for more accurate estimation [20].

Later, genetic programming (GP) was used for effort estimation using the Desharnais dataset [21]. The effectiveness of the machine learning algorithm-naive-Bayes classifier for software effort estimation was demonstrated in a paper published [22] utilizing the Benchmark 6 datasets from the ISBSG.

Newer paradigms like fuzzy logic models may offer accurate software effort estimates. Martin explained a fuzzy logic application and compared the findings to those of a multiple regression model. For the study, a selection of 41 modules from ten programs was chosen as the dataset. The fuzzy logic model was even extended to the reusable components or the reusable code [23]. Based on the input of 60 programs produced by ten developers, four fuzzy logic systems (FLS) were developed to estimate the effort. The findings suggest that the FLS can be used to estimate software effort at a personal level [24, 25]. Fuzzy models were also developed using the standard COCOMO dataset and an artificial dataset and were found to produce better results [26]. Effort estimations using regression approaches are also compared in another comparative study [27]. A novel algorithm based on fuzzy logic with 2D Gaussian membership functions was developed to get better estimates [28]. Further, the accuracy of fuzzy models was improved using cascading and clustering techniques [29]. A comparative empirical study was presented on the fuzzy analogy-based effort estimation [30]. In the work by Nassif, regression fuzzy models are used for the calculation of effort [31].

For calculating the effort, a soft computing paradigm employing the NFIS was applied [32], and the findings suggest that the model worked well for industry applications. In a paper on software effort estimation using ML techniques [33], several models were developed for estimation based on the public datasets, and it was concluded that the usage of a particular model cannot always produce better results. In addition, a Sugeno fuzzy inference system (FIS) approach was used to improve the accuracy of software effort estimation [34]. Another study used the class point approach with adaptive NFIS to estimate the cost of various software projects [35]. The implementation analysis of FCM-based ANFIS and ELMAN neural networks for software effort estimation was done in another study [36]. An adaptive neuro-fuzzy inference system (ANFIS) and NNs were utilized to develop an efficient software effort estimate approach based on functional points [37]. Use case points and expert-based software development effort estimates were thoroughly analyzed by Mahmood [38].

In another study on effort estimation, two models were proposed using PSO for fine-tuning of parameters of COCOMO [39]. The models handle imprecise or ambiguous input data well, increasing the accuracy of effort estimation. An improved PSO algorithm was also developed for effort estimation [40]. For software effort estimation, a hybrid model is suggested and tested that combines particle swarm optimization (PSO), K-means clustering methods, neural networks, and the ABE approach [41]. A method of improving case-based effort estimation by the ant colony optimization (ACO) algorithm is experimented with [42]. Another method of estimation is done by designing the networks using self-organizing maps (SOM) [43]. In a work by Azath, software effort estimation was done using modified FCM clustering and neural networks [44]. The work by Pillai for software effort estimation experiments with the deep learning models [45].

Effort estimation can also be done using the support vector regression method [46]. The accuracy of estimation improves with the combination of feature selection and parameter tuning in support vector regression [47]. Another experiment is done by using the random forest technique for effort estimation at an early stage based on use-case points [48]. An experiential study and evaluation of software development effort estimation were carried out using the random forest method [49]. The implementation of random forest regression for COCOMO II software effort estimation was presented in another paper by Suherman [50].

The literature includes a few cost-effective supervised learning algorithms for estimating software effort in agile contexts [51]. Similarly given is an improved model for assessing the estimation based on support vector regression and grid search method [52]. A review article on estimation in agile methodology summarizes the complete research on agile methodology, its implementation strategy, and its characteristics [53]. In an article, a comparison of machine learning algorithms for software effort estimation in various software sizes was offered [54, 55]. Another study gave a rigorous evaluation of 14 algorithms widely utilized in the data science field for effort estimation [56]. A work by Al-Rubaie suggests a complementary approach by performing data mining on a pre-processed NASA dataset [57]. Three machine learning approaches were used to make this prediction: naive Bayes, logistic model tree (LMT), and adaptive boosting (AdaBoost). A new framework for effort estimation was proposed by Khatib where the procedure for adapting the various models for estimation was presented [58].

An examination of the utilization of delicate registering procedures like fluffy logic, NNs, ANFIS, random forest, and SVM for programming exertion assessment was introduced utilizing the NASA and Desharnais datasets [59]. In another work, a set of soft computing techniques were applied for effort estimation, and it was concluded that decision trees and random forest performed better [60]. A novel method, namely AGS, was developed for software effort estimation which was proven to improve accuracy [61]. In all the above cases, the effort estimation was considered a regression problem, and an attempt was made efficiently by considering it as a classification problem as well [62].

Software effort estimation using a neural network ensemble was presented by Pai in his research work [63]. Kumar outlines how several ANNs, such as basic NNs, higher order NNs, and deep learning networks, were utilized by the investigators for software effort estimation in his publication [64]. A comparison of ML and deep learning methods for effort estimation was offered in a recent publication [65]. The machine learning hyper-parameter tuning techniques for effort estimation comparing all the previous techniques, along with the challenges, are presented in a study by Villalobos. Another review study examines machine learning–based software effort estimation approaches, their application domains, methods for calculating software effort estimation, and an examination of existing ML techniques to see where more research may be done [66]. Finally, to conclude, a substantial amount of research was done in the past on software development effort estimation using AI techniques and this process of estimation is continuing for better accuracy using several ensemble techniques.

16.3 RESEARCH OUTCOMES IN SOFTWARE EFFORT ESTIMATION

16.3.1 Scopus database search

Globally, there exist many widespread databases, including Scopus, Web of Science, Google Scholar, Scimago, etc. Scopus, the most widely utilized database, is used for the study among these databases. The source used for the search is www.scopus.com. The query used for searching the Scopus database is shown in the following. No restrictions on year, country, language, etc. are considered. The search was carried out on 31 May 2021 and the result is a list of 219 publications. The resultant Scopus database retrieved after applying the search query is used for the statistical analysis and the network analysis.

(TITLE-ABS-KEY (Software Effort Estimation) AND TITLE-ABS-KEY (Machine Learning) OR TITLE-ABS-KEY (Artificial Intelligence) OR TITLE-ABS-KEY (Soft Computing) OR TITLE-ABS-KEY (Software Development Effort Estimation))

16.3.2 Initial search outcomes

As mentioned in section 16.3.1, the search query yielded 219 publication documents. When language is considered as one of the parameters for analysis, it was observed that the majority of the publications are in English. There are 209 publications in English, three publications in Spanish, two publications in Chinese, two publications in Turkish, one publication in Arabic, one publication in Portuguese, and one publication in Russian.

In addition to the essential keywords like software effort estimation, machine learning, artificial intelligence, etc., many other keywords were discovered during the search. Software effort estimation is the keyword present in 166 publications and software design is the next highest keyword present in 94 publications.

16.4 SYSTEMATIC ANALYSIS

On the Scopus database results of the query search, two types of analysis can be performed [67]. First is the statistical analysis that includes documents by source, year, subject area, type, country, author, affiliation, and top funding agencies. Second is the network analysis of databases that includes relationships such as co-authorship, co-occurrences, citation investigation, bibliographic reference, and co-reference. Factual analysis reports are consequently produced by Scopus. Network analysis is carried out by using VOSviewer software. The tool used for network analysis based on the Scopus database is VOSviewer version 1.6.16. VOSviewer is a helpful way to analyze the parameters like co-authorship, co-occurrences, citation, bibliographic citation, and co-citation.

16.4.1 Statistical analysis

Using the query search given in section 16.3.1, a statistical analysis is done on the Scopus database acquired from the Scopus site. The result is a Scopus database of 219 records named SE-DB. The analysis is performed on this database in different ways as presented in the following, i.e., analysis of documents by source, year, subject area, type, country, author, affiliations, and funding sponsors.

The SE-DB includes publications from different sources including conference proceedings, journals, book chapters, notes, etc. The graphical representation of the year-wise statistics of the publications from the top five sources is shown in Figure 16.1.

The SE-DB database contains publications from 1995 through 2021 from a variety of sources, including conferences, journals, book chapters, and more. The graphical representations of the documents per year are shown in Figure 16.2. It has been discovered that the year 2019 has the most publications, followed by the year 2020.

The SE-DB consists of documents searched using the fundamental keyword software effort estimation. Software effort estimation is purely related to software engineering, which in turn is related to computer science. Hence most documents are found under the computer science category (55.7%).

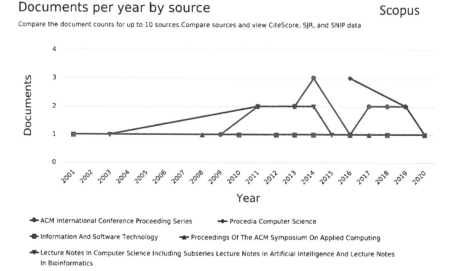

Documents per year by source   Scopus

Compare the document counts for up to 10 sources. Compare sources and view CiteScore, SJR, and SNIP data

- ACM International Conference Proceeding Series   Procedia Computer Science
- Information And Software Technology   Proceedings Of The ACM Symposium On Applied Computing
- Lecture Notes In Computer Science Including Subseries Lecture Notes In Artificial Intelligence And Lecture Notes In Bioinformatics

Figure 16.1 Documents per year by source.

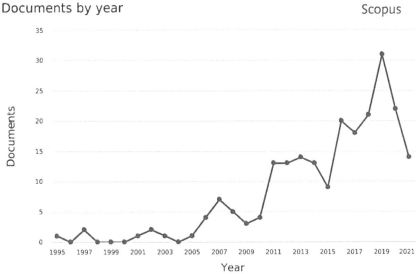

Figure 16.2 Documents by year.

There are most documents in the engineering (14.8%) category following the computer science category. The graphical representation of the documents by subject area is shown in Figure 16.3.

According to the SE-DB, most distributions are from conference proceedings, followed by journal publications, which were retrieved using the query search. The graphical representation of the documents by type is presented in Figure 16.4, and the number of documents by type is presented in Table 16.1.

Based on the Scopus database, the authors with the most publications can also be identified. The graphical representation of the top ten authors based on their number of publications is shown in Figure 16.5. A. Idri is identified to be the author with the most publications (19) in the space of programming effort estimation.

The number of publications based on affiliations is also analyzed based on the Scopus database. It is found that Mohammed V University in Rabat has the highest documents by affiliation, followed by the École Nationale Supérieure d'Informatique, Rabat Information Technology Centre, etc. The SE-DB is investigated to see the publications done country-wise. It illustrates that India is the highest contributor followed by Morocco, Canada, Australia, and Brazil.

From the SE-DB, it was observed that the Centre National pour la Recherche Scientifique et Technique in Morocco is the top funding sponsor. The next top four funding sponsors are the Universidad de Costa Rica,

Documents by subject area

Scopus

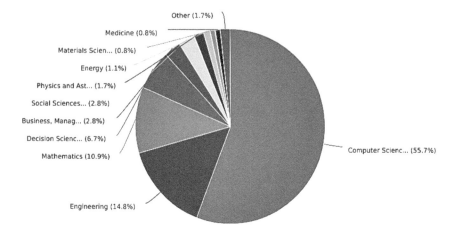

Figure 16.3 Documents by subject area.

Documents by type

Scopus

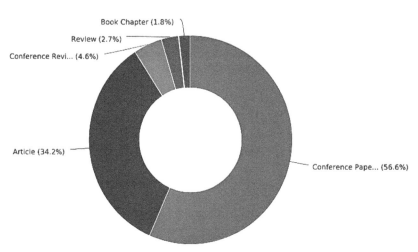

Figure 16.4 Documents by type.

Table 16.1 Number and type of documents

S. no.	Type of document	Documents count
1.	Conference paper	124
2.	Article	75
3.	Conference review	10
4.	Review	6
5.	Book chapter	4
Total		**219**

Documents by author

Scopus

Compare the document counts for up to 15 authors.

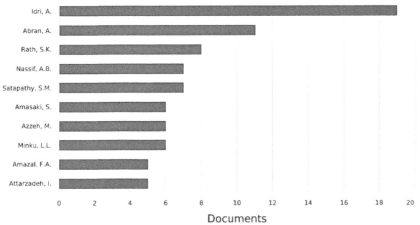

Figure 16.5 Documents by author.

Japan Society for the Promotion of Science, Universiti Teknologi Malaysia, and Conselho Nacional de Desenvolvimento Científicoe Tecnológico.

16.4.2 Network analysis

A network analysis can also be presented on the SE-DB retrieved from the Scopus site using the query search presented in section 16.3.1. The resulting database of 219 records is used in VOSviewer for performing the network analysis. Co-authorship analysis, co-occurrence analysis, citation analysis, bibliographic coupling analysis, and co-citation analysis are all types of network analysis that can be generated and seen.

As for co-authorship analysis, the author A. Idri has the highest publication count of 19, the author Oliveira has got the most citations, i.e, 202, the Centre of Informatics, Federal University of Pernambuco has the most co-authorship citations of 164, and Canada has the highest number of co-authorship citations, i.e., 567. In this chapter, the citation analysis and co-citation analysis are presented in more detail. Citation analysis can be measured based on documents, sources, authors, organizations, and countries. The network analysis of co-citation is also performed by modifying the units of analysis such as cited references, cited authors, and cited sources.

16.4.2.1 Citation analysis of documents

If the minimum number of citations for a document is 1, 155 documents fit the requirements out of the 219 total. K. Srinivasan is the author with the highest number of citations at 292. The citation analysis of documents is presented in Figure 16.6. If a document's minimal number of citations is deemed to be five, 94 documents fulfill the requirement.

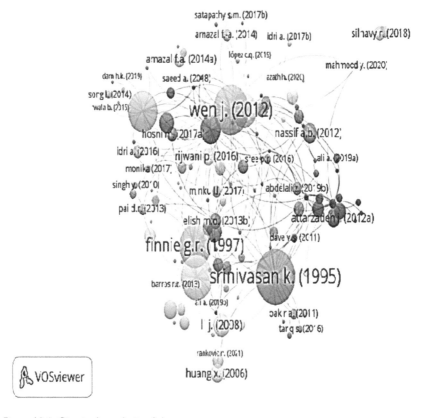

Figure 16.6 Citation's analysis of documents.

16.4.2.2 Citation analysis of sources

Sources may also be considered as an analysis parameter. If a source must have a minimum of five documents and no citations, then six of the 141 sources meet these requirements. The assessment shows that the record number of documents from the source ACM International Conference Proceedings is 15. The source *Information and Software Technology* has the most citations at 680, with the highest link strength of 23. If the minimum number of documents of a source is considered as three, out of 141 sources, 16 meet the criteria.

16.4.2.3 Citation analysis by authors

Assuming that the author's minimum number of documents is considered to be five and the minimum number of citations for an author is assumed to be zero, 14 out of 397 orders fulfill the minimal criteria. The author A. Idri has the most cited documents at 19, with the highest link strength of 24. The author with the most citations is Oliveira (202 citations). The citation analysis by author is shown in Figure 16.7. If the minimum number of documents of an author is considered as three, 36 of 397authors meet the threshold.

16.4.2.4 Analysis of citations by organization

For citation analysis by an organization, the minimal number of documents and citations for citation analysis by organization are considered three and zero, respectively. There are a total of 361 organizations linked with this database and six meet the threshold. The most citations of 164 are for the organization Centre of Informatics, Federal University of Pernambuco. If the minimum number of documents published by an organization is two, then 17 organizations meet the requirement.

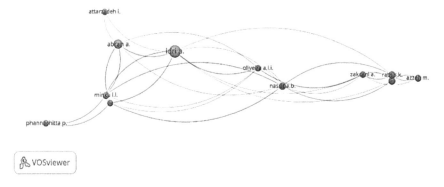

Figure 16.7 Citation analysis by authors.

16.4.2.5 Citation analysis by country

There are only 15 nations out of 51 that match the criteria for citation analysis by country when the minimum number of publications for a country is considered five and the minimum citations are considered zero. The country with the most publications is India with 61 documents and the country with the most citations is Canada with 567 citations. The citation analysis by country is shown in Figure 16.8.

16.4.2.6 Co-citation analysis by cited references

For co-citation analysis by cited references, when the minimal citation of a cited reference is considered as five, out of 6,123 cited references, 18 fit the criteria. The cited reference of Shepperd has the most citations at 14 and the highest total link strength of 19. If the minimum number of citations for a cited reference is three, only 103 of the 6,123 cited references fit this criterion.

16.4.2.7 Co-citation analysis by cited sources

When the minimum number of citations of a source is regarded as 20, only 24 sources out of the 3,335 sources meet the requirements for co-citation

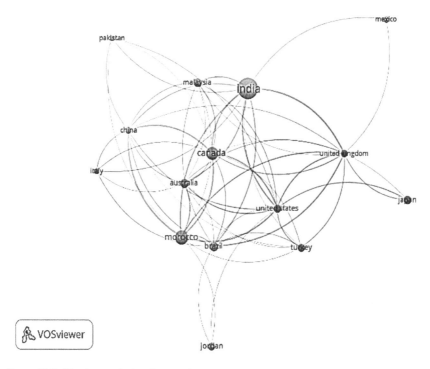

Figure 16.8 Citation analysis of countries.

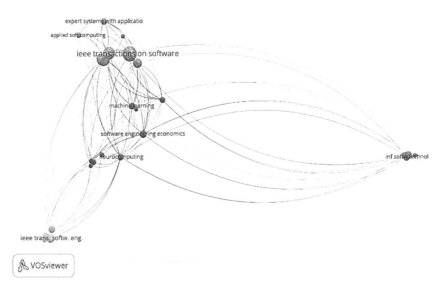

Figure 16.9 Co-citation analysis by cited sources.

analysis by cited sources, according to the results of the study. The source IEEE Transactions on Software Engineering has the most citations at 229 and the source *Information and Software Technology* has the highest total link strength of 2,552. The co-citation analysis by cited sources is shown in Figure 16.9. Out of 3,335 cited references, 57 meet the requirement if the minimum number of citations of a cited reference is taken into account.

16.4.2.8 Co-citation analysis by cited authors

If the minimum number of citations for an author is 20, out of 4,760 authors, 124 meet the criterion for co-citation analysis by cited authors. The author Idri has the most citations at 274 and the highest total link strength of 14,757. The co-citation analysis by cited authors is shown in Figure 16.10. If the minimum number of citations expected for an author is ten, then 276 authors out of 4,760 match the criteria.

16.5 RESULTS AND DISCUSSIONS

The exhaustive survey was carried out using the Scopus database on the topic of software effort estimation using AI techniques. There are 219 documents published between 1995 and 2021 on this topic. The statistical analysis is done using the Scopus data and network analysis is done using VOSviewer software. The analysis was done by considering different parameters.

Figure 16.10 Co-citation analysis by cited authors.

By statistical analysis, it is observed that 209 articles were published in English on the topic and the English language was majorly used for writing the research findings. India is the country that published more articles in this area. A. Idri is the author who has published 19 documents, the highest number of documents in this area. A maximum number of 31 articles in this area were published in 2019. The biggest source type of document is conference proceedings with 110 documents. Most documents are produced under the document type conference paper with 124 documents. A majority of 15 articles are from the source ACM International Conference Proceeding Series. Nearly 55.7% of the documents were in the topic area of computer science. When considering the documents by affiliation, Mohammed V University in Rabat has published the most documents at 22. Considering the documents by funding sponsor, Centre National pour la Recherche Scientifique et Technique is the biggest sponsor with five documents being published.

Network analysis was done using the VOSviewer software. The various types of network analysis performed are co-authorship analysis, co-occurrence analysis, citation analysis, bibliographic coupling analysis, and co-citation analysis. Using the network analysis, various other significant issues are identified. Oliveira has the most co-authorship citations at 202.

Canada is the country that has the most co-authorship citations at 567. The keyword which is often used in the articles is software effort estimation with 166 occurrences. K. Srinivasan is the author who has received the most citations, 292, for his publications. The source *Information and Software Technology* has the most citations at 680. The organization Federal University of Pernambuco has the most citations at 164. M. Sheppard has the most co-citations at 14. Under co-citation analysis, the source IEEE Transactions on Software Engineering has the most citations at 229.

16.6 RESEARCH DIRECTIONS

From the exhaustive statistical and network analysis, it is observed that the analysis has given a deep insight into the research carried out in the domain of software engineering and in particular, software effort estimation. Though several algorithmic techniques and expertise models were existent in the literature to estimate the cost of development of software, these techniques have failed to estimate the cost accurately. In this context, the latest AI techniques or machine learning techniques have given solutions to the problem of accuracy by efficiently estimating software costs. Many funds were also given to the researchers who carry out research in the area of software effort estimation using machine learning techniques. The best models which accurately estimate the cost can be used by the software industry to overcome unnecessary expenditures. If the expenditure is beyond budget, the project would be a failure. If a project is as per the requirements of the customer and is developed within the given budget, the project is said to be successful. Hence, there is a high scope for carrying out research in software engineering in the areas of estimation, reusability, reliability, metrics, product line feature model defects [66–71], etc. where researchers can aim at deriving better models using machine learning, artificial intelligence, deep learning techniques, etc., which can give more accurate estimations. The intelligent models can also be developed for other related works in software engineering.

16.7 CONCLUSION

Estimations play a vital role in software development. Early estimations must be accurate for any project developed in the software industry during the SDLC. In this regard, several intelligent software estimation models were developed using AI techniques in the past. This chapter presents a more systematic and exhaustive survey of all the intelligent effort estimation models developed from 1995 to 2001. The intelligent software estimation models were developed using AI techniques like neural networks, fuzzy logic, neuro-fuzzy approaches, particle swarm optimization techniques, ant colony optimization, genetic programming, ensemble learning, etc. Statistical analysis and network analysis were performed on all the relative research works done in this area. Based on the statistical analysis, a report is presented on the number of articles published per year, articles published from various sources, articles published by authors, articles published by countries, articles published by organizations, articles published by funding sponsors, and articles published by types. Based on network analysis, a report is presented on the citations per author, co-author citations, citations by source, citations by organization, co-citations by source, citations by country, etc. From this exhaustive review, it can clearly be concluded that there are many possibilities for investigation in this area of accurate effort estimation using AI techniques. Industries could use more precise intelligent models at large to increase projects' success rates. Further, these types of intelligent models could also be altered for their use in other patterns of estimations.

REFERENCES

1. Davis, Alan M., Edward H. Bersoff, and Edward R. Comer. "A strategy for comparing alternative software development life cycle models." *IEEE Transactions on Software Engineering* 14.10 (1988): 1453–1461.
2. Strike, Kevin, Khaled El Emam, and Nazim Madhavji. "Software cost estimation with incomplete data." *IEEE Transactions on Software Engineering* 27.10 (2001): 890–908.
3. Ramil, Juan F. "Algorithmic cost estimation for software evolution." Proceedings of the 22nd International Conference on Software Engineering. 2000.
4. Boehm, Barry W. "Software engineering economics." *IEEE Transactions on Software Engineering* 1 (1984): 4–21.
5. Benediktsson, Oddur, et al. "COCOMO-based effort estimation for iterative and incremental software development." *Software Quality Journal* 11.4 (2003): 265–281.
6. Jørgensen, Magne. "A review of studies on expert estimation of software development effort." *Journal of Systems and Software* 70.1–2 (2004): 37–60.
7. Devnani-Chulani, Sunita. "Results of delphi for the defect introduction model." (1997).
8. Baskeles, Bilge, Burak Turhan, and Ayse Bener. "Software effort estimation using machine learning methods." 2007 22nd International Symposium on Computer and Information Sciences. IEEE, 2007.
9. Srinivasan, Krishnamoorthy, and Douglas Fisher. "Machine learning approaches to estimating software development effort." *IEEE Transactions on Software Engineering* 21.2 (1995): 126–137.
10. Finnie, Gavin R., Gerhard E. Wittig, and Jean-Marc Desharnais. "A comparison of software effort estimation techniques: Using function points with neural networks, case-based reasoning and regression models." *Journal of Systems and Software* 39.3 (1997): 281–289.

11. Pendharkar, Parag C., and Girish H. Subramanian. "Connectionist models for learning, discovering, and forecasting software effort: an empirical study." *Journal of Computer Information Systems* 43.1 (2002): 7–14.

12. Foley, D. G., and B. K. Wetzel. "Object-oriented software cost estimation methodologies compared." *Journal of Cost Analysis and Parametrics* 1.1 (2008): 41–63.

13. Ross, Michael A. "Next generation software estimating framework: 25 years and thousands of projects later." *Journal of Cost Analysis and Parametrics* 1.2 (2008): 7–30.

14. De Barcelos, Tronto, Iris Fabiana, José Demísio Simões da Silva, and Nilson Sant' Anna. "An investigation of artificial neural networks-based prediction systems in software project management." *Journal of Systems and Software* 81.3 (2008): 356–367.

15. Singh, Yogesh, et al. "Predicting software development effort using artificial neural network." *International Journal of Software Engineering and Knowledge Engineering* 20.03 (2010): 367–375.

16. Kaushik, Anupama, A. K. Soni, and Rachna Soni. "An adaptive learning approach to software cost estimation." 2012 National Conference on Computing and Communication Systems. IEEE, 2012.

17. Idri, Ali, Wafa, and Abdelali Zakrani. "Comparing the performance of RBFN networks based software effort estimation models." Decision Making and Soft Computing: Proceedings of the 11th International FLINS Conference. 2014.

18. Rijwani, Poonam, and Sonal Jain. "Enhanced software effort estimation using multi layered feed forward artificial neural network technique." *Procedia Computer Science* 89 (2016): 307–312.

19. Titov, Alexandr Igorevich. "Software development effort estimation using a neuro network approximation approach." *Informatics and Automation* 44 (2016): 20–30.

20. Rankovic, Nevena, et al. "A new approach to software effort estimation using different artificial neural network architectures and Taguchi orthogonal arrays." *IEEE Access* 9 (2021): 26926–26936.

21. Burgess, Colin J., and Martin Lefley. "Can genetic programming improve software effort estimation? A comparative evaluation." *Information and Software Technology* 43.14 (2001): 863–873.

22. Stewart, B. "Predicting project delivery rates using the Naive–Bayes classifier." *Journal of Software Maintenance and Evolution: Research and Practice* 14.3 (2002): 161–179.

23. Martín, C. L., J. L. Pasquier, C. M. Yanez, and A. G. Tornes "Software development effort estimation using fuzzy logic: a case study." 2005 Sixth Mexican International Conference on Computer Science (ENC'05) (pp. 113–120). IEEE.

24. Lopez-Martin, C., C. Yanez-Marquez, and Gutierrez-Tornes. "A fuzzy logic model based upon reused and new & changed code for software development effort estimation at personal level." 2006 15th International Conference on Computing. IEEE, 2006.

25. Lopez-Martin, Cuauhtemoc, Cornelio Yanez-Marquez, and Agustin Gutierrez-Tornes. "Fuzzy logic systems for software development effort estimation based upon clustering of programs segmented by personal practices."

Electronics, Robotics and Automotive Mechanics Conference (CERMA'06) (Vol. 2). IEEE, 2006.

26. Attarzadeh, I., and S. H. Ow. "Proposing a new high-performance model for software cost estimation." 2009 International Conference on Computer and Electrical Engineering, ICCEE 2009 (Vol. 2, pp. 112–116).

27. Nadgeri, S. M., Vidya P. Hulsure, and A. D. Gawande. "Comparative study of various regression methods for software effort estimation." 2010 3rd International Conference on Emerging Trends in Engineering and Technology. IEEE, 2010.

28. Attarzadeh, Iman, and Siew H. Ow. "A novel algorithmic cost estimation model based on soft computing technique." Journal of Computer Science 6.2 (2010): 117.

29. Sree, P. Rama, and Ramesh SNSVSC. "Improving efficiency of fuzzy models for effort estimation by cascading & clustering techniques." Procedia Computer Science 85 (2016): 278–285.

30. Idri, Ali, Aya Hassani, and Alain Abran. "RBFN networks-based models for estimating software development effort: A cross-validation study." 2015 IEEE Symposium Series on Computational Intelligence. IEEE, 2015.

31. Nassif, Ali Bou, et al. "Software development effort estimation using regression fuzzy models." Computational Intelligence and Neuroscience 2019 (2019).

32. Huang X., D. Ho, J. Ren, and L. F. Capretz. "A soft computing framework for software effort estimation." Soft Computing 10.2 (2006): 170–177.

33. Ahmed BaniMustafa, "Predicting Software Effort Estimation Using Machine Learning Techniques 2018." 8th International Conference on Computer Science and Information Technology (CSIT), 11–12 July 2018, Jordan, IEEE, 2018.

34. Nassif, Ali Bou, Luiz Fernando Capretz, and Danny Ho. "Estimating software effort based on use case point model using sugeno fuzzy inference system." 2011 IEEE 23rd International Conference on Tools with Artificial Intelligence. IEEE, 2011.

35. Satapathy, Shashank Mouli, Mukesh Kumar, and Santanu Kumar Rath. "Optimised class point approach for software effort estimation using adaptive neuro-fuzzy inference system model." International Journal of Computer Applications in Technology 54.4 (2016): 323–333.

36. Edinson, Praynlin, and LathaMuthuraj. "Performance analysis of FCM based ANFIS and ELMAN neural network in software effort estimation." The International Arab Journal of Information Technology. 15.1 (2018): 94–102.

37. Rama Sree, S., R. SNSVSC, and P. R. Ch. "An effective software effort estimation based on functional points using soft computing techniques. International Journal of Innovative Technology and Exploring Engineering 8.10 (2019): 3729–3733.

38. Mahmood, Yasir, Nazri Kama, and Azri Azmi. "A systematic review of studies on use case points and expert-based estimation of software development effort." Journal of Software: Evolution and Process 32.7 (2020): e2245.

39. Hari, C. H., and P. V. G. D. Reddy. "A fine parameter tuning for COCOMO 81 software effort estimation using particle swarm optimization." Journal of Software Engineering 5.1 (2011): 38–48.

40. Benala T. R., R. Mall, and S. Dehuri. "Software effort estimation using functional link neural networks optimized by improved particle swarm optimization." 2013. Lecture Notes in Computer Science (including subseries Lecture Notes in Artificial Intelligence and Lecture Notes in Bioinformatics), 8298 LNCS, PART 2 (pp. 205–213).
41. Nagarajan, Shivakumar, and Balaji Narayanan. "K-means clustering algorithms to compute software effort estimation." *Journal of Computational and Theoretical Nanoscience* 13.10 (2016): 7093–7098.
42. Fellir, Fadoua, Khalid Nafil, and Lawrence Chung. "Improving case based software effort estimation by an ant colony algorithm." 2018 6th International Conference on Control Engineering & Information Technology (CEIT). IEEE, 2018.
43. Idri, Ali, and Ibtissam Abnane. "Fuzzy analogy based effort estimation: An empirical comparative study." 2017 IEEE International Conference on Computer and Information Technology (CIT). IEEE, 2017.
44. Azath, Hussain, Marimuthu Mohanapriya, and Somasundaram Rajalakshmi. "Software effort estimation using modified fuzzy C means clustering and hybrid ABC-MCS optimization in neural network." *Journal of Intelligent Systems* 29.1 (2020): 251–263.
45. Pillai, S. P., and SD. Madhu Kumar "Evaluating deep learning paradigms with TensorFlow and Keras for software effort estimation." *International Journal of Scientific and Technology Research* 9 (2020): 2753–2761.
46. Braga, Petrônio L., Adriano LI Oliveira, and Silvio RL Meira. "A GA-based feature selection and parameters optimization for support vector regression applied to software effort estimation." Proceedings of the 2008 ACM Symposium on Applied Computing. 2008.
47. Oliveira, Adriano LI, et al. "GA-based method for feature selection and parameters optimization for machine learning regression applied to software effort estimation. " *Information and Software Technology* 52.11 (2010): 1155–1166.
48. Satapathy, Shashank Mouli, Barada Prasanna Acharya, and Santanu Kumar Rath. "Early stage software effort estimation using random forest technique based on use case points." *IET Software* 10.1 (2016): 10–17.
49. Zakrani, Abdelali, Mustapha Hain, and Abdelwahed Namir. "Software development effort estimation using random forests: an empirical study and evaluation." *International Journal of Intelligent Engineering and Systems* 11.6 (2018): 300–311.
50. Suherman, Ilham Cahya, and Riyanarto Sarno. "Implementation of random forest regression for COCOMO II effort estimation." 2020 International Seminar on Application for Technology of Information and Communication (iSemantic). IEEE, 2020.
51. Moharreri, Kayhan, et al. "Cost-effective supervised learning models for software effort estimation in agile environments." IEEE 40th Annual Computer Software and Applications Conference (COMPSAC) (Vol. 2). IEEE, 2016.
52. Zakrani, Abdelali, Assia Najm, and Abdelaziz Marzak. "Support vector regression based on grid-search method for agile software effort prediction." 2018 IEEE 5th International Congress on Information Science and Technology (CiSt). IEEE, 2018.

53. Sudarmaningtyas, Pantjawati, and Rozlina Mohamed. "A review article on software effort estimation in agile methodology." *Pertanika Journal of Science & Technology* 29.2 (2021).

54. Valerdi, Ricardo. "Pioneers of parametrics: Origins and evolution of software cost estimation." *Journal of Cost Analysis and Parametrics* 8.2 (2015): 74–91.

55. Rahman, Md Tanziar, and Md Motaharul Islam. "A comparison of machine learning algorithms to estimate effort in varying sized software." 2019 IEEE Region 10 Symposium (TENSYMP). IEEE, 2019.

56. Phannachitta, Passakorn, and Kenichi Matsumoto. "Model-based software effort estimation: A robust comparison of 14 algorithms widely used in the data science community." *International Journal of Innovative Computing Information and Control* 15.2 (2019): 569–589.

57. Al-Rubaie H. A., and A. S. Abbas "Software effort estimation using data mining techniques based on improved precision." *Journal of Advanced Research in Dynamical and Control Systems* 12.5 (2020): 176–185.

58. Khatibi Bardsiri, Amid. "A new combinatorial framework for software services development effort estimation." *International Journal of Computers and Applications* 40.1 (2018): 14–24.

59. Rama Sree S., and C. Prasada Rao "A study on application of soft computing techniques for software effort estimation." *Intelligent Systems Reference Library* 185 (2020): 141–165.

60. Sharma, S., and S. Vijayvargiya "Applying soft computing techniques for software project effort estimation modelling." *Lecture Notes in Electrical Engineering* 692 (2021): 211–227.

61. Ananth, V. V., and S. Srinivasan. "AGS: a precise and efficient AI-based hybrid software effort estimation model." *International Journal of Business Intelligence and Data Mining* 18.1 (2021): 1–16.

62. Bakır, A., B. Turhan, and A. Bener "Software effort estimation as a classification problem." International Conference on Software and Data Technologies (Vol. 2). Scite p$ress, 2008.

63. Pai, D. R., K. S. McFall, and G. H. Subramanian. Software effort estimation using a neural network ensemble. *Journal of Computer Information Systems* 53.4 (2013): 49–58.

64. Kumar, P. Suresh, et al. "Advancement from neural networks to deep learning in software effort estimation: Perspective of two decades." *Computer Science Review* 38 (2020): 100288.

65. Priya Varshini, A. G., and Vijayakumar Varadarajan. "Estimating software development efforts using a random forest-based stacked ensemble approach." *Electronics* 10.10 (2021): 1195.

66. Sinha, R. R., and R. K. Gora "Software effort estimation using machine learning techniques." *Lecture Notes in Networks and Systems* 135 (2021): 65–79.

67. Bhushan, Megha, and Shivani Goel. "Improving software product line using an ontological approach." *Sādhanā* 41.12 (2016): 1381–1391. https://doi.org/10.1007/s12046- 016-0571-y

68. Bhushan, Megha, Shivani Goel, and Karamjit Kaur. "Analyzing inconsistencies in software product lines using an ontological rule-based approach." *Journal of Systems and Software* 137 (2018): 605–617.

69. Megha, Arun Negi, and Karamjit Kaur. "Method to resolve software product line errors." *International Conference on Information, Communication and Computing Technology (ICICCT)* (2017): 258–268. https://doi.org/10.1007/978-981-10-6544-6_24

70. Bhushan, Megha, Shivani Goel, Ajay Kumar, and Arun Negi. "Managing software product line using an ontological rule-based framework." *2017 International Conference on Infocom Technologies and Unmanned Systems (Trends and Future Directions) (ICTUS)* (2017): 376–382. https://doi.org/10.1109/ICTUS.2017.8286036

71. Bhushan, Megha, Shivani Goel, and Ajay Kumar. "Improving quality of software product line by analysing inconsistencies in feature models using an ontological rule-based approach." *Expert Systems* 35.3 (2018): e12256. https://doi.org/10.1111/exsy.12256

Index